# THE RIGHT TO DIE

# The Right To Die

## UNDERSTANDING
## EUTHANASIA

*Derek Humphry*     *Ann Wickett*

## THE BODLEY HEAD
### LONDON

Grateful acknowledgment is made for permission to reprint:

Excerpt from 'Hospital Horror: How Patients Are Run Down by the Health-Care Steamroller' by Elliot Carlson. First appeared in the October–November 1984 issue of *Modern Maturity*.

Excerpt from 'When Suicide Prevention Becomes Brutality: The Case of Elizabeth Bouvia' by George Annas. First appeared in the April 1984 issue of *Hastings Center Report*.

Excerpt from 'The Sanctity of Life' by John Sutherland Bonnell. First appeared in the May–June 1951 issue of *Theology Today*.

Excerpt from a story about Kenneth Wright which first appeared in the April 28, 1981, issue of *The Hartford Courant*.

Excerpt from 'Murder by Request' by Anthony M. Turano. First appeared in *American Mercury* (1935).

Excerpt from Arthur Koestler's suicide note. Reprinted by permission of Harold Harris, Literary Executor of the Estate of Arthur Koestler.

British Library Cataloguing in Publication Data
Humphry, Derek
The right to die; understanding euthanasia
I. Euthanasia—Moral and ethical aspects
I. Title II. Ann Wickett
174'.24        R726
ISBN 0 370 31009 8

Printed in Great Britain for The Bodley Head Ltd
30 Bedford Square London W C I B 3RP
by Redwood Burn Limited, Trowbridge, Wiltshire

*First published in New York by Harper & Row Inc 1986*
*First published in Great Britain 1986*

For Garth (1927–1986)

Whose untimely death showed that modern
medical technology can take away life as
well as save it.

When life is so burdensome, death has become
for man a sought-after refuge.

*Herodotus (c. 485–425 B.C.)*

# Contents

# Preface

Pope John Paul II predicted in 1978 that the great moral issue of the 1980s would be euthanasia. He was correct. It turned out to be a towering legal issue too.

Already in this decade the number of pro-euthanasia groups has trebled. Western society, cushioned by a high-technology, high-expectation lifestyle, goes from one *cause célèbre* to another, trying to come to grips with the complexities of dying. The cry 'Save me, doctor!' has turned to 'Save me from machines, doctor!'

The courts reviewed a succession of deeply troubling cases. Quadriplegic Elizabeth Bouvia was refused permission to starve to death in a hospital, highlighting the conflict between the handicapped individual and the rights of health workers. Karen Ann Quinlan, whose landmark case in 1976 publicized the right of a comatose patient to be disconnected from oppressive life-support machinery, finally died in 1985. William Bartling pleaded with the world and the courts to be allowed to discontinue use of his respirator, but justice moved too slowly to free him in time. Claire Conroy's family won the watershed right to disconnect her from artificial feeding, setting a precedent that pleased some and dismayed others.

Mercy killings rose ten times in the 1980s compared to any five-year period since 1920, while murder-suicides, double suicides, and assisted suicides involving the terminally ill increased forty times as desperate elderly people felt obliged to take the law and fate into their own hands. Suicide rates for the elderly are nearly double that of youth suicide. But it took a twenty-five-year prison sentence for septuagenarian Roswell Gilbert in the mercy killing of his wife to arouse the nation to the realization that something was wrong in the care of the dying.

For every court case that took us further forward to a compassionate, commonsense position, another reflecting other, usually traditional values, set us back. A middle ground proved elusive.

This book is an attempt to explain the complexities of the most controversial issue of the decade against the historical, cultural, and legal background.

Derek Humphry
Ann Wickett

*Los Angeles, January 1986*

# Acknowledgments

Without the patience, skill and consistent good humour of Susan Waller, chief researcher for this book, our task would have been much more difficult. She was ably assisted in research by Joyce Rotheram and in word processing by Diane Kenworthy.

Special thanks for advice and manuscript checking are due to Curt Garbesi, Linda Worthman, George Annas, Norman Goldman, David B. Clarke, Joseph Fletcher and Alan Johnson. Any errors and omissions are the fault of the authors. Tim Saclier in Australia and Frank Dungey in New Zealand were tireless advisers on law and policy.

# CHAPTER ONE

# Historical Perspective

Martha Schirmer was eighty-six years old when she died in a nursing home, where relatives had put her only a few weeks before. Organically there was nothing wrong with her. 'She just lost interest in everything,' her grand-daughter said. 'She wasn't interested in food or anything.'

Only a year before, she had been alert, involved, and physically active. Her niece lived across the street; they did crossword puzzles together and played Scrabble. Every spring, when the baseball season began, Martha Schirmer walked a half mile to the bus stop in Mount Vernon, New York, where she lived, and took a bus to the Dyre Avenue subway, which took her to Ebbets Field. She never missed a Dodgers game. Even though the trip took well over an hour, she attended every game when the Dodgers were in town—usually twice a week—as she had for more than twenty years. She knew every player, every batting average, every score, every coach.

However, during the summer of her eighty-sixth birthday, the Dodgers moved to Los Angeles. Her niece died. Her favourite granddaughter was leaving for college. There was nothing left to do.

She stopped eating. There was nothing the family could do to persuade her to try and get better. 'We were frustrated and annoyed with her,' her granddaughter says. 'She'd always been so full of life. We wanted her to be the way she was.'

Nothing worked. Her weight dropped. She grew more feeble. In desper-ation, her family put her in a nursing home, where doctors pronounced her health 'frail but sound'. In less than a month, Martha Schirmer was dead. 'Maybe she was ready to go,' someone suggested, years later. The grand-daughter replied, 'We couldn't accept that then. We wanted her to be like she had always been. We couldn't accept the fact that she was dying.' She paused. 'That maybe she wanted to die.' Could she accept that now? 'Only now can I see there was nothing going for her. She had nothing left to live for.'

I

Compare this with an elderly Aymara Indian of Bolivia. When he becomes terminally ill, relatives and friends are summoned to the home to keep a death vigil. If death is slow, the ill person may ask for help. The family will withhold food and drink until the dying person slips into unconsciousness and dies. Medical examination of these deaths (reported in the *Journal of the American Medical Women's Association*) indicates that they appear to have been caused not by starvation or thirst but by the simple will to die.

Some societies consider this sort of practice, one demanded by the sick and dying themselves, an act of mercy. For instance, in some Eskimo cultures, an old or sick Eskimo tells his family he is ready to die and the family, if it is a good one, will immediately comply by abandoning the aged person to the ravages of nature or by killing him. (Many Eskimos believe that anyone who has courageously faced a violent death spends eternity in the highest heaven.)

Similarly, consider travellers' tales and written accounts of suicides/ deaths by the elderly or ill in other primitive cultures. What are we to make of Pliny's stories of old men of northern barbarian tribes who jumped into the sea from overhanging rocks, 'having no pleasure to look forward to', of aged Ethiopians who allowed themselves to be tied to wild bulls, of the natives of Amboina in Indonesia, who ate their failing relatives out of charity, and the Congolese who jumped on the tired and old until life was gone? There were the Formosans who, with a little more hospitality, choked the sick and the aged with strong drink, the Hottentots who gave a lavish feast in honour of an ailing senior citizen before abandoning him in a hut in the wilderness, and the legendary islanders who had special officials called Caritans to perform the noble duty of stifling the aged 'to prevent them suffering.'[1] It is as if nature provided these barbaric examples as a contrast to those of the overcivilized twentieth century.

Indeed, in more primitive societies, death—as a result of illness, injury, or old age—was treated more realistically than it is today. It was treated as a natural part of life. Aiding death was often done out of respect for an ill person.

Today things are different. The average life expectancy has increased. We have medical advances—such as organ transplants and long-term-care institutions—that people did not dream of three or four decades ago. Yet we've observed that such progress can be a double-edged sword. People are kept alive against their wishes. Medicine caters to the biological man, often abandoning the psychological and social one. Hospitals are antiseptic and impersonal. Pneumonia, formerly the 'old man's friend', is treated with antibiotics. The patient lingers—often in pain. Afraid of litigation, the medical team persists.

Martha Schirmer was lucky. She died when she wanted to. She was ready to go. Her death was a kind of suicide, the kind many older, ailing (or younger, terminally ill) people desire. Still, such an end is not easy. Medical ingenuity largely prevents it, as it searches for and treats the physical malaise, often neglecting the patient as a whole and ignoring his wishes.

And, in the Western world, suicide is considered a strange, forbidden practice. For several centuries it was a crime. Many people—Christians or ex-Christians or Jews—experience the traditional Judeo-Christian inhibition against suicide. They choose to linger on, lonely and unhappy, often sick and suffering. Like Martha Schirmer, they're ready to go, but too often they can't.

## GREECE AND ROME

In classical times, attitudes were different. A tolerance of suicide began with the Greeks, although there were qualifications. Greeks never abandoned elderly or helpless adults,[2] and there *were* taboos against the taking of one's life. Aristotle argued that 'to kill oneself to escape from love or poverty or anything else that is distressing is not courageous.'[3] He went on to define suicide as an offence against the state. A penalty was imposed and dishonour attached to the family—usually the right hand of the dead person was cut off, he was buried separately, and his descendants were disfranchised.[4]

Indeed, in the golden age of reason, most of the disapproval of suicide was tied either to loyalty to the state or to the residual Greek horror of killing one's kin.[5] On the other hand, with greater wealth and luxury, there was growing emphasis on the revered principle of *kalokagathia*, the ideal of a perfect balance of physical and mental well-being. The Greeks embraced the concept of *euthanasia*, meaning well (*eu*) death (*thanatos*). Illness became a kind of curse. There is some evidence that in Ceos there was an ancient custom requiring people over sixty to commit suicide—a 'utilitarian practice'.[6] Similarly, both Aristotle and Plato endorsed infanticide as a means of ensuring the worthiest state with the worthiest individuals. In the *Republic*, Plato scorned the idea of 'weak fathers begetting weak sons'.[7] He went on to outline a crude form of eugenics, having Socrates say to Glaucon: 'The offspring of the inferior, or of the better when they chance to be deformed, will be put away in some mysterious, unknown place, as they should be.'[8]

Further, when suicide was state approved, it was not only encouraged but endorsed. In Athens (as well as in Ceos and in Marseilles) magistrates kept a supply of poison for anyone who wished to die. All that was needed was official permission:

Whoever no longer wishes to live shall state his reasons to the Senate,

3

and after having received permission shall abandon life. If your existence is hateful to you, die; if you are overwhelmed by fate, drink the hemlock. If you are bowed with grief, abandon life. Let the unhappy man recount his misfortune, let the magistrate supply him with the remedy, and his wretchedness will come to an end.[9]

It was Socrates who, according to Plato, saw painful disease and suffering as good reason not to cling to life. In the *Republic*, he condemns the physician Heroditus—teacher of Hippocrates—for 'educat[-ing] diseases ... and invent[ing] lingering death.'[10] He goes on to say: 'Being a trainer, and himself of a sickly constitution, by a combination of training and doctoring [he] found out a way of torturing first and chiefly himself, and secondly the rest of the world.'[11]

Socrates goes on to praise Asclepius, god of healing and medicine, for his more humane and practical policies. Bodies that disease had penetrated 'through and through' Asclepius would not have attempted to cure: 'He did not want to lengthen out good-for-nothing lives . . . Those who are diseased in their bodies, [physicians] will leave to die, and the corrupt and incurable souls they will put an end to themselves.'[12] It's entirely possible that many physicians practised this policy then, if for slightly different reasons. During the classical period, doctors were itinerant and had the status of craftsmen. Competition demanded that they diagnose accurately and cure effectively—if at all. In an essay entitled 'The Arts' in the *Hippocratic Collection*, the physician as healer was required to 'do away with the sufferings of the sick, to lessen the violence of their diseases, and to refuse to treat those who are overwhelmed by their diseases, realizing that in such cases medicine is powerless.'[13] (Indeed, before Socrates himself drank hemlock, he made death sound highly noble and desirable. The philosopher Cleombrotus, apparently inspired by the eloquence of the deathbed scene as described in the *Phaedo*, drowned himself. The Roman statesman Cato, similarly inspired, read the book through twice before falling on his sword.[14])

Equally, the Stoics embraced suicide, an option they chose when life was no longer in accordance with nature—because of pain, grave illness, or physical abnormalities. Zeno, the founder of Stoicism, hanged himself at age ninety-eight after falling and wrenching a finger. Cleanthes, another Stoic philosopher, continued starving himself after a doctor recommended it as a remedy for a gumboil. Even when the gumboil healed, he continued his fast to death. As one historian noted, 'He had advanced too far on his journey towards death, he would not now retreat.' In short, he was ready to die.[15]

Perhaps the best indication that suicide was committed as a form of euthanasia in Greece is the fact that the practice was condemned by other groups—Pythagoreans, Aristotelians, and Epicureans.[16] Still, the influence of Socrates, Plato, and the Stoics was far-reaching. It was one achievement of the Greeks that they stripped suicide of many of its primitive horrors and superstitions. They elevated it as a subject—and practice—worthy of rational discourse and consideration. It was, given certain circumstances, a worthy and reasonable choice. Not least important, it was often the most humane thing do to.

In Rome, suicide was punishable only if it was irrational. Anyone who killed himself without cause was looked down on, because 'whoever does not spare himself would much less spare another.' On the other hand, ending one's life because of a terminal illness was considered good cause. Suicide brought on by 'impatience of pain or sickness' was perfectly acceptable, as was that induced by 'weariness of life . . . lunacy, or fear of dishonour.'[17] The idea of dying well (*eu thanatos*) was a *summum bonum*.

To the Romans, living nobly meant dying nobly. It's hardly surprising that under the principate, aristocrats were often allowed to commit suicide as an alternative to execution. Certainly, killing oneself was an acceptable form of death as an escape from disgrace at the hands of an enemy.[18]

Roman attitudes towards suicide as a release from unendurable suffering reflect a synthesis of the Stoic, Pythagorean, Platonic, Aristotelian, and Epicurean influences. Seneca, the Stoic wrote:

> It makes a great deal of difference whether a man is lengthening his life or his death. But if the body is useless for service, why should one not free the struggling soul? Perhaps one ought to do this a little before the debt is due, lest, when it falls due, he may be unable to perform the act.[19]

## CHRISTIANITY

In the second and third centuries, Stoicism was seriously undermined by the growing influence of Christianity. Suicide was denounced. As a result, church law was profoundly affected. Anyone who took his own life was denied Christian burial. Civil legislation was influenced as well. Not only were the victim's goods and property confiscated by civil authorities; the body received an ignominious burial on the highway, impaled by a stake. There were no exceptions—not even for those who had endured prolonged suffering due to an incurable illness.[20] Every suicide was branded a *felo de se* (self-murder).

For the Romans and Greeks, dying decently, rationally, and—not least—with dignity had mattered immensely. In a sense, how they died was a measure of the final value of life, especially for a life wasted by disease and suffering. For Christians, however, this was not a consideration, nor was it a prerogative. It was God's will and God's only. Similarly, Neoplatonism, which arose in the third century, held that man should not abandon the post assigned him by God; suicide adversely affected the soul after death. With this influence, and that of Christianity—which was flourishing—the strictures against taking one's own life became fearsome.

To gain any kind of merciful release from an affliction, however grave, became unthinkable. Man owed all to God. By the fifth century, St Augustine felt called upon to decry suicide as 'detestable and damnable wickedness'. His ardour was fuelled by the Christian mania for martyrdom. He presented arguments: First, taking one's own life defied the Sixth Commandment, 'Thou shall not kill.' By committing suicide, a man was usurping the function of church and state. Finally, Augustine held that life and its sufferings are divinely ordained by God and must be borne accordingly.[21]

Not surprisingly, condemnations of suicide soon became more official. In 533 the Council of Orléans declared that funeral rites would be denied to anyone who had killed himself while accused of a crime. Three decades later, the Council of Braga denied funeral rites to *all* suicides—regardless of social position, method or circumstances. (This would have included most of those who martyred themselves for the church.) Finally, in 693, the Council of Toledo announced that anyone who *attempted* suicide would be excommunicated. (It was not until 824 that the penalties were somewhat lessened: England's Parliament permitted a suicide's burial in the churchyard, but only between nine and twelve at night.[22])

It's interesting to note that during this time, the relationship between the medical and the lay communities had become more structured. By the sixth century, contractual agreements between a doctor and a patient were drawn up, often in writing. By the twelfth century, groups of practitioners had banded together into worker associations. This meant more tightly controlled standards of training, education, and performance. In 1140, state examinations were held in Sicily for those who wanted to practise medicine. Similar legislation evolved in other countries over the next two centuries. Recognition of the physicians' guilds (which in time became medical schools) was exchanged for the public's right to play a role in setting the terms of professional practice.[23] Physicians were not indifferent to the open condemnation of suicide; such widespread disapproval affected their attitudes, especially towards patients wanting to be put out of their misery. As had been proclaimed by church and state, the taking of one's own life—under any circumstance—was prohibited. Any upright citizen was expected to abide by this, not least of all the physician/healer.

Intolerance towards suicide culminated in the thirteenth century with St Thomas Aquinas. In his *Summa Theologica* he presented to the world the medieval synthesis of the philosophical and theological arguments against the practice. According to Aquinas, not only was suicide sinful because it violated the Sixth Commandment;[24] it was the most dangerous of sins because it left no time for repentance. It was against the law of nature and contrary to charity; it was not lawful because each man belongs to his community; and it was a sin against the deity because life was a gift and subject only to God's powers.[25] In short, over a period of twelve centuries, suicide had become the most mortal of Christian sins.

## THE RENAISSANCE

With the revival of arts and letters in Europe in the fourteenth century, attitudes towards suicide changed radically. The Renaissance, a time of intense learning and scientific discovery, was beginning. A more worldly attitude meant that many superstitions and misconceptions were dispelled. In a sense, the world was turned on its axis. Educated opinion began to swing steadily away from the medieval condemnation of suicide. The movement continued and gathered momentum through the late 1600s and early 1700s.

With a reaffirmation of Greek and Roman values, the concept of an 'easy death' gradually came to be regarded as an ideal once again. A sudden and intense strengthening of religious feeling in the fifteenth and sixteenth centuries was offset by a renewed enthusiasm for rationalism. Both the Catholic and the Protestant churches continued to condemn suicide, but most enlightened people no longer saw it as an inexpiable sin. As Montaigne observed: 'The voluntariest death is the fairest.'[26]

In 1516, Sir Thomas More's *Utopia* was published. It depicted an ideal society in which voluntary euthanasia was officially sanctioned. Of terminal illness, the noted Catholic wrote:

> If, besides being incurable, the disease also causes constant excruciating pain, some priests and government officials visit the person concerned and say... Since your life's a misery to you, why hesitate to die? You're imprisoned in a torture chamber—why don't you break out and escape to a better world... We'll arrange for your release... If the patient finds these arguments convincing, he either starves himself to death, or is given a soporific and put painlessly out of his misery. But this is strictly voluntary.[27]

What distinguished the sixteenth-century attitude towards suicide from that of the Middle Ages was a reawakened interest in individualism. The shift in emphasis made the morality of life-and-death decisions more fluid and complex. Certainly, they were open to question. Montaigne, for instance, argued that man's dignity and ability to evaluate himself in the scale of nature made suicide justifiable. It was no disadvantage, in his eyes, if humanistic reflections of the period provided an opportunity to cast

7

doubts on the teachings of the Church. Quite the contrary. With Cato as his model, he intended to restate Stoic ideas in his writings, tempered somewhat by a moderating Christianity.[28] 'Death,' he wrote, 'is a most assured haven, never to be feared, and often to be sought.' And later he said: 'All comes to one period, whether man make an end of himself, or whether he endure it.'[29]

It's recorded that in 1537, Ambroise Parè, surgeon to Francis I, mentioned finding several severely wounded and unconscious men. 'An old soldier,' he noted, 'asked me if there was any way to cure them. I said "No." Then he went up to them and cut their throats, gently and without ill will. I told him he was a villain; he answered he prayed God that when he should be in such a plight, he might find someone to do the same for him.'[30] By the same token, less than a century later, Francis Bacon insisted that doctors should help dying patients 'to make a fair and easy passage from life.'[31] And in 1647, John Donne, in *Biathanatos*, argued in favour of suicide as a form of voluntary euthanasia. The taking of one's life, he insisted, is not incompatible with the laws of nature, of reason, and of God. Speaking of a disease for which there is no cure, he said:

> When the disease would not reduce us, [God] sent a second and worse affliction, ignorant and torturing physicians. I must say the same of this case, that in punishment of Adam's sins God cast upon us an infectious death with so much horror and fright that it can hardly be made wholesome and agreeable to us.[32]

He closes by quoting a physician: 'Let him who cannot digest sleep.'

The expansiveness of the Renaissance, then, not only enhanced man's sense of himself. It also, through scientific discovery, gave rise to innovative methods for treating disease. At the same time, efforts to keep patients alive often caused suffering—which threatened to diminish the value of life. Bacon, Montaigne, More and Donne were among the first to recognize this dilemma. They were among the first to demand a merciful release from the new 'technology' of their times.

## THE EIGHTEENTH CENTURY

Still, those men were essayists and philosophers. Fortunately, by the eighteenth century, a few members of the medical profession had begun speaking about their responsibility to the patient. They stressed the importance of a natural and humane way of dying. For instance, in his 'Oratio de Euthanasia of 1794, Paradys, a physician, recommended an "easy death" for a patient, especially one who is incurable and suffering.'[33] Like More and Donne, he saw medical progress as a sword that cut both ways, with the patient sometimes a victim.

Further, by this time, it was not just the physician who had views on life and death. One result of the Renaissance and the Reformation was a general humanitarian enlightenment. The common man was more informed. For example, he knew that suicide was no longer an unforgivable sin, and that civil and criminal law had softened towards the victim. Between 1770 and 1788, the coroners for the county of Kent returned only fifteen verdicts of *felo de se* out of approximately 580 suicides. Although the penalty for the fifteen cases is unknown (dishonour for the family? confiscation of goods and property?), public opinion was opposed to punishment of any kind; the average eighteenth century suicide and his family could count on a sympathetic jury. In France, likewise, between 1700 and 1789, there were only eighteen successful actions taken against suicides.[34] In Geneva, in 1770, indignities to the corpse were officially abolished; confiscation of a suicide's property had ended many years before.[35]

For the eighteenth-century rationalists, then, it was ridiculous and presumptuous to inflate suicide, an intensely private act, into a monstrous crime. In 1777, a year after his death, the Scottish philosopher David Hume's essay 'Of Suicide' was published. 'When life has become a burden,' he had written, 'both courage and prudence should engage us to rid ourselves at once of existence.'[36] With this more informed attitude on the part of Hume and others, another phase had begun. A supportive attitude towards suicide surfaced publicly. For instance, Joseph Addison's play *Cato*, extolling the noblest Roman suicide of all, was greeted each night by thunderous applause from Whigs and Tories alike. In 1788, Horace Walpole, commenting on the statutes and penalties imposed on suicides, referred to such practices as the 'absurd stake and highway of our ancestors.'[37]

Similarly, in France—where suicide laws and penalties had once been equally stringent—there were references in Rousseau to a 'virtuous suicide' due to increased suffering and wastefulness: *'être rien, ou être bien'*— 'to be nothing, or to be well.' It was believed that when incurable pain overwhelmed man—when he was dehumanized by suffering, when the soul was no longer the soul—death was indeed a merciful release and suicide a laudable act.[38] It took nearly a century in France, but by 1870, with a swing back to liberal and democratic ideals, the government eventually forbade discrimination against anyone—even suicides—in the matter of burial, and insisted on the application of proper honours, whether in religious or in civil funerals.[39]

## FROM THE NINETEENTH CENTURY TO 1940

In the early part of the nineteenth century, one Carl F. H. Marx presented an oral thesis, 'Medical Euthanasia'. In it he criticized physicians who treated diseases rather than the patient, and who, as a result, lost interest and abandoned the patient when they couldn't find a cure. Marx insisted that the physician 'is not expected to have a remedy for death, but for the skilful alleviation of suffering, and he should know how to apply it when all hope has departed.'[40] Several years later, Schopenhauer stressed man's 'unassailable title to his own life and person . . . It will be generally found that, as soon as the terrors of life reach the point at which they outweigh the terrors of death, a man will put an end to his life.'[41]

While Schopenhauer may have been speaking of a more general malaise as a basis for contemplating suicide, man's right to define the quality of his own life and death was an inalienable assertion of his will, whatever the reasons. (It was Nietzsche who, only a few years later, spoke of the thought of suicide as 'a strong consolation . . . one can get through many a bad night with it.') Both physicians and philosophers were speaking about a person's right to decide for himself. Man was increasingly in charge of his environment. The Renaissance had rekindled many classical values, not the least of which was that a man was a free agent, provided he was acting rationally. He could applaud and draw on the 'natural and obscure instinct' (as did Montesquieu) which enabled him, like the ancient Romans, to love what was worthy in himself more than mere life or a collective ideal.[42] A life wasted by persistent and unrelenting pain was not worthy; it was a useless life, often demanding a merciful release. In short, a man living such a life was no longer a man.[43]

In the latter half of the nineteenth century, even more medical writers addressed the subject. Much of the fascination lay in precisely what caused a suicide—imbalance in the brain, thick cranium, genetic defects—but a handful of physicians wrote and spoke about suicide and the dying patient. Didn't every patient deserve to die 'well'? In 1869, William Lecky referred to euthanasia as an act of 'inducing an easy death'.[44] In 1873, L. A. Tollemache, in an eloquent article entitled 'The New Cure of the Incurables', made a strong plea for the legalization of voluntary euthanasia. 'Need I not add,' he wrote, 'that, if a doctor, even at an agonized patient's entreaty, takes a course likely to hasten death, he is doing that for which, under the present law, he might be severely taken to task; nay, that he is hovering on the brink of manslaughter, if not of something worse?'[45]

In 1889, while speaking to the Maine Medical Association, Dr Frank E. Hitchcock urged physicians not to ignore the needs of terminally ill patients, especially those in pain. Such suffering should be relieved, he argued; ultimately, fairness and justice 'would regard the intent of the physician who humanely assists the patient in and out of his suffering.'[46] Only twenty years earlier, a plea had been put forth in an essay published by the Birmingham Speculative Club: The writer, S. D. Williams, held that it was the responsibility of the physician to 'destroy consciousness at once and put the sufferer to a quick and painless death' when the illness was agonizing and hopeless.[47]

In 1897, French sociologist Émile Durkheim published *Le Suicide*, which examined suicide as a social fact and analyzed it accordingly, somewhat demystifying the phenomenon.[48] A few years later, the German psychiatrist/philosopher Alfred Hoche coined the term *Bilanz Selbstmord*—'balance-sheet suicide'—in citing examples of apparently rational suicide by those who had reviewed their lives, weighed the pros and cons, and decided, quite deliberately, that death was preferable to life. The concept of physical and mental pain, then, was considered by physicians and writers as a possible justification for ending one's life.

In fact, in both America and Europe over the next three decades, the subject of euthanasia was becoming less academic and more a matter of what *should* be done—not only by physicians but by the law and governing bodies. For instance, in England in 1901, Dr C. E. Goddard addressed the Willesden and District Medical Society in northwest London. His speech, 'Suggestions in Favour of Terminating Absolutely Hopeless Cases of Injury and Disease', made an appeal for legalizing euthanasia as a way to avoid suffering for terminal patients. Hopeless idiots, imbeciles, and 'monstrosities' were included—'Those having no will power nor intelligence of their own, and being a burden to themselves, and especially their friends and society, [and] of course absolutely incapable of improvement.'[49] Goddard's speech was received with both interest and alarm.

Five years later, in the United States, a bill dealing with euthanasia was introduced in the Ohio legislature. An editor of the *Independent* wrote about the bill:

> When an adult of sound mind has been fatally hurt and is so ill that recovery is impossible or is suffering extreme physical pain without hope of relief, his physician, if not a relative and if not interested in any way in the person's estate, may ask his patient in the presence of three witnesses if he or she is ready to die... Three other physicians are to be consulted.[50]

The writer went on to say that although the bill was supported by some eminent people, civilization at that time was not ready to consider such legislation seriously. An article in the *Outlook* ('Shall We Legalize Homicide?') listed some dangers: Guardians and relatives could rid themselves too easily of 'burdens', inept doctors could conceal their failures, inheritors would be tempted to stoop to corrupt practices and pressures, and confidence in doctors would be undermined. 'It would add to the terror of the sickbed by stimulating fears... The patient would look forward to the visit of the physician with dread.'[51] A *New York Times* editorial compared the practice of euthanasia to 'practices of savages in all parts of the world.'[52]

Not surprisingly, when the Ohio bill was sent to the Committee on Medical Jurisprudence, it was defeated by a vote of seventy-eight to twenty-two.

Still, the fact that the bill was proposed at all—and received almost 25 per cent of the vote—indicated that people were concerned about controlling the manner of their dying. In 1911 in Europe, the Laforgues—he a French writer and socialist, she the daughter of Karl Marx—committed suicide. In a written statement, Laforgue pointed out that he had orchestrated his own death 'before pitiless old age (which is taking from me one by one the pleasures and joys of existence, and depriving me of my intellectual strength) paralyzes my energy, breaks my life, and makes me a burden to myself and others. Years ago I promised myself not to live beyond seventy.'[53] Similarly, in 1912, a woman petitioned the New York state legislature to allow her physician to put her to death painlessly—and not charge him with homicide—because she was suffering from an incurable disease and was in constant pain. The petition caused a sensation. Despite the appeal, still no legal sanctions for euthanasia were secured.

Such efforts to change the law provoked much debate, especially among doctors. Responding to the New York petition, the president of the American Medical Association declared that allowing physicians to practise any form of euthanasia would demean the profession; it would be 'no respectable calling'.[54] Disagreeing with him was Dr William J. Robinson, who argued that euthanasia measures were perfectly reasonable and justified when the incurably ill and hopelessly insane were involved. Life was sacred, he said, but only if it was 'pleasant, wanted, and bearable.'[55]

One of the most important attempts to incorporate euthanasia into law took place in England in 1931. Dr C. Killick Millard, health officer for the city of Leicester, gave his presidential address before the Society of Officers of Health. It was during this time that there had been a spate of scholarly articles and two books in support of euthanasia and its legalization. Perhaps Millard's speech was inevitable. Still, he startled his audience by devoting his entire talk ('A Plea for Legalization of Euthanasia') to an appeal for a change in the law. He quoted extensively from More's *Utopia* and spoke of the anguish of those who die lingering deaths, 'by inches'. In a subsequent article in *Fortnightly Review*, he presented his specific proposals in a draft bill entitled 'The Voluntary Euthanasia Legalization Bill'. It included the following provisions:

1. An application for a euthanasia permit may be filed by a dying person stating that he has been informed by two medical practitioners that he is suffering from a fatal and incurable disease, and that the process of death is likely to be protracted and painful.
2. The application must be attested by a magistrate and accompanied by two medical certificates.

3. The application and certificates must be examined by the patient and relatives interviewed by a 'euthanasia referee'.
4. A court will then review the application, certificates, the testimony of the referee and any other representatives of the patient. It will then issue a permit to receive euthanasia to the applicant and a permit to administer euthanasia to the medical practitioner (or euthanizer).
5. The permit would be valid for a specified period, within which the patient would determine if and when he wished to use it.

Millard added that the final responsibility might lie with either the physician or the patient—that a lethal dose could, in fact, be placed by the patient's bedside to be taken at his discretion. ('I am inclined myself to think,' he wrote, 'that the responsibility for the actual *coup de grâce* should rest with the patient.')

Despite a mixed reaction to Millard's proposals, much support came from prominent people—churchmen, academics, writers, aristocrats, and other physicians. Eventually, in 1935, the British Voluntary Euthanasia Society was formed, specifically to promote the bill drafted by Millard. (And it was around this time that an anonymous doctor granted an exclusive interview to the London *Daily Mail*, citing numbers of cases in which he had put suffering patients out of their misery. The article, which described the physician as a 'kindly-faced, elderly family doctor', caused a stir in both Britain and America. The November 16 issue of *Newsweek* commented that the article 'looked suspiciously like publicity for England's Euthanasia Legalization Society which this Winter hopes to introduce a bill in Parliament.')

Unfortunately for Millard and his colleagues, the bill had as many—if not more—opponents as supporters. In 1936 it was defeated in the House of Lords, after a heated discussion, by a vote of thirty-five to fourteen. The Euthanasia Society, however, continued to campaign for the rights of the terminally ill and for appropriate legislation (which was not considered in Parliament again until 1950). Millard continued as spokesman. After the bill was defeated, he said he believed that 'the substitution of a quick and painless death in certain cases for a death which was slow and agonizing would be regarded hereafter as one of the great reforms of the age.'[56]

In 1937 in Nebraska, a bill modelled after its English predecessor was introduced in the state legislature by Senator John Comstock. Entitled the Voluntary Euthanasia Act, the bill was sponsored by Dr Inez Philbrick, a former member of the University of Nebraska faculty. It was, however, referred to a committee, indefinitely postponed, and never acted upon.

Concern about the failure to enact legislation and inspired by the British model led to the founding in 1938 of the Euthanasia Society of America. Announcing the formation of the Society, Reverend Charles Francis Potter explained that members 'subscribed to the belief that, with adequate safe-guards, it should be made legal to allow incurable sufferers to choose im-mediate death rather than await it in agony.'[57]

Yet their founding principles were widespread, to say the least. Dr Foster Kennedy, a member of the advisory board and the Society's second president, concentrated solely on the 'congenitally unfit'. In speaking of 'nature's mistakes', Kennedy argued that what was questionable was 'per-mitting a life that is young . . . to continue when that life is at once defec-tive, without value and tortured . . . I believe it would be for the general good that euthanasia be legalized for creatures born defective, whose pres-ent condition is miserable and whose future . . . hopeless.'[58] Later he would modify his views. Dr Alexis Carrel, another supporter, was even more radical. 'Sentimental prejudice,' he had declared four years earlier, 'should not obstruct the quiet and painless disposition of incurables, crimi-nals, and hopeless lunatics.'[59]

On January 26, 1939, a bill to legalize euthanasia in New York was pro-posed by the Society's treasurer, Charles Nixdorff. 'Spurred by recent "mercy killing" cases,' the January 27 New York Times reported, 'and by mounting inquiries from persons suffering from incurable diseases, the Eu-thanasia Society of America offered yesterday a proposed legislative bill which would legalize the putting to death of incurables in this State when the patient wants to die.' Similar to the British bill, which concentrated on terminally ill adults, it was never introduced into the legislature and was shelved until after the war. Efforts at legislation on both sides of the Atlan-tic had been useless.

The reasons for such interest in legalizing euthanasia were twofold. First, there were more doctors who were willing to speak publicly about their responsibilities to the dying patient. For instance, in the May 17 issue of Medical Record, Abraham Wolbarst, in 'The Doctor Looks at Eutha-nasia', defended the practice and the proposed New York bill. (It was, ap-parently, the first article in an American medical journal to advocate legaliz-ing euthanasia.) 'The vast majority of thinking people,' Wolbarst wrote, 'favour euthanasia as a humanitarian principle... The human mind revolts at the thought of unnecessary suffering... It is not how long we humans live, but how we live, that is important.' (Four years earlier, in an article in Forum, Wolbarst had advocated euthanasia for the incurably ill, imbeciles, the mentally defective, and the chronically insane. Naturally there were many opponents, among them physicians, psychoanalysts, and Catholic churchmen. One of the latter, in Commonweal, defined all suffer-ing generically, as 'the greatest possible source of heroism, purification and redemption.')

Equally important in fuelling the debate was the growing number of court cases in England and America since 1920 that revolved around mercy killings, assisted suicide, and suicide due to terminal illness. No two results were the same. In 1920 in Michigan, Frank Roberts was convicted of wilful murder and sentenced to life imprisonment and hard labour, as well as solitary confinement. His crime? At the urging of his wife, who suffered from multiple sclerosis and had attempted suicide before, Roberts had mixed Paris green (containing arsenic) with water and given it to her. The court's decision was upheld by the Supreme Court of Michigan.[60]

In 1925 in Colorado, Dr Harold Blazer was tried for killing his daughter, an incurable invalid he had cared for for more than thirty years. The case was dismissed when the jury could not reach a verdict. In 1933, a coroner's jury attributed the death of Allie Stephens, a cancer sufferer for six years, to natural causes—not to the violent blow given at her request by a nephew. Apparently Stephens had pleaded with him to hasten her death. Driven to distraction, he struck her violently, but since her skull was not fractured the blow was not considered the cause of death.[61]

In 1934 in England, sixty-two-year-old May Brownhill killed her thirty-one-year-old imbecile son. The case received a good deal of publicity in England and America. 'I have just put Denis to sleep,' she told a doctor. 'I gave him one hundred tablets and then placed a gas tube in his mouth.' Mrs Brownhill was about to undergo a serious operation and had been worried that there would be no one to care for her son. The judge warned the jury of the law as it stood: 'The time may come when it may be the law of this country that an imbecile or idiot may be sent to a merciful death. [But] that is not the law at present.' The jury, absent only five minutes, returned a verdict of guilty—although they added 'the strongest possible recommendation for mercy.'[62] Still, the defendant was sentenced to die for 'mercy murder'; the death penalty was mandatory in England for wilful murder. Within two days of the sentencing, however, the home secretary pardoned Mrs Brownhill. She was set free, recuperated from her operation, and went on holiday with her husband.

The question of mercy killing was also raised in cases where, out of self-pity and fear, terminally ill people took their own lives. The most widely publicized of these suicides was that of Charlotte Perkins Gilman, an early feminist crusader. When she killed herself in 1935, she left a note saying: 'The time is approaching when we shall consider it abhorrent to our civilization to allow a human being to lie in prolonged agony which we should mercifully end in any other creature... I have preferred chloroform to cancer.'[63] In an essay published posthumously, she had written: 'The record of a previously noble life is precisely what makes it sheer insult to allow death in pitiful degradation. We may not wish to "die with our boots on", but we may well prefer to "die with our brains on".' Before her death she publicly appealed for legislative changes to sanction euthanasia for anyone suffering from an incurable mental or physical illness.[64]

Three years later, in New York in 1938, a grand jury refused to indict Harry C. Johnson for asphyxiating his wife, who had reportedly wanted to die. Johnson was charged with first-degree murder. Mrs Johnson, who had had cancer for four and a half years, pleaded with her husband, according to his accounts, to end her agony. Finally, he dismissed a nurse, went to the basement, attached fifty feet of garden hose to the gas jet, and hauled the line upstairs to his wife's bedroom. He then sealed the room and turned on the gas.[65] Three psychiatrists judged Johnson temporarily insane. The grand jury deliberated two hours before it agreed to free him without a trial.

Four months later, in early 1939, Louis Greenfield was acquitted by a jury of the murder of his seventeen-year-old 'incurable imbecile' son, his only child. 'Father on Trial as Mercy Killer' read the headlines. Soaking two handkerchiefs in chloroform, Greenfield had placed them over the face of his sleeping child. Afterwards he informed the doorman of his apartment building, who summoned authorities; Greenfield was subsequently charged with first-degree murder.

In a mild opening address, the district attorney failed to ask openly for a conviction, but told the jury he would prove that Greenfield was sane when he chloroformed his son. As a result, Greenfield based his defence on 'defective reasoning'—brought on by years of physical and mental torture caused by the suffering of the boy. 'I knew it was against the law of man,' Greenfield said, 'but not against the law of God. . . . The law of God is mightier than the law of man.'[66] After deliberating four hours, the jury acquitted him. Curiously, New York psychiatrists promptly condemned Greenfield, calling him a murderer who had tired of his son. *Time* magazine, however, in its January 23 issue, was quick to report their findings—based on statistics provided by the Euthanasia Society:

> Few hardheaded psychiatrists or soft-hearted laymen realize that: 1) mercy killings now occur in the US at the rate of one a week; 2) mercy killers are almost never convicted; 3) stiffest penalty imposed in recent years was three months in prison. If a grand jury refuses to indict Louis Greenfield, it will add one more brick to the foundation of unwritten laws condoning mercy killings. It will also strengthen the case of euthanasia advocates, headed by Manhattan's famed Neurologist Foster Kennedy. Euthanasists decry mercy killings by overwrought relatives, plump for a tightly written law which will set up impartial committees of physicians to examine hopeless invalids to recommend scientific extinction.

After having read newspaper accounts of the Greenfield case, ten months later, in October 1939, Louis Repouille chloroformed his thirteen-year-old son, described as another 'incurable imbecile'. Repouille called his act one 'of mercy'. The boy, deformed and mute since birth, was bedridden; five years earlier, because of a brain tumour, he had become blind. Repouille said: '[The Greenfield case] made me think about doing the same thing to my boy. I think Mr Greenfield was justified. They didn't punish him for it. But I'm not looking for sympathy. I don't care what happens to me. My boy is dead and his suffering is over.' Repouille was arraigned on a homicide charge, and later he told detectives: 'If I had to do it again, I'd do it. I know I did the right thing in ending my boy's misery.'[67]

Two months later, Repouille was found guilty of manslaughter in the second degree. The district attorney declared that the verdict demonstrated that 'mercy killings are not countenanced by society.' Despite the fact that the judge suspended Repouille's sentence, he commented:

> This type of killing has become associated in the public mind with the thought that, on certain occasions, it is an act of mercy. The words mercy killing have no sanction in our law. The fact that you were the father of an imbecile did not give you the right to kill him. There is grave danger that the leniency extended to you may encourage others to do what you did.[68]

Released on probation, Repouille announced to the public that he was looking for a job 'to support my wife and four children.'

During the last half of the decade, several polls tapped public opinion on mercy killings. In 1937 a survey conducted by *Fortune* magazine posed two questions:

> Some people believe that doctors should be permitted to perform mercy killings upon infants born permanently deformed or mentally handicapped. Under what circumstances would you approve this?
> The same thing is suggested for persons incurably and painfully ill. Under what circumstances would you approve this?[69]

Although 40.5 per cent of the respondents unconditionally rejected euthanasia for defective infants, 14.5 per cent were undecided and 45 per cent approved of the practice with the following breakdown: 13.9 per cent with the permission of the family, 23.3 per cent with the approval of a medical board, and 7.8 per cent with the approval of a medical board and the family's permission.

Similarly, 47.5 per cent rejected, unconditionally, euthanasia for the incurably ill; 15.2 per cent were undecided; and 37.3 per cent approved its practice with the following differences: 11.6 per cent with the permission of the patient, 4.2 per cent with the family's permission, 10.9 per cent with the approval of a medical board, 1.7 per cent with patient and family permission, and 8.9 per cent with patient, family, and medical board permission.

In 1936 and 1939, the American Institute of Public Opinion asked people: 'Do you favour mercy deaths under government supervision for hopeless invalids?' In 1936, 38.64 per cent of the respondents said yes; 45.36 per cent said no; and 16.0 per cent had no opinion. In 1939, 41.40 per cent said yes; 48.60 per cent said no; and 10.0 per cent had no opinion. Doctors who were polled separately voted 53 per cent in favour and 47 per cent opposed.[70] A similar poll conducted by the British Institute of Public Opinion showed that, of those responding, 69 per cent—more than two thirds—endorsed the principle of euthanasia.[71]

The end of the nineteenth century and the beginning of the twentieth was a time when people were increasingly concerned about the quality of life, the impact of sophisticated medical techniques, and the ability to control the environment. Questions about protracted death-beds, unnecessary suffering, the chronically insane, and defective infants prompted growing support for euthanasia and its legislation—in both America and Europe. Mercy-killing trials dramatized these situations. Yet despite the efforts of the American and British voluntary-euthanasia societies, all attempts at legislation failed, even with a significant proportion of the public—a third or more—supportive of such efforts.

Attempts to establish the practice of euthanasia, however, took a radically different turn in Germany. The concept of *lebensunwerten Leben*— 'life not worthy of life'—had surfaced as early as 1920. Arguments for terminating these lives—'wasted' or 'useless'—appeared in German medical and legal literature throughout the 1920s and 1930s. This was similar to literature in America and Britain,[72] but in Germany the notion gained governmental approval. As a result, *lebensunwerten Leben* provided the rationale for the Nazi practice of senselessly murdering thousands of Germans who were mentally and physically handicapped. Improperly labelled 'euthanasia', such a practice would forever affect the meaning of mercy killing and good death.

Euthanasia would never again be defined as the Greeks and Romans understood it.

# CHAPTER TWO

## *Euthanasia's Nazi 'Albatross'*

Without question, the most totally evil crime of this century was the Jewish Holocaust. Germany, under Nazi rule between 1935 and 1945, ruthlessly exterminated an estimated six million European Jews. The victims were shot, gassed, starved, beaten, or tortured to death. In the name of science, experiments on live humans were carried out in fiendishly cruel ways, causing unimaginable agony—and producing no significant advances in medical knowledge.

The mass extermination of Jews by gassing—a method that accounted for some two-thirds of the deaths—was preceded, from 1939 to 1941, by the elimination of approximately 100,000 men, women, and children, none of them Jewish, all Aryan Germans, who were handicapped, mentally or physically, or both. Most were murdered with equipment that resembled shower stalls; the victim was lured to his death under the guise of personal hygiene. Instead of water, the nozzles emitted the lethal Zyklon B gas especially developed for mass murder.

For the four decades since the discovery (at the Nuremberg war crimes trial) of the extent of the Nazi extermination programmes, the intellectual and legal progress of the euthanasia movement, particularly in the English-speaking world, has been seriously hampered by the haunting memory of German atrocities.

The conscience of many people is troubled by three features: (1) that a nation so highly educated and cultured as Germany, birthplace of universally venerated musicians, poets, philosophers, and physicians, could permit such evil; (2) that German adherence to the democratic rule of law and its highly structured bureaucracy—often ludicrous in its efficiency—could degenerate so far as to permit such extensive and persistent violations of the basic human and legal right to life; and (3) that if such atrocities could happen in Germany, they might happen in Britain or the United States, given a change in social attitudes and the election of a tyrannical politician. Could a small amount of justified legalized voluntary euthanasia today become the 'thin end of the wedge' for enforced euthanasia tomorrow?

From the proceedings of the Nuremberg trials in 1946–47, German trials of war criminals in the 1950s and 1960s, and the ongoing investigations by historians of the Holocaust, it is now possible to see the sequence of events against the climate of political and racial policies that existed in the 1930s and 1940s in Germany.

There is in German nationalist and racial ideology a long history of obsession with racial purity, an urge to acknowledge the Aryans as the finest, strongest race in the world and thus the most dominant. In the 1920s, Hitler and his Nazi colleagues developed this historical belief into a mystique: A racially pure Germany that would no longer lose wars and that would never again be humiliated by the rest of the world.

In 1924, Hitler wrote in *Mein Kampf* (My Struggle): 'All who are not of good race in this world are chaff. And all occurrences in world history are only the expression of the races' instinct of self-preservation, in the good or bad sense.'[1]

If there was a fearsome hint as to what havoc the man intended, it must be another short passage from *Mein Kampf*: 'And if there were ever really one healthy man among the cripples, he used up all his strength just to keep the others on their feet, and in this way he himself was crippled.'[2]

It is one of the worst lessons of history that the world ignored this book containing Hitler's crazed predictions, even when he took power. One of the first laws the Nazis enacted in 1933 was compulsory sterilization of persons who had hereditary illnesses. The condemned person had no say in the matter. The court-authorized operation was forcible.

Hitler ignored whatever criticisms there were and proceeded with a programme of indoctrinating health professionals with Nazi racial ideology. 'Eugenics, or race hygiene' (*Rassenhygiene*), was taught to all health workers—including those in psychiatric institutions.

Craftily, the Nazis waited for this propaganda to sink in. Then, at the start of World War II, they launched their 'euthanasia' programme, at a time when people were distracted by the fighting and were receptive to the idea that those who could not help the nation might just as well be dead.

The concept of the *Volk*—pure Aryan Germans, destined to rule the world—had been around for centuries. The German term for those who stood in the way of this was *lebensunwerten Leben*. As noted, this means 'life unworthy of life'. The Nazis thought up a phrase more apposite to wartime: *unnütze Esser*—'useless eater'.

While the sterilization programme was being carried out openly and legally, the euthanasia programme was top secret and cloaked under wartime furtiveness. Hitler instructed his aides that he was not to be connected with the programme at all—at least not officially—and in late October

1939 he signed a secret decree, backdated to September 1, 1938. (Britain and France declared war on Germany on September 3, when Hitler refused to withdraw from Poland.) The decree, found after the war, read: 'Reich leader Bouhler and Dr Brandt are charged with the responsibility for expanding the authority of physicians, to be designated by name, to the end that patients considered incurable in the best available human judgment, after critical evaluation of their state of health, may be granted a merciful death.'[3]

Covertly, Hitler's aides set up front organizations such as the Charitable Foundation for Institutional Care which worked from an obscure office in Tiergartenstrasse 4, hence the infamous code name 'T4' for the extermination programme. Patients shipped to the euthanasia camps had absolutely no say in their fate, nor did their next of kin—if, indeed, they had any idea what was happening. Anyone who asked about the legality of the programme was told that Hitler's decree had full legal force and that elimination of the handicapped was already being legally carried out in Russia and America. It was almost impossible in wartime Germany for anybody to confirm this.

When some physicians asked why the law was not made public, they were told by the bureaucrats that this would upset the patients who were to be killed, thus requiring the drafting of a new type of law.

Initial gassings took place at the end of 1939 and early 1940 at Brandenburg an der Havel, the first of a dozen or so institutions converted for the programme in Germany and Austria. Covert organizations back in Berlin arranged the transportation of the victims, tidied up their financial and legal affairs, and concocted letters to next of kin giving phony reasons for death. The letters often read:

We regret to inform you that your——, who was recently transferred to our institution by ministerial order, unexpectedly died on —— of ——. All our medical efforts were unfortunately without avail.

In view of the nature of his serious, incurable ailment, his death, which saved him from a lifelong institutional sojourn, is to be regarded as a release.

Because of the danger of contagion existing here, we were forced to have the deceased cremated at once.[4]*

An urn containing what purported to be the dead person's ashes was for-

---

* A variation: 'For purposes of avoiding the outbreak or the communication of infectious disease, the local police authorities, as per §22 of the ordinance concerning the combating of communicable diseases, have ordered the immediate cremation of the corpse and the disinfection of any remaining effects.' (Gerald Fleming, *Hitler and the Final Solution* [Berkeley: University of California Press, 1982], p. 26.)

warded to the family. Often relatives of the deceased were warned not to demand further explanations or to 'spread false rumours'.[5]

German public opinion was alerted to the programme by the often demonstrable falsity of the death certificates. For instance, some documents claimed that death occurred during an appendectomy, when the family knew the appendix had already been removed. Some death certificates referred to a long illness, whereas the family had seen their loved one fit and well in recent times. Occasionally two urns came to the same family.

Officials, physicians, and at least fifty psychiatrists involved in the programme, used pseudonyms to conceal their identities. Some of Germany's most eminent psychiatrists, holding professorial chairs, took part in the selection procedures.[6] One professor received six hundred brains from euthanasia institutes for scientific study. 'They were shipped to him,' one historian writes, 'in accordance with instructions he gave, in batches of 150 to 250 by the Non-Profit Patient-Transportation Corporation.'[7]

There is no record of the Nazis assisting in a suicide or killing anyone suffering intolerably from a fatal illness. Quite the contrary, every killing was unexpected by the victim and involuntary. The operators liked to call their work 'mercy killing', but the quality of 'mercy' was something they—and only they—decided. The victims ranged from the grossly deformed to the mentally handicapped to the treatably neurotic.

A nonexistent registry, documents with false reports and circumstances of death, the pretence of an epidemic hazard as justification for the cremation of corpses, cover names for physicians and officials, fabricated medical histories, gas chambers disguised as tiled shower facilities with dummy shower nozzles, hypocritical demonstration of sympathy and condolence, deceptive claims about the purpose of patient relocations and the registration forms: this is what actually constituted the euthanasia programme, which was so readily termed a programme of 'mercy killing' (*Gnadentod*), and about which no one—least of all, the victims—was permitted to know for whom, when, and where 'mercy' would be granted.[8]

Despite the elaborate precautions taken to ensure secrecy, within two years many Germans were becoming aware of what was happening. Nearby residents could not help but notice the busloads of people entering the extermination centres and the nauseating smells emerging from the chimneys. Children shouted in the streets, 'There comes the murder van again!' Bogus death certificates were prompting more and more discussion. The Nazis explained away the enforced cremations by saying that there were epidemics of disease—but no one in the community saw any evidence of this. SS men posted newly painted signs in front of estates that had never been used as hospitals, warning: 'Keep Away! Danger of Pestilence!' Anyone who made inquiries—even relatives—was warned off.[9]

Although Hitler declared in the autumn of 1941: 'The law of existence prescribes uninterrupted killing, so that the better may live,'[10] the euthanasia programme was slowing down considerably by then. There was a growing fear that the elderly, regardless of the state of their health, would be next. The minister of justice had written to Hitler that people 'are disquieted by the question of whether old folk who have worked hard all their lives and may merely have come into their dotage are also being liquidated. There is talk that homes for the aged are to be cleaned out too.'[11] Even worse, rumours—demoralizing for the war effort—were circulating that soldiers with grievous wounds, particularly head wounds, would be 'eliminated' when they were sent home.

The demoralization became so serious that at the end of 1940, Heinrich Himmler, head of the SS, wrote to a Reich official:

I hear that there is great unrest in the Württemberg mountains on account of the Grafeneck Institution. The people know the grey SS bus and think they know what happens in the crematory with its ever-smoking chimney. What does happen there is a secret, and yet it is a secret no longer. The public temper is ugly and in my opinion there is nothing to do but to stop using this particular institution. Possibly one might initiate a skilful and reasonable programme of enlightenment by running films on hereditary and mental disease in this particular region. May I ask you to let me know how this difficult problem was solved.[12]

Fortunately, there were a few who protested. In the early part of 1941, several prominent members of the various churches voiced their opposition to Hitler. Pastor Braune of the German Protestant Church stated: 'It is urgently necessary to halt [the extinction programmes] as quickly as possible, since they strike sharply at the moral foundations of the nation as a whole. The inviolability of human life is a pillar of social order.'[13] The bishop of Limburg wrote of the horrors of people in his community, who were well aware of the euthanasia programme being carried out nearby. And the archbishop of Munich-Freising wrote to the minister of justice in 1940: 'Even in time of war, the inalienable foundations of moral order and the fundamental rights of the individual must not be revoked.'[14]

Other people, including physicians, lodged formal complaints (one doctor wrote: '[With such destruction], the law must guard against undermining the patient's faith in the medical profession'[15]), embarrassing law enforcement officers who still believed in the rule of law. In addition, there were rumours that mental patients were being eliminated because of food shortages, indicating to many Germans that the nation might be on the verge of starvation.

In August 1941, Hitler was bowing to these pressures; he gave a verbal order for the programme to be 'stalled'. Historians differ as to whether Hitler was willing to consider abandoning the programme for reasons of morale or because he had killed all he needed to. Until then, there were only estimates of how many 'unpure' had died, mainly because of the furtiveness of the programme. The general guess was about ninety thousand. However, official documents found after the war showed that while the killings slowed, they were never entirely stopped.

Hitler had learned from these purges that he could not safely carry out the mass extermination of the Jews from bases within Germany—but there might be alternatives. The special gas chambers for the euthanasia programme were dismantled and shipped to Poland. And within Germany, many killings were continued under the auspices of the Ministry of the Interior, a unit that acted under Hitler's orders. In fact, in the light of the war trials since Nuremberg, it has emerged that the killing of defective children went on until 1945. For instance, Alfons Klein, a director of the Hadamar psychiatric institution, declared at his trial in 1946 that three thousand patients had been killed after August 1941.[16] They were eliminated by starvation or injection of lethal drugs. How many children died will never be known, but there were undoubtedly many thousands.

In evidence at the Nuremberg war trials, Dr Karl Brandt, one of the two men charged in Hitler's original decree with carrying out the programme, recalled: 'In the case of children the purpose was to prevent their development at an early age, if only for reasons of family difficulties, etc. The goal was to make it possible to locate and kill these cases of congenital malformation as soon as possible after birth.'[17] There is no proof that the parents of these children had any say at all in their children's fate.

Regardless of how many children were murdered, there is no doubt that the twelve or more institutions used for such German domestic extermination programmes were also schools for mass murder. The Nazi plan for the extermination of the racially 'valueless' had been spoken of since 1935. From the Nazi point of view, then, the euthanasia 'camps' provided a felicitous twofold use of their facilities.

In his book *The Murderers Among Us*, Simon Wiesenthal, the Nazi-hunter, pinpoints the value of the elimination centres. Writing about Castle Hartheim in Austria, he notes:

Hartheim graduates later became teachers of future cadres of scientifically trained killers. After some practice, the 'students' became insensible to the cries of the victims. The 'teachers' would watch the reaction of their 'students'. It was a brilliant psychological touch to use Germans and Austrians as victims in the basic training for mass murder. If a 'student' did not break when he had to kill his own people, he would have no moral scruple about exterminating thousands of *Untermenschen*. A 'student' who couldn't take it was sent to the front, where his commander would assign him to *Himmelfahrskommando*, a suicide squad.[18]*

Why did many Germans either take part in the exterminations or tolerate them? One historian suggests that Hitler's greatest asset was his country's 'inferiority complex. He knew well that Germans would put up with anything provided that something worse was reserved for "lesser breeds".'[19] Germany's outstanding postwar novelist Heinrich Böll has observed: 'The Nazi period could have happened only in Germany, largely because of the German education of obedience to any law and order.'[20]

The bigger puzzle is why so many psychiatrists and physicians participated. There were, of course, German physicians who refused to take part and asked to be excused, without apparent recriminations. Then again, there was evidence that some protesting physicians would be exterminated as well. One doctor, quoted in the *Hastings Center Report*, said that he and many other physicians knew about the 'poison vans', yet they did nothing.

If anyone had protested or undertaken some positive action against the murder squad, he would have been arrested twenty-four hours later and would have disappeared. It was one of the most ingenious stratagems of the totalitarian system that they gave their opponents no opportunity to die a martyr's death for their convictions. But a man who chose his death, rather than the silent toleration of such atrocities, would have sacrificed his life in vain.[21]

As it was, the programmes of experimentation and extermination continued because resistance was scattered. Letters of protest—individual outcries of indignation—were infrequent. The medical establishment as a whole, well aware of what was occurring, did nothing to interfere with or condemn what was clearly offensive to many doctors. Their turning away was indirect collusion.

The Nazi indoctrination programme on eugenics and racial purity had done most of its groundwork by the time war broke out in 1939. If it had pleased the Führer, it had unsettled the public. The declining of moral standards during combat lowered spirits even more and generated distrust. Still, even though one senior German official wrote in 1941, 'Confidence in the German medical profession, especially the administration of mental institutions, is being severely shaken,'[22] the effect was not enough to discourage certain bizarre rituals. For instance, there was a celebration cere-

---

* Just how ruthless Germans could be is pointed out by Leo Alexander in 'Medical Science Under Dictatorship' (*New England Journal of Medicine*, July 14, 1949, p. 42): 'The [German] physician gradually became the unofficial executioner, for the sake of convenience, informality, and relative secrecy. Even on German submarines, it was the physician's duty to execute any troublemakers among the crew with a lethal injection.'

mony in 1941 when the Hadamar psychiatric institution performed the ten thousandth cremation of a mental patient. Each of the psychiatrists, nurses, attendants, and secretaries received a bottle of beer for the occasion. One staff member dressed up as a priest and pretended, to the amusement of his audience, that he was performing funeral rites.[23]

Looking at what he considered the causes of the German euthanasia programme, Dr Leo Alexander, an investigator for the War Crimes Tribunal, attributed much of the moral decline to the attitudes of the physicians:

> The beginnings at first were merely a subtle shifting in emphasis in the basic attitude of the physicians. It started with the acceptance of the attitude, basic in the euthanasia movement, that there is such a thing as life not worthy to be lived. This attitude in its early stages concerned itself merely with the severely and chronically sick. Gradually the sphere of those to be included in this category was enlarged to encompass the socially unproductive, the ideologically unwanted, the racially unwanted and finally all non-Germans. But it is important to realize that the infinitely small wedged-in lever from which this entire trend of mind received its impetus was the attitude towards the nonrehabilitable sick.[24]

Dr Alexander's essay, published in 1949, has become part of the textbook for the right-to-life movement, because of its 'wedge' argument.

While Alexander was correct inasmuch as the extermination of one set of people *did* lead to worse atrocities, there is no evidence that the Nazis, or those doctors who supported them, even gave their services—requested or unrequested—to the sick or dying. Alexander's significant and lengthy article, frequently reproduced, takes no account of the racial aspect and ideological factors that were the core of the Nazi movement. He gives no credit to the fact that there were those Germans who did protest (some of the most prominent were church leaders), which led to a temporary halt of the programme, at least an official halt. Telford Taylor, a professor of Law at Columbia University Law School who was chief counsel for the prosecution at the Nuremberg trials, points to the power of public resistance: 'In the published record of the medical trial, we entered a number of medical pieces of correspondence on this issue and the official reaction to the correspondence. It is one of the few areas where it is possible to see that public protest and opposition had an effect on the Nazis.'[25]

Those opposing Alexander maintain that the Nazi experience is historically irrelevant to the contemporary euthanasia debate. For instance, Professor Lucy S. Dawidowicz, a historian and sociologist and author of *The War Against the Jews, 1933–1945*, has argued that studying the Nazi experience does not enlighten us as to the problems we confront in making decisions today about euthanasia. '"Euthanasia" as the Nazis used the term,' she writes, 'is not euthanasia in our terms. "Euthanasia" was only a code

name which the Nazis used as both camouflage and euphemism for a programme of murder—killing various categories of persons because they
were regarded as racially 'valueless': deformed, insane, senile, or any combination thereof.'[26]

Philosophers such as Joseph Fletcher and Marvin Kohl have also argued
that there can be no comparison of the Nazi experience and modern euthanasia. Fletcher notes that it was merciless, not mercy, killing. Considering
other Nazi atrocities—such as the elimination of the entire populations of
the villages Lidice and Oradour-sur-Glane and the carnage of the Jews—it
is hard to argue with this.[27] Kohl notes:

> The motivation behind and the nature and consequences of acts of bene-
> ficient euthanasia are radically different. In the Nazi example, the motiv-
> ation, aside perhaps from sadism, was solely that of maximizing 'benefit'
> for the state. In cases of beneficient euthanasia the motivation is essen-
> tially and predominantly that of maximizing benefit for the recipient, of
> helping most where and when the individual needs it most. The Nazi
> form was involuntary: the form advocated here is voluntary.[28]

Winston Churchill, writing of this period in history, observed that 'conditions in Germany bore no resemblance to those of a civilized State. A Dictatorship based upon terror and reeking with blood had confronted the
world. Anti-Semitism was ferocious and brazen, and the concentration-
camp system was already in full operation for all obnoxious or politically
dissident classes.'[29]

As for the clergy, if there were some protests, there was an even graver
silence—although the Holocaust occurred in a deeply Christian country.
(A 1940 census showed that 95 per cent of Germans were affiliated with a
church.)

Many of those who carried out Hitler's orders were church-oriented and
continued to think of themselves as such, in spite of what they were doing.
For instance, Franz Stangl—commandant of the Treblinka concentration
camp, in which about 700,000 people died—was a lifelong Roman Catholic, even though he had to sign a statement that he was a *Gottgläubiger*, a
believer in God without a religious affiliation.[30] He stated that this was not
easy for him to do; the Germans were fond of their church rituals and membership. Similarly, Hermann Göering told the Nuremberg court: '[I]
always considered I belonged to the church.' He noted that the party represented a 'positive Christianity . . . [fighting] the spirit of Jewish materi-
alism.'[31] In his speeches, Hitler frequently invoked the Deity.

Historian William Sheridan Allen argues that it would have been counterproductive for the church to oppose Hitler publicly, even on those occasions when he openly espoused murder. There was, Allen holds, too

much of a 'lack of focus on moral fundamentalism' and too much concern for the church's survival, even when many of the basic tenets of the Christian religion were being so obviously violated: 'The failure of the [German] church leaders to remain faithful to their own doctrines [e.g., to love and protect thy neighbour], to oppose the regime in obedience to the principles they taught their congregations, meant in effect that they were supporting it, except on those few occasions when Hitlerian policies ran directly counter to their obvious organizational self-interest.'[32]

It is not the intention of this book to lay unfair blame on the German churches for not acting against the Nazis, though it is true that they did very little. Earlier protests—the bishop of Münster, the bishop of Berlin, Bishop Preysing, all in 1941,[33] had a negligible impact. As one observer noted: 'Nobody cared about what those fellows said in church. Hardly anybody went to church anyway. All we cared about was our crust of bread and getting the war over and done with.'[34] And as historian Gerald Fleming argues, Hitler was too shrewd to assume that the majority of Germans would share his hatred for the Jews; thus he insisted that the 'total solution' of the Jewish question be painstakingly masked. The church, caught in the midst of ignorance and self-interest, 'did not publicly protest the deportation of Jews from the Reich [except] with one bold exception.'[35]

Fleming is referring to the bishop of Württemberg and his denouncement of the Holocaust, which did not come until 1943. (He had spoken out against the regime publicly—but in Latin—in 1941.) The bishop wrote an open letter of protest to a ministerial office on January 28, 1943, denouncing the 'systematic murder of Jews and Poles'; he wrote further letters of protest to Gauleiter Mürr on February 8, 1943, to the Reich minister of the interior on March 14, 1943, and to Hitler on July 16, 1943.[36] Similarly, Pope Pius XII did not publicly condemn Hitler's euthanasia programme until June 1943—in his pastoral letter *Mystici Corporis*—although he had been told of it by German bishops in 1941.[37]

In looking back, the facts of the Nazi 'euthanasia' programme are now fairly well known. It took some twenty years for them to emerge, because many of the war criminals were killed or disappeared. Of the fifteen doctors tried at Nuremberg—some of them well-known medical men—seven were hanged and the others sentenced to prison. Some, like Stangl, were caught later; he died while serving a twenty-year prison sentence.

The excessive secrecy in which the Nazis cloaked their extermination programmes means that precise figures of those killed are unobtainable. As stated earlier, the death toll—until August 28, 1941—was estimated to be ninety thousand.[38] Until the end of the war, the killings continued at a slower pace, with at least one witness at a peacetime trial, Alfons Klein, noting that he knew of three thousand deaths in one camp. So it seems that the most accurate figure is somewhere close to 100,000, give or take a few thousand.

Today we have enough facts to ask ourselves: Could it happen again?

The right-to-life movement and its principal supporter, the Roman Catholic Church, believe it could. They distrust the constitutional, legal, and voting protections that countries like the United States, Britain, and her former colonies have enacted over centuries. Their 'slippery slope', or 'wedge', hypothesis is based on the German experience. As Alexander wrote: 'It should be realized that this [euthanasia] programme was merely the entering wedge for exterminations of far greater scope'[39] — despite such eminent historians as Winston Churchill pointing out the freakishness of German behaviour at that time.

While the Nazi slaughter of the handicapped and the Jews was the worst such manifestation of this century, genocide has been a feature of man's inhumanity to man over the centuries. For example, Christopher Columbus and his men virtually wiped out the Arawak Indians over a period of thirty-five years. One historian compares Columbus's behaviour to that of other explorers: 'What Columbus did to the Arawaks of the Bahamas, Cortes did to the Aztecs of Mexico, Pizarro to the Incas of Peru, and the English settlers of Virginia and Massachusetts to the Powhatans and the Pequots.'[40]

The native American Indian was reduced from an estimated ten million to one million over an extended period. The Armenians say that 1.5 million of their people were slaughtered by the Turks in 1915, a claim that Turkey denies. Still, there *were* massacres. Genocidal actions in Cambodia and Africa in the past thirty years have cost millions of lives, causing Lord Young, chairman of International Alert, an organization that monitors genocide, to say: 'Genocide has cost more lives since World War II than the six million Jews who were exterminated in Nazi Germany.'[41]

Perhaps what happened in Germany is more shocking to us not only because it was within our own time but because it was carried out so effectively through a well-organized bureaucracy, with modern means of mass transportation — principally railway train — and modern technology (gas). It appears, then, that in bursts, mankind will resort to genocide, and that neither religious beliefs nor law will be a deterrent once there is the belief that such actions are 'justified'.

Euthanasists argue that the Hitler experience was so singular and unusual that it should not be compared to the present crusade for euthanasia legislation, nor should the memory of the experience deprive a helpless, suffering terminal patient the help he seeks in dying. There is simply no comparison. Instead, there is always the question: Should such a massive abuse mean that all euthanasia — even that based on personal autonomy and informed consent — be dismissed? Euthanasia crusaders point to the fact that the Nazis (like the pro-lifers today) opposed abortion, although for very different reasons. The Nazis wanted a huge population with which to dominate the world; the pro-life movement detests abortion on sanctity-of-life grounds. No thinking person would equate pro-lifers with Nazis; why, then, the reverse?

The pro-life position holds that this is the thin end of the wedge, or the slippery slope: one day a government might utilize minor euthanasia laws to make sweeping clearances of unwanted sections of the population.

Few people have expressed this fear better than Laurence McCullough, a postdoctoral fellow who took part in the seminal 1976 conference on 'Biomedical Ethics and the Shadow of Nazism', organized by the Hastings Centre. He said:

> Our slippery slope might yet be analogous to Nazi Germany's in a more abstract way. If we consider the rationale which gives social utility or economic returns precedence over individual freedom, then we might see how our society could approach the kind of thinking that underlay the Nazi experience. There, racism overrode personal autonomy; here it might be an economic rationale—the attitude that we won't spend so much per year to keep somebody alive on the slim chance of recovery. The slippery slope then is not the precipating act; it's the context in which that act takes place.[42]

In later chapters, we will discuss the problems of an ageing population and rising medical costs within the context of the euthanasia debate. In Nazi Germany, extermination programmes were based on the double motivation of racism and so-called mercy; could euthanasia in Western societies be justified by social and economic interests and 'mercy'?

Would it lead to a coarsening of attitudes towards life? The Nazis started out with compulsory sterilization, moved on to 'euthanasia' and then to mass murder of the Jews. Within the past twenty years, sterilization—or restricted families—has been compulsory in India and China, but these nations have not progressed, as the Nazis did, to exterminations. Presumably, their institutions, religions, and governments are in a position to prevent abuse.

Medical costs rise in tandem with the expectation of a long and good life. Might there come a point when the younger generation, finding itself in harsher economic times, would turn against the elderly and rule: You are dying; why should we spend our scarce resources on prolonging the inevitable?

This line of argument confuses economic and technological issues with the murderous tactics of the Third Reich. An estimated ten thousand people lie in irreversible comas in American hospitals, mostly the result of traffic accidents, and there would be a justifiable howl of protest at the first person who suggested that they are useless and should be eliminated on grounds of cost.*

The quintessence of Nazism was total social and political control through the S S and the Gestapo. The individual was a pawn in the mania for a perfect race; the end justified the means, however horrible. So-called euthanasia was just one of the 'means' inflicted. If a murderous, autocratic political group seized control of the United States, the extermination of the handicapped and the elderly might be among atrocities perpetrated against the population. This is exactly why we nurture our democracy and maintain the fabric of our society—to protect, through sound laws and humanitarian principles, the individual and his rights, especially those of the helpless and vulnerable.

* On March 15, 1986, the Judicial and Ethical Council of the American Medical Association announced a major opinion stating that it is ethically permissible for doctors to withhold all life-prolonging treatment, including artificial nutrition and hydration, from patients in irreversible coma, even if death is not imminent, as well as from dying patients. 'However, he should not intentionally cause death,' said the statement, unanimously arrived at.

# CHAPTER THREE

## *1940 to 1950*

Naturally, the war itself absorbed the energy and attention of America and the Allies. Full and accurate reports of the Holocaust did not surface until later. In the meantime, there was a general lull on both sides of the Atlantic concerning the euthanasia question, although in 1941 the Euthanasia Society of America had sent a questionnaire to more than twenty thousand physicians. Were they, it asked, in favour of legalizing voluntary euthanasia for incurable adult suffers? Were they in favour of legalizing euthanasia for 'congenital monstrosities, idiots, and imbeciles?'

At their general meeting in November 1941, the society's vice-president, Mrs F. Robertson Jones, announced that just over three thousand physicians had replied to the questionnaire.[1] (Ultimately the number would total about four thousand.) Four out of five doctors responded that they favoured legalizing euthanasia for incurable adults *who asked for it*; one out of four favoured legalizing euthanasia for severely defective infants and children.

Encouraged by the results, the society voted to seek, for the third consecutive year, the introduction of a 'mercy death' bill in the New York state legislature—limited to voluntary euthanasia for terminally ill adults. This stipulation was the result of the physicians' response to the questionnaire, an interesting decision in the light of the response of the public to more than one poll: Roughly as many people favoured euthanasia for grossly defective infants as for incurable adults.[2]

Once again, the society's attempt to introduce such a bill in the legislature failed for lack of a sponsor. Undaunted by failure, they pressed on with the campaign. In 1945, they sought the official backing of clergymen, doctors, and other prominent professionals. In 1946, fifty-four eminent Protestant ministers signed a statement endorsing voluntary euthanasia for those suffering from a painful, incurable disease. Signers included Dr Henry Sloane Coffin, president of Union Theological Seminary, and Dr Henry Emerson Fosdick, minister of the Riverside Church, both in Manhattan. That same year, the society announced that a committee of 1,776 physicians had been formed which backed the programme. This led to a petition signed by 1,100 doctors, urging members of the state legislature to provide support for victims of painful, terminal illnesses.

The petition pointed out that the proportion of old people subject to painful, chronic, and degenerative diseases was increasing rapidly; that the cancer death rate had reached a new high in 1946, and that 'many incurable sufferers, facing months of agony, attempt crude, violent methods of suicide while in other cases distraught relatives of hopeless incurables who plead for merciful release secretly put them out of their misery and thereby render themselves liable to prosecution as murderers.' Moreover, to permit the termination of useless, hopeless suffering at the request of the sufferer was to accord with the humane spirit of that age. The petition, presented to the legislature in 1947, specified that:

1) Any sane person over twenty-one years old, suffering from an incurably painful and fatal disease, may petition a court of record for euthanasia, in a signed and attested document, with an affidavit from the attendant physician that in his opinion the disease was incurable;

2) The court shall appoint a commission of three, of whom at least two shall be physicians, to investigate all aspects of the case and then report back to the courts whether the patient understands the purpose of the petition and comes under the provisions of the act;

3) Upon a favourable report by the commission the court shall grant the petition, and *if it is still wanted by the patient*, euthanasia may be administered by a physician or any other person chosen by the patient or commission.[3]

Again, the Euthanasia Society was unable to find a sponsor for the bill. However, it had succeeded in calling public attention to the question of euthanasia. Also, it had attracted a number of prominent supporters, including Dr Walter C. Alvarez, Robert Frost, W. Somerset Maugham and Margaret Sanger. Not surprisingly, such support, along with that of the physicians and clergy, prompted outcries of indignation from similarly distinguished opposing quarters. Public opinion became divided into two camps, each equally ardent.

Dr R. E. Dyer, the director of the National Institute of Health, discounted the euthanasists' arguments, commenting: 'It is silly to talk about "hopeless" [diseases] in these times.'[4] Monsignor Robert E. McCormick, presiding justice of the ecclesiastical tribunal of New York, at an annual communion breakfast for the University of Notre Dame Club of New York, called euthanasia 'the basest of tyrannies'. In a manner reminiscent of Hawthorne's *The Scarlet Letter*, he demanded that every physician who was a member of the Euthanasia Society state his membership 'on his shingle and in his hospital and telephone listings; this will protect ethically-minded doctors [from those] who have advocated medical murder.'[5]

After the breakfast, Dr Charles Potter, the society's president, who had clandestinely bought a ticket and was seated at the front table, disclosed his presence and approached Monsignor McCormick. Would he be willing to engage in a public debate—especially since he had identified Potter more than once as *persona non grata*, a 'leader in the movement to legalize mercy killing'?

The Monsignor deigned to shake hands but dismissed the idea of a debate, declaring: 'There is only one law and I have stated it: the law of God. This is not a debatable issue.'[6] A week later, Dr Potter replied from his pulpit, saying that no priest or church had the right to decide—without public debate—what was morally right or wrong for the American people. He quoted Sir Thomas More and described him as 'one of the most enthusiastic supporters of voluntary euthanasia in cases of incurable and painful illness.'[7]

Similar opposition to the petition came from medical quarters. A resolution condemning euthanasia was unanimously adopted by the American Physicians Association (one hundred members) and the New York State Naturopathic Association (thirty members) at a joint convention in November 1948. (Naturopathy is a system of therapy that relies exclusively on natural remedies.) Stating that life and death were God given rights, Dr J. Forest Witten, president of the Naturopathic Association, warned that euthanasia would give to a small group of doctors 'the power of life and death over individuals who have committed no crime except that of becoming ill or being born, and might lead towards state tyranny and totalitarianism.' He added that no one knew for certain whether a disease was incurable.[8]

A good deal of opposition to euthanasia was reflected in a poll conducted by George Gallup in 1947. People were asked: 'When a person has a disease that cannot be cured, do you think doctors should be allowed by law to end the patient's life by some painless means if the patient and his family request it?' Responses were: Yes, 37 per cent; No, 54 per cent; No Opinion, 9 per cent. Similarity of responses to an earlier poll (*Fortune*, July, 1937) is notable: The percentage of 'Yes' answers is the same. In contrast, the Gallup polls of 1937 and 1939 registered 'Yes' answers of 46 per cent, indicating a significant decline in support of legislation for the incurably ill in 1947. Perhaps the war and Nazi 'euthanasia' practices—by then well known to the American public—produced enough of a backlash to swing 9 per cent of those polled away from considering euthanasia of any kind. Certainly the pronouncements of well-known Catholics like Monsignor McCormick, physicians, and other public figures might have held some sway as well. Declarations of euthanasia as 'immoral', 'un-American', and 'medical massacre' cannot have escaped the attention of many.

In fact, aside from the publicized efforts of the American Euthanasia Society to obtain legislation, there was little literature on the subject in the 1940s, and what did exist was sporadic and reached a small minority of the public. In 1940, Judge W. C. Earengey, in an address that later appeared in the *Medico-Legal and Criminal Review* in Great Britain, defended the Voluntary Euthanasia Legalization Bill proposed by the Voluntary Euthanasia Society of Britain, and recently considered by the House of Lords. While noting a man's responsibility to his community ('If a useful citizen, by taking his life, diminished that return, he does an anti-social act to the detriment of his community'[9]), he acknowledged the exception: The invalid, suffering from a painful and incurable disease, had nothing but additional pain to look forward to, as did his family. In such a case, Judge Earengey argued, the state, 'far from receiving an adequate return from his continued existence, would benefit from his early demise.'[10] However, any doctor who assisted in accelerating death, even for the most humane reasons, would run grave risk of prosecution—and any judge would have to direct the jury to the fact that intentional curtailment of life, even to eliminate suffering, amounted to murder. Some juries might 'take the bit between their teeth,' he pointed out, 'but no doubt others would feel bound ... to bring in a verdict of guilty.'[11] He urged full support of the bill, which, he said, 'carries out broad humanitarian and ethical principles.'

Support for Judge Earengey came from Protestant theologian R. F. Rattray, who argued that decisions of such a delicate and important nature should not be left to the discretion of one doctor.[12] Opposition to both men came from a physician, Sir Arthur Hurst, who maintained that a humane doctor should have such decisions left to his discretion precisely because every humane doctor always kept a dying patient's pain under control— even if it accelerated death. (Notably, he seemed more interested in euthanasia for deformed infants and adults, but avoided any mention of appropriate legislation.)[13]

In 1944 a San Francisco physician, Frank Hinman, presented a paper in which he weighed two kinds of euthanasia, therapeutic and 'decreed'. Considering the fact that the Nazi *Gnadenstod*, the 'mercy deaths', were no longer a complete secret,* Hinman's article is a chilling acknowledgment of the old argument for 'improvement of the race through control of breed-

---

* For instance, in 1941, William L. Shirer's *Berlin Diary* was published. In a condensed chapter in *Reader's Digest*, entitled '"Mercy Deaths" in Germany,' Shirer pointed out that the Gestapo, with the approval of the German government, had been systematically putting to death the Reich's mentally deficient and other 'undesirables'. Other accounts surfaced intermittently after that, until the end of the war, when the full story came out.

ing, environment and nutrition, and through elimination of the unfit.'[14] Therapeutic euthanasia was the term he used for what Judge Earengey and others had argued for: allowing an incurable sufferer to die painlessly.

Going further, Hinman raised the possibility of decreed euthanasia, 'which [to] require legalizing, distinguishes the following varieties: (1) voluntary euthanasia ... and (2) imposed euthanasia, or death for unfitness.'[15] Comparing man's world to that of animals, he commended those phyla (e.g., arthropods) whose 'well-organized communities' were the reward of a society in which the 'good of the individual is subordinate to that of the race.'[16] Nonadaptive organisms—the unfit—were effectively weeded out.

Three years later, a Canadian magazine published an article by a noted journalist, Sidney Katz. 'Are They Better Off Dead?' dealt with cases in which relatives had been charged with murder for ending the life of someone either incurably ill or grossly deformed ('unfit', in Hinman's terminology). Several doctors confided to Katz that they had practised euthanasia more than once with hopeless sufferers. Not to help, not to act, seemed 'barbarous and stupid'.[17] In one case, where parents had ended the life of a two-and-a-half-year-old son, blind and dying from cancer, the jury returned a verdict of not guilty after ten minutes of deliberation. 'If you acquit them,' the judge had instructed them, 'it may begin a new era in which decent people will not be classed with murderers and cutthroats because they have been merciful.'[18]

In a subsequent article, Selwyn James, a former journalist and teacher, quoted physicians from Britain and America, many of whom admitted—as with Katz, off the record—that they had practised euthanasia. Many others supported the idea of legislation. As one doctor said: 'The stark fact is that euthanasia, in one form or another, is practised by many sincere and able physicians in cases where doomed patients, faced with months of intolerable agony, plead for it.'[19] In bits and pieces, the public was being educated about the pros and cons of euthanasia.

In 1949 the Euthanasia Society reported that another petition, signed by 379 Protestant and Jewish clergymen, had been sent to the New York state legislators. Like the previous petition, the document proclaimed the signers' belief that a person suffering continual pain from an incurable illness 'has the right to die'. It urged the legislature to enact a law permitting voluntary euthanasia, or 'mercy killings'.

We no longer believe that God wills the prolongation of physical torture for the benefit of the sufferer. For one enduring continual and severe pain from an incurable disease, who is a burden to himself and his family, surely life has no value.

We believe that such a sufferer has the right to die, and that society should grant this right, showing the same mercy to human beings as to the sub-human animal kingdom. 'Blessed are the merciful.'[20]

Republican Senator Wallace J. Mahoney of Buffalo called the appeal 'shocking'. He claimed that euthanasia paved the way for a 'complete breakdown of the moral tone of a nation,' pointing to the mercy killings in Nazi concentration camps.[21] A Monsignor Middleton condemned the petitions too, equating mercy killings with murder. Those who sought legislation were motivated by a 'pagan mentality', he declared, as he extolled 'the mystical beauty of pain'.[22]

By the end of the year, the bill still had not been introduced into the legislature. In fact, further efforts were shelved until 1952, when a final attempt was made.

In January 1950, the Euthanasia Society in England sent a petition to be presented by its American counterpart in New York to the United Nations. The document, signed by 379 prominent Britons (including six members of Parliament), requested an 'Amendment of the Declaration of Human Rights to Include the Right of Incurable Sufferers to Voluntary Euthanasia.' More than two thousand Americans—two-thirds of them clergymen and physicians—added their signatures. The petition called for a world in which 'human beings shall enjoy . . . freedom from fear.'[23]*

In 1950, in a move that surprised many, the General Assembly of the World Medical Association voted to admit physicians from West Germany and Japan, despite the fact that some of the German doctors had admitted their participaton in war crimes. They presented a 'Solemn Document' to the assembly, admitting their guilt but ending on a note of contrition.

We . . . acknowledge our participation . . . in numerous acts of cruelty and oppression, and in the organization and perpetration of brutal experiments on human beings without their consent.

We acknowledge that in performing these acts and experiments, which have resulted in the deaths of millions of human beings, the German medical profession has violated the ethical tradition of medicine . . . and has prostituted medical science in the service of war and political hatred.

We express our regret that no protest was made by the organized medical profession in Germany . . . and we now place on record our condemnation and abhorrence of the crimes committed by members of our profession. . . .

We hereby solemnly give our promise . . . to the medical profession

---

* The petition was not presented to Eleanor Roosevelt (chairman of the Commission on Human Rights) until two years later. Mrs Roosevelt expressed sympathy for the plight of the incurably ill, but advised the New York society that the commission was concerned with the Genocide Convention, and it would be inappropriate to present the petition at that time.

throughout the world never again to participate in or permit such a betrayal of medicine. . . . We will exact from our members a standard of conduct that recognizes the sanctity, moral liberty and personal dignity of every human being.[24]

The vote to approve the German and Japanese doctors to full membership was thirty-three to three, after a strong protest from two Israeli delegates, former victims of Nazi atrocities. The third dissenting vote came from Dr E. A. Gregg of the British Medical Association.

A heated discussion of euthanasia followed the vote. The assembly voted again, to approve a resolution recommending to all national medical associations that they 'condemn the practice of euthanasia under any circumstance.'[25] Despite pleas from delegates representing India and Great Britain to consider a 'merciful end to intolerable suffering when there is no longer any hope,' there was no further consideration of this aspect of 'merciful dying'.*

The assembly also voted to disapprove of attempts by 'various governments' to 'dictate judgments on such biological and medical questions as genetics, anthropology and even physiology in order to make them serve political ends.'[26] There was agreement to delete references to Nazi Germany and Soviet Russia as the 'various governments' in question. Many euthanasists were repelled and discouraged by such decisions, as if the scapegoats for the genocide revulsion were indeed the right-to-die movement and the terminally ill sufferer. As usual, opinion was divided. While the World Medical Association was voting to condemn euthanasia 'under any circumstance', a Gallup poll of 1950, asking 'Would you approve of ending a patient's life if a board of doctors appointed by the court agreed the patient could not be cured?' showed a notable increase in the number of 'Yes' responses. In contrast to 37 per cent who voted 'Yes' in 1947, the number was now 43 per cent, nearly half of those asked.

As there had been in the 1930s, there were a number of mercy-killing cases to dramatize the plight of the incurable sufferer as well as to crystallize public opinion. On the whole, judgments tended to be harsh. Where there was mercy, it was tempered. For instance, in 1942 a twenty-nine-year-old Brooklyn housewife, Edith Reichert, shot and killed her brother, a long-time mental patient, 'to put him out of his misery.'[27] Despite the fact that their mother had given Mrs Reichert unconditional support and had been present at the shooting of her son, the defendant was charged with first-degree murder. Her attorney stated that Mrs Reichert's defence would be 'legal insanity rather than the mercy killing angle'.

* Delegates from Ireland, France, and the United States—representing conservative factions—were particularly opposed to this.

38

Although the jury found Mrs Reichert not guilty due to temporary insanity at the time of the killing, the judge—who could have freed her (psychiatrists for the prosecution and defence declared her 'now sane')—committed her to a state hospital for indefinite observation. Not only was there 'still a question of her mental health', but it was not in the best interests of society to release Mrs Reichert immediately. 'To permit this girl to go absolutely free now,' the judge said, 'might influence the relatives of some of the 21,000 patients in state hospitals in Suffolk County to go out and do the same thing as she did.'[28] Mrs Reichert had confided to two psychiatrists that she had been influenced in her plan to kill her brother by two newspaper accounts of people acquitted in 'mercy slayings'.

A year later, in a much-publicized case, forty-six-year-old Massachusetts attorney and Harvard graduate John Noxon was charged with first-degree murder in the killing of his six-month-old mongoloid child. Noxon pleaded innocent. The child had been electrocuted; a radio wire was found around his arm. He was on a metal tray and in wet diapers; the live wire caused acute heart failure induced by the passage of electric current through the chest from forearm to forearm.

After deliberating nearly five hours, the jury found Noxon guilty. Death in the electric chair was mandatory. Noxon continued to protest his innocence. Two years later, and eight days before the execution date, the governor of Massachusetts commuted Noxon's sentence to life imprisonment, citing 'extenuating circumstances'. Unwilling to identify exactly what these circumstances were, the governor hastened to add that 'mercy killing, so-called, could not be considered extenuating circumstances and was not a factor in his decision.'[29] (It was acknowledged, however, that hundreds of letters urging leniency had been received, including recommendations from the attorney general and the State Advisory Board of Pardons and Paroles. The state corrections commissioner pointed out that Noxon, who had been crippled for more than twenty years from polio, was 'a great sufferer. . . . And because of this fact, it is reasonable to assume that his mongoloid son would have caused him greater concern than a physically normal person.'[30] After serving four and a half years, Noxon was released on parole. He announced that the first thing he would do was go job-hunting. 'I don't know what I'm going to do,' he told the press, 'but I've got to do something.'[31] Later he was disbarred from practising law in the state of Massachusetts.

In a similar case in Great Britain, forty-six-year-old paper-mill worker Gordon Long was sentenced to hang because he gassed to death his seven-year-old deformed daughter, an imbecile. 'I sent my wife to the garden,' he recalled. 'Then I locked the back door, shut the windows and placed Jessie in the corner by the gas copper. I gave her a piece of chocolate to suck. I laid my Home Guard respirator beside me and turned on the gas. I played with

Jessie and kissed her goodbye. Then I had to put on my respirator. She closed her eyes and went limp.' Long spoke of how much he loved his daughter. 'Bringing about her death was the hardest thing I've ever done.'[32] A week after being sentenced to hang, Long received a reprieve from the Home Secretary. He was given a life sentence, which was later commuted.

In 1947 in Pennsylvania, forty-seven-year-old Ellen Haug admitted having killed her ailing seventy-one-year-old mother with an overdose of sleeping pills. 'I couldn't endure her crying and misery any longer,' she said. 'She had suffered too long already and I was on the verge of collapse myself. Then what would have become of her?'[33] Mrs Haug herself was recovering from an overdose of sleeping pills she had taken after giving them to her mother. When the jury brought in a verdict of not guilty, many courtroom spectators stood and cheered.

In 1950 there were four mercy-killing cases. Again in Pennsylvania, Harold Mohr, thirty-six years old, was convicted of voluntary manslaughter in the shooting of his blind, cancer-ridden brother, who was fifty-five. Mohr told police that his brother had begged to be killed. The prosecutor pointed out that Mohr had made a round of taprooms for seven hours before the killing and drank 'ten to twelve glasses of beer.' Further, he denounced the defendant as someone 'who tried to step into the shoes of God' when he killed his brother.[34] Giving their verdict, the jury recommended mercy. The judge sentenced Mohr to three to six years in prison and fined him five hundred dollars. Mohr had, he said, acted through 'the dictates of his conscience' and thus become 'a martyr'. As a martyr, he had to 'accept willingly the punishment that goes with the breaking of the laws of the state.'[35]

In Detroit, by a verdict of not guilty by reason of temporary insanity, Eugene Braunsdorf, a fifty-two-year-old musician, was freed in the mercy killing of his spastic daughter, who, at twenty-nine, had been four feet tall, could not hold her head upright, and talked in gobbling sounds only her father could understand. People in the courtroom cheered the verdict, while some jurors wept.

At one time, Braunsdorf had held four jobs just to keep his daughter at home and well looked after. In 1942, however, he fell ill, was forced to sell his business at a loss, and resigned himself to leaving his daughter in a sanatorium. Then he lost his main job with the Detroit Symphony and underwent three operations. Fearing he would die, he was worried that his death would deprive his daughter of the means for hospitalization she required. One morning in the spring, he took her for a ride, stopped the car, and shot her. Then he shot himself four times.

He survived to stand trial and to be accused by the prosecutor of slaying his daughter because she was a 'burden to his pocketbook'. When he was found not guilty, it left the press free to ask: 'What is justice for the distraught who kill in the name of mercy?'[36]

In a similar case in Connecticut, a twenty-one-year-old college girl, Carol Paight, was charged with second-degree murder in the shooting of her father. His doctor had just pronounced him 'riddled with cancer'. *Time* magazine commented: 'On an afternoon four months before, Carol had become one of a legion of transgressors who, either out of love or pity, have assumed a right that is not theirs: the right to take a human life.'[37]

Despite such editorials, sympathy for Carol ran high. Forty-seven witnesses were called by the defence, thirty of them to attest to her character. Her mother observed: 'She had the old Paight guts. She only did what I would have done if I'd had the courage.'[38] Neighbours and civic leaders raised a defence fund. Carol was acquitted on the grounds of temporary insanity, the defence having argued that she had a 'cancer phobia'. Still, *Time* could not resist asking: 'Could a "mercy killer" be forgiven?'[39]

In the most highly publicized case of all, New Hampshire physician Hermann N. Sander was charged with first-degree murder in the mercy killing of an incurably ill cancer patient, Abbie Borroto.* Dr Sander had injected Mrs Borroto with forty cc's of air, and then, a week later, dictated into the hospital record: 'Patient was given ten cc's of air intravenously, repeated four times. Expired ten minutes after this was started.'

The record librarian related the entry to her superiors, who promptly reported Dr Sander to the authorities. When arrested, Sander told the sheriff that Mrs Borroto's husband had pleaded with him repeatedly to end her life in order to end her suffering; during the trial, the sheriff also quoted Sander as having claimed he gave Mrs Borroto the injections because he felt she 'had suffered so much and her husband was so run down [and] she wouldn't live more than a week and she couldn't eat or drink.'[40] Later Sander claimed he had done no legal or moral wrong: 'I did it in a moment of weakness, but what I did was morally right. I have no regrets. I have broken the law, but I committed no sin.' On the witness stand, however, he denied any intention of killing Mrs Borroto. 'I can't explain exactly what action I took then,' he said. 'Why I did it I can't tell. It doesn't make sense.'[41]

The trial, which lasted three weeks and ended in acquittal, centred on lack of causation, the defence's conviction that Mrs Borroto may have been dead when Dr Sander gave her the injection. In that sense, the mercy-killing issue was avoided, at least in the courtroom. Outside it, many

---

* In England that same month, an article by an anonymous doctor appeared in the *Sunday Empire News*. He revealed that he had given three patients 'mercy' deaths and had no regrets. 'Some people would call me a killer,' he said. 'If they mean I have deliberately taken a human life, they would be right.' However, he wanted to put on record what many doctors like himself thought and did.

people, including some physicians, wondered why Dr Sander had committed the indiscretion of noting his action on record. As the county medical referee observed: 'Had [Dr Sander] omitted the notation, it would have been impossible to detect the cause of death as an air injection.'[42]

The jury deliberated one hour and ten minutes before handing down a verdict of not guilty, which was received with gasps of joy by many of the spectators.* (Among them was novelist John O'Hara.) In fact, the Sander case had galvanized the community, the nation, and euthanasia supporters and opponents. Local support was overwhelming. Sander was the first first-degree-murder defendant allowed free on bail ($25,000), mainly because of the attorney general's awareness of his 'high moral character and standing in the community.'† After Sander's arrest, neighbours circulated a petition that stated: 'We have known [Dr Sander] as a man of Christian virtue devoted to the highest interests of human welfare at all times . . . and unselfish devotion to his tasks.'[43] When Sander was acquitted, neighbours blew automobile horns and rang church bells and held an hour-long celebration in front of the Sander home. They announced that they had collected $11,500 from 1,800 contributions to help meet the estimated $40,000 in trial expenses.[44]

After Sander's arrest, the Euthanasia Society in New York took a firmly supportive stand, announcing that the law lagged behind public opinion.‡ Dr Potter stated 'Overwhelmingly the people of New Hampshire who know him and the facts of the case say that Dr Sander was morally right but legally wrong. We maintain that what is morally right should be made legally right, or else all respect for law will be gone.'[45]

At the annual meeting of the society's board of directors a week later, a New York physician, Dr A. L. Goldwater, admitted that he had given overdoses of morphine to incurable patients and that other doctors did the same. 'I tell [my patient] one tablespoon will ease the pain,' Goldwater said, 'but warn him to be careful, because if he takes the whole bottle he may not wake up. If that be murder, make the most of it.'[46]

Opposition to Sander was inevitable. 'Suffering on earth is useful in the sight of God,' Reverend Napoleon Gilbert declared, and Reverend Dr

---

* Despite his acquittal, Sander remained stigmatized. Following the trial, the New Hampshire Medical Society condemned measures for relieving suffering in the deliberate termination of life. Hospitals in Manchester banned Sander from practising on their staffs. The New Hampshire Board of Registration rovoked his licence. The American Academy of General Practice and the Hillsborough County Medical Society dropped him from membership.

† Curiously, the prosecuting attorney was a boyhood friend of Sander's. They had also attended Dartmouth College together. The trial brought them together for the first time since their graduation.

‡ In England, Dr C. Killick Millard, the Euthanasia Society's secretary, commented that there had never been a doctor prosecuted in Britain for a mercy killing; Dr Sander's case would help bring home the need for legal euthanasia.

Franklin Frye said that he considered 'all mercy killing wrong, even when legalized' (although he added that he hoped that some way would be found to restore Dr Sander to practise without condoning euthanasia).[47]

In Boston, before an audience of six thousand, evangelist Billy Graham held that Dr Sander should be punished as 'an example'. 'Anyone who voluntarily, knowingly or premeditatedly, takes the life of another, even one minute prior to death, is a killer. I don't say Dr Sander deserves death, but if we let this pass, who is to say who is to live and who is to die?'[48]

As if attempting to put the matter into a more balanced perspective, one minister responded to the Sander case differently. Reverend William Pick, a Unitarian, noted that he was one of many clergymen who had been requested not to discuss the case. (He would not say by whom.) His reaction: 'This highly charged atmosphere is due to the persistence of ancient beliefs of the early church fathers whose authority supersedes today the authority even of doctors. I think the discussion evoked by the current discussion is a beneficial one, as quickening the intellectual interests in searching for that which is true and right.'[49] Indeed, as *Time* put it: 'Is there an eternal law that transcends man's best intentions, and if there is, how are men to interpret it?'[50]

The answer to such a question does not come easily, nor did it come easily to people in the postwar era trying to weigh the behaviour of people such as Sander, Carol Paight, Harold Mohr, and others against the connotations 'mercy death' had assumed after World War II. Although neighbours, friends, and communities were supportive of the defendants, the law was still the law. In each of the trials, the mercy-killing aspect was neatly dodged. As Judge Earengey and others had said, murder is murder in the eyes of the court, regardless of the motive.

Temporary insanity, the most artfully used defence in most of the mercy-slaying cases, was unfortunate and inaccurate in considering the motives of each of the defendants. Undoubtedly, exhaustion and desperation contributed to their actions, especially those of Eugene Braunsdorf, Carol Paight, Harold Mohr, and Edith Reichert. But to interpret such actions as the result of temporary insanity and derangement was to miss the point. In every case, it was an awareness of the alternatives—or lack of them—that prompted these people to act, and the belief that there was recourse to little else.

Dr Alexander had warned, in 'Medical Science Under Dictatorship', that the dangers of doing away with the 'useless eaters' began with acknowledging such a thing as a life—any life—deemed unworthy. He pointed out that the Nazi war crimes started from such small beginnings: 'They started with the acceptance of an attitude, basic to the euthanasia movement, that there is such a thing as a life not worthy to be lived, and then spread to all

43

'useless eaters' and politically and socially unwanted persons.'[51]

Many people condemning euthanasia at the time of the mercy-killing trials were reacting to such a notion: that from such small beginnings, greater abuses could occur. Couldn't they see what sanctioned mercy killings had led to in the last war? The law, equally uncomfortable with the 'euthanasia question', simply avoided dealing with it, as had Governor Tobin of Massachusetts, who, when commuting John Noxon's death sentence, refused to identify any of the 'extenuating circumstances' he cited. He refused to acknowledge the mercy-killing angle at all.

It was easier to sidestep the issue. Or, like the General Assembly of the World Medical Association, to categorically condemn euthanasia, regardless of circumstances. There was no distinction made between the war crimes committed by the Third Reich, where there was furtiveness and egregious cruelty, and mercy killings such as Sander's, in which compassion and openness were primary factors. In fact, euthanasia legislation aimed to protect the individual, not make him subservient to the state and a collective ideal. Its objective was to oversee certain medical practices through legislation, with built-in safeguards and humanitarian principles. The horrors of Nazi Germany reached the extent they did precisely because the operations were clandestine. There was nothing voluntary about any of it. Mercy was nonexistent.

The euthanasia bills, then, backed, at least in spirit, by a substantial portion of the population in both America and Britain, emphasized the rights of the individual, the quality of the patient's life, control of medicine through legislation, and the need to protect the physician and family who wished to honour a patient's request. Whatever laws existed were painfully inadequate. The sole legal options to a mercy 'killer' were to plead not guilty to temporary insanity to charges of murder or manslaughter. The danger lay, not in the proposed legislation, but in the lack of it, and in the sheer absence of guidelines for the terminally ill.

By 1950, the euthanasia question was as unresolved as it had been ten years earlier, with both camps—supporters and opponents—even more alienated. The rift widened despite indications that the general public was beginning to sense that helping an incurably ill patient to die—given the appropriate safeguards—might be preferable to anything else.

As Hermann Sander said, 'If I've broken the law, then the law should be changed.'

# CHAPTER FOUR

# *1950 to 1960*

Undaunted, those who believed in legalizing euthanasia continued to press for changes. In England, in November 1950, Lord Chorley introduced a motion in the House of Lords 'to call attention to the need for legalizing voluntary euthanasia.' He reiterated some of the details of the bill proposed by the Euthanasia Society.[1] The motion led to a debate, and the majority of objections were predictable: Euthanasia was contrary to God's law. Once a 'licence to kill' was granted, where would it stop? Today's incurables could be cured tomorrow. The criterion of 'sound mind' when requesting help was questionable. Pain had a 'natural and supernatural value'. Euthanasia was deplorable because it was a confession of failure.[2] Not surprisingly, due to strong opposition, the motion was withdrawn without a vote.[3] (It was not until 1962 that a new bill was drafted and proposed; in 1969, a bill was finally voted on.)

Two years later, in 1952, the Euthanasia Society in New York, with extensive support from prominent Protestant clergymen, physicians, and other public figures, made its final attempt to obtain legislative backing for its bill. In a dramatic attempt to capture the attention of state politicians, representatives from the society submitted to the president of the Senate a petition (measuring nine feet) signed by two thousand voters. However, the Senate president, Arthur H. Wickes, refused to act on behalf of the petition, and the bill was not introduced into the legislature.

For the time being, the Society decided to concentrate on other areas, one of which was the provision of speakers requested by dozens of organizations all over America.

By the early 1950s, the subject of euthanasia and mercy killing had begun to capture the interest of both lay people and scholars. Women's clubs, public libraries, ministers, schools and colleges discussed this topic, provoked especially by Hermann Sander's trial.[4] For instance, in 1951, debating teams from Norfolk Prison Colony in Massachusetts and from Williams College addressed the question 'Should Euthanasia—Mercy

Killing—Be Legalized?' The prison team, which took the negative, won the debate in their auditorium.[5]

That same year, one of the nation's leading Protestant ethicists, Joseph Fletcher, published an article in *Theology Today* in which he challenged the legal definition of euthanasia. Fletcher objected to the categorization of euthanasia as murder, which was defined as 'the killing of one human being by another *with malice aforethought*.'[6] Arguing that mercy killings involved *mercy* aforethought, Fletcher pointed out that euthanasia is indeed planned and deliberate, but it is also 'excusable and justified, unless ... the law wishes to accept a purely vitalistic doctrine of the human being.'[7]

He supported the bill presented by the Euthanasia Society to the New York legislature, and went on to respond to the ten most common objections to euthanasia.[8] To the charge that euthanasia is suicide, Fletcher argued that certain qualities—such as freedom, knowledge, self-possession, and control—are sufficient to justify the taking of one's life. To the charge that voluntary euthanasia is murder, Fletcher responded that, again, the law should carefully weigh the motive and end sought: In euthanasia cases, it is absurd to assume that premeditation necessarily means malice.

Fletcher dismissed the belief that only God decides when life should cease by pointing out that if the argument were strictly followed, it would be equally immoral to lengthen life through medical advances. He went on to reinterpret the biblical commandment 'Though shalt not kill.' 'The translation, "Thou shalt not kill," is faulty; it should be ... "Thou shalt do no *murder*," i.e., *unlawful* killing.' To the argument that suffering is part of God's divine plan, his response was that were this literally true, we would have to withhold all anaesthetics and medical relief that alleviated suffering. While Fletcher conceded that occasionally 'incurables' were cured, he reminded the reader of those cases in which, 'by no stretch of the imagination, can we foresee a discovery that will restore health to a life already running out. A patient dying of metastatic cancer may be considered already dead, though still breathing.'

The safeguards of the proposed bill would, he said, counter a patient's impulsive and ill-considered request for euthanasia: The law would rule out hasty euthanasia in nonfatal illness, and would provide an interval between application and administration. To the charge that euthanasia would minimize the importance of life and weaken our moral fibre, Fletcher maintained that, quite the contrary, to ask for euthanasia 'would call for courage and resolution, and encourage us to live without fear of the unknown.' He went on to compare euthanasia to therapeutic abortion, which was a common exception to the rule that forbids physicians to take life—arguing that euthanasia was indeed less reprehensible, since 'a merciful death is co-operation with a person whose integrity is threatened by disintegration . . . an embryo in therapeutic abortion has no personal value or development at stake.'

Finally, Fletcher pointed out, since doctors admit that euthanasia is already being practised, it should not be done furtively—as the American Medical Association had implied, since they were strictly opposed to the legalization of euthanasia. Again, the safeguards of the proposed law would ensure that euthanasia would be sanctioned and regulated by statutes; its practice would be brought out into the open and would be subsequently protected from abuse by erratic or irresponsible physicians. Such a law would also ensure that a physician acting with the consent of the patient would not be liable for criminal prosecution.

In short, Fletcher argued for the quality of life, the quality of death, and the right to choose: 'The issue is *which kind of death*, an agonized or a peaceful one, death in personal integrity or in personal disintegration, a moral or demoralized end to mortal life.'[9]

Of course, opposition to any form of euthanasia continued to surface, equally avid. By the time Fletcher's article appeared, the American Academy of General Practice had succeeded in blocking the issue of euthanasia from its agenda at its annual conference. The Medical Society of New York had voiced its official disapproval, and the Massachusetts Medical Society categorically denied that mercy killing was common among doctors.[10]

The American Council of Christian Churches had already voted disapproval of euthanasia. In 1951 the General Council of the Presbyterian Church, noting that many Protestant clergymen—including members of their own church—had signed petitions favouring euthanasia legislation, denounced mercy killing as being 'in direct conflict with . . . the Sixth Commandment. Legislation would open the door to more dangerous and vicious practices.'[11] In 1952 members of the General Convention of the Protestant Episcopal Church approved a resolution reminiscent of that of the World Medical Association: It opposed the legalization of euthanasia *under any circumstances*.

John Sutherland Bonnell, in an adversarial companion piece to Fletcher's article in *Theology Today*, referred to his 'pastoral experiences' and held that sanctioning the idea that death might be preferable to life would promote a wave of suicides among the neurotic and unbalanced.[12]

Bonnell went on to state other familiar reasons for resisting attempts to legalize euthanasia:[13] Infanticide would appear to be morally sanctioned, since it could fall under the category of 'justifiable homicide'; the state, like Nazi Germany, once endowed with the ability to authorize the destruction of incurables, would be tempted to 'usurp and abuse' that right; euthanasia would spread from incurables to the deformed and crippled, and society would be confronted with the problem of selectivity—who would be permitted to survive? It's notable that Bonnell's argument dealt with none of the safeguards of the proposed legislation; all examples were of involuntary cases. As an addendum, Bonnell reminded us that suffering edifies: 'The complete elimination of pain would probably have serious consequences in the character of the human individual.'[14]

In a distinctly cheery fashion, he suggested, at the close of the article, that the most significant and hopeful development on the frontier of relief of intractable pain is a 'relatively simple' surgical procedure, available to all, offering 'unlimited vistas of hope': the unilateral prefrontal lobotomy. For cases in which the unilateral lobotomy fails to arrest pain, Bonnell quoted a physician who recommended a 'second lobotomy', on the remaining side of the brain. All this, indeed, to 'preserve the sanctity of human life ... [to prevent] evils only dimly apprehended today in the proposed legislation of euthanasia.'[15]

A gentler approach ('Is Euthanasia Christian?') appeared in a Protestant periodical, *Christian Century*. Discussing the medical, theological, and legal aspects of helping a suffering, incurably ill patient to die, Edgar Jackson made important concessions. The right to end someone else's life, he noted, could not be properly evaluated without considering related questions—for instance, capital punishment and the declaration of war, practices that were, at that time, approved.

Further, suffering had to be regarded as capable not only of ennobling men's souls but of destroying them. Would it not, Jackson asked, benefit society 'to provide for easing of suffering of those who would soon be released by death anyway, if there were the assurance that the concept of the value of persons as individuals would not be endangered in the process?'[16] He went so far as to suggest, without actually endorsing euthanasia legislation, that with the proper safeguards (stressing the *voluntary* element), people could decide whether an 'early release from suffering' was appropriate. And in the cases of the patients not in full possession of their mental powers, the right to decide would be passed on to the next of kin.

The majority Catholic view remained orthodox: Euthanasia was absolutely contrary to God's divine rule. It was strongly condemned in the journals *Catholic World* and *America*.[17] Similarly, Dr Thomas Owen Martin, a Catholic theologian, in an address at the Catholic University of America, unconditionally opposed the legalization of euthanasia. Leaning heavily on the wedge argument, Martin, like Bonnell, disregarded the voluntary aspect of the proposed legislation. Instead, he pointed to the 'gratifying progress' made in controlling diseases, especially cancer, and the notion that '"hopeless" or "incurable" disease is an outmoded medical concept.'[18]

In *Hospital Progress*, Gerald Kelly, of the Society of Jesus, had reiterated, in an article entitled 'Medico-Moral Problems', of the prescribed

Catholic stance on euthanasia: Only God has the right to take away the life of the innocent, and human suffering has a special value.[19] In the next issue, Kelly elaborated on these points, with one minor but significant concession—which Catholic thinkers would debate over the next few decades with elegant precision, and which would resolve itself in the principle of 'double effect'. In 1950, Kelly could only state it simply and vaguely: 'Let me mention the fact that some Catholic theologians speak of euthanasia as 'the giving of drugs to a dying person to relieve him of pain.' This is not absolutely forbidden, even though the drugs induce unconsciousness. In fact, with very definite restrictions, it is permitted by the hospital code.'[20]

Although easy to pass over at first, Kelly's point is well worth noting: It foreshadowed Pope Pius XII's subsequent ground-breaking pronouncements on the treatment of the dying, with reference to ever-increasing questions about passive and active euthanasia, and ordinary versus extraordinary means.

In a 1956 broadcast to the Seventh International Congress of Doctors in The Hague, the Pope reiterated the Catholic position: Physicians could not obey laws that called for actions which contradicted the clearly manifested law of God, especially euthanasia and abortion. 'Medical law can never permit the doctor or the patient to practise direct euthanasia. . . . Thanks to such an objective orientation of the conscience, the Christian doctor will avoid falling into the condemned forms of situational ethics.'[21]

However, in an address to an international group of physicians gathered in the Vatican in 1957,[22] the Pontiff answered in more detail questions about the use of painkillers and anaesthesia. Acknowledging that avoidance of physical pain is permissible if 'an advantage of higher worth is gained', he replied to three questions about the religious and moral implications of pain prevention. To the question 'Is there a moral obligation to refuse analgesia and to accept physical pain in the spirit of faith?' the Pope responded that anaesthesia 'is in accordance with the ordinance of the Creator to bring suffering under man's control.' The second question was about the use of drugs and loss of consciousness: Was it in keeping with the spirit of the Gospel to bring about by means of drugs loss of consciousness and the use of man's higher faculties? Here the Pontiff noted that it occurred in natural sleep and was 'permitted'.

The third and fourth questions were perhaps the most important: Was it lawful for the dying to make use of drugs if that was medically indicated? Could drugs be used—*even if relief of pain shortened life?* Here the Pope replied: 'Yes, provided that no other means exist and if in the given circumstances [administration of such drugs does] not prevent carrying out other moral and religious duties.' For instance, in cases of inoperable cancer, drugs to relieve unbearable pain could be administered even if they shortened life, 'if there exists no direct causal link either through the will of the interested parties or by the nature of things.'

Despite his previous responses, the Pontiff hastened to add that euthanasia, or mercy death, is 'unlawful, because man is not master and owner but has only the use of his body and life.' In a later address to anaesthetists,[23] he made similar contradictory statements. First, he declared that a patient and his or her family were under a moral obligation to receive only conventional medical treatment; further, if artificial respiration or other advanced techniques in 'seemingly hopeless cases' represented a burden for the family and great hardship, they could ask the doctor 'to end his efforts and the doctor may lawfully comply.' (The Pope labelled artificial respiration in these 'seemingly hopeless cases' and other advanced reanimation techniques as going beyond generally accepted medical practices and, therefore, 'not obligatory'.)

However, the Pope was quick to deny that such cases had anything to do with euthanasia, which he added would 'never be lawful'. He made little mention of the voluntary aspect of treatment (or lack of it). Nor did he consider the need for legal safeguards, or for the confirmation of diagnosis by at least one other doctor. Quite the contrary, power of decision lay heavily with the single attending physician.

Still, some attempt was made to clarify the issues of pain control for the terminally ill. Rather than cling to the orthodox argument that life and death were God-given and that pain ennobled, the Pontiff clearly sanctioned passive euthanasia under certain circumstances—despite his denunciation of it as a concept. He also officially introduced the 'double effect' principle:

> If there exists no direct or causal link, either through the will of interested parties or by the nature of things, between the induced unconsciousness and the shortening of life—as would be the case if the suppression of the pain could be obtained only by the shortening of life; and if, on the other hand, the actual administration of drugs brings about two distinct effects, the one the relief of pain, the other the shortening of life, the action is lawful.[24]

Catholic theologian Gerald Kelly, elaborated on this theory in his book *Medico-Moral Problems*. The principle of double effect justified certain actions that produced 'indirectly' evil consequences, provided four conditions were met: the action, by itself and independently of its effect, could not be morally evil; the evil effect could not be a means of producing the good effect; the evil effect was sincerely not intended but merely tolerated; and there was a proportionate reason for performing the action, in spite of its evil consequences.[25] For example, giving a potentially lethal dose of morphine *to relieve pain* in a cancer patient, who then dies, is different from deliberately administering an overdose, *knowing it would be lethal*, on the grounds of mercy. Or, Mercy aforethought, in Joseph Fletcher's words.

By 1954, Fletcher's book *Morals and Medicine* had been published. One chapter, entitled 'Euthanasia: Our Right to Die', would become a classic treatise on mercy deaths. Directly contradicting the Catholic denunciation of a causal link between intent and effect, Fletcher insisted that it is that very deliberation that makes the action moral. 'Euthanasia is obviously planned and deliberate,' Fletcher argued. 'It is precisely this that gives it its ethical quality!'[26]

Reiterating much of his 1950 article, 'Our Right to Die', Fletcher insisted that both the intent and the effect in euthanasia are morally justified and that the law should recognize this. Further, he made no distinction between a lethal dose taken by a patient and one furnished by a doctor.

As moralists, those who would justify euthanasia have to ask the lawyers and lawmakers to recognize it as justifiable homicide rather than a felony, whether it is merciful death self-administered by the patient, with medical advice, or administered by the physician. There is, at bottom, no real moral difference between self-administered euthanasia and the medically administered form when it is done at the patient's request.[27]

Pointing to the double standard in many Christian societies, Fletcher observed how the church might condemn capital punishment, claiming life and death were God-given, then, when church and state 'became partners', perform an about-face, consenting to the practice. 'We are ... willing to impose death but unwilling to permit it: we will justify humanly contrived death when it violates the human integrity of its victims, but we condemn it when it is an intelligent voluntary decision.'[28] Fletcher spoke of a committee of American Protestants who had concluded that the mass extermination of civilians by an atomic bomb could be 'just'; at the same time, many of the committee's members would hesitate to agree that fatal suffering could be ended for a victim 'burned and charred externally and internally, not even as a response to the victim's plea.'[29] In short, we are left with the knowledge that we are not free to die decently, even if we are free to live 'indecently'. Sadly, the suffering, terminal patient rarely has the last word.

The psychiatrist K. R. Eissler addressed this issue in a book published a year after Fletcher's, *The Psychiatrist and the Dying Patient*. Commenting on the 'sinfulness' of euthanasia, Eissler noted: 'A deity which permits human beings to be exposed to such awful sufferings as are caused by some diseases must be called unjust in forbidding man's charitable impulse to curtail such sufferings.'[30] He argued that euthanasia is in no way an offence against ethics in general, nor is it incompatible with past or present Christian ethics.

However, Eissler doubted whether the medical establishment could accept this: 'The question is . . . whether psychiatry will be able to live up to the requirements of the new ethics . . . and, if so, why so little has been done in the past.'[31] He even went so far as to suggest that physicians who denounce euthanasia do not always do so out of the most impeccable motives: 'Actually some of those physicians who uncompromisingly deny patients the beneficence of euthanasia are not superior to their contemporaries in their general ethics, and it is quite possible that this moral stringency is often a concealed manifestation of their sadism.'[32] On the whole, Eissler was sceptical about the immediate future of euthanasia, despite his concern for the patient: 'I believe . . . that the tendency of modern ethics may go contrary to euthanasia.'

Certainly, some of Eissler's scepticism was borne out. More medical journals were publishing articles on euthanasia and the dying in the 1950s than before, but the majority of them were either against euthanasia or, if supportive, were vague and unfocused. For instance, when the World Medical Association was categorically condemning euthanasia in 1950, there appeared in a New York medical journal an article in which a physician/barrister denied that most terminal patients demand help in dying. The writer maintained that if there is a 'voluntary' request for death, the patient has been prodded into it.

> Most doctors have reason to reflect on the sinister truth of the saying 'Where the carcase is, there will the vultures be gathered together,' for when all sort of lost or forgotten relatives begin to assemble about the patient's bed, eagerly looking for pickings before life is extinct, most patients sense that the end is not far off and few are deceived by the affection displayed; a feeling of hopelessness or weariness overcomes them and they give up the struggle.[33]

More enlightened articles appeared, but invariably disclaimers were inserted. In 1952, physician Walter C. Alvarez spoke of his concern for the dying patient, emphasizing the importance of kindness, candour, comfort, and pain relief. While he conceded that some physicians wisely don't prolong life at all costs and are guided by the family's wishes, he quickly added: 'I do not wish here to advocate euthanasia or the neglect of patients; rather I am talking about relaxing some effort for old persons when they are obviously beyond help.'[34]

In 1953, in a symposium on euthanasia sponsored by the Maryland Medical and Bar Association,[35] George Boas, professor of the history of philosophy at Johns Hopkins, argued the pro side of euthanasia without ever mentioning it specifically. Instead, he reviewed the double standard in Christian times and the Bible, and spoke of how the concept of 'sanctity of life' was disregarded by those in power.[36] He concluded that the courts and the state had systematically condemned suicide, while they did nothing to improve the quality of life. Any support of euthanasia could only be inferred from Boas's argument, and not without some effort. (A lawyer at the symposium, taking an adversarial position, observed that a mercy killing would and should remain a felony. Courts were not concerned with motive or patient consent: 'It is not up to the prosecuting officer to determine whether, when the law has been violated, the act was "meritorious in character".'[37]*)

A physician who spoke at the symposium held that 'life should be preserved to its ultimate, regardless of the conditions at hand.'[38] The physician should never be 'executioner'; his sole activity is prolonging life; no doctor he knew ever knowingly ended a life; and the 'desolation [sic] of life' was entirely out of a physician's reference.[39] Indeed, '. . . let me go a little further. The mere degree of illness, however extreme, should never be mistaken for the signs of impending death. The inevitability of death in any disease is never more than an estimate passed upon an opinion and experience.'[40]

Dr John Farrell, in 'The Right of a Patient to Die', was concerned with the needs of terminal patients, but hastily added: 'I am *not* discussing euthanasia, for which I hold no belief.'[41] In a similar vein, Dr Edward H. Rynearson argued, in 'You are Standing at the Bedside of a Patient Dying of Untreatable Cancer', that a physician should not needlessly prolong life, although 'The present piece has nothing to do with euthanasia.'[42] (In an address to the American Medical Association three years later, in 1960, Rynearson denied that he had ever discussed or advocated positive steps to hasten death.)

Many of the questions about the care of the dying—those raised by Fletcher and discussed by physicians—had not escaped the attention of other professionals as well. Two years after *Morals and Medicine* was published, the *New York University Law Review* reported on a symposium in response to Fletcher's book.[43] Whereas many physicians had been reluctant to tackle euthanasia directly, participants in this symposium (each representing a different point of view: philosophy, Catholicism, Protestantism, Judaism, medicine, the law) responded pointedly to, among other things, a patient's right to die and the euthanasia bill endorsed by Fletcher.

* It's worth noting that this lawyer committed some serious sins of omission in presenting his facts. Stressing that juries invariably follow the letter of the law—as he argued they should—he related how May Brownhill (see p. 15) was 'sentenced to be hanged' for the murder of her son; he failed to explain (as any one of the newspaper clippings reported) that she was subsequently reprieved and pardoned. In the case of Hermann Sander (pp. 41–43), he stressed the charge of murder in the first degree, adding unconvincingly that he was 'unable to ascertain' exactly what the issue was before the jury. From 1950 to 1953, more than two dozen articles appeared in the *New York Times*, *Time*, and *Newsweek* about the trial.

Horace M. Kallen, a professor of social philosophy, argued that since human existence is consciousness, any pain or suffering that reduces consciousness to a subhuman level can only be deemed undesirable. Euthanasia is neither justifiable homicide nor murder; it is, instead, the 'essence of humanity'—that which distinguishes man from animal: 'That a human being whose consciousness is all hurt beyond endurance should appraise its extinction as better and more desirable than its existence, that he should aim at and seek to effect its lasting termination, is one of the prime attributes of his humanity.'[44]

The Catholic view, expressed by Reverend Joseph D. Hassett, S.J., embraced the traditional argument that no one has the right to take the life of another, 'unless the latter is an unjust aggressor against an individual or the common good.'[45] He condemned the proposed euthanasia legislation, as 'a deliberate and direct attack on human life.'[46]

Paul Ramsey, professor of religion at Princeton, represented the Protestant position. Although he supported Fletcher's concern for the rights of the patient, Ramsey questioned whether the intervention of a second or third party might not introduce additional complex issues. Noting that the proposed bill 'puts the state and the medical profession in the killing business and involves a "direct" taking of life,'[47] Ramsey suggested that the bill be rewritten with this in mind, allowing the patient to indicate his or her wishes well in advance. He also expressed his concern for a clearer definition of extraordinary means: 'Have we not gone too far in thoughtlessly supposing that any means for prolonging life, once made available, becomes ordinary and mandatory upon both patient and doctor?'[48]

Rabbi Emanuel Rackman declared, quite simply, that petitions for euthanasia would 'definitely be objectionable from Judaism's point of view.' Seeing sanctioned mercy killings as homicide by physicians 'playing God', Rackman, less simply, denounced the suggested legislation: 'The misery of the few who might take advantage of the legislation proposed is naught by comparison with the misery of multitudes whom the Leviathan will destroy when and if we raze the ramparts which religion has reared for millennia around the sanctity of life.'[49]

In more subdued rhetoric, Dr Phillips Frohman dismissed euthanasia as totally unnecessary. Almost all pain is relievable, he remarked; the doctor's main concern is preservation of life, there *are* miracle cures, and no decision is valid that is made at a time of emotional upset and intractable pain.[50]

Attorney Morris Ploscowe, like the attorney at the Maryland symposium, held that euthanasia is still unjustifiable homicide under the existing statutes. He also acknowledged that no provision of law should 'encourage the killing of human beings.'[51] Citing the Nazi abuses, Ploscowe predicted that such a law would be too easily extended to include other objectionable groups or races.

54

Harry Kalven, a professor of law, deplored the inadequacy of existing legislation, noting the 'apparent elegance of some of the continental modes', which considered motivation and mitigation.[52] Still, Professor Kalven was somewhat 'repelled' by a court's issuing a licence for death. Like Ploscowe, who thought it better that the law 'limp along in these areas' as it had been doing,[53] Kalven concluded: 'In the end and with no great conviction in my conclusion, I would favour leaving things as they are and trusting for a while yet to the imperfect but elastic equity in the administration of the law as written.'[54]

Aside from that one point of agreement, it seemed that no one in the symposium in response to Fletcher's arguments could concur on what would or wouldn't work.

By this time, a new advocate had appeared on the scene, to provide the euthanasia movement with fresh impetus. In 1955, Glanville Williams, Fellow of Jesus College and Rouse Ball Professor of Laws at Cambridge University (and a member of the Standing Committee on Criminal Law Revision), addressed the Euthanasia Society in London at its annual meeting. Williams analyzed the failure of the 1936 bill and the continuing opposition from members of Parliament. Repeating statements made during the 1950 debate, Williams said he could only assume that euthanasia was widely practised by the medical profession, and he felt there was no 'logical or moral chasm' between cutting short the act of dying (passive euthanasia) and accelerating or precipitating death.[55]

Two years later, in his book *The Sanctity of Life and the Criminal Law*, Williams expanded many of these points. Reviewing the prohibition of suicide over the centuries, he went on to discuss objections to euthanasia on religious and secular grounds. Williams noted the Catholic arguments against any form of mercy killing and observed: 'According to the usual view of the Christian religion ... the greatest of all commandments is to love, and this surely means that euthanasia is permissible if performed truly and honestly to spare the patient and not merely for the convenience of the living.'[56]

Williams's interpretation of the principle of double effect was that making a choice of values (e.g., an overdose for pain relief? or an overdose to end a patient's life?) could be avoided by keeping one's mind off the consequences, and this in turn could only encourage hypocrisy in dealing with such weighty moral matters. Like Fletcher, Williams saw desire, intent, and result as inextricably tied together. 'What is true of morals is true of the law. There is no legal difference between desiring and intending a consequence as following from your conduct, and persisting in your conduct with a knowledge that the consequence will inevitably follow from it, though not desiring that consequence. When a result is foreseen as certain, it is the same as if it were desired or intended.'[57]

Williams was far more receptive to the doctrine of necessity, which amounts to a choice of the lesser of two evils. 'The ordinary rule,' he explained, 'has to be departed from in order to avert some great evil.'[58] For instance, if a patient is experiencing intolerable pain, a physician would have to choose between administering a quantity of narcotic that would relieve suffering but would sooner or later cause death, or leaving the patient without relief. 'The more violent and protracted the pain to be relieved,' Williams stated, 'the greater the dose of the drug required to be administered, and the more the doctor is justified in ignoring the risk that this drug will immediately or indirectly bring about a curtailment of life.'[59] The legality or morality of the act, then, is not determined by the doctrine of double effect, for it would be 'both human and right for [the physician] in these circumstances to welcome his patient's death as a merciful release.'[60]

As for the proposed legislation on euthanasia, Williams chose to bypass the safeguards, noting that they provoked more criticism than support: 'Did the opposition like these elaborate safeguards? On the contrary, they made them a matter of complaint. The safeguards would, it was said, bring too much formality into the sickroom, and destroy the relationship between doctor and patient.'[61] He recommended, instead, that the reformers of the proposed law abandon something so 'cumbrous': that a bill be adopted that quite simply relieved the doctor of criminal liability in helping a patient to die—provided the doctor acted in good faith, with the consent of the patient, and to save him from severe pain in an illness both incurable and fatal.

> There should be no formalities and everything should be left to the discretion of the doctor.... It would simply legalize a practice that, according to Lord Dawson and many other eminent medical men, is already widespread and beneficial.... Under the bill proposed here, the rightness or wrongness of euthanasia would not be directly an issue, for the bill would merely leave this question to the discretion and conscience of the individual medical practitioner.... In other words, *the moral question would no longer be whether euthanasia is right, but whether the doctor should be punished.* [Emphasis added.][62]

Ironically, not unlike the Pope's pronouncements made the same year, Williams's proposals concentrated exclusively on decisions and actions instigated by the physician. Although the consent of the patient was a consideration, Williams's plan neither adequately recognized a patient's right to choose nor provided any safeguards to protect the patient. As a result, supporters of euthanasia laws, although appreciative of Williams's efforts, could only express disappointment in a suggested bill that would reduce mercy deaths to an essentially one-dimensional issue, one that avoided such salient points as patient autonomy and abuse.

In New Jersey that same year, a petition was presented to the state legislature. It bore the names of 166 physicians (many of whom denied, when the list was made public, that they had in fact signed the petition) and emphasized patients' rights. The petition specifically requested that the legislature 'amend the law to permit voluntary euthanasia for incurable sufferers, when authorized by a Court of Record, upon receipt of a signed and attested petition from the sufferer and after investigation of the case by a medical committee designated by the court.'[63] Several religous and medical groups objected to the proposal; the Medical Society of New Jersey immediately issued a statement declaring that 'the practice of euthanasia has been and continues to be in conflict with accepted practices of morality and sound medical practice.'[64] No legislative action was taken.

In 1959, a bill was presented to the Connecticut general assembly by the state chapter of the Euthanasia Society. It differed from the New York bill in not restricting the age of the patient to twenty-one. It also provided for the signing of a request for euthanasia in advance of any illness. The purpose of the bill was 'to legalize euthanasia to allow those afflicted with severe physical suffering to have their lives terminated by painless means under the sanction of law.'[65] Despite the efforts of the drafters of the bill to avoid extensive use of the word 'euthanasia' (the Connecticut Medical Society's House of Delegates had just passed a resolution opposing it), the proposal was defeated.

It seemed, then, that whatever the variations—from Williams's proposal to the more intricate bill outlined in Connecticut—any version of a euthanasia bill would be received with enough suspicion and disapproval to ensure defeat.

Over the decade, the courts continued to deal inconsistently with mercy-killing cases. Charges ranged from murder to manslaughter; verdicts varied from guilty, to acquittal by reason of temporary insanity, to probation. In many instances, leniency was displayed by judge and jury.

From 1950 to 1959, more than a dozen cases were reported in America and abroad. In Copenhagen in 1950, a forty-three-year-old woman turned on the gas jet and killed her seventeen-year-old son, an epileptic who had spent most of his life in mental institutions. She was released on probation.[66] In Ontario, an all-male jury acquitted Ralph Kilbon of the shooting murder of his mentally ill wife.[67] Albert Sell, a forty-four-year-old tavernkeeper in New Jersey, was declared not guilty by reason of temporary insanity in the shooting of his five-year-old crippled son. He was placed in a mental institution and released after a year.[68] In 1953 in Arizona, fifty-four-year-old Herman Nagle, a former policeman, charged with the shooting of his adult daughter who suffered from cerebral palsy, was found innocent of first-degree murder.[69]

In the Netherlands in 1952, a physician, Dr Arnold J. Berman, received a one-year suspended sentence for putting his pain-racked brother out of his misery. The brother, who had suffered from tuberculosis for eight years, had pleaded for an end to his torture. 'I did not take his life,' Berman told the court. 'His existence no longer deserved the name of life. I only shortened his suffering. I could not refuse his last wish.'[70] After the doctor's confession and trial, his medical practice increased by 30 per cent.

In England, John S. Marples, a village postman, returned home after a year in prison for killing his elderly cancer-ridden mother. He found a new trailer and a bank account provided by sympathetic villagers; they had petitioned the Post Office to reinstate him.[71] At the same time, Dr Maurice Millard, son of the founder of the British Euthanasia Society, admitted at a Rotarians' meeting that a woman incurably ill with cancer had died after he gave her sleep-inducing drugs. 'I did not kill her,' Millard remarked. 'I kept her asleep until death took over.'[72] Unaware that his speech would be publicly reported, Millard found himself at the centre of renewed controversy over mercy killings, much of it supportive.

A young farm worker awaiting recommittal to a mental hospital in Maine was slain by his father, Charles M. Collins, who told the county attorney: 'The boy has never been right. When he went bad he was violent. He thought it would kill his mother and me to have him go back to the hospital.'[73] Collins was charged with murder, found guilty, and sentenced to life imprisonment.

The following year, William R. Jones was tried for having electrocuted his wife, an amputee and a diabetic, who had been in constant pain. The judge, who wept as he considered Jones's case, explained that he could not condone the killing, but would 'show [him] every consideration.'[74] Jones, who wept too, thanked him. He was found guilty, and sentenced to more than a year in jail.

In October 1953, John Petyo, a janitor, was charged with murder and sent to prison for the slaying of his wife, who had suffered from a paralytic stroke. After Mrs Petyo begged her husband to kill her, Petyo said, he struck her on the head with a claw hammer and then strangled her by wrapping an electric cord around her neck.[75]

The response of the courts to these mercy killings, then, depended in part on the nature of the slaying: Petyo's and Jones's acts were particularly brutal. Yet equally important, if not more so, was the rapport between the judge, the defendant, and, when applicable, the jury. In the case of *People v. Werner*, presiding Chief Justice A. L. Marovitz displayed a boldly unorthodox attitude towards the defendant, Otto Werner, a sixty-nine-year-old man who had used rags to suffocate his wife, a hopelessly crippled, bedridden patient. In the arraignment proceedings, the state waived a charge of murder and permitted Werner to enter a plea of guilty to manslaughter, punishable by one to fourteen years in prison. Werner was found guilty on his own admisson.

However, after hearing the testimony of Werner's children and his pastor, describing in detail Werner's devoted care of his wife (after suffocating her, he took an overdose of drugs, but was resuscitated), and a letter from Mrs Werner's doctor describing the severity of her illness, the judge allowed Werner to change his plea. The transcript is worth noting:

> *Chief Justice Marovitz*: Well, folks, how would the family and neighbours feel if I permitted the defendant to withdraw his plea of guilty and I found him not guilty?
>
> Here is a man sixty-nine years old, in the twilight of his life, and he has been so devoted and attentive to his wife. . . .
>
> I would rather send him home to his daughter and son without the stigma of a finding of guilty, and I am not reluctant to do it if the family feels they wouldn't have any objection.
>
> I won't ask the state's attorney for his consent to [the change of plea]. I know him well enough to know he would be inclined to do the same thing. . . .
>
> Mr Werner, this is a time in one's life where good reputation and decency over a span of years pay off. I can't find it in my heart to find you guilty. I am going to permit you to go home with your daughter and live out the rest of your life in as much peace as you can find it in your heart to have.[76]

A plea of not guilty was entered and accepted by the court. Otto Werner was freed and spent his final years with his son and daughter.

# CHAPTER FIVE

# *The 1960s*

Until the sixties, death and dying were subjects that were largely avoided. Except for the few specialists—attorneys, physicians, ethicists, and euthanasia society members—who had a reason for studying the subject, the general public remained relatively ignorant about the intricacies of dying.

And indeed, why shouldn't they be ignorant? One sociologist estimated that the average American family went for more than twenty years without encountering a relative's death. Even then, most adults, and especially children, were insulated from the realities of dying, except as it was portrayed on television. In one family, when the children were informed of their grandfather's death, the response was: 'Who shot him?'[1]

Throughout America, death was being defied, if not denied. Hospitals and medical laboratories became bastions of eternal optimism: the glories of technology promised a solution for every ill. In its turn, religion emphasized man's immortality: Death was a 'transition' from a mundane to a celestial state of being. Not surprisingly, people rarely spoke of the fact that someone had died. Phrases like 'passed away', 'went to meet his maker', and 'resting quietly' achieved new currency. Corpses were 'loved ones'.

At funeral parlours, the dead reclined in the 'slumber room' or 'reposing room', while cosmeticians beautified them. One mortician advertised 'Nature-Glo—the ultimate in cosmetic embalming.'[2] Coffins were sold with innerspring mattresses and perfect-posture beds. Undertakers sold 'fashions for the dying—styles from the best in life for the last memory.'[3] Cemetery plots were 'resting places'.

In intensive care units, where most dying took place, relatives were excluded while a medical team surveyed the failing vital signs of the patient, who was probably kept in ignorance about the details of his condition: A poll showed that 60 to 90 per cent of physicians were opposed to telling a patient his illness was terminal.[4] Usually the dying person was surrounded in his final moments, not by loved ones, but by harsh lights, IV needles, catheters, beeps, and endless sterility. The atmosphere was one of crisis, not of human contact.

In one year in the early 1960s, the public spent more than $5 billion on cosmetics and youth-enhancing products, while the government spent a fifth of that amount on old-age assistance. Few people wanted to face up to the final reality of death. A new way was discovered to stay alive indefinitely, or so it was advertised: Cryonics societies promised to freeze your body for an indefinite number of years until cures were found for all diseases and a way to avoid natural death was discovered. People spent thousands of dollars to ensure that their corpses would be frozen. One cryonics society newsletter included a poem entitled 'My Will: To Be an Icecube.'[5]

As spectacular breakthroughs in medicine took on a new urgency, circumstances surrounding death and dying had to be reevaluated. Unanticipated dilemmas accompanied the progress.

With the first human heart transplants came demands for other transplantable organs. How, and on what basis, should they be distributed? As cures were found for formerly lethal diseases, the cost of medical care rose at an alarming rate. And where there were now more patients, there was a shortage of personnel to care for them. Taxpayers and patients' families became increasingly aware of the cost of prolonging useless treatment for the dying. Patients who were 'saved' vegetated indefinitely in comas. Physicians expressed more and more dissatisfaction over the prescribed method of defining when a person was legally and medically dead.

In a decade when many traditional attitudes were being reexamined and thrust aside, additional questions arose. What were the ethics of transplants? Did medical advances prolong dying as well as living? Why keep a brain-dead person alive indefinitely on a life-support system? What constituted the precise moment of death? How did the dying feel about dying? Should doctors tell a terminal patient the truth?

It was during this time that radically new attitudes towards the terminal patient and the patient's rights surfaced. Here was an era that seemed determined to overthrow much of the stuffiness of the past. If death was a taboo, it was now a subject that could no longer be avoided. The problems of the dying were too pressing, medically, ethically, and, not least, economically.

Physicians, lawyers, ethicists, theologians, and journalists published, from 1960 to 1969, more than four dozen articles and one dozen books on euthanasia, the terminal patient, and laws (or lack of them) about mercy killings. Many expressed indignation over the useless drawing out of life. 'What have we wrought?' one doctor protested; and in a Protestant periodical, a writer asked: 'When *is* man justified in tampering with the transition between life and death?'[6]

Psychiatrists and physicians began to pay attention to the physical *and*

61

emotional needs of the dying. At the same time, committees were set up to establish a stricter, more binding definition of death. A lawyer drafted a patient directive that stipulated, in advance of a grave illness, how much treatment the person agreed to, thereby empowering the patient to decide more and more for himself.

The statements of Pope Pius XII in 1957 (see pp. 49–50), differentiating between ordinary and extraordinary means, foreshadowed the debate over what was appropriate treatment for a patient, a debate that would swell in the next thirteen years. More than a third of the articles published, most of them by non-Catholics, addressed the issue of ordinary versus heroic means for the patient; many specifically mentioned the Pontiff's directive.[7] Clearly, such a concession from the most conservative voice of authority signalled a new era.

Before the 1960s, with one exception (in 1906),[8] there had been no attempts to study how the elderly and the terminally ill felt about dying. Yet between 1961 and 1969, researchers expressed a new interest in this previously ignored group. Nine articles and one book appeared, all measuring the attitudes of older people and terminal patients towards death. On the whole, the studies showed that most people fear *prolonged* dying, regardless of whether their health is failing; at least one in five terminal patients experiences physical suffering in the final stages, and many more experience prolonged mental distress or anxiety. The grief of dying patients was considered, as well as how others should deal with their grief.

In a pioneering study in 1958, Wendell Swenson, a psychologist at the Mayo Clinic, investigated how older people feel about death. The report was published in a symposium on 'Death Attitudes' published in 1961. None of the subjects was dying. Questioning 210 people, all over sixty, Swenson asked his subjects to check any words or phrases that described present attitudes towards death. For example:

—Happiness
—Don't think about it
—Pleasant
—Sadness
—Fear leaving loved ones
—Something you face every day
—Peaceful bliss
—Hell's torments
—Deliverance from pain and difficulty[9]

Combining the list with several others (religious affiliation, education, marital status, living conditions, personality), Swenson concluded that attitudes to death and dying could be measured in a structured way. The aged person rarely admits to a fear of death; religion plays a significant part in one's attitude (religiously oriented people feel more positive about death than do others); people in homes for the aged apprehend death more than those outside institutions. 'Solitary existence in old age,' Swenson noted, 'is somewhat associated with a fearful contemplation of the experience of death.'[10]

A subsequent study reported in the same journal showed that older people who feared death most were less religious and more isolated, and had significantly fewer leisure activities. The authors, also studying non-terminal subjects, found, as Swenson had, that only a minority (10 per cent in both instances) acknowledged fear of dying. The authors concluded that denial is an important mechanism in dealing with anxiety in old age, 'promoted chiefly by ... perceptual distortions ... changes in body image with age and chronic disease ... [and] gradual deterioration of the central nervous system.'[11]

Both studies in the 'Death Attitudes' symposium had confined themselves, however, to health subjects. A 1960 study by psychiatrist Daniel Cappon of the University of Toronto dealt with this omission specifically, comparing attitudes of the dying and nonpatients. The questions were arranged in three groups: How much information did a sick or injured person want? What was the preferred mode of death? What was the subject's opinion of euthanasia?

Results showed that, whether sick or healthy, most people desired at least minimal information: 'They wanted to be told whether or not they were going to die.'[12] An overwhelming majority—90 per cent of the dying—said they wanted to die suddenly rather than slowly, even if it meant some shortening of life. Finally, a majority of people interviewed, with the greatest response from the terminally ill (73 per cent), favoured euthanasia, leading Cappon to conclude:

> ... the majority of subjects wanted some control over the time and manner of their exit from life.... Euthanasia would be well worth the study by both the law-givers and the physicians whose dual function is to 'enter the house for the benefit of the sick' and to foster optimal attitudes to death and dying. In this age of anxiety, the question of giving the dying patient a painless and untroubled passage must not be obscured by a society which seems uneasy and denying of death.[13]

A follow-up study by the *Toronto Daily Telegram*, surveying more than three hundred Toronto residents, found that—combined with Cappon's study—more than 80 per cent of the people questioned wanted to die suddenly; 70 per cent favoured euthanasia.[14]

In England in 1961, physician A. N. Exton-Smith undertook a study to measure the pain and distress of 220 patients during their terminal illnesses.[15] One-fifth of the patients with cardiovascular, respiratory, or nervous disorders complained of moderate to severe pain, not always relieved; in those with a malignant disease, pain was of a relatively short duration and could be controlled by analgesics or narcotics. In contrast, patients with locomotor disorders (especially rheumatoid arthritis) experienced severe and prolonged pain, aggravated by the fact that these people were mentally alert and recognized their helplessness.

The following year, J. M. Hinton, a London psychiatrist, conducted an extensive investigation into the thoughts and behaviour of terminally ill patients at King's College Hospital.[16] Dying patients were matched with those suffering from serious but not lethal illnesses. Hinton hoped to measure the amount of physical and mental distress in the terminally ill, the relationship between distress and certain features of the patient's personal life, and whether there was any alteration in distress as death approached.

Results showed that physical distress from moderate to severe was more common in the terminally ill (66 per cent), and that half of those who were expected to die within six months openly acknowledged and accepted their dying. One-third to one-half of the dying patients were able to have their physical distress relieved, but they experienced persistent, often relentless discomfort from nausea, breathlessness, vomiting, or exhaustion.

Nearly half of the terminal patients had a distressing degree of depression; several were suicidal. Anxiety was greatest among the dying, especially those who were younger and had family responsibilities. As with Swenson's subjects, those patients who were the most religious were found to be the least anxious. Commenting on Hinton's and Exton-Smith's studies, the *British Medical Journal* suggested that doctors make extra efforts to be sensitive to the mental and physical suffering of the terminally ill: 'The distress of the dying patient cries out for prompt and effective treatment.... No one should be tempted into believing that because the patient's expectation of dying is not expressed, it is not in his mind.'[17]

In a book published in 1967, *Dying*, Hinton addressed these issues more thoroughly: Do we fail to provide adequate care for the dying? What is done to help those in unusual anguish? What treatments bring most relief? Are dying people better cared for at home or in hospital? What do they dread most, death itself or physical suffering? Can doctors relieve their sorrow?[18] However, Hinton disapproved of euthanasia. Ending distress by deliberately ending the sufferer's life was unacceptable to him: Some religions forbade such a practice; there were too many problems in deciding who was suitable for euthanasia; and 'it is impossible to define by logical argument the exact circumstances when taking life is permissible and when forbidden.'[19]

Still, Hinton's work was unique in the extent to which it addressed the problems of the terminally ill patient, not least of which was the patient's emotional needs. Hinton, in *Dying* and two articles,[20] noted the terror of progressive helplessness and the loneliness of the dying, especially of those isolated in intensive care units or wards for the terminally ill. These were areas that had never before been explored, and his work paved the way for subsequent studies aimed at relieving the distress of the dying.

In 1963, psychiatrist C. Knight Aldrich studied the mourning responses of the terminally ill in 'The Dying Patient's Grief'. Observing that knowledge of dying brings about a similar grief in both the patient and his loved ones, Aldrich showed the different ways patients accept their illness and mourn, depending on their readiness to take in the reality of imminent death. Such readiness, for Aldrich, is determined by the extent and quality of the patient's close relationships, the use he makes of denial, and 'the extent of his regression and the retraction of his ego boundaries secondary to his illness.'[21]

To help accommodate the patient through his grief—and accept that some patients can't confront their dying while others are more realistic—Aldrich suggested a technique for physicians that balances optimism and concern: 'Inform a patient of the serious nature of his illness and at the same time . . . couch it in terms which indicate confidence as well as apprehension, so that the patient can choose, then and later, whether or not to face death.'[22] Such a technique acknowledges the patient's needs rather than the physician's needs and preconceptions, many of which have been directed exclusively towards healing and a denial of impending death, as Aldrich and others have observed.

In her book *The Nurse and the Dying Patient*, J. C. Quint noted the same trait in nurses. In their training, highest priority is given to lifesaving goals and activities, and the reality of death is avoided. Many instructors concentrate almost solely on recovery goals, even when dealing with the terminal, without working towards the distinctly different goals of helping people to live while they're dying. As for euthanasia, 'the usual response [of nurses] is that "no one has the right to make this decision about another person's life".'[23]

Similarly, sociologists B. G. Glaser and A. L. Strauss, in a 1965 study, observed the evasiveness of physicians in dealing with dying patients.[24] It's clear, then, that the elderly and a good proportion of the terminally ill are not the only ones who avoid thinking about death. Despite a more enlightened attitude of some medical workers towards the dying, as Glaser and Strauss pointed out, too often there remains a conspiracy of silence among much of the attending staff, not least the physicians, in caring for patients who will never recover.

A classic study, which would have a significant impact both inside and outside terminal wards, appeared in 1969, in psychiatrist Elisabeth

Kübler-Ross's book *On Death and Dying*. Dr Kübler-Ross followed the emotional responses of dying patients and recorded interviews with them and their relatives. She attributed her ability to work with the terminally ill to the fact that she grew up in Europe, in an era when medical technology did not interfere with or adulterate the straightforward process of dying. Recalling a neighbour who had a severe fall, she remembers that when he was dying, 'he was left at home, in his own beloved home which he had built, and among his friends and neighbours who went to take a last look at him where he lay in the midst of flowers in the place he had lived in and loved so much. In that country today there is still no make-believe slumber room, no embalming, no false makeup to pretend sleep.'[25]

From her interviews, Kübler-Ross inferred that there were five emotional stages a patient could experience, although not always successively:

- Denial, which acts as a buffer after unexpected shocking news, allowing the patient to collect himself and, with time, to mobilize other, less radical defences.
- Anger, directed randomly towards doctors, family, friends, and at the thought of losing so much.
- Bargaining, an attempt at negotiating with oneself or the attending staff—or even God—to stave off the inevitable by striking a bargain: 'If I behave, God will give me an extension', or 'If I'm nice, this disease will abate'.
- Depression, an inevitable reaction, when the patient becomes increasingly ill and denial and bargaining are no longer of any use.
- Finally, acceptance, often preceded by depression, when the patient, having mourned so many impending losses, will think about his coming end with a certain degree of quiet expectation.[26]

As Kübler-Ross, Aldrich, and others have observed, acceptance is far more difficult to achieve for those who are younger (under fifty) and have active family responsibilities, especially dependent children.

Kübler-Ross's book and her subsequent publications[27] elevated the subject of death and dying to a new plateau. The subject of dying, for so long a process shrouded in mystery, was no longer the great taboo. In large part because of her work, the terminally ill would no longer be considered outcasts.

Those who have the strength and the love to sit with a dying patient in the silence that goes beyond words will know that this moment is neither frightening nor painful, but a peaceful cessation of the functioning of the body... To be a therapist to a dying patient makes us aware of the uniqueness of each individual in this vast sea of humanity. It makes us aware of our finiteness, our limited lifespan.[28]

Preceding the work of Kübler-Ross and others were several articles and questionnaires measuring attitudes towards the terminally ill. As early as 1960, the entire January–February issue of CA (*Bulletin of Cancer Progress*) had been devoted to the subject of death. Many of the articles and letters were in response to the Rynearson article ('You Are Standing at the Bedside of a Patient Dying of Untreatable Cancer', see p. 53) that had appeared six months earlier. The editor published excerpts from thirty-nine letters, five dissenting from and thirty-four concurring with 'allowing the suffering, incurable, moribund patient to die quietly without the annoyance of radical procedures for short-period extension of life.'[29] There was a seven-page summary of the literature on terminal care. Articles ranged from 'A Psychiatric Approach to the Dying Patient', similar to Aldrich's ('To spend time learning about the emotional reactions of the dying patient . . . may be unpalatable to many physicians . . . [but] it is the physician's responsibility to see his patient through to the end'[30]), to 'The Misuse of Narcotics by Patients Suffering from Cancer.' A Catholic philosopher discussed the Pope's directive about ordinary and extraordinary means for dying patients. A cancer specialist argued, in 'Why Prolong the Life of a Patient with Advanced Cancer?' that it is the doctor's responsibility to save lives at all costs, and that cancer patients provide the physician with an invaluable opportunity for experimenting with and learning more about the disease. (For a more detailed discussion of both articles, see pp. 72–3, 77–8.)

As the debate continued, additional questionnaires and polls appeared. In 1961, Dr Arthur A. Levisohn, professor of medical jurisprudence at the University of Chicago Medical School, sent 250 internists and surgeons a series of questions, including 'Do you think that in the case of incurable adult sufferers, physicians are strongly tempted to practise euthanasia?' and 'In your opinion, do physicians actually practise euthanasia in instances of incurable adult sufferers?' Of the 156 physicians who responded, 61 per cent agreed that doctors *did* practise euthanasia, either accelerating death or omitting life-saving measures. Despite this, 72 per cent disapproved of proposed legislation to legalize euthanasia.[31] Still, Levisohn held that legislation *is* needed so that the doctor may know where he stands: 'He should not have to make decisions on his own, "in his own secret heart", without consulting with his medical colleagues, with the family, or with the patient.'[32]

In a questionnaire Levisohn sent to 146 non-doctors, 80 per cent of the 116 respondents said 'Yes' to the question 'Would you welcome euthanasia if you were incurably ill and were suffering unendurable pain?' Asked

'Would you favour legalizing euthanasia for incurable adult sufferers at their own request?' 102 of the 134 people who replied said 'Yes'. In both instances, affirmative answers came from 74 per cent of the Protestants, more than 70 per cent of the Jews, 100 per cent of those who had no religion, and 20 to 25 per cent of the Catholics.[33] Levisohn concluded that basic objections to euthanasia were based on religious beliefs, and that the punishment for its practice does not belong in the realm of criminal law. To remedy this, he called for a better public policy:

> Today our society has no laws by which use of the instruments of advanced medicine, which were designed to prolong human life, may be limited so that it serves only to improve the condition of human life as it increases the life span, and not the useless prolongation of human suffering which it is inadvertently causing in an increasing number of instances.[34]

A year later, *New Medica Materia*, a monthly periodical concerned with medical and socioeconomic problems, polled a cross-section of American doctors on whether euthanasia was justified in the case of:

1. A patient in great pain without hope or relief of recovery.
2. An infant born with serious abnormalities and with no chance of a normal life.[35]

In the first case, 31.2 per cent of the doctors signalled their approval. A breakdown of their religions showed that, of those approving: 38.5 per cent were Protestant; 38.8 per cent Jewish; and 6.7 per cent Catholic.

In the case of a defective infant, 32 per cent felt that euthanasia was justified. The breakdown by religious affiliation was: 40.7 per cent Protestant; 48.8 per cent Jewish; and 6.2 per cent Catholic.

The *American Journal of Psychiatry* noted that the opinions expressed in the study 'illustrate the perennial division between religious and non-religious thinking,'[36] reinforcing Levisohn's argument that opposition to euthanasia is religiously oriented.

In England in 1964 and 1965, a National Opinion Poll was taken of two thousand general practitioners, chosen randomly from the *Medical Register*.[37] Although there was no religious breakdown, results are notable because of their relative similarity to those on the other side of the Atlantic: 48.6 per cent said they had been asked by a dying patient to give final relief from suffering; 53.9 per cent said that this created a conflict for the physician because of existing laws. One-third (35.8 per cent) said they would be willing to administer voluntary (positive) euthanasia if it became legally permissible, and three-quarters (75.5 per cent) thought that some doctors already administered treatment that caused shortening of life. (Levisohn noted 61 per cent.) The physicians were divided equally on whether adequate legal safeguards could be devised.

In 1967, *Good Housekeeping* polled one thousand members of its Consumer Panel.[38] Statements about relief from prolonged and hopeless suffering, euthanasia as a basic human freedom, and the moral right of an incurable sufferer to end his life were used as the basis for sampling opinions. Half the panel members (53 per cent) agreed about the rights of a terminally ill person to get relief from suffering, even if it accelerated death. (Most of them had witnessed the agony of a loved one's protracted dying.) The majority of people who disagreed did so for religious reasons. Three-quarters of the panel said that extraordinary measures should be withheld in hopeless cases, while two-thirds approved of discontinuing medication.

Finally, Dr Robert H. Williams of the University of Washington in Seattle sent a questionnaire to each member of the Association of Professors of Medicine and the Association of American Physicians. All but eleven of the 344 physicians polled answered. Regarding euthanasia, Williams asked:

1. With (A) appropriate change in laws, (B) detailed consideration of the status of the patient and others by the physicians and two or more additional professional hospital personnel, and (C) with consent of the patient and/or appropriate relative, do you favour in certain carefully selected circumstances:
   (a) Negative euthanasia (planned omission of therapies that probably would prolong life)?
   Yes_____No_____
   (b) Positive euthanasia (institution of therapy that is hoped will promote death sooner than otherwise)?
   Yes_____No_____
2. Have you ever practised negative euthanasia to some extent?
   Yes_____No_____[39]

Regarding negative euthanasia 1(a), 87 per cent voted in favour, with an even distribution among religious affiliations. More than three-quarters—80 per cent—of the physicians admitted having practised negative euthanasia (2), Protestants the most (88 per cent), and Catholics the least (62 per cent).

However, in answer to question 1(b), on positive euthanasia, only 15 per cent voted their approval. Catholic doctors were the greatest dissenters—virtually 100 per cent. Protestant and Jewish doctors were the most progressive, with approximately 10 to 15 per cent of each group signalling their approval. Williams's findings led him to conclude that negative euthanasia, with proper safeguards, should be incorporated into a medical/legal framework, while a longer interval would be required before a serious consideration of positive euthanasia could take place.[40]

In fact, the entire decade had been characterized by the debate that Williams and others attempted to measure: how the dying felt, attitudes towards negative and positive euthanasia (later known more commonly as passive and active), and the difference between ordinary and extraordinary means of treatment. For doctors arguing in favour of any kind of euthanasia disclaimers such as those used in the 1950s were no longer necessary. More and more physicians and other professionals were willing to express their discomfort at the double-edged sword called medical progress. As Dr Perrin H. Long noted, while surveying a ward full of patients 'vegetating': 'Who among us can be proud of [this]?'

That kind of indignation characterized Long's article and many others that appeared. There was barely muted horror over what 'modern miracles' had produced. Recalling the ward in which the patients had all been 'saved' by medical technology, Long observed: a cancer patient, suffering the 'tortures of the damned,' being vigorously treated with penicillin; a coma patient kept alive to endure a painful, hopeless existence; a thirty-five-year-old mongoloid, saved from an early death by '"miracle" drugs,' playing in a pool of faeces and urine; a senile patient, gibbering senselessly, banished to an 'overcrowded, understaffed modern Bedlam,' the base of her spine exposed because of bedsores.[41]

Expressing his concern over the effects of our increasing ability to prolong life, Long argued that keeping the patient alive at all costs is cowardly. Such an attitude is the easiest way to avoid decision-making and a sense of defeat. Also, noting the Catholic directive of ordinary and extraordinary means, Long responded: 'What is "reasonable"? What is excessive? What is extraordinary?'[42] And who is to decide what the answers are: the patient? the patient's family? the physician?

Quoting a fellow physician, Long pointed out that such a policy leads only to quantity of life, not quality. It also causes untold anguish to the patient and his friends, intolerable financial burdens for family and community, the diversion of medical resources from those who could use them more effectively, and a great increase in the cost of hospitalization for the average patient.

A comparable article appeared in a Canadian family magazine in 1962. Science professor N. J. Berrill of McGill University wrote about 'The Crime of Keeping Worn-Out Bodies Alive.' Like Long, Berrill deplored the unnatural prolongation of life, maintaining that such a practice had no sanction either in the Hippocratic oath or in Christianity; in effect, keeping insensible bodies alive was a moral crime. As for euthanasia:

If a person is in the terminal stages of cancer, under such heavy sedation to reduce the pain that little consciousness remains, and that little consciousness is aware only of pain, the question is whether it is morally and ethically justified to administer so much sedation that not only is the pain killed but also the person. Of course it is![43]

In a gentler article, Catholic psychiatrist Frank J. Ayd emphasized the patient's right to live—and die—in peace, and he insisted that physicians must recognize this right. Ayd noted typical intrusions imposed on the dying: oxygen, which only prolongs the patient's ordeal; stimulants; and endless tubes inserted in natural and artificially created orifices. The patient's family 'resent being deprived of the opportunity to share the waning moments of life with the one they love,' he stated. 'Why, when they face the greatest of all crises together, must they be shoved out of the room, displaced by gadgets and personnel striving to delay the inevitable?'[44]

Further, deciding whether ordinary or extraordinary means are best for the patient should not be a matter solely for the attending physician or physicians; aspects of the patient's life—family and personal obligations, financial resources, the seriousness of the illness, the pain, the likelihood of success, and the cost of proposed therapy—are all-important factors. Although Ayd's article did not deal with euthanasia as such, it is still an impressive assertion of patients' rights, heralding concepts that would become standard thought decades later: If the patient is unable to consent to treatment, permission must be sought from relatives or guardians; a sane adult has the right to accept or reject a recommended treatment; a doctor does not have the right to urge a dangerous remedy or a new procedure without just cause; a doctor is not under any compulsion to make ceaseless efforts to prolong a patient's life. As Ayd stated, simply and eloquently, 'All men have inalienable rights which transcend any consideration of science or of the good of others.'[45]

In stronger language, a surgeon writing in the *Medical Journal of Australia* condemned the abuse of a patient's right to die peacefully:

Any such surgery which inflicts an unutterable burden on patients and relatives in exchange for slender and irrational hope is difficult to justify. The abasement of an individual to a vegetable status ... is not an achievement to awaken pride ... The most brilliant victories of techniques and surgical enterprise are sometimes won in the territory of poor humanitarianism and bad citizenship.

That a patient's final weeks should be characterized solely by 'the rhythmic click of the respirator, the periodic jab of the antibiotic needle, and the scientific surveillance of an enthusiastic and fascinated attendant' is nothing less than inflicting 'surroundings of horror'.[46]

Physician C. G. Riley, in a more cautious address to doctors and clergy in Christchurch, New Zealand, while defending a doctor's right to save lives, conceded that 'it is the doctor's duty to make [dying] easy if he can. He should not intentionally accelerate it, but he should not give treatment that prolongs an inevitable end.'[47] In a similar article published two years later, the *Medical Journal of Australia* reasserted the ultimate right of the patient to die in peace.[48]

Along the same lines, Dr William P. Williamson, addressing the First National Congress on Medical Ethics and Professionalism, in Atlantic City, New Jersey, in 1966, spoke of the primary decision which belongs rightfully to the dying patient, who deserves nothing less than a peaceful ending. Commenting that progress in medicine had created as many ethical, moral, and economic problems as it had solved, Williamson emphasized that decision-making has to be team oriented, with the terminal patient and his spiritual needs at the centre: 'The physician should treat the patient within the dictates of the patient's religion, and not force his religious convictions upon [him].' Although no specific mention was made of euthanasia, the patient and his family should ultimately be consulted by the physician and the clergy, as well as by a lawyer, a social worker, and a nurse, if necessary in decision-making. It is essential that doctors 'still treat the patient, not just the disease; that we be merciful humanitarians, not cold, aloof scientists; and that we not delude ourselves and become "medically omniscient".'[49]

Not everyone agreed. There was plenty of caution, as well as an early backlash to the growing awareness that a patient could and should decide his own fate. Cancer specialist David Karnofsky had argued, as early as 1960, that a physician's priorities were to save life at all costs, to learn more about disease, and to further medical progress. Unlike Williamson and others, Karnofsky believed that the patient and his wishes came last, not first.

> The physician who treasures his patient's life, *without trying to judge its value to the patient, his family, or to his community*, will in the end make fewer mistakes, will learn more about the disease he is treating, and will have the satisfaction of giving his best efforts against difficult odds. [Emphasis added.]

Perceived as a kind of guinea pig, then, the patient presents the medical team with the opportunity for invaluable research: Physicians, both in training and in practice, Karnofsky argued, can learn a great deal from the study of these patients. Extraordinary measures should never be withheld, regardless of the patient's wishes, since medical progress can be advanced only by 'those doctors who do too much—who continue to treat the patient when the odds are overwhelming—and not from those who do too little.'[50]

Although less extreme than Karnofsky, editors of *The Lancet* had also expressed their apprehension over the dangers of sanctioning the end of a patient's life. Expressing repugnance at the idea that there would be a team of medical men specially endorsed to give help of this sort, one editor acknowledged the 'sinister possibilities attendant on the giving of increased licence to the less-reputable members of their profession.'[51] The writer pointed to the slippery slope dangers, quoting from Exton-Smith's study: If those suffering from locomotor diseases—not strictly terminal—endured the most relentless pain, why, then, should they not be candidates for euthanasia, and, indeed, anyone else 'whose life [is] useless, burdensome to others, [and] unhappy, if not painful?'[52]

In another editorial in *The Lancet*, a different physician lamented the tragic consequences of those 'fragmentary creatures' kept alive beyond anything that appears reasonable. 'Is this really prolonging life, or merely prolonging dying?' the writer asked, adding that the efforts of doctors to save the dying are sometimes out of all proportion to the advantages.

However, like the physician in the previous editorial, the writer suggested that doctors should always be regarded as preservers of life. Hospital beds and personnel should be increased to accommodate these patients, since 'in Medicine ... such extravagances are justified because they enable people to feel that, whatever the expense or inconvenience, everything possible will be done for them.'[53]

Similar conservatism was expressed by Australian physician K. S. Jones, who, in 'Death and Doctors', restated the by now familiar arguments against decision-making by the patient, the patient's family, and the doctor. Ultimately, for Jones, the patient wants to be saved ('the patient rarely demands euthanasia'), the family has no right to decide the patient's fate, and the physician should not be a traitor to his charge.[54] Likewise, in England, Professor David Daube declared, in a symposium on the cost of life, that any policy on euthanasia would undermine the basic trust between patient and doctor.[55] In an 'Editor's Soliloquy' in *Minnesota Medicine*, Carl Rice, M.D., defended a doctor's right to save a patient, regardless of the severity of the disease: 'Only when your sands run out is your life finished. Doctors should be charged with neither the responsibility nor the culpability for making it different.'[56]

Psychiatrist Adriaan Verwoerdt, discussing euthanasia in *Geriatrics*, admitted that passive euthanasia might be acceptable as a cooperative act between physician, patient and family, but held that it should never, under any circumstance, be authorized by legislation. He stated, 'There are no instances where euthanasia in the sense of mercy killing is justified, even if both the patient and the family insist on it.'[57]

In the same spirit, at the meeting of the World Medical Association in Sydney in 1968, physicians adopted a statement confirming their opposition to euthanasia: They did not see themselves as agents of death. In 1969, the British Medical Association passed a similar resolution condemning euthanasia. Despite an outcry of indignation from many British physicians, the decision was based on a report by the BMA's Central Ethical Committee, allegedly manned by elderly, conservative physicians or specialists unaware of the suffering of the terminally ill. The report completely ignored the patient's rights, instead asserting that pain can be controlled and that most deaths are tranquil.[58] The debate raged on.

The medical community was not alone in its interest in the terminally ill. Ethicists and religious leaders were equally concerned about needlessly protracted dying. As one Presbyterian minister asked: 'What is life? When is death? When is man justified in tampering with the transition between the two? What problems does this "tampering" create?'[59]

Since 1957, there had been a steadily increasing protest in all denominations against useless prolongation of life. Joseph Fletcher led the campaign on the Protestant front. In 1960, in 'The Patient's Right to Die', he had quoted Nietzsche: 'In certain cases it is indecent to go on living.' Remarking on how artificial respirators and kidneys, organ transplants, antibiotics, intravenous feeding, and other techniques prolong life and dying, Fletcher buttressed his argument, as did Long, by giving examples of patients kept alive beyond anything that seemed humane: a twenty-year-old man in the living death of a coma for four years; a seventy-year-old woman, suffering from cancer, who begs to die; another patient, edging his way to an agonizing death from pneumonic suffocation. 'Now,' Fletcher wrote, 'due to the marvels of medicine, all kinds of things can keep people "alive" long after what used to be the final crisis.' Instead of the classic deathbed scene, with loving partings and solemn last words, we are left with a 'sedated, comatose, betubed object, manipulated and subconscious, if not subhuman.'[60]

Fletcher's conclusions? That the appropriateness of medical aid—itself and interference with nature—cannot be evaluated without considering the patient's circumstances and wishes; that decision-making by the patient is all-important; that death control, like birth control, is a matter of human dignity; and that doing nothing to keep the patient alive is morally no different from administering a fatal dose of a painkilling drug. 'A decision *not* to keep a patient alive is as morally deliberate as a decision to *end* a life,' Fletcher stated.[61]

In his book *Moral Responsibility: Situation Ethics at Work*, Fletcher explained in a more scholarly manner how his conclusions about euthanasia are based on the requirements of love in relation to the needs of the dying patient. His situational—or contextual—approach presupposes a theological 'positivism' that has as its basis the supreme act of faith (*agape*): God is love.

Three working principles inherent in this system are pragmatism, relativism and personalism. For instance, a terminal patient's choices (taking into account his spiritual values as well as practical considerations) should be honoured, and decisions about his welfare ought to be made situationally, not prescriptively. For Fletcher, the end result always justifies the means, there is a premium on freedom and responsibility, and every decision made about the patient should be 'concrete and focused, concerned to bring Christian imperatives into practical operation.'[62]

Fletcher challenged the vitalism—or fixed rules—of conventional medical ethics, suggesting that they be replaced with the personal values of human dignity, self-possession, and freedom of choice. 'We cannot separate the social from the personal,' he said.[63] Proposing the terms 'anti-dysthanasia' for (indirectly) permitting death—i.e., withholding treatment—and 'euthanasia' for directly inducing death, Fletcher repeated that since the goal of the two—death of a patient—is the same, there is absolutely no moral difference between anti-dysthanasia and euthanasia, or passive and active euthanasia.

In a later article, 'Elective Death', Fletcher tackled Karnofsky, attacking his absolutist view that biological life is better than anything else. Fletcher summarized his feelings by saying that

> life [is] good sometimes, and death good sometimes, depending upon the case, the circumstances, the total context. In this view life, no more than any other good thing or value, is good in itself *but only by reason of the situation*; and death, no more than any other evil, is evil in itself *but only by reason of the situation*. This is the method by which medicine makes decisions, and there is every reason why it should do so from first to last. [Emphasis added.][64]

More modified views were expressed by other Protestants, but significant questions were raised. Chaplain Edgar Filbey, while noting the often-quoted objections to euthanasia, maintained that the onus of decision-making should not rest solely with the physician but, instead, belongs to the patient and those closest to him. Still, he asked, can anyone— patient, loved ones, physician, chaplain—be totally impartial? 'When a tortured man asked, "For God's sake, Doctor, let me die, just put me to sleep," we have yet to find the answer as to whether to comply *is* for God's sake, the patient's sake, our own, or possibly all three.'[65]

Indeed, as physician Duncan Vere pointed out in 'Why the Preservation of Life?' one's religious and moral frame of reference will always determine the rightness or wrongness of one's decision-making: 'Given a utilitarian basis, assisted suicide is very plausible; given a conventional Christian basis, the reverse is the case. The real point is not whether mercy killing can be right or wrong, but which basis of ethics is to be given the most respect.'[66]

Mary McDermott Shideler, writing in the Protestant *Christian Century*, argued that, from a Christian point of view, there are those who, like herself, believe it is a greater desecration to maintain a human being in a vegetable state or hopeless torment than to kill him. Recalling how her ailing mother had begged to be put to death for months before she finally died, Mrs Shideler related how neither she nor her mother's physician was capable of acceding to the sick woman's wishes.

Questioning a society that empowered no one to give or take responsibility for such decisions, she maintained: 'We are behaving irresponsibly. We are so afraid that someone will make a wrong decision that we take refuge in the maxim that because we can keep these persons alive, we *must*.'

Following Fletcher's argument that medicine can be an interference with nature, Mrs Shideler suggested that 'many years ago, God did give my mother the gift of death, when her disease was in its early stages, and ... we consistently frustrated His will by repeated surgery and protracted periods of intensive care.... During this time, however, it was death which was "natural" for her, and her artificially maintained life which was "unnatural".'[67] Mrs Shideler likened a chosen death to that of Socrates or Jesus, both of whom expressed a commitment to a community and an ideal. Further, the biblical commandment 'Thou shalt not kill' is 'ambiguous, if not irrelevant, when the person is already dead or dying in all but the most technically biological sense.'[68]

In the same issue of *Christian Century*, Charles Blaker reviewed the case of Kurt Staesen, who, after a car crash, remained in a coma for eight years before he died. Criticizing the anachronistic attitude of the church, Blaker blamed the unnecessary prolongation of life on the secular resurgence influencing the church in the sixteenth century, 'when men became interested in *this* life as inherently worthwhile rather than an uncomfortable anteroom to the next.'[69] Blaker held that few Christians believe that God sends suffering as a necessary prerequisite for spiritual growth. 'For each person who matures on the wheel of suffering,' he asked, 'how many are broken by it?'[70]

Echoing Fletcher, Blaker argued that for patients like Kurt Staesen, situation ethics sums up and extends the demands of legalistic ethics in a single, flexible requirement: 'To love.'

Similar articles appeared in other Protestant periodicals, one of the most forceful being 'What Are We Doing with Our Power over Death?' in *The Episcopalian*. This was reprinted by the United Church of Canada, retitled 'Privilege of Dying: We Have the Power to Deny Death, What Are We Doing with This Power?' A flood of letters followed, most of them favourable.[71]

In England in 1965, the Church Assembly Board for Social Responsibility of the Church of England published a monograph entitled

'Details About Life and Death: A Problem of Modern Medicine'. The board asked such questions as: At what moment, if any, may the doctor and nurse give up and strive no further? At what point may the patient be allowed to die and be pronounced dead?

The patient's wishes, age, general condition, as well as the nature of the disease and the possibility of cure or relief, were factors in arriving at answers to such questions. Noting that there was no clearly prescribed code of ethics for the physician in the treatment of terminal patients, the committee also questioned whether someone in an incurable coma is actually dead, or is alive and thus entitled to all the protection the law affords a living person. The *Canadian Medical Association Journal*, commenting on the monograph, summarized its findings:

> In so far as it can reach any conclusion, the committee decided that society cannot take the duty of decision away from the physician by some such expediency as creating tribunals to decide the different cases. The doctor must be left with his decisions, but he must remain answerable for them to society and, the religious man would add, to God.[72]

In a more assertive manner, the British Humanist Society, in 1968, called for early and prompt passage of voluntary-euthanasia legislation. Also in England in 1968, the National Secular Society and the National Council for Civil Liberties passed at their annual meetings a resolution for the 'natural right of individuals to seek euthanasia for themselves when their lives became intolerable, and for their doctors to be able to help them without risking a criminal prosecution.'[73]

From a different perspective, most Catholics continued to oppose euthanasia on the basis of the underlying Catholic principle of natural law: that good is to be done, and evil is to be avoided.[74] From this point of view, a basic precept for man is to preserve life and health, and the basic position of the Catholic Church on euthanasia is derived from a strict interpretation of natural law. Not surprisingly, articles that appeared in Catholic periodicals like *America*[75] continued to condemn euthanasia as immoral and dangerous.

Still, given the Pope's earlier statements, more thoughtful Catholic theologians considered the implications of ordinary and extraordinary means for the hopelessly ill. In a nicely reasoned article, E. Paul Betowski, S.J., acknowledged the apparent contradiction in applying lifesaving techniques to someone who won't recover. On the one hand, 'refusal of the everyday means of sustaining life, such as nutrition, rest and relaxation, is, in effect, a self-destruction which clearly violates the divine dominion over human life. On the other hand, the common consent of mankind clearly recognizes the fact that a man is not expected to sustain his life at all costs.'[76]

Betowski conceded that ordinary treatment is not always discernible from extraordinary treatment ('what is extraordinary in one stage of cultural or scientific development may be ordinary in another'), allowing that, occasionally, what has been regarded as ordinary (e.g., intravenous feeding) can be 'licitly discontinued' on the grounds that—while Catholic theologians might differ as to why—the prolongation of such means is *relatively* useless. 'Relative to what?' Betowski asked. His answer? 'The meaning of "relativity" in the preservation of human life seems to be the relation of a due proportion between the cost and effort required to preserve this fundamental context, and the potentialities of the other goods that still remain to be worked out within that context.'[77] Betowski further pointed out that the patient should have some say in what type of treatment is appropriate, at least in terms of what is excessive.

Along the same lines, an editorial in *America*, 'Keeping the Dying Alive', acknowledged that, as well as preserving life, doctors and nurses are confronted with difficult and troublesome moral dilemmas as medical science's ability to artificially prolong life grows. The writer maintained that Catholic moral theology does see a decisive difference between killing a person and ceasing to make extraordinary efforts to keep him alive: 'A civilized society will continue to draw the line between euthanasia and unnecessary efforts to keep the dying alive.'[78]

Or, as the Most Reverend Fulton J. Sheen said when asked what he would do if he were a cancer patient kept barely alive by a battery of tubes and devices: 'I would ask them to take them out. I find no moral difficulty in this.'[79]

In his well-researched 'Jewish Attitude Toward Euthanasia', Fred Rosner, M.D., reviewed the dilemmas of treating the dying. Traditionally, he pointed out, Jews have regarded any form of euthanasia as prohibited: A *gosses*—someone in whom death is imminent—is still considered a living person in all respects; interfering in any way with the passage from life to death is forbidden. Rosner quoted an excerpt from the fifth-century *Talmud*: 'He who closes the eyes of a dying person while the soul is departing is a murderer.'[80]

Conversely, to perform an act that prevents an easy death is equally prohibited. 'If a person is dying and someone near his house is chopping wood so that the soul cannot depart, then one should remove the [wood] chopper from there'—*Sefer Chasidim*. Also: 'It is forbidden to hinder the departure of the soul by the use of machines.'[81]

Thus, since hastening death is not allowed, any form of active euthanasia is regarded as murder. But what of interference, such as the woodchopper and the machines? As Rosner observed, Jewish law sanctions the withdrawal of any factor, whether extraneous to the terminally ill patient or not, that may artificially delay his death in the final phase. Still, this kind of passive euthanasia is acceptable only in a patient not expected to live more than three days.

In other words, discontinuing medical treatment is permissible only if one is absolutely sure that in doing so, one is shortening the act of dying and not interrupting life. How analogous is extraordinary treatment with the woodchopper and machines? Which interferes, which hastens, and which eases the passage from life to death? Or as Rosner put it: 'Who can make the fine distinction between prolonging life and prolonging the act of dying? The former comes within the physician's reference, the latter does not.'[82]

As more articles and books on euthanasia appeared, a smaller number of mercy-killing cases were reported than in either of the two preceding decades. Did this mean there were actually fewer cases? Or that mercy killings were less newsworthy, or that doctors were more unwilling to report such cases? Or that, in a sub rosa way, doctors were cooperating with the dying patients more often than they had in the past?

Five cases of child mercy killing were reported, with penalties ranging from acquittal to probation, to imprisonment, to death. In England in 1960, George Ernest Johnson, forty, gassed his three-month-old son to death. Johnson, a major in the Royal Corps of Signals, carried his son, physically and mentally retarded, into the kitchen, where he baptized him with tap water. Then, placing a flexible gas pipe on the baby's pillow, Johnson turned on the gas and left the kitchen. When he returned five minutes later, the baby was dead. Johnson called his family physician, telling him, 'I have murdered David.' Later, telling the authorities that the boy could never have earned a living or properly taken care of himself, Johnson recalled the doctor's earlier words about David's condition: 'There's no cure.'

The jury, deliberating for ten minutes, found Johnson innocent of murder but guilty of manslaughter, a permissible charge if the accused at the time of the killing suffered from impaired mental responsibility. The presiding judge commented: 'No thinking person could feel other than the greatest sympathy for you. I accept that your terrible deed was done ... solely to put your child out of its misery. But you knew you were breaking the law. I cannot pass over what you did, lest other people think they can do likewise.'[83] Johnson served twelve months imprisonment, the minimum sentence under the law.

In a sensational trial in Liège, Belgium, in 1962, Suzanne Vandeput was charged with the murder of her seven-day-old daughter, who had been born badly deformed because of the tranquillizer drug thalidomide her mother had taken during pregnancy. After the killing, Mme Vandeput said: 'I knew I could not let a baby live like that.... If only she had been mentally abnormal. . . . She would not have known her fate. But she had a normal brain. She would have known.'[84]

In the five-month interval between the killing and the trial, a 'sympathy movement' gave support to Vandeput and her codefendants—her mother, sister, husband, and her physician, who had prescribed the barbiturates he knew Vandeput might use to murder her child. The case even led to a referendum, approved by the city of Liège, in which 16,732 people voted their approval of Suzanne Vandeput's act, while only 938 disapproved. During the trial, many described Vandeput's act as 'courageous'.

Despite the judge's warning—'A not guilty vote would set a terrible precedent. Thousands of thalidomide mothers . . . have their eyes riveted on your verdict'—the twelve-man jury found Vandeput not guilty. Defence attorneys wept. Wild applause broke out in the courtroom. After the acquittal, two other Belgian mothers killed their deformed children, it was reported: one by strangling, the other by gas.[85]

In Israel in the autumn of 1964, a mother was convicted of the mercy killing of her three-year-old retarded son. Thirty-four-year-old Gizela Kafri had confessed to drowning him in the bathtub. Her petition for a pardon was rejected by President Zalman Shazar. Kafri was sentenced to twelve months in prison, although Shazar later reduced the sentence.[86] That same year in Perth, Australia, a lecturer was charged with the killing of his four-year-old handicapped son. He was found guilty without mitigating circumstances and sentenced to death.[87]

The following year, in London, Arthur Gray, forty-four, pleaded not guilty to murdering his only child, twelve-year-old Richard, who was suffering from cancer of the spine. During the trial, both the defence and the prosecuting attorneys spoke of the devotion of the parents to the boy, who had been in constant pain. Gray ended his son's life while his wife was in church; he gave the boy sleeping tablets and gassed him after he was asleep. He then went to the police station, where he confessed.

In considering the case, the judge commented: 'I am the last person in the world to think of punishing you for this offence, dreadful though it was.' The court accepted Gray's plea of guilty of manslaughter on the grounds of diminished responsibility; he was placed on probation for two years.[88]

Two cases that involved the mercy killing of an adult took place in Chicago in 1967. 'Slays Mother in Hospital', read the headline[89] to the story of Robert Waskin, a twenty-three-year-old college student, who shot his mother three times as she lay in her partitioned hospital room, in the final stages of leukemia. A nurse, hearing the shots, rushed to Mrs Waskin's bedside, where she saw Robert place a twenty-two-calibre pistol on the table. He got up, walked past her, and stood with his father in the corridor. When the police arrived, he said, 'She's out of her misery now. I shot her.'[90]

Mrs Waskin's doctors said that, at the most, she'd had only a few days left to live; she wanted to die and had begged her son to kill her. Only three days before, she had tried to commit suicide by taking an overdose of sleeping pills. According to her husband and the doctors, she was suffering deep pain at the time she was killed.

At the trial, a jury deliberated forty minutes before finding Waskin not guilty by reason of insanity, adding, 'We further find that he is no longer insane.' Later, the jury foreman commented on the difficulty of the trial. 'I think all the jurors were relieved when it was over,' he said. After his release, Waskin told the press: 'I feel the moral issue of euthanasia, mercy killing, has not been decided, and I believe that it should be.'[91]

In August of the same year, William Reinecke, eighty-four, was charged with murder after strangling his cancer-riddled wife, who was seventy-four. He was found guilty but placed on probation.

Between 1965 and 1969, there were three cases in which a terminally ill person was slain, and the mercy killer then committed suicide. Double (or multiple) suicide, a distressing and desperate act and a relatively new phenomenon, would increase in time (or at least the reporting of it would).

In 1965, Dorothy Butts, a Methodist, shot and killed her friend Mary Happer, a patient at High Oaks Home for Christian Scientists in Philadelphia. Happer, like Butts a teacher, suffered from a stomach tumour and apparently could no longer keep her suffering to herself. During their last visit together, Butts stayed for an hour before taking out the newly purchased gun and shooting her friend twice. As a nurse rushed in, Butts fled, climbing into her car, which she drove to a police station in Bethesda, Maryland. She wrote a note—'Today I killed my best friend, Mary Happer. . . . I had to let her find relief from the cancer pain that was killing her so cruelly'—before firing a bullet into her own brain.[92]

Dean Jerald Brauer of the University of Chicago Divinity School, commented: 'The incident dramatizes the situation in which we find ourselves in regard to mercy killings. The religious community will quite soon have to rethink its whole stand on this.' And Unitarian minister Jack Mendelsohn, of Boston's Arlington Street Church, remarked: 'There are occasions when mercy killing is justified because it is desired by the person who is ill.'[93]

In Paris in 1969, Claude Auzello, seventy-seven, retired director of the Ritz Hotel, and his ailing wife, Blanche, were found shot to death in their apartment. Police said that M. Auzello, depressed by his wife's painful and incurable illness, killed her and then committed suicide.[94]

In Montclair, New Jersey, only four months later, an eminent cancer specialist, J. Thompson Stevens, seventy-nine, was found shot to death, as was his wife, seventy-eight, and their forty-nine-year-old mongoloid son. Dr Stevens left a note, explaining that his wife was being treated for cancer of the throat and that he suffered from emphysema: he felt both would die soon.

Mrs Stevens, the note said, was feeding the son in his second-floor bedroom when Dr Stevens shot them. Shortly after signing the note at one o'clock in the morning, he shot himself in the head.[95]

Why, one wonders, do the unailing partners choose to kill themselves? This is especially pertinent in the case of Dorothy Butts, who was fifty, in good health, and had had an active career as a teacher.

Is it that the prospect of life without the loved one is unendurable? Or does the possibility of standing trial for murder drive them to do away with themselves? If the victim—wishing to have his or her suffering ended—had indicated that wish earlier, would it have saved the mercy killer from the thought of a trial and the air of suspicion that surrounded his or her motives? As one attorney noted, the dying can only lie helpless, unable to argue for their preference, incapable of asserting their rights.[96]

In fact, two voices surfaced in the 1960s to address this issue. Earlier in the decade, physician/lawyer Arthur Levisohn had argued:

Instead of the victim having to wait until he is in extremis, let it be enacted that any believer in the principle of euthanasia should be permitted to make his decision known while he is in the best of health and strength. He should be permitted to make a declaration in a prescribed legal form, that in case he should ever be in such a condition that his physician consider him a fit subject for euthanasia, it should be administered without legal penalties attaching to anyone.[97]

No further mention was made of this proposal for a patient-instigated directive until the summer of 1969, when Louis Kutner's ground-breaking article, 'Due Process of Euthanasia: The Living Will, A Proposal', appeared. Reviewing, like Levisohn and others, the flaws in American law in mercy-killing cases, Kutner demonstrated how neither the defendant nor the victim, whose death may have been unwarranted, has sufficient protection. In addition, when a terminal patient has requested help in accelerating death, 'the current state of the law does not recognize the right of the victim to die if he so desires. He may be in a terminal state suffering from an incurable illness and literally forced to continue a life of pain and despair. Such a denial may well infringe upon an individual's right of privacy.'[98]

Arguing that it is, by law, a patient's right to consent to or refuse treatment, and arguing that, hence, the law recognizes the inviolability of the human body, Kutner proposed a living will, 'analogous to a revocable or conditional trust with the patient's body as the res, the patient as the beneficiary and grantor, and the doctor and the hospital as the trustees.'[99]

In short, while still healthy and mentally competent, the individual would indicate in the document to what extent he would consent to treatment in the future. With the right to refuse treatment unquestionably valid, a person could record his refusal, *even if such treatment were to prolong his life*. Further, if a doctor acted contrary to the patient's wishes, he would be subject to liability.

> The law ... does recognize that a patient has a right to refuse to be treated, even when he is *in extremis*.... Where the patient is incapable of giving consent, such as when he is in a coma, a constructive consent is presumed and the doctor is required to exercise reasonable care in applying ordinary means to preserve the patient's life. However, he is not allowed to resort to extraordinary care, especially where the patient is not expected to recover from the comatose state.[100]

Every treatment considered for the dying person, and every therapy and medication prescribed, should reflect the current medical practices, the wishes of the relatives, and, not least, the condition and wishes of the patient.[101] Kutner's proposal for a patient-instigated directive was perhaps the single most important event in euthanasia in the 1960s.

During this time, the Euthanasia Society in New York made no further efforts to press for legislation. As one observer commented: 'This has been a great disappointment to many members, but the board adopted a policy of limiting its efforts to education rather than legislation.'[102] It was felt that further attempts at enacting laws would be fruitless until the public was more receptive to the problems of the terminally ill.

In 1967 the Society established a tax-exempt branch, the Euthanasia Education Fund (EEF), which concentrated solely on distributing information about the dying. Its first president, Donald McKinney, said he doubted the appropriateness of any laws regarding the right to die; issues were too complex to be covered by legislation. In a letter to the president of the Voluntary Euthanasia Society in Victoria, Australia, McKinney, reviewing the history of the American society, explained that 'Roger Baldwin, America's most distinguished civil libertarian, cautioned me about being wedded to that [legislative approach] tactic.'[103]

The EEF's newly conferred tax-exempt status, granted by the government on the understanding that an educational corporation is prohibited from attempting to influence legislation, may have been a factor in the decision not to make any further efforts to change the law. To such a non-profit corporation, all donations were tax exempt, thus, as historian Stephen J. Kuepper pointed out, 'encouraging a greater flow of money into the organization.'[104] Indeed, over the next seven years, substantial amounts of money were donated to the EEF; one bequest was for $1.25 million.

There were isolated attempts at legislation by individuals not associated with the New York group. In 1967 in Florida, Dr Walter W. Sackett, a Catholic physician and a member of the Florida House of Representatives, sought to amend the state constitution with the concept of 'death with dignity'. Sackett hoped for some legal authority for doctors in Florida who ended treatment for the hopelessly ill. Later, he decided that legislative action would be more appropriate, and for several years he tried to pass a bill in the legislature.[105]

In Idaho in 1969, the Health and Welfare Committee of the House of Representatives introduced a Voluntary Euthanasia Bill to legalize, at the patient's request, the painless inducement of death 'when the patient is suffering from an irremediable condition.'[106] Safeguards were built into the bill, but like Sackett's, it failed to pass.

In England, the Euthanasia Society, unlike its American counterpart, continued with plans to get a euthanasia bill enacted. As early as 1962, the society had started drafting a bill for introduction into Parliament. In 1967 a public furore over a resuscitation policy at London's Neasden Hospital stoked the controversy even more, reminding both advocates and opponents of euthanasia legislation of the need for better regulations to protect the patient. A notice that had been posted for more than a year before it was reported to the authorities read: 'The following patients are not to be resuscitated: very elderly, over sixty-five; malignant disease. Chronic chest disease. Chronic renal disease. Top of yellow treatment card to be marked NTBR [not to be resuscitated].'

The controversial notice was seen by a patient and reported to the Ministry of Health. Sir George Godber, the ministry's chief medical officer, replied: 'No patient should be excluded from consideration for resuscitation by reason of age or diagnostic classification alone, and without regard to all the individual circumstances.' Hundreds of letters to editors were written, defending or attacking the directive. A cartoon appeared in the *Evening Standard*, in which an elderly hospitalized man in a wheelchair asks: 'Is this one of those hospitals where one daren't stop breathing?'[107]

Dr William McNath, Neasden's medical superintendent, took sick leave after the directive was reported, admittedly upset by the controversy[108]; yet a hospital management board supported the notice, explaining that the medical staff should be allowed to choose between which patients should be allowed to die and which should be resuscitated. A member of the board pointed to distressing and unprofitable procedures in which incurably ill patients had been revived, only to survive a day or two in agony.

In the winter of 1969, Lord Raglan, a Labour peer, introduced the Voluntary Euthanasia Bill (drafted from 1962 on) into the House of Lords. The bill was passed without debate on its first reading. It contained fewer safeguards than the 1936 version, and stipulated that a person who could not communicate his wishes would still be a candidate for euthanasia, provided he had signed a declaration of his wishes. It excluded those who were comatose and had not signed such a declaration, just as it excluded defective infants and mental incompetents.[109]

While euthanasia supporters staunchly defended such legislation, opposition came from several fronts. Conservative member of Parliament St John-Stevas launched a 'Human Rights Society' to fight the bill.[110] The British Medical Association stated that, notwithstanding the attempt at legislation, the association was not likely to change its opposition to euthanasia. The Right Reverend Christopher Butler, Roman Catholic auxiliary bishop of Westminster, commented: 'Catholics regard euthanasia as a breach of the commandment "Thou shalt not kill". They believe that it is always wrong deliberately to end the life of an innocent person, even if he is incurably sick and even if he himself wishes his life to be taken.'[111] A rabbi explained his opposition to the bill: 'We cannot agree to purchasing the relief from pain at the cost of life itself. . . . One of the reasons for our position is that we consider human life to have infinite value and therefore every fraction of human life, even only one hour of it, has precisely the same infinite value as the whole of life.'[112]

Dr Cicely Saunders, medical director of St Christopher's Hospice in London, denying that doctors actually practise euthanasia, argued that almost all pain can be abated. 'The statement [made by the Euthanasia Society's secretary] that doctors do in fact give euthanasia unasked,' she wrote to the *Times* editor, 'is just not true. . . . Few deliberately kill them. . . . There are few forms of physical distress which cannot be dealt with by good medical and nursing care.'[113]

On the second reading in the House of Lords, the bill was rejected by a vote of sixty-one to forty. Although discouraged, supporters of the bill said that the forty supporting votes (40 per cent of the total) were a substantial increase over 1936. Several members who had voted against the legislation indicated that their objections were to specific details of the bill instead of the idea as a whole, which they supported in principle.[114] Still determined, the bill's drafters returned to the drawing board to rethink their position and consider amendments in their plans to resubmit the bill at a later date.

On both sides of the Atlantic, then, significant advances had been made in the 1960s, despite the continuing controversy. Attempts at legislation, even if unsuccessful, had drawn attention to the issues of euthanasia and gathered additional supporters. And with dramatic advances in medical technology, more people were aware of the dilemmas that extraordinary and heroic treatment provoked. While many lives were saved and happily prolonged, others were needlessly extended, leading to an increased interest in patients' rights and in the strength and morality of informed consent.

Still, until legislation could be successfully passed in England and America, no amount of interest could provide the right kind of help for the dying. Without proper guidelines and laws for both physician and patient, the terminally ill would remain isolated and unprotected. As one writer commented, those who would be most affected by a change in the euthanasia laws were least able to speak for themselves.[115]

# CHAPTER SIX

# *The Early 1970s*

In the summer of 1975, Lois Phillips, an Oakland, California, housewife, shot herself in the head. Before the shooting, she was in good health. She used the same small-calibre handgun on herself that she had used, two months earlier, to kill her husband, William, to whom she had been married for thirty-two years.

After she shot her husband, Mrs Phillips kept his body hidden under sheets. 'Who would have understood?' she said later. Phillips had been an invalid for more than twelve years, suffering from a painful spinal deterioration. For the last five years of his life, he had been virtually unable to move. He had repeatedly begged his wife to end his misery by killing him.

The body remained concealed under bedclothes for the entire summer. In August, relatives announced they were coming to visit. Anticipating their discovery, Mrs Phillips shot herself. She survived, however, and later told the police, 'He wanted to die.'[1]

The shooting occurred at a time when Americans were embracing the subject of death and dying with a fervour that could not have been predicted ten or fifteen years earlier. The public appetite for dying was fed by a huge crop of books, magazines, and newspaper articles. 'Death is now selling books', *Publishers Weekly* announced wryly.[2] Elisabeth Kübler-Ross's *On Death and Dying* was on the best-seller list. By one estimate, publishers were turning out two or three full-length books a week on death, ranging from highly personal accounts to specialized works for professionals.

The first American hospice, a hospital devoted to care of the dying, was about to be opened in New Haven, Connecticut. Membership of the Euthanasia Educational Council had swelled from 600 in 1969 to more than 300,000 in 1975. Courses and symposia on death became popular at colleges and universities; nearly 200 regular courses were offered by the mid-1970s, organized by a new group of scholars calling themselves 'thanatologists'. The subject became an important part of many medical school curricula.

In New York, the Foundation of Thanatology held regular conferences on death and dying; its aim was to get medical and nursing schools to teach students how to deal with dying patients and their families.[3] In Philadelphia, a number of physicians, nurses, churchmen, and others formed Ars Morendi, to explore death 'as a part of life, as a part of the health of the individual.' At the University of Minnesota, a Center for Death Education and Research was formed.[4] Physicians at the Yale University School of Medicine reported that they had allowed forty-three severely deformed infants to die by withholding treatment. What was unusual was not the decision to let the infants die, but the doctors' willingness to talk publicly about what they had done, in the hope of 'breaking the public and professional silence as a major social taboo.'[5]

Yet despite what one observer called the 'cascading forth' of interest in death and dying,[6] an individual like Lois Phillips remained isolated and unaffected. If death was no longer a taboo, an ordinary housewife had recourse to relatively little assistance, if any. Whatever books, thanatology foundations, or university courses existed on the treatment of the terminally ill were irrelevant. As Bernard Shaw once commented, 'Most professions are a conspiracy against the laity.'

After surviving the self-inflicted gunshot wound, Mrs Phillips was questioned by the police, who debated whether to charge her with murder or a lesser offence. Because of notes found in the apartment verifying William Phillips's wish to die, the 'most appropriate charge', according to the Alameda County district attorney, was aiding and abetting a suicide. He expressed concern that he would be unable to get a conviction. Recovering at Highland Hospital in Oakland, Mrs Phillips said, 'There was nothing left to do.'[7]

In the early 1970s, then, there was a somewhat startling preoccupation with death, as if the subject had never before been properly explored or confronted.* Yet there was also, as there would continue to be, a gap between what people felt was an intolerable burden for a dying person, and the actual condition that, more often that not, had to be endured.

Surveys and questionnaires revealed that more than half the people polled—both medical and lay—believed that the life of an incurably ill, suffering person should not be prolonged, despite existing mores and laws

* Some observers related the new concern over death to the dawn of the nuclear age, when all people, not just the old and weak, were threatened with premature death. Others suggested that the technological 'covering over' of death had led to a psychic numbing and massive denial in which 'something had to give'. The fact that, for many, death was no longer a transition to an after life encouraged some writers to suggest that, thrown back on his own resources, man finally had to confront his mortality. Still others mentioned the counterculture movement of the 1960s, when people tended to be more concerned about others, especially the weak. (See 'Attitudes to Death Grow More Realistic,' *New York Times*, July 21, 1974.)

that insisted on the contrary. A survey of physicians in Seattle hospitals[8] indicated a desire for change that would permit a doctor to practise euthanasia without fear of penalty. 59 per cent said they would practise negative (passive) euthanasia *with a signed statement by the patient or family*; a quarter—27 per cent—said they would practise positive (active) euthanasia with such a statement if there were a more tolerant climate. The author of the study concluded that factors influencing doctors are essentially cultural.[9]

In other words, more than half those physicians felt that it was unnecessary to preserve the life of a terminal patient who wished to die, and one-fourth would hasten death if social attitudes and the law permitted such acts. What specifically inhibited them? Many of the doctors mentioned fear of malpractice suits, the commandment 'Thou shalt not kill', and the Hippocratic Oath with its emphasis on the administration of 'no deadly drug'.*

A survey of medical students and nurses at the University of Washington School of Medicine[10] showed even more radical views. 90 per cent of fourth-year medical students and 69 per cent of first-year students said they would practise passive euthanasia with a signed statement. Half of the students (46 per cent in both cases) favoured changes permitting active euthanasia. The authors suggested that, as in the former study, such attitudes indicated growing pressures to change existing ethical considerations and practices. Another physician reviewing the material commented that, considering the difference between these attitudes and present customs, the medical profession 'faces difficult problems in changing mores.'[11]

A significant majority of the nurses questioned[12] indicated the same need for social change that would permit euthanasia. 85 per cent said they would practise negative/passive euthanasia with a signed consent. A third to half of the nurses, depending on their specialities, said they would be willing to practise positive or active euthanasia with a signed statement. (Notably, nurses were even more eager than doctors for these social changes. Undoubtedly their daily contact with patients increased their sensitivity to the patients' needs. For instance, the *Washington Post* reported on December 13, 1973, that in Japan, 28 per cent of the nurses questioned at 70 hospitals said they had carried out mercy killings of patients when requested—without consulting the attending physicians.)

Another gap was uncovered by *Life* magazine in 1972.[13] Of the 41,000 readers who responded to the questions regarding 'What do you think of your medical care?' 70 per cent said that a patient should be told he is dying,

---

* Of 3,000 randomly selected doctors polled in 1974 by the magazine *Medical Opinion*, 79 per cent agreed that people have the right to make their wishes known before a serious illness strikes. 82 per cent said they would practise passive euthanasia on family members; 86 per cent, on themselves. The magazine concluded that 'the medical mandate for euthanasia is far stronger than was previously known.' (*New York Times*, June 16, 1974.)

while in only half (55 per cent) of the families that had experienced a terminal illness had the patient been told the truth. Almost unanimously— 91 per cent—readers endorsed the right of a dying patient to refuse further treatment. 'To torture a terminal patient with tests, X-rays, injections, and various other treatments, when it is certain they cannot help, should be forbidden by law,' wrote an angry reader.[14]

A Gallup poll conducted the following year showed that more than half of Americans—53 per cent—answered 'Yes' to the question: 'When a person has a disease that cannot be cured, do you think doctors should be allowed by law to end the patient's life by some painless means if the patient and his family request it?'[15] Commenting on the poll, Dr Walter Alvarez noted the two biggest problems in medicine: 'When can a doctor "pull out the tubes", and who has the right to say "Pull out the tubes".'[16] A Louis Harris poll conducted the same year showed 62 per cent sanctioning passive euthanasia, 37 per cent approving of active.[17]

In a 1973 survey on attitudes towards death, Dr John W. Riley, Jr, of the Equitable Life Assurance Society's Office of Social Research, reported that only 26 per cent of his national sample expressed the belief that doctors should use any means possible for keeping a patient alive.[18] And in 1975 in California, 87 per cent of the people questioned backed passive euthanasia.[19] 77 per cent of the Catholics surveyed agreed. Another majority— 63 per cent—insisted that an incurably ill patient has the right to ask for and get medication that would end his life. Here the Catholics were divided: 49 per cent agreed, 43 per cent disagreed, and 8 per cent had no opinion.

In fact, more people—physicians, attorneys, ethicists, and lay people— were openly crusading for changes that would affect euthanasia. The indignation was often unconcealed. If a significant majority endorsed the belief that a suffering patient should not be kept alive against his will, why did customs and the law lag behind?

Dr R. H. Williams, long concerned with the plight of the dying, deplored the options left for a terminal patient. 'Underscoring the extent of their suffering,' he wrote, 'are the terrible means of death elected by some, such as jumping into a fire, leaping in front of a train or a car or from a building, cutting the wrists or throat, and shooting oneself.'[20] Reviewing his survey, in which more than 80 per cent of physicians and lay people favoured negative (passive) euthanasia, and approximately 15 per cent of physicians and 35 per cent of the lay group favoured positive (active), he pointed to the need for changes in laws, religious policies, and public attitudes before active euthanasia could exist. As for passive euthanasia, too often it is 'too late, too little, or nonexistent in more than 99 percent of the instances where it should be applied.'[21]

Arthur Schiff, a general practitioner in Miami, argued that every physician should act according to his conscience. If a doctor believed euthanasia to be reasonable, he should work to introduce new laws, advancing solid arguments to his legislators. Schiff wrote: 'You should urge relatives and friends who have lived through a trying experience with a dying loved one to contact their lawmakers.'[22] (He added that a physician can continue to practise clandestine negative euthanasia.)

Walter Sackett, Florida physician and legislator, continued his crusade by writing and speaking about the need for a change in the laws, which would permit death with dignity.[23] In his 1973 article 'I've Let Hundreds of Patients Die. Shouldn't You?' Sackett presented his no-nonsense approach, stressing the enormous cost—$100 million a year—of life-prolonging procedures for people who are no more than human vegetables. 'We must stop this waste. That's why I've introduced a death-with-dignity bill at several sessions of the Florida State Legislature. It would halt the tragedies that occur every day because relatives or . . . spouses can't persuade a physician to take the risk of discontinuing useless treatment.'[24]

Joseph Fletcher, pressing on with his argument for passive and active euthanasia, deplored, as he had earlier, lifesaving procedures that transformed a human life into subhuman dying. Insisting that there is very little difference between omission and commission, Fletcher maintained that it is 'naïve and superficial to suppose that because we don't "do anything positively" to hasten a patient's death, we have thereby avoided complicity in his death.' He added: 'Not doing anything is doing something; it is a decision to act every bit as much as deciding for any other deed.'[25]

Additional articles surfaced, reinforcing the position Fletcher and others took—that to prolong living at all costs makes a mockery of life and death, and the patient should not be trapped into protracted dying against his wishes.[26] While there were critics of euthanasia—doctors shouldn't play God, life should be preserved at all costs[27]—these articles were outnumbered by the abundance of commentaries on the plight of the dying. As Kübler-Ross wrote: 'It says nowhere in the Hippocratic Oath that you have to prolong suffering. . . . That subtle line between prolonging life and dying is part of the art of medicine. Unfortunately, that chapter isn't in medical school text books.'[28]

To dramatize the argument, personal testimonials began to appear with regularity not only in specialized journals but in newspapers and family magazines. In 1971 the *Hastings Center Report*, in a piece entitled 'On Drinking the Hemlock', published a letter from Dr Arthur E. Morgan as a reminder that the 'ethical issues with which the Institute deals are not just abstract, but human problems of the most poignant sort.' In his letter, ninety-three-year-old Dr Morgan spoke of his ninety-four-year-old wife's existence in a nursing home, where—blind, deaf, and having suffered a

severe cerebral hemorrhage—she 'has not had the best of mental health.'
He went on to say, in a quiet but forceful manner:

> I sometimes think that living does not seem an asset to her.
> I know of no local agency with which to share this problem. To talk the
> matter over with her might infer that I am weary of her company.…
> I was ninety-three on June 20 and am as active as my strength and mental
> conditions permit.… My age is evident and a similar issue may be
> facing me in a year or two. It occurs to me that you might not dislike to
> have such a situation presented.[29]

Dr Morgan enclosed a letter written by his wife years before, in which she
stressed the importance of never being a burden. 'We are none of us afraid
of the grave,' she had written, 'and have no feeling of desire for life when
usefulness is over.'[30]

In the *New York Times*, in what might be an appropriate reply to David
Karnofsky (see pp. 72–3), Deborah Josephs, a New York secretary,
spoke of the agonizing dying of her twenty-three-year-old brother-in-law.
Relating how 'Flip' was moved to a hospital specializing in cancer research,
she noted how wrong the decision had been: 'It only served to postpone,
tortuously, the inevitable.' Bombarded with an endless—and, to Deborah,
useless—series of treatments, Flip, often against his will, was 'treated as a
research specimen for the remainder of his life.'

> He lived for eleven months … never once out of pain, never once feel-
> ing good, and, in the end, telling us that he was more afraid of living than
> dying.… In the eleven months, Flip had not a day without pain, and
> most of his pain was created by doctors continuing in their efforts to help
> him.…
> We saw people an hour away from death being taken out on stretchers
> to be X-rayed. We saw dying patients who had contracted pneumonia
> treated rigorously so that they would not die of pneumonia but live a few
> days longer until their inevitable death from cancer. We were told that
> Flip could receive no stronger pain killers because of the dangers of
> addiction.[31]

When the family disapproved of a particular treatment (accelerated chemotherapy), one Flip did not wish, the doctors informed them that he
would have to leave if the treatment was discontinued. Josephs emphasized
the importance of a patient's wishes while she lamented the paternalistic
attitude of a medical staff that denied a person the right to die as he
pleased—'with love, compassion, and dignity.'

*Life* magazine explored many of these same points in a 1972 article,
'When Do We Have the Right to Die?' The subtitle was 'There are times

when keeping someone alive may be crueller than death.' Using two examples of adults whose lives were prolonged to the point where quality of life was questionable, the author prefaced the case histories with the comment that death is, quite simply, not always worth fighting for. For instance, Tony Gallo was kept alive for two years with the help of a kidney machine. However, the physical discomfort that accompanied the treatment made him question whether the effort was worth it. His wife had spent five thousand dollars of their savings and had remortgaged their house to support him in his illness. 'Why do I have to be around? Why do I have to live like this?' he asked her daily. A few days after his wife's birthday in 1969, he ripped the tubes from his arm and walked out of the treatment room. Despite the pleadings of his family and his priest, he insisted that enough was enough. 'He told me it wasn't worth it any more,' his wife said. Tony Gallo was dead within a week.

In Pennsylvania, Ray Whittemore, a robust six-foot-two-inch middle-aged ticket agent, was diagnosed as having a tumour on his brain. As his mind and health deteriorated, his wife, Anne, began to foresee a horrible future for her husband, immobile in a cancer ward, bandages covering his eighty-pound body, tubes thrust in each opening, machines and needles everywhere. When cobalt treatments—extremely unpleasant—were begun, Anne countermanded them. 'Of course I knew his life might be extended,' she said, 'but what kind of life did he have? Ray was a dignified man and I wanted him to have a dignified death.' When the hospital called to tell her that her husband had died, her only comment was 'Thank God, his suffering is over.' Later she would say: 'I did what I thought was right. . . . I guess you could call it a sort of euthanasia, a mercy killing, but when I get too bad, I hope somebody will love me enough the way I loved Ray, and do the same thing for me.'[32]

The *Chicago Tribune* in 1972 noted two similar cases in '"Right to Die": a Growing Debate.'[33] One man was kept alive from 1957 to 1966, despite brain death as a result of an automobile accident. The state of Indiana paid $122,459.49 in hospital costs. Another man, eighty-five, suffering from a stroke, diabetes, inflammation of the veins, a fatal blood disease, and blood clots in the lungs, was kept alive in the hospital long after there was any hope for recovery. His daughter, a medical technologist, recalled: 'My father suffered the agonies of the damned. He should have been permitted to die. If I had had a syringe in my house, I would have gone into the hospital and injected air into him and killed him, and I would have taken the consequences.' As the author of the article stated, 'When are we prolonging life, and when are we merely prolonging death?'

By the same token, journalist Stewart Alsop, in 'The Right to Die with Dignity', argued that cancer patients should be able to decide for themselves what quantity of painkilling drugs they need, as well as when to end their suffering. Alsop, a leukemia sufferer, remembered his experiences in cancer wards and asserted:

> a cancer patient in full command of his faculties should be permitted to ask a committee of experienced doctors about his future, and if he is told that it holds nothing but suffering and death at the end, he should have the right to demand, and to receive, a pill or some other painless means of ending his life. But the right to end his own life should be *his* right, not a doctor's.

Alsop had been particularly influenced by a twenty-eight-year-old roommate in a cancer ward, who was given insufficient doses of painkilling drugs. After two hours, when the pain returned, 'he would begin to moan, or whimper very low. . . . Then he would begin to howl, like a dog. . . . [The painkiller] affected him no more than half an aspirin might affect a man who had just broken his arm.'[34]

In Montana, Joyce Franks, a housewife, recalling the agony of her father's dying, pleaded with the Bill of Rights Committee at the Montana Constitutional Convention to make a provision for the right to die in the new state constitution. Sobbing, Mrs Franks described the suffering her father went through, with no relief from the pain. 'For eight weeks he died,' she said, 'little by little, minute by minute, day by day. He was denied a release from the suffering and torture which he knew, and we knew, and the doctor knew he faced.'[35] Referring to the merciful death her father, a farmer, had given to sick animals, she said, simply, 'He asked for the same mercy for himself.' When Mrs Franks was unsuccessful in persuading the convention to include the right-to-die provision in the revised Declaration of Rights, she took her campaign to the state legislature. A voluntary-euthanasia bill was introduced in the 1973 session of the Montana legislature, but was defeated by a vote of eighty-three to fifteen.

Mrs Franks was not alone in her crusade for legislation. Dr Sackett continued to introduce into the Florida legislature bills that would enable doctors to terminate treatment for dying patients without being penalized.* He was not successful. In 1971 and 1973, death-with-dignity bills were presented in the Wisconsin and the Washington state senates, but received insufficient backing. In 1973, on Governor Tom McCall's recommendation that legislation for the terminally ill be considered in Oregon, a strong voluntary-euthanasia bill was introduced in the legislature; it was tabled after one hearing.

That same year, bills to legalize the Living Will (distributed by the Euthanasia Educational Council) were introduced in the legislatures of Massa-

---

* Sackett (along with Dr Morgan, Dr Kübler-Ross, and others) testified at the 1972 Senate Special Committee on Ageing and Death with Dignity, a spirited debate that pitted crusaders like Sackett against traditionalists who emphasized the sanctity of life.

chusetts and Delaware, but met with powerful opposition. A similar defeat occurred in the Maryland senate in 1974. In the Virginia legislature in 1975, Ira Lechner campaigned vigorously for a death-with-dignity bill that would honour the Living Will and affirm a person's right to refuse extraordinary measures. He failed to gain committee approval for the bill, despite considerable support from colleagues and from many physicians.

In all, by the end of 1975, bills had been introduced in fifteen states. The others were West Virginia, Idaho, Illinois, Rhode Island, Hawaii, and California. Only in California would such a bill be passed. In October 1976, Governor Brown signed into law a bill legalizing voluntary euthanasia: the Natural Death Act. Introduced in the assembly by Barry Keene, the bill recognized the legitimacy of the Living Will. Governor Brown commented: 'For too long, people have been unwilling to talk about death. This bill gives recognition to the human right that people have to let their life come to its natural conclusion.'[36]

By this time, the American Hospital Association had endorsed, after a three-year study, a twelve-point Patient's Bill of Rights. In 1973 the document had been approved as a national policy statement, affirming, among other things, a person's right to choose death by rejecting medical therapy and to obtain a full explanation of his medical condition in clear, concise terms. As one journalist observed: 'Medical paternalism is rapidly being challenged by health consumerism as patients are demanding a greater role in making decisions about their medical care.'[37]

In fact, the Patient's Bill of Rights expressed what doctors and hospitals had long recognized as logical but had lagged behind in communicating directly to the public. A further offshoot of the bill was the patient representative—or ombudsman—a professional whose job it was to ensure that patients' rights were fulfilled. By the end of 1973, more than four hundred hospitals employed ombudsmen.[38]

For four years after its inception in 1969, the Euthanasia Educational Council distributed more than a quarter of a million copies of the Living Will, a pointed attempt at ensuring a patient's right to a natural death, unencumbered by heroic efforts or unnecessary resuscitation. Although the will was not legally binding at that time, it made a person's wishes clear and provided direction for the attending physician. As the Council's president, Donald McKinney, said: 'Its great value is that a tremendous burden of guilt is lifted from the family and children when a person signs the will. And it is also a great deal of help to doctors.'[39]

The politically active counterpart of the Council, the Euthanasia Society of America (called the Society for the Right to Die after 1975), was reactivated in 1974; the group's aim was to legalize the Living Will in individual states. Both groups restricted themselves to endorsing passive euthanasia, a notable departure from the position of founder Dr Charles Potter, whose earlier euthanasia bills embraced active euthanasia as well. Thus the Living Will became the sole vehicle for expressing the aims and goals of both the Council and the Society. '[It] embodies all we have to say about passive euthanasia,' Elizabeth Halsey, the council's head, stated.[40] Neither group sanctioned legislation supporting active measures.*

In contrast to this more cautious approach, a 'Plea for Beneficent Euthanasia' appeared in the summer issue of *The Humanist*. The document supported both passive and active euthanasia, and stated 'On the basis of a compassionate approach to life and death, it seems to us at times difficult to distinguish between passive and active approaches. The acceptance of both forms of euthanasia seems to us implied by a fitting respect for the right to live and die with dignity.'[41] Among the forty signers were three Nobel Prize laureates (including Linus Pauling), five physicians, twelve religious leaders (including Joseph Fletcher), five philosophers, and Catholic professor of theology Daniel Maguire. The 'Plea' was followed by six articles, almost all of which dealt with the need for better care and legislation for the dying.

Physicians' organizations were also taking firmer stands on the issue of euthanasia. Although not as bold as the 'Plea', statements were being made that clarified what had, until that time, been avoided or condemned. In 1972 (perhaps foreshadowing the 1976 Natural Death Act) a committee of the California Medical Association issued a statement: 'Society as a whole will decide sometime in the future whether negative legislation will become accepted practice. . . . The burden of the vital decision should not rest on the individual physician.'[42] In 1973 the New York State Medical Society adopted a resolution affirming a patient's right to die with dignity when there was irrefutable evidence that death was inevitable. While pointing out that 'The use of euthanasia is not in the province of the physician,' the statement went on to say: 'The right to die with dignity, or the cessation of the employment of extraordinary means to prolong the life of the body when there is irrefutable evidence that biological death is inevitable, is the decision of the patient and/or the immediate family, with the approval of the family physician.'[43]

Indeed, six months later, the president-elect of the American Medical Association (AMA) conceded at a press conference (in response to a physician's being charged with a mercy killing; see p. 98) that some mercy killings 'have their place'.[44] Dr Malcolm Todd, a Long Beach, California, surgeon, told reporters that doctors should not be forced to make decisions about mercy killings themselves, but that a board might decide when such

---

* In Denver, a grass-roots version of the council surfaced in 1972. Called the Good Death Fellowship, the group published a newsletter and hoped for changes in legislation primarily through educating the public. In Washington, Frances Graves, a radio broadcaster, circulated a 'Death-with-Dignity Newsletter', with goals and aims similar to those of the Good Death Fellowship.

an act is justifiable. He asserted that the AMA should develop its own euthanasia policy.

Six months after that, at its convention, the AMA—despite Dr Todd's suggestion—officially condemned mercy killing, although it adopted a death-with-dignity report advising doctors that they should respect a dying person's wishes. The report stated, like the endorsement of the New York State Medical Society, that a patient and his family should have the right to insist that extraordinary measures be withdrawn when the person is dying.[45] Together with the newly enacted Patient's Bill of Rights, then, a patient could be assured of more autonomy, more authority, and better protection, at least in theory. (Notably, the AMA refused to endorse any form that permitted the expression of a patient's wishes.)

In other countries: The Canadian Medical Association's General Council voted, seventy-six to sixty-six, that in some cases a doctor could ethically write 'no resuscitation' on the chart of a dying patient.[46] In England, the debate over appropriate means for treating the terminally ill continued, with physicians (among others) divided over whether euthanasia legislation should be applauded or condemned. In the early 1970s, *Your Death Warrant? The Implications of Euthanasia* had appeared. Written by Catholic doctors, lawyers, and members of Parliament, the book—a reaction to the proposed 1969 bill—warned of the dangers of euthanasia legislation.

In turn, in 1971, the British Medical Association voted strongly against euthanasia. Emphasis was placed on the need for more and better resources for the sick and elderly; the panel studying the issue held that most people die peacefully and well.[47] In 1972 the Council of Social Services of the Department of Health and Social Security in England had a conference in which euthanasia legislation was hotly debated. A similar conference was sponsored by the Royal Society of Health in 1973. The debate continued, although there was general agreement on the need to prevent lingering misery by extraordinary measures, with some emphasis on hospice as a workable alternative.[48]

Initiatives by Australian members of the British Voluntary Euthanasia Society, working independently in their home states, saw the formation in 1974 of the Voluntary Euthanasia Society of Victoria and of the subsequently named Voluntary Euthanasia Society of New South Wales. The New South Wales society grew out of preparatory work supported and guided by the N.S.W. Humanist Society.[49] In 1974, South Africa launched its own Voluntary Euthanasia Society. All three groups emphasized the need to change existing laws and enact proper legislation that would protect the rights of a terminal patient.

The euthanasia movement, then, was broadening its base to include groups crusading actively in four countries. Over the next decade, it would expand to twenty-seven societies in sixteen countries.

Even in the midst of such campaigns in the United States, England, Australia and South Africa, there still were people like Lois Phillips, who, unaided, were driven to desperate measures. The courts were relatively lenient in most cases.

In England, for instance, in the winter of 1971, thirty-five-year-old James Price drove his retarded six-year-old son to a secluded river in the Midlands, kissed the boy goodbye, and drowned him. Afterwards Mr Price drove to the local police station and confessed, saying his son was 'just a living cabbage'. In court, Price was placed on probation for a year. 'I am taking an exceptional course in an exceptional case,' the judge said, as Price stood weeping in the witness stand. 'I am quite sure that in the passage of time, you will be able to forget about this matter.' The judge admitted later that he had been partly influenced by a petition signed by six hundred people in Mr Price's neighbourhood.[50]

A year later, in Liège, where Suzanne Vandeput had killed her deformed baby daughter, a court acquitted a man who strangled his wife to relieve her suffering. Jean Picquereau, seventy-four, had nursed his wife, Suzanne, since 1969, when cerebral sclerosis incapacitated her. He told police he had decided to kill her when the disease caused her unendurable pain and a mental breakdown.[51] And in the Netherlands in the spring of 1973, Dr Geertruida Postma received a one-month suspended sentence and a year's probation for killing her dying mother by lethal injection.

In America in 1973, two almost simultaneous cases galvanized the public. Twenty-three-year-old Lester Zygmaniak, in New Jersey, was charged with the slaying of his twenty-six-year-old brother, George, who had reportedly begged to be killed after a motorcycle accident paralyzed him. Lester took a sawed-off shotgun to his brother's bedside. 'Close your eyes now, I'm going to shoot you,' he said before firing at George's head. George was comatose for twenty-seven hours before he died. Later his widow testified on behalf of her brother-in-law:

> [George] said they were torturing him. He didn't want to go on living. . . . He said, 'Lester, promise me.' Then he said, 'Swear to God that you're not going to let me live like this.' Lester was crying and my husband was also crying, and I kept saying, 'Don't talk like this.' Then my husband said, 'Jean, you have to promise me you're not going to interfere.' And the look on his face and the way he said it got to me so bad that I had to tell him what he wanted me to tell him. Lester also. . . . Then the three of us said the Lord's Prayer and the Hail Mary out loud.[52]

Zygmaniak's lawyer argued that the act was not a felony, since George Zygmaniak had consented to his own death; the lawyer added that since suicide was not a crime, no crime had been committed. The jury acquitted the defendant, but on grounds of temporary insanity. As the defence attorney stated, Lester Zygmaniak was 'crazed with love' when he shot his brother. 'The only crime Lester is guilty of was having his power to reason overwhelmed by events,' he said.[53]

On Long Island, the chief surgical resident of the Nassau County Medical Center was indicted on a charge of wilful murder. Dr Vincent Montemarano was accused of killing fifty-nine-year-old Eugene Bauer, who was suffering from cancer of the throat and given two days to live. A nurse witnessed Montemarano's administering an injection of potassium chloride. Bauer died within five minutes.

District Attorney William Cahn, who had not personally prosecuted a case in eleven years, decided to conduct the case himself. Initially he characterized Bauer's death as a mercy killing, but later he described the death as a murder of convenience so that Dr Montemarano would not have to return that night to pronounce Bauer dead. The defence never conceded that an injection had been given, insisting instead that Bauer was already dead when Dr Montemarano was called by the nurse to examine him,—or, lack of causation, the same defence used in the Sander case. 'It's not a case of mercy killing,' Montemarano's lawyer declared. 'The state must prove a case of murder—pure and simple murder.'[54]

After deliberating fifty-five minutes, the jury returned a verdict of not guilty, which caused pandemonium in the courtroom. 'There was never any doubt,' said one juror as he left the courtroom. 'We were one mind and we just went and did it.'[55] Reviewing both the Montemarano and the Zygmaniak cases, a *Time* essay, 'Deciding When Death Is Better Than Life', noted that with mercy killings and passive euthanasia, there remain too many unanswered questions: 'Doctors will have to live with these grey areas, perhaps indefinitely.... The fundamental question, however, is humane rather than legal.' Recalling Freud's death by a requested injection of morphine to end his long and painful struggle against cancer, *Time* concluded: 'To die as Freud died should be the right of Everyman.'[56]

In Copenhagen, a twenty-three-year-old apprentice nurse received a one-year suspended sentence in the mercy killing of her fifty-three-year-old fiancé, who had suffered from polio for twenty-one years and could only move one finger and turn his head. The girl testified that he had repeatedly asked her to end his misery. Finally, she did so by injecting a drug that induced a coma, and then switching off his respirator.[57] Six months later, also in Copenhagen, a physician, Bjoern Ibsen, admitted in a radio interview that hopelessly ill patients in the intensive care unit were often allowed to die by doctors or nurses who shut off respirators or administered huge doses of morphine. 'One can ask,' the physician said, 'if it is not more humane to take a patient into a room, give him morphine and let him have peace, if it becomes clear during an operation that nothing possible can be done to help him.' Dr Ibsen was not charged with crime, but he was rebuked by the National Board of Health for 'destroying public confidence in the country's medical profession and hospitals.'[58]

In England in 1974, Elizabeth Wise, a third cousin of the Queen, was placed on probation for twelve months after pleading guilty to manslaughter on grounds of diminished responsibility for the mercy killing of her blind, deaf and retarded infant daughter. The child's brain had been destroyed by disease; Mrs Wise was told by doctors that she had no hope of living. The trial judge commented: 'I have little doubt it was your devotion which kept her alive. . . . Therein lies the tragic irony of this case. I accept that you acted as you did, although wrongly, in what you considered to be the child's own interest.'[59]

In Tel Aviv, a court sentenced a sixty-year-old woman to a year in prison for killing her thirty-seven-year-old son, who suffered from cancer. Aliza Hellman testified in court that the shooting was tragic, but the five years of her son's suffering had been a greater tragedy.[60] And in Cape Town, a physician, Alby Hartman, was charged with murder in the mercy killing of his cancer-stricken eighty-seven-year-old father. Dr Hartman pleaded not guilty, adding that his father, whom he loved deeply, was in great pain and nodded when asked if he would like to be put to sleep. He put Sodium Pentothal—which he said he knew was lethal—into his father's intravenous bottle. He was found guilty of murder, but received a one-year suspended sentence. 'This is a case which calls for a total suspension of sentence,' the presiding judge said.[61]

In the autumn of 1972, the bodies of Charles and Helen Croadsdill were found in their Seattle home. Both were in their eighties. Friends attested that they had been despondent over failing health and the fact that Mrs Croadsdill had to move to a nursing home. Police said the deaths were part of a suicide pact: Mr and Mrs Croadsdill were found side by side on their bed with plastic bags over their heads.

The following year, an elderly San Francisco couple named Sanderson carried out a suicide pact. The Sandersons' son spoke of his parents' fear of nursing homes and deteriorating health. 'Years before,' he said, 'they told me that if one became terminal, they planned to go together. The idea of letting death take you—they didn't like that at all—they wanted to control it.' When he received a telegram from them, as planned, he flew to San Francisco, where he found them in their bedroom, dead from cyanide. 'I was relieved and I was proud of them,' he said.[62]

In Princeton, New Jersey, in early 1975, Dr Henry (Pitney) Van Dusen, former president of Union Theological Seminary and a member of the Euthanasia Education Council, and his wife took overdoses of sleeping pills in a suicide pact. Friends said they entered into the pact rather than face the prospect of debilitating old age. In a letter left to friends and family,

Mrs Van Dusen said: 'Since Pitney had his stroke five years ago, we have not been able to do any of the things we want to do . . . and my arthritis is even worse. There are too many helpless old people who without modern medical care would have died, and we feel God would have allowed them to die when their time had come.'

After taking the pills, Mrs Van Dusen died immediately. Mr Van Dusen vomited up the pills and died fifteen days later, apparently of a heart ailment.[63] The double suicide provoked Norman Cousins, editor of the *Saturday Review*, to comment: 'Death is not the greatest loss in life. The greatest loss is what dies inside us while we live. The unbearable tragedy is to live without dignity or sensitivity.'[64]

That same winter, in Pittsburgh, a sixty-five-year-old retired maintenance man, Joseph Saveikis, was charged with third-degree murder in the stabbing of his wife, who was afflicted with multiple sclerosis. His lawyer argued that the act was a mercy killing, but Saveikis was convicted.[65]

And in Palm Springs, California, in August 1975, four days before Lois Phillips put a gun to her head, William Plachta was arrested for manslaughter when he told police he had stood by while his terminally ill wife committed suicide with an overdose of drugs. Perhaps because the manner of her death was less brutal than Mrs Saveikis's and was self-inflicted, there was no conviction. 'I could not let her go on like this,' Plachta told the police, as he described a deathwatch of twenty-four hours when his wife slipped into a coma. Mrs Plachta had been suffering from a degenerative nervous disorder for two years; it affected the motor centre of her brain and partially paralyzed her. In a farewell letter she dictated to her husband, her final words were 'Goodbye, rotten world.'[66]

# CHAPTER SEVEN

# *Significant Developments,*
# *Late 1970s to 1985*

On the night of April 15, 1975, Karen Ann Quinlan, a pretty, bright, twenty-one-year-old, was rushed to a New Jersey hospital in a coma. While waiting to hear further news, Karen's friends told her parents that she had eaten very little in the last four days and had taken some drugs (reports varied from one Valium to methadone, heroin, and cocaine) with alcohol while celebrating a birthday. Without warning, 'Karen began to act kind of strange,' one friend said. 'We thought she was drunk, so we all went out to the car and drove back to the house.'[1] Later, when they checked on her, friends found she wasn't breathing. They tried mouth-to-mouth resuscitation, but Karen started turning blue. A rescue squad was called; a policeman revived her breathing, but, still in a coma, she was rushed to the hospital. She would never recover.

Why Karen Ann Quinlan stopped breathing was never clearly determined, but the interruption in her normal breathing process apparently caused anoxia, an insufficient supply of oxygen to parts of the body, and coma. She was placed on a respirator, in what her physician called an altered state of consciousness. Dr Robert Morse, a neurologist, maintained that although she had suffered irreparable brain damage, Karen was not brain-dead, referring to the Ad Hoc Committee of Harvard Medical School criteria: She reportedly did not have a flat electroencephalogram (EEG), and she exhibited involuntary muscle activity, responding to pain, light, sound and smell.

Three months later, Karen's father, Joseph Quinlan, signed a release to permit the physicians to turn off the respirator. 'After many prayers,' he said, 'I'm convinced it is our Lord's will that Karen be allowed to die.' Mrs Quinlan said of her daughter: 'She is just a vegetable. She is not alive.'[2] However, Karen's physicians refused to remove the respirator, arguing that to do so would be an act of homicide.

# Checklist Chart
# Of 36 Living Will Laws

The 36 living will laws enacted between 1976 and 1985 legally recognize the individual's right to die with dignity. They authorize an adult to execute an advance declaration instructing that, in the event of a terminal condition, life-sustaining procedures shall be withheld or withdrawn.

No two statutes are precisely alike. This chart shows their principal similarities and differences. Also shown are the provisions of the 'Uniform Rights of the Terminally Ill Act', recommended by the National Conference of Commissioners on Uniform State Laws.

The Checklist Chart is intended to serve as a quick reference source for many of the most significant provisions of the laws. For more complete information, the full statutes should be consulted.

# CHECKLIST CHART OF 36 LIVING WILL LAWS

| | AL | AZ | AR | CA | CO | CT | DE | DC | FL | GA | ID | IL | IN | IA | KS |
|---|---|---|---|---|---|---|---|---|---|---|---|---|---|---|---|
| Law contains declaration form. | x | x | | x | x | x | | x | $x^{10}$ | x | x | x | $x^{14}$ | x | x |
| Form must be precisely followed. | | | | x | | | | | | x | x | | | | |
| Form permits personalized instructions. | x | x | | | x | x | | x | x | | | x | x | x | x |
| Declaration in effect until revoked. | x | x | x | | x | x | x | x | x | | | x | x | x | x |
| No. Number of years effective: | | | | | 5 | | | | | 7 | 5 | | | | |
| Law specifies proxy provision. | | | | | | | | x | | x | | | $x^{15}$ | $x^{15}$ | |
| To be binding, declaration must be executed after terminal diagnosis. | | | | | $x^3$ | | | | | | $x^{13}$ | | | | |
| Declaration invalidated during pregnancy. | x | $x^1$ | | x | $x^1$ | x | x | | x | x | | x | x | $x^1$ | x |
| Declaration may be executed for a minor. | | | x | | | | | | | | | | | | |
| Law establishes decision-making for comatose patients who have not executed a declaration. | | | x | | | | | | x | | | | | x | |
| Declarant must notify physician of declaration, physician must file in patient's medical record. | x | x | | x | x | | | x | x | | | x | x | | x |
| Declaration signing must be witnessed by 2 adults. They must not be: | x | x | x | x | x | x | x | x | x | x | x | x | x | x | x |
| Related to declarant by blood or marriage. | x | x | x | | | | x | x | $x^{11}$ | x | x | x | $x^{16}$ | | x |
| Heir or claimant to any part of declarant's estate. | x | x | | x | x | | x | x | | x | x | x | x | | x |
| Declarant's physician or physician's employee. | | | | x | $x^4$ | | | x | | x | x | | | | |
| Patient's health facility's employee. | | | | x | $x^5$ | | x | x | | x | x | | | | |
| Responsible for patient's health care costs. | x | x | | | | | | x | x | x | | x | x | | x |
| Nursing home patient's declaration requires special witness. | | | | x | | | x | x | | $x^{12}$ | | | | | |
| Other formalities of execution are specified. | | | $x^2$ | | | | | $x^9$ | | | | $x^2$ | | | |
| Law provides immunity to health professionals complying with declaration. | x | x | x | x | x | $x^6$ | x | x | x | x | x | x | x | x | x |
| Physician must comply with qualified patient's directive or transfer patient to another physician. | x | x | | x | x | | | x | x | x | | x | x | $x^{17}$ | x |
| Penalty may be incurred by failure to do so. | | | | | x | x | | x | | | | | x | | x |
| Compliance requires confirming consultation and written certification of terminal condition. | x | x | | x | x | $x^{7,8}$ | x | x | x | x | | $x^7$ | $x^7$ | x | x |
| Law addresses provision of nutrition and hydration. | | x | | | x | x | | | x | x | | x | x | x | |
| Recognizes living wills from out of state. | | | | | | | | | | | | | | | |

| MD | MS | MO | MT | NV | NH | NM | NC | OK | OR | TN | TX | UT | VT | VA | WA | WV | WI | WY | Uniform Act* |
|---|---|---|---|---|---|---|---|---|---|---|---|---|---|---|---|---|---|---|---|
| x[14] | x[19] | x[19] | x | x | x |  | x | x | x | x | x[10] | x | x | x[10] | x | x | x[28] | x | x |
|  |  |  |  |  |  |  |  |  |  |  | x |  |  |  |  |  |  |  |  |
| x | x | x | x | x | x |  | x | x |  | x |  | x | x | x | x | x | x | x | x |
| x | x | x | x | x | x | x | x | x | x | x | x | x | x | x | x | x |  | x | x |
|  |  |  |  |  |  |  |  |  |  |  |  |  |  |  |  |  | 5 |  |  |
|  |  |  |  |  |  |  |  |  |  |  | x | x[25] |  | x |  |  | x |  |  |
|  |  |  |  |  |  | x[3] |  |  |  |  |  |  |  |  |  |  |  |  |  |
| x | x | x | x[1] | x | x |  |  |  |  |  | x | x |  |  | x |  | x | x | x[1] |
|  |  |  |  |  |  | x[18] |  |  |  |  | x |  |  |  |  |  |  |  |  |
|  |  |  |  |  |  | x | x |  | x |  | x | x[26] |  | x |  |  |  |  |  |
| x | x[20] | x | x | x | x |  |  | x | x | x | x | x | x | x | x | x | x | x | x |
| x | x | x[21] | x | x | x | x | x | x | x | x | x | x | x | x | x | x | x | x | x |
| x | x |  |  | x | x |  | x | x | x | x | x | x | x | x | x | x | x | x |  |
| x | x |  |  | x | x |  | x | x | x | x | x | x | x |  | x | x | x | x |  |
| x | x |  |  | x | x |  | x | x | x | x | x | x | x |  | x | x | x |  |  |
| x |  |  |  | x |  |  | x | x[5] | x |  | x[5] | x |  |  | x | x | x |  |  |
| x |  |  |  |  |  |  |  | x |  |  |  | x |  |  | x |  | x |  |  |
|  |  |  |  |  | x[12] |  |  | x |  |  |  |  |  |  |  |  |  |  |  |
|  | x[20] |  |  | x[2] | x[22] | x[2] | x[23] | x[22] |  | x[22] |  |  |  |  |  | x[22] |  |  |  |
| x | x | x | x | x | x | x | x | x[24] | x | x | x | x | x | x | x | x | x | x | x[24] |
| x | x | x[17] | x[17] |  | x | x |  | x | x | x | x | x | x | x | x | x | x | x | x |
|  |  |  | x |  |  |  |  | x | x |  |  |  |  |  |  |  | x |  | x |
| x | x[8] |  | x[7] | x | x | x[8] | x | x[8] | x |  |  |  |  | x[27] | x | x | x[29] | x | x |
| x |  | x | x |  | x |  |  | x |  | x |  | x |  |  |  | x | x | x | x |
| x |  | x |  |  |  |  |  |  |  |  |  |  |  |  |  |  |  |  | x |

*"Uniform Rights of the Terminally Ill Act," adopted August 1985 by the National Conference of Commissioners on Uniform State Laws, which seeks to promote uniformity in state laws where appropriate. *Numbered notes appear on reverse side.*

# NOTES

1. Declaration shall be given no effect as long as foetus could develop to point of live birth with continued application of life-sustaining procedures.
2. Must be executed with same formalities as required for executing will of property.
3. If not executed/reexecuted after terminal diagnosis, directive may be given weight as evidence of patient's wishes, and attending physician may determine whether or not it should be implemented.
4. Nor may any other physician witness signing of declaration.
5. Nor may witness be co-patient in declarant's health facility.
6. To be assured of immunity from liability, attending physician must obtain informed consent of next of kin, if known, or legal guardian, if any, before life-support systems may be removed.
7. Requires diagnosis and written verification by attending physician only.
8. Does not specify certification in writing.
9. Each witness must verify in writing that he/she is not prohibited from being a witness by any of the disqualifications specified in statute.
10. Statute also provides that oral declaration may be made in presence of two witnesses by competent adult who has been diagnosed as being in terminal condition.
11. Only one of two witnesses must not be spouse or blood relative.
12. Declaration executed by patient in skilled nursing facility must be witnessed by medical director; in hospital, by chief of medical staff.
13. Statute nowhere addresses subject of declaration executed before terminal diagnosis.
14. Statute also provides for execution of declaration requesting administration of life-sustaining procedures. Indiana's statute contains suggested form for this, Maryland's does not.
15. Does not directly address proxy appointment; but by providing for consultation between attending physician and patient's representative under specified circumstances, statute by inference provides for appointment of proxy (or, in Iowa, of attorney in fact).
16. Statute bars only declarant's parents, spouse, and children from acting as witnesses to declaration.
17. Obligation to comply or transfer applies not only to physician but also to health care facility in which declarant is patient.
18. Declaration executed on behalf of minor who has been certified in writing by two physicians to be terminally ill must be certified by district court judge. In Louisiana, declaration must be executed in presence of witnesses as stipulated in statute's definition of 'witness.' In New Mexico, it must be executed with same formalities as will of property.
19. Mississippi's statute also contains a revocation form. In Missouri's, revocation form is included as part of suggested declaration form.
20. Requires that declaration be filed with Bureau of Vital Statistics of state Department of Health. Revocation must be similarly executed and witnessed

unless declarant is physically unable to do so, in which case a clear oral or other expression of intent to revoke will suffice. Before implementing patient's directive, physician must obtain certified copy of it, and certificate that no revocation has been filed with Bureau of Vital Statistics.

21. If declaration is entirely handwritten by declarant, no witnessing of its execution is required.
22. Affidavit must be made before notary public (or, in New Hampshire, before notary public or justice of the peace or other official authorized to administer oaths).
23. Declaration must be certified by clerk of the court or notary public.
24. Immunity from liability provided unless physician is negligent.
25. Statute contains Special Power of Attorney form, to be substantially followed, which must be executed before notary public.
26. Law establishes decision-making for any incompetent patient.
27. If patient is competent, only attending physician's diagnosis and written certification is required.
28. Statute stipulates that state's Department of Health and Social Services must distribute the declaration form contained in the statute; it is not otherwise obligatory to use this form.
29. Physicians must determine that death will occur within 30 days with or without application of life-sustaining procedures.

# STATUTORY CITATIONS

**Alabama Natural Death Act,** ALA. CODE §§ 22-8A-1–10 (1981).

**Arizona Medical Treatment Decision Act,** ARIZ. REV. STAT. ANN. §§ 36-3201–3210 (1985).

**Arkansas Death with Dignity,** ARK. STAT. ANN. §§ 82-3801–3804 (1977).

**California Natural Death Act,** CAL. HEALTH & SAFETY CODE §§ 7185–7195 (1976).

**Colorado Medical Treatment Decision Act,** COLO. REV. STAT. §§ 15-18-101–113; see also §§ 12-36-117 (1985).

**Connecticut Death with Dignity Act,** Public Act No. 85–606 (1985)

**Delaware Death with Dignity Act,** DEL. CODE ANN. tit. 16, §§ 2501–2509 (1982).

**District of Columbia Natural Death Act of 1981,** D.C. CODE ANN. §§ 6-2421–2430 (1982).

**Florida Life Prolonging Procedure Act,** FLA. STAT., Chap. 84–58, §§ 765.01–.15 (1984).

**Georgia Living Wills Act,** GA. CODE ANN. §§ 31-32-1–12 (1984).

**Idaho Natural Death Act,** IDAHO CODE §§ 39-4501–4508 (1977).

**Illinois Living Will Act,** ILL. ANN. STAT. ch. 110½ §§ 701–710, (Smith-Hurd 1984).

**Indiana Living Wills and Life-Prolonging Procedures Act,** IND. CODE 16-8-11 (1985).

**Iowa Life-Sustaining Procedures Act,** IOWA CODE ch. 144A.1–144A.11 (1985).

**Kansas Natural Death Act,** KAN. STAT. ANN. §§ 65-28, 101–109 (1979).

**Louisiana Life-Sustaining Procedures,** LA. REV. STAT. 40:1299.58.1–.10 (1984, amend. 1985).

**Maine Living Wills Act,** ME. REV. STAT. ANN. tit. 22, ch. 710a (1985).

**Maryland Life-Sustaining Procedures Act,** MD. HEALTH GENERAL CODE ANN. §§ 5-601–614, subtitle 6, Life-Sustaining Procedures (1985).

**Mississippi Act,** MISS. CODE ANN. §§ 41-41-101–121 (1984).

**Missouri Act,** MO. REV. STAT. §§ 459.010–459.055 (1985).

**Montana Living Will Act,** MONT. CODE ANN. §§ 50-9-110–104, §§ 50-9-111, §§ 50-9-201–206 (1985).

**Nevada Withholding or Withdrawal of Life-Sustaining Procedures,** NEV. REV. STAT. §§ 449.540–690 (1977).

**New Hampshire Living Wills Act,** N.H. REV. STAT. ANN. ch. 137H (1985).

**New Mexico Right to Die Act,** N.M. STAT. ANN. §§ 24-7-1–11 (1977).

**North Carolina Right to Natural Death Act,** N.C. GEN. STAT. §§ 90-320–322 (1977, amend. 1979, 1981, 1983).

**Oklahoma Natural Death Act,** OKLA. STAT. tit. 63, §§ 3101–3111 (1985).

**Oregon Rights with Respect to Terminal Illness,** OR. REV. STAT. §§ 97.050–.090 (1977, amend. 1983).

**Tennessee Right to Natural Death Act,** TENN. CODE. ANN. §§ 32-11-101–111 (1985).

**Texas Natural Death Act,** TEX. STAT. ANN. art. 4590h, (1977, amend. 1979, 1983, 1985).

**Utah Personal Choice and Living Will Act,** UTAH CODE ANN. §§ 75-2-1101–1118 (1985).

**Vermont Terminal Care Document,** VT. STAT. ANN. tit. 18, §§ 5251–5262 and tit. 13, § 1801 (1982).

**Virginia Natural Death Act,** VA. CODE §§ 54-325.8:1–13 (1983).

**Washington Natural Death Act,** WASH. REV. CODE ANN. §§ 70.122.010–70.122.905 (1979).

**West Virginia Natural Death Act,** W. VA. CODE. Chap. 16. Art. 30 §§ 1–10 (1984).

**Wisconsin Natural Death Act,** WISC. STAT. §§ 154.01 *et seq.* as created by 1983 Wisconsin Act 202 (1984).

**Wyoming Act,** WY. STAT. §§ 33-26-144–152 (1984).

Consequently, Joseph Quinlan went to court to be appointed Karen's guardian, with the express power of authorizing discontinuance of all extraordinary means of sustaining vital processes. The Quinlans, both Catholics, had been advised by priests that Catholic doctrine distinguished between acting to take a life and removing devices that artificially sustained life in a hopeless case. They also testified that only weeks before she went into a coma, Karen had told her mother and sister that if she ever became ill beyond hope, she would not want to be kept alive by extraordinary medical procedures.

However, the judge of the superior court decided in favour of the hospital. Noting that Karen did not meet the Harvard criteria for brain death, he held: 'There is a duty to continue the life-assisting apparatus. . . . There is no constitutional right to die that can be asserted by a parent for his incompetent adult child.'[3] The Quinlans then appealed to the New Jersey Supreme Court, which overturned the lower court ruling. A major concern was the violation of Karen's right to privacy:

> We think the State's interest contra weakens and the individual's right to privacy grows as the degree of bodily invasion increases and the prognosis dims. . . . It is for this reason that we determine that Karen's right of privacy may be asserted in her behalf, in this respect, by her guardian and family under the particular circumstances presented by this record.[4]

As a result, Karen Ann Quinlan was weaned from the respirator. However, she did not die as expected and was transferred to a nursing home, where she remained in a coma, fed through tubes, until she died in July 1985, ten years later.

While Karen's removal from the respirator did not end the ordeal of the Quinlans, it had a profound effect on public opinion and the law regarding care of the terminally ill. Before 1975, right-to-die legislation had been introduced in only five states. The following spring, after the lower court's denial of Joseph Quinlan's request and during the supreme court's consideration of it, seventeen such bills were introduced in different states, although all were defeated.

However, in 1977, fifty bills were introduced in thirty-eight states, and in Arkansas, California, Idaho, Nevada, New Mexico, North Carolina, Oregon, and Texas, they were signed into law. 'The Quinlan case has had a strong effect on bringing this out in the open,' said Alice Mehling, executive director of the Society for the Right to Die. 'Many legislators have referred to [it] in presenting or discussing their bills.'[5] From 1969 through to September 1975, when the case first became news, the Euthanasia Education Council distributed 750,000 copies of its version of the Living Will. For the next year and a half, when the Quinlan case had its greatest impact, the council had 1.25 million requests for the document from people who were apparently afraid of ending their days as Karen Ann Quinlans.

Since that time, Living Will laws have been enacted in thirty-six states at the time of this writing.* The Society for the Right to Die, dedicated to promoting such legislation, has defined Living Will laws as those that 'give legal recognition to an individual's advance declaration directing the withholding of life-sustaining medical measures in the event of terminal illness or injury.'[6] (The society adds that Living Will legislation—as it is referred to in society literature and here—is used generically and identified by a variety of phrases, such as 'natural death', 'death with dignity,' and 'right to die'.[7]) The society provides a Checklist Chart of 36 Living Will Laws (see pages 103–9).

Similarly, the Durable Power of Attorney, recommended by the 1983 President's Commission for the Study of Ethical Problems in Medicine and Biomedical and Behavioural Research, has received widespread approval. Such a directive—which appoints an 'agent' to represent a person's health care decisions if that person becomes incompetent—has been endorsed in the form of durable power statutes that exist in all fifty states.

However, as the Society points out, 'This application of the durable power . . . has not been widely used, and is not completely certain.'[8] With the exception of California, which amended its Uniform Durable Power of Attorney Act in 1983 and specifically authorizes refusal of life-sustaining treatment on behalf of the appointer if he or she is incompetent, the power of such statutes is questionable. 'Even less certain,' the Society notes, 'except in . . . California, is whether or not the durable power authorizes the attorney-in-fact to refuse life-sustaining treatment for the incompetent principal who is in a terminal condition.'[9]

Still, the fact that such statutes exist, along with massive distribution of the Living Will, is a tribute to the dual efforts of both the Society for the Right to Die and the Euthanasia Education Council. Together, they responded to and filled a pressing need dramatized by the Karen Ann Quinlan case.

Until 1979, the Society and the Council operated as separate arms of the American right-to-die movement, sharing the same offices and concentrating on passive euthanasia. The Society focused on enactment of state right-to-die laws, while the nonprofit council stressed educational and philosophical issues of dying with dignity. Because of the Council's non-profit status, contributors were encouraged to send donations; it, in turn, financed the Society's programmes.

In 1979 the working relationship between the two groups ended, however. The Council's president wrote to the Society board, informing them

* In December 1983, the Natural Death Act was passed in Australia, the only 'letting die' statute enacted outside the United States.

of the council's decision to end financial support of the Society, based mainly on reservations about its more activist, legislative approach.[10] In September 1980, the Council—now called Concern for Dying—issued a statement indicating its disapproval of 'indiscriminate or ill-conceived legislation', thus reinforcing its stand against overt efforts to introduce laws into state legislatures; the statement pointed out that such legislation was not an effective way of securing decision-making power for the terminally ill patient and those caring for him. Directly contradictory to Concern's founder Charles Potter's beliefs, the opposition was grounded in the conviction that 'legislation may have the unintended effect of limiting rather than broadening the individual's decision-making power.'[11]*

The rift between the two groups widened in October 1980, when the Society brought suit against Concern, eighteen of its directors and former directors, and its executive director, Ann Jane Levinson. The charges were that in 1978, when Concern requested Society to cease its fund-raising activities, it breached the agreement both groups had. (The mutual bylaws provided that anyone who donated three dollars or more became a member of both organizations.)

Further, Society held that a bequest of $1.25 million left to the 'Euthanasia Fund' by Mr Hugh Moore in 1973 was transferred to Concern, when in fact, as Society argued, the funds were meant for activist pursuits. The Society also charged Concern and its directors with libel.[13]

An out-of-court settlement was not arrived at until the spring of 1985, when Concern agreed to provide a grant of $275,000 to Society (now a non profit corporation as well). Both groups decided they would not publicize the costly lawsuit. Commenting on the rift—which caused bitterness to both groups and dismay to right-to-die organizations in other countries—the former president of the Voluntary Euthanasia Society of Victoria, Australia, observed:

> The Society's roots were radical ones, and it's a matter of regret to some of us that both the Society and its originally conceived educative arm, Concern, have become so entrenched in the 'passive' philosophy, which seems to have become a principle rather than a tactical weapon. . . . I suspect that very few Concern/Society members are aware of the schism and bitterness. They are impressed by the public labours of their respective groups, and it's for that very valid reason that they continue to give their support.[14]

In 1979, during the Society/Concern break, the Voluntary Euthanasia Society in London—then called EXIT—considered publishing a practi-

---

* Concern's president, Donald McKinney, continued to emphasize the organization's commitment to education versus legislation. As he later explained, 'Legalisms are not what must dictate health care; rather, common sense and respect.'[12]

cal guide to rational suicide for the dying. While EXIT's board was divided over publication of such a booklet and attempted to deal with its own inner turmoil, the newly formed Scottish EXIT brought out its own guide, modelled after the London draft.*

In America, Derek Humphry, who retained close ties with EXIT, considered publishing a similar book that would be lengthier and less of a 'suicide recipe book,' as many critics had dubbed the Scottish EXIT booklet. Humphry, a former journalist, who was investigated by the Department of Public Prosecution in London in 1978 for aiding in the suicide of his cancer-stricken wife, was now living in Los Angeles; much of the feedback he had received in 1978 convinced him that in America, right-to-die groups should campaign for active as well as passive euthanasia for the terminally ill in accordance with strict guidelines—thus departing radically from the firmly entrenched commitment to passive euthanasia held by Concern for Dying and the Society for the Right to Die.

In August 1980, Humphry and his second wife, Ann Wickett, formed the Hemlock Society, an organization 'supporting the option of active voluntary euthanasia for the terminally ill.' It stated as its principles:

- Hemlock will seek to promote a climate of public opinion which is tolerant of the right of people who are terminally ill to end their lives in a planned manner.
- Hemlock does not encourage suicide for any primary emotional, traumatic, or financial reasons in the absence of terminal illness. It approves of the work of those involved in suicide prevention.
- The final decision to terminate life is ultimately one's own. Hemlock believes this action, and most of all its timing, to be an extremely personal decision, wherever possible taken in concert with family and friends.
- Hemlock speaks only to those people who have mutual sympathy with its goals. Views contrary to its own which are held by other religions and philosophies are respected.[15]

Humphry also announced his intention of publishing the first U.S. guide to self-deliverance, *Let Me Die Before I Wake*, which appeared in early 1981, its copies at first available to members only.

Within a month of Hemlock's inception, Concern for Dying issued a statement condemning such books. Referring to EXIT's plans as well, Concern's president, Donald McKinney, said: 'We oppose the publication of material offering advice or counselling on specific aspects of suicide because we believe that such material is likely to be misused and that it is not possible to give effective standardized advice about drug dosage for the

---

* Such a publication was made easier in Scotland because specific laws against assisting suicide did not apply there.

purpose of suicide.'[16] In response to Hemlock's emergence and its more 'direct approach' (which she conceded resembled the goals of Dr Potter in 1938), Concern's executive director, Ann Jane Levinson, wrote to Humphry: 'The potential for abuse is . . . still too great. I only hope the backlash doesn't sink us all. I'd like to wish you luck but I'm not sure it would be honest.'[17]

In 1980 the World Federation of Right-to-Die Societies was founded, with twenty-seven groups from eighteen countries joining.* A year later, four books (or booklets) on self-deliverance for the terminally ill were available: Scottish EXIT's 'How to Die with Dignity' (thirty-one pages), Hemlock's *Let Me Die Before I Wake* (one hundred and ten pages), Holland's 'Justifiable Euthanasia: A Manual for the Medical Profession' (nine pages), and London EXIT's 'A Guide to Self-Deliverance' (thirty-two pages). In 1985, Concern reiterated its disapproval of such books: 'We oppose organizations which offer practical help or disseminate printed material describing methods of committing suicide,' the statement read, although it acknowledged: 'We realize this leaves unanswered the question of how a terminally-ill person needing assistance can implement a decision if family, friends, and professional advisors all refuse to help. . . . We have no ready remedy.'[18]

Given the ideological differences and estrangement between the American groups, Donald McKinney commented: 'What concerns me most . . . is that there continues to be so little contact and dialogue among us. . . . We seem to spend so much time in the totally non-productive machinations of behind the scenes in-fighting, rather than keeping clearly before us the far larger goal of helping society wrestle with these critical and highly complex issues.'[19]

Indeed, disagreements between the American organizations—and between groups in other countries—reflected the different and provocative points of view on a subject that attracted a great deal of attention. For instance, between 1976 and 1985, nearly five hundred articles could be found under 'Euthanasia' in the *Cumulated Index Medicus*, representing attitudes that stressed the sanctity of life, preserving life at all costs, who should decide the patient's fate, removing life-support systems, and accelerating the death of a hopelessly ill, suffering patient. The annual *Bibliography of Bioethics*, by the 1980s, contained roughly two thousand new articles every year. More than a hundred books had appeared, addressing euthanasia, biomedical ethics, and the law. Again, opinions differed rad-

* Concern for Dying joined in 1982. Its application was opposed by Society for the Right to Die on the grounds that Concern had sabotaged attempts at legislation—McKinney before the President's Commission and Mrs Levinson while testifying against the proposed District of Columbia bill. Still, Concern was admitted to the federation.

ically. Courses on death and dying proliferated on college campuses as students tackled the same, unresolved questions; as a result, more textbooks on the subject surfaced.[20]

A 1977 Harris survey showed that half of the people questioned (49 per cent) condoned active euthanasia—that a terminally ill patient has the right to tell his doctor to put him out of his misery—while 38 per cent were opposed. A 71 per cent majority endorsed passive euthanasia—the same patient should be allowed to die rather than have his life extended—with 18 per cent opposing. (Two-thirds of those surveyed felt that the family of a comatose patient had the right to instruct a doctor to remove life supports.)

While the results showed a significant increase in support of euthanasia since 1973 (an 11 to 12 per cent increase: four years earlier, only 37 per cent supported active measures, 60 per cent passive), one-quarter of the population could go only so far as to endorse passive but non active means. Opinions were still divided. One-fifth to one-third of those questioned resisted one or both measures, with, predictably, urban residents, whites, liberals, and better-educated people more in favour of euthanasia. (Contrary to many previous polls, the survey found that Catholics and Jews were more supportive of euthanasia than Protestants.[21]* A 1978 poll conducted by the American Council on Life Insurance supported these findings, adding that approval of euthanasia was highest among the young and lowest among the elderly.[23]

Nevertheless, differences in attitudes and apparent contradictions emerged in much of the literature. For instance, a 1983 survey by the American Hospital Association—while showing that 71 per cent of those polled supported passive euthanasia—found that younger people were more likely to prefer continued use of life-support systems in contrast to older people.[24] Similarly, an earlier (1979) study in a Seattle nursing home had shown that doctors (50 to 70 per cent) were sensitive to the futility of lifesaving procedures on hopelessly ill patients and either withdrew or withheld treatment; 30 per cent favoured accelerating death.[25]

Two studies in 1984, however, published in the *New England Journal of Medicine*, maintained that doctors often ignore their elderly or ailing patients' desires to be allowed to die. One study found that even though at least one patient in three about to die would reject any medical intervention, patients were seldom asked whether they wanted their doctors to practise aggressive measures. Only one doctor in ten actually discussed resuscitation with his patient; one in five consulted family members, even when the patient was fully competent. But most consulted neither. The study, one physician said, 'reveals some longstanding attitudes and prac-

* A sociologist, in "Correlates of Attitudes Towards Euthanasia",[22] published in 1979, found similar results—that race, religious behaviour, attitudes towards freedom of expression, and regional patterns significantly affected one's attitudes to euthanasia and suicide.

tices that tend to limit the autonomy of patients,' foremost among them doctors' reluctance to discuss painful prospects with their patients.[26]

Taking a more personal approach, physician David Hilfiker, in 'Allowing the Debilitated to Die',[27] agonized over whether he had done enough to treat an eighty-three-year-old chronically ill patient in a nursing home. Was aggressive treatment excessive, was too little treatment inappropriate and uncaring? When the patient finally died, Hilfiker observed: 'We have been forced into the role of God, yet we hardly seem to have recognized it. For my part . . . the life-and-death importance of my actions has kept me awake at night; the guilt and depression of never really knowing whether I have acted properly have been overwhelming.'[28]

Yet another physician, reviewing the article, felt that Dr Hilfiker had done too much rather than too little. Clearly, there were no guidelines, no real agreement. 'The group of patients representing the sort that caused Dr Hilfiker to philosophize needs further, nonfurtive attention. . . . Interestingly, the plaintive voices are often those of physicians who feel they have themselves been victimized by an intolerable system.'[29]

In fact, more attention was being paid to the psychic toll on doctors who worked with dying patients, the suggestion being that the pain suffered by patients affected the physician in a number of different ways, ways that could not always be quantified or evaluated. As the *Los Angeles Times* noted in 1984, in 'Doctors Share the Pain of Their Dying Patients': 'How does a person whose career is dedicated to saving, healing, and prevention deal with agony, disfiguration, and death?'[30]

Predictably, there has been no consensus. While there have remained those physicians who insist on preserving life at all costs, maintaining that pain can always be controlled, more doctors have emphasized the importance of the patient's needs and wishes. For instance, in 1976, one physician recommended the following considerations in deciding when and how life-prolonging treatment has ceased:

- The expressed wishes and attitudes of the patient towards death and dying, whether religious, cultural, family, or personal.
- The age, responsibilities, and anticipated quality of life of the patient.
- The mental and/or physical state of the individual prior to the present illness.
- Have all reasonable treatments been employed?
- The financial resources of the patient and his family.[31]

Most physicians who have acknowledged patient needs have condoned passive euthanasia for the hopelessly ill who wanted to be allowed to die.*

* Roughly more than half the articles that appeared in the *Cumulated Index Medicus* were concerned with some aspect of passive euthanasia—in many cases, both passive and active means were addressed.

Yet who would provide the guidelines for the decision-making has been disputed: doctors and lawyers together with the patient,[32] public opinion,[33] or doctors exclusively? As one physician argued, citing the number of right-to-die cases in court and Living Will legislation: 'Such decision-making is a matter within the medical domain and also is a matter of privacy between patient and physician and, therefore, is not a judicial or legislative matter.'[34]

Nurses, too, have been struggling with these issues. If doctors were debating the appropriateness of treatment or nontreatment, it was—and remains—the nurse who cares for the patient and invariably has to carry out a physician's orders. In an article published in 1979, 'Euthanasia: When You Can't Stand the Agony', one nurse described her feelings:

> If my patient is screaming and yelling in pain, begging to be put out of his misery, I say to the doctor, 'His respirations are shallow, but he desperately needs more pain medicine.' If the doctor says 'Give him morphine; we have to help his pain,' both of us know what the other is saying. Both of us know that a side effect of morphine is depressed respiration. But it's still theoretical. Once I pick up the needle and syringe and draw up the morphine, once I inject it into him and fifteen minutes later he stops breathing because of what I did, it *feels* like euthanasia. To everyone else, his death was only a side effect, but to me ... it's my patient who stopped breathing, it doesn't feel like a side effect. It feels like I killed him. ... [A nurse] can't cop out by pretending it's all the doctor's responsibility. The law may say it is, but when she looks down, she's the one holding the empty syringe in her hand. She feels the guilt.[35]

Another nurse wrote of her helplessness when confronted with a suffering terminal patient who wanted to die. The attending physician refused to listen to the pleas of the patient, the patient's family, and the nursing staff, claiming the woman was not rational. Instead, she continued treating the woman's condition as a medical emergency rather than a sign of impending death. The nurse's conclusion: 'The right to consent seems to me our greatest right.' She added:

> Not only was [the patient] not given the option to consent or to have her refusal to consent respected, but the doctor was initiating painful procedures and [the patient's] family had to leave her bedside because they could not watch her being 'tortured'. The fact that the family and the nurse had discussed with [the patient] how she wanted to be cared for ... before her pain was excruciating was of no consequence.[36]

Similar articles appeared in other issues of the *American Journal of Nursing*, in which nurses discussed how they were often put in an impossible situation. If they followed a physician's orders (such as the case above), they felt they were betraying the patient. On the other hand, if they followed the wishes of the patient, they had disobeyed physicians' orders and risked losing their job and incurring a lawsuit—especially in cases where resuscitation orders had been defied. 'If there is an explicit order to resuscitate,' one nurse wrote, 'the nurse may decide to follow it as part of her role obligation to the physician. Or, she may decide not to follow it as part of her role obligation to the patient based on her ethical reasoning that . . . the patient wants to die.'[37]

In a subsequent article, two nurses complained of cases in which patients' lives were hopelessly prolonged by doctors, causing grief to the patients, their families, and the nursing staff. As one nurse explained:

From the start, I was angry with the physicians for performing extensive surgery without Mr J's informed consent. I became more angry that they were letting him linger in such a miserable existence. But I was even angrier at myself that I was not able to grant Mr J's wish, especially since I would not be actively killing him, but just letting him die.[38]

In advising this particular nurse, a nurse/ethicist recommended 'blowing the whistle' on the attending physician, since Mr J's right to informed consent (and refusing treatment) was violated—although in doing so, the nurse might jeopardize her position. Again, her obligation to obey a physician's orders was in conflict with what she felt was her obligation to the patient: 'Standing up for a patient's rights is a professional duty that can conflict with the nurse's position as an employee. The nurse must decide which obligation to fulfil and must recognize the negative consequences of abandoning one to adopt the other.'[39]*

In an excellent overview of nurses' dilemmas, Marie Hilliard pointed out that in many cases a nurse must implement a 'code'—life-sustaining efforts—even in the absence of specific instructions from a physician. Doctors are often reluctant to write 'no code' orders, either because the hospital lacks explicit policies on such orders or because recent litigation has left many physicians uncertain as to whether the decision is theirs to make. Whatever the case, too often the onus falls on the nurse:

In general, nurses are expected to obey a written 'No Code' order which follows hospital policy. However, neither the physician's orders nor the agency's policies protect the nurse from legal and ethical accountability

---

* A 1983 poll reported by United Press International on February 16, 1983, noted that 9 per cent of the 5,000 nurses surveyed said that they had given a narcotic overdose to a dying patient and would do so again. The associate publisher of *Nursing Life* commented: 'What nurses are legally bound to do may not be what they feel is right. . . . Nurses may feel [some] situations are cruel for the patient and the family.' The survey also showed that more nurses in 1983 than in 1974 were writing up doctors' errors and going before review boards to report what they had seen.

for her actions.... Often the nurse's implementation of professional legal and ethical duties may be hampered by the legal privilege and conventional ethical rights of the physician who is considered to have ultimate accountability for patient care or by institutional limits on the nurse's authority to act.[40]

Over the years, nurses have been taught to follow the rule-ethics of obedience to authority. However, as more nurses are discovering, a moral dilemma, often impossible to resolve, is unavoidable when a nurse who values functioning within the system disagrees with a health professional of a higher ranking. Unfortunately, nurses must work within such a system, one that rarely allows them any formal input into decision-making. As Hilliard concludes: 'It is not surprising that in the face of such confusion, some nurses may opt for a conventional level of ethical behaviour.'[41] Indeed, in a 1984 poll for nurses cited by *Good Housekeeping*,[42] of those nurses who said they had imposed a code on a dying patient who had beseeched everyone to let him die, 49 per cent answered that they did so to protect themselves legally, and 26 per cent answered that it was the only way to avoid conflict with the doctor and the hospital administration. (In reply to other questions, 84 per cent favoured withholding life-sustaining procedures for dying patients, 70 per cent disapproved of extraordinary means for the terminally ill, and 97 per cent felt that the patient's desire to end life-sustaining efforts, despite family resistance, should be honoured.)

And what of those nurses who rebel? In February 1985, a New Jersey appellate court ruled that a hospital had the right to dismiss a nurse who refused, for 'moral, medical, and philosophic' reasons, to administer kidney dialysis treatments to a terminally ill double amputee. The nurse, Connie Warthen, had periodically dialyzed a patient in his seventies, someone Mrs Warthen described as 'debilitated and unresponsive'. At one point during treatment, the patient's heart stopped beating; he was resuscitated and placed on a respirator. Following other treatments, he bled internally. Mrs Warthen asked to be replaced, arguing that she could not submit the man to dialysis because he was dying and the procedure was causing additional complications. Taken off the case, Mrs Warthen was later reassigned to it. She refused to dialyze and was fired. (Another nurse performed the dialysis; the patient died several days later.).

Mrs Warthen sued the hospital, alleging that she had been wrongfully discharged. She insisted that her actions were consistent with the 'Code for Nurses', an ethics code adopted by the American Nurses' Association, which states that a nurse respects the 'human dignity and uniqueness' of all patients. However, the three-judge appellate panel agreed with the hospital that the nurses' code was not public policy; the code, ruled the court, set standards 'beneficial to the individual nurse and not to the public at large.'

The attorney for the hospital held that it was the duty of the hospital to preserve life, saying a nurse could not take it upon herself to decide whether or not a treatment was unjustified, even if the point of view was 'humanistic'.

Mrs Warthen responded: 'Nurses are supposed to be patient advocates. I may be an employee of the hospital, but my duty is to the patient, too. It's frightening if nurses have to fear being fired if they speak up for patients.'

At the time of this writing, Mrs Warthen's lawyer has filed an appeal with the state supreme court. He will argue that the nurses' code can be construed as public policy.[43]

Mrs Warthen's case typifies much of what plagues the medical community today. What is public policy, and what applies, as the appellate court panel argued, solely to the individual? While some guidelines—like those provided by the American Nurses' Association—provide instructions or recommendations, which are legally binding?'

If medical inventions such as dialysis have contributed to the dilemma, the system within which Mrs Warthen and others work has failed to provide a clear, universal set of legal and ethical guidelines on when certain treatments are appropriate and, if they're not desired by the patient, when they can be withdrawn. 'Everyone is confused,' said Dr Willard Gaylin, president of the Hastings Center, commenting on the substance and reasoning behind many bioethical decisions. 'No one is quite sure what the rules are. Doctors get in trouble when one virtue conflicts with another virtue. People of good will can come down on opposite sides. We are still in the stage of consciousness-raising.'[44]

What many doctors, lawyers, and philosophers have attempted to do to reduce the confusion is standardize guidelines and rules, just as Living Will legislation emphasized a patient's right to forego medical treatment.* For instance, in 1981, a joint committee of the Los Angeles County Medical Association and the Los Angeles County Bar Association issued formal guidelines for doctors on withdrawing life-support systems from hopelessly ill patients. Three circumstances were listed in which life supports could be stopped without the necessity of prior approval of the courts:

- If two physicians confirm that the person has suffered a total and irreversible cessation of brain function and is pronounced brain dead before the systems are disconnected.

---

* Despite the fact that critics of such legislation claim it is seriously flawed—many of the laws contain ambiguous language, they create bureaucratic burdens for patients and physicians, and have limited applicability—supporters respond that the rights and responsibilities of patients and physicians have been clarified, the doctor–patient relationship has been strengthened, and the terminally ill patient is treated with more respect and concern.[45]

- If the hopeless patient has signed a valid directive to physicians requesting that life not be artificially maintained.
- If the doctor and an appropriate consultant such as a neurologist make a written diagnosis of irreversible coma. The medical record must also state that the patient did not request indefinite life support and that the patient's family or guardian or conservator concurs in the decision.[46]

In 1982 the Medical Society of the State of New York issued its first set of guidelines for withholding emergency resuscitation from a terminally ill patient whose heart or breathing has failed.* Concerned hospital administrators and physicians, torn by ethical considerations and worried about possible criminal and civil consequences, welcomed such recommendations: in many instances, do-not-resuscitate (DNR) orders were communicated orally, or were written in pencil or on blackboards so that they could be erased later out of fear of malpractice charges.

Although the guidelines are strictly advisory and have no legal authority, the Medical Society advised that they be used as a legal defence. In order for a physician not to implement a do-not-resuscitate order, it was stipulated that:

- It shall be written by the attending physician. 'A verbal or telephone order for DNR cannot be justified as sound medical or legal practice.'
- The attending physician is responsible for ensuring that the order is discussed with hospital staff members.
- Facts and considerations involving the order should be made part of the patient's progress notes.
- The order shall be made 'subject to review' at any time and 'may be rescinded at any time.'[47]

A similar ruling in September 1983 occurred when the Veterans Administration, under a new policy that recognized a patient's right to die, permitted doctors practising in the nation's 172 veterans' hospitals to write explicit orders denying lifesaving medical therapy to certain critically ill patients. Specifically, the new rules allowed doctors to signify a 'No Code' or do-not-resuscitate order in advance so that a dying patient whose heart and lungs fail should not be revived. The orders are to be written on a patient's medical chart, the decision has to be made by a senior physician with the patient's permission, or, if the patient is not legally competent, with the consent of the family. The guidelines replaced those of 1979, which formally prohibited such measures.[48]

* New York was the fourth state to do so: Minnesota, North Carolina, and Alabama had issued similar guidelines earlier. Outside America, the Swiss Academy of Medical Sciences, in 1976, published its guidelines on caring for the dying, which stressed the physician's duty to offer personal support and care, as well as medical treatment.

In Minnesota in 1983, following the 1981 DNR guidelines proposed by the Minnesota Medical Association, the Board of Ageing outlined rules and recommendations on which of the state's more than forty thousand nursing home residents should be given only supportive care if near death. If a patient is terminally ill and imminently dying; severely and irreversibly mentally disabled, unable to communicate, and unaware of self and environment; and/or severely and irreversibly disabled and, despite normal mental functions, unable to interact in a meaningful way with the environment because of pain or impairment, he is a candidate for supportive care only. Such care means that a patient is kept as comfortable as possible; however, he is not treated for infections that, without treatment, would threaten his life. Perhaps most important, the guidelines do not apply to any mentally aware patient who wants to live.[49]

Recognizing the need for such standardized policies in hospitals and health care institutions, the President's Commission for the Study of Ethical Problems in Medicine and Biomedical and Behavioural Research in 1983, after a two-year study, recommended that when death looms as a certainty, a mentally competent and fully informed patient should be allowed to halt the treatment that keeps him alive. 'Competent patients' decisions regarding medical treatment should almost always be honoured,' said Morris Abram, the commission's chairman, 'even when they lead to an earlier death.'[50] If a patient is incapable of making such a decision, the family should be permitted to take that responsibility.

The commission urged hospitals to establish formal policies about the resuscitation of patients whose hearts have stopped. 'There are cases in which it is appropriate not to resuscitate,' the report stated. 'Such decisions should not be made covertly, however. When cardiac arrest is likely, a competent patient (or an incompetent patient's surrogate decision-maker) should usually be informed and offered the chance specifically to decide for or against resuscitation.'[51]

The commission also recommended that health care institutions develop internal review mechanisms to hear all points of view regarding dilemmas over life-sustaining treatment. It suggested that dying patients be provided with as wide a range of treatment choices as possible, including outpatient home care. Patients refusing life supports or life-prolonging measures should not be deprived of other forms of medical care, especially those 'needed to relieve pain and maintain dignity.'[52]*

A year later, in line with the principles articulated by the commission, ten prominent physicians proposed a bill of rights for dying patients (published in the *New England Journal of Medicine*), outlining criteria for the appropriate withdrawal of medical care. Noting that in modern medi-

* Months later, in Canada, doctors, nurses, and hospitals approved a policy guideline that authorized doctors to let some terminally ill patients die.

cine and treatment of the dying, 'Technology competes with compassion, legal precedent lags, and controversy is inevitable,' the authors said: 'The problem is least troublesome when an informed patient and an empathetic physician together confront a clearly defined outlook.'[53]

Such an outlook would be elucidated by the following guidelines:

- Physicians should either cease or diminish aggressive treatment if it would only prolong an uncomfortable process of dying.
- Doctors and hospitals should respect a patient's right to refuse treatment. As well, doctors should take the time to inform patients of their choices, rather than leaving them adrift in a 'mess of medical facts and opinion'.
- A patient should be told the truth about his condition, so he can make decisions regarding future care.
- A patient's refusal of treatment should not be a reason to question his competency.
- A doctor who is not sure of a patient's chances of recovery should consult specialists.
- 'Appropriate and compassionate care' should have priority over fears of criminal or civil liability, or advice of lawyers 'whose primary objective is to minimize liability'.
- It is justifiable to withhold antibiotics and artificial nutrition from a patient in a 'persistent vegetative state', or one who is hopelessly ill and 'severely and irreversibly demented and merely passively accepting food and care'—if the patient, by prior wishes, agrees and the family agrees.
- Even in elderly patients with permanent mild impairment of competence (the 'pleasantly senile'), emergency resuscitation and intensive care should be provided sparingly, guided by the patient's wishes, if known, the patient's family, and the patient's prospects.[54]

The guidelines were distilled from a meeting organized by the Society for the Right to Die, held at Harvard Medical School in 1982. The proposals were applauded by many doctors for their approach to such complex medical issues, and commended for their boldness in stating specifically that drugs, surgery, and other measures (including nutrition, in some instances) be withheld; there could be more focus on individualized care for the dying. 'It's going to get really crowded in emotional reaction,' one physician commented, 'until society is brought up—psychologically, socially, and culturally—to accept the fact that nutrition, hydration, medicines, and technology do little for a dying patient except prolong dying.' He added that guidelines would decrease liability for medical professionals and not force them to treat a patient 'in a manner that would be horrifying if they ever did that to you.'[55]

Commendable as such guidelines are, whether issued by a presidential commission, Harvard Medical School, or a community hospital, their effectiveness is limited. Arthur Caplan, a Hastings Center philosopher, commenting on the Harvard recommendations and a similar article published in the *Hastings Center Report*, said that few doctors follow such guidelines. His estimate? That only 5 per cent of physicians would agree to withhold fluids and food, and only 15 to 20 per cent would withdraw antibiotics.[56] Nor do all institutions care to follow the recommendations, even if they're aware of them. For instance, a June 28, 1985, *Los Angeles Times* article pointed out that the California Department of Ageing had been quietly advising their nursing homes to reject doctors' orders to remove tubes that provide water and nutrition to unconscious dying patients. The attorney for the department explained: 'A conservative approach is warranted until the law is further clarified.'

Despite the advances, then—a small but growing number of ethics committees in hospitals, more ethics courses in medical schools, more bioethical philosophers, more explicit guidelines—their impact on the medical community as a whole is relatively small. Experts point out that whatever consensus they do reach usually involves only an elite community of scholars, many of whom are connected to such prestigious groups as the Hastings Center, the Kennedy Institute, or the President's Commission. 'What we agree upon is by no means the same as what's felt out in the general medical community,' Hastings director Daniel Callahan said. 'Only some of our writings filter through. My general impression is that people who make actual decisions base it on religion if they have a strong faith, or else they grab a principle from the current culture that they can use for their purposes. This is rarely preceded by systematic thinking.'[57]

Moreover, where there have been guidelines, the courts have confounded the issue by delivering conflicting judgments, a bewildering phenomenon to physicians, who are increasingly concerned about litigation. In New Jersey, for example, a trial judge agreed to remove a nasogastric tube from an incompetent patient, Claire Conroy, but an appeals court reversed the decision. In January 1985, the New Jersey Supreme Court, a single judge dissenting on narrow grounds, reversed the appellate court decision and ordered the tube removed. Similarly, a Los Angeles superior court denied William Bartling the right to have his respirator disconnected, but an appellate court overturned the decision. (For a lengthier discussion, see Chapter 16, Is There a Constitutional Right to Die?)

As it stands, for doctors and nurses and other health professionals, there are no easy answers. In the case of a patient who is terminal and suffering, and does not want to live, is it ethically and legally permissible for a hospital to cut off nutrition? Dr Eric Cassell of Cornell University School of Medicine observed: 'It's ugly both ways.' If no effort is made to feed the patient, he said, then the hospital staff, committed to fighting death, must watch him slowly die from starvation. If the decision is to feed the patient against his wishes, then a tube may have to be inserted in the patient's stomach and his hands may have to be tied to the bed, another 'ugly scene'.

Dr Cassell suggested a preferable approach based on an 'unspoken agreement' between the patient who desires death and a hospital staff that sees its mission as something more than just keeping the body alive. The staff's duty would be to help the patient die in as 'pleasant' and 'congenial' a way as possible.[58]

However, a small but increasing number of patients and their families are going beyond an unspoken agreement and arranging what is called a 'negotiated death'. Carried out quietly and with a deliberate minimum of legal fuss or public attention, a patient's death is planned by the hospital, initiated either by the patient or by his physician and family. Such arranged deaths are rarely discussed or acknowledged outside the hospital, mainly because they could be construed as assisting a suicide or murder—by, for instance, an overzealous district attorney—and result in a lawsuit. As well as fearing a court fight, many doctors are aware that, failing resolution, keeping a hopelessly ill patient alive against his will is draining for everyone and incurs tremendous social, financial and emotional costs.

Typically, over days or weeks, the patient, his physician, his family, the hospital ethics committee (if there is one), hospital administrators, and sometimes lawyers form an ad hoc committee, concurring that death is inevitable and that prolonging life only adds to the patient's suffering. At a time agreed on, equipment is unplugged or other forms of treatment are discontinued. That such a phenomenon exists is perhaps inevitable in a world where technology has enabled doctors to extend the life of a dying person but has provided no explicit set of ethical and legal guidelines that will be universally applied and consistently upheld by courts. One doctor noted: 'Our medical inventions have invented our own dilemma. Sometimes the machines are a blessing. And sometimes they are a curse. But we haven't invented laws or rules yet to tell the difference.'[59]

Experts maintain that negotiated deaths happen every day and have become a fact of American life.[60] Often they take place with the tacit approval of law enforcement officials, most of whom wink at such cases since complaints are rarely filed. Many hospital ethics committees, when involved in a negotiated death, do not keep formal minutes for fear they could be used against them in a court case for murder conspiracy.

Such a form of euthanasia is endorsed by those physicians and health care professionals who argue that it is the only humane alternative in an area where neither law nor science has provided a solution. As one prominent bioethicist, Robert Veatch, said, commenting on terminal care decisions: 'It is increasingly clear that the health professional has a moral duty as well as a legal duty to stand aside and refuse to intervene to force treatment on a patient against that patient's wishes.'[61]

Yet other experts fear that the secretive, ad hoc nature of negotiated deaths could lead to fatal abuses. 'The problem is,' one lawyer said, 'that there is no legislation that details when and under what circumstances and with whose consent the life support can be withdrawn.'[62] Indeed, without legally binding rules, who and what ensures that a hospital ethics committee, if there is one, has acted correctly? What checks and balances are there to oversee such decision-making, especially when there is not a consensus of opinion? What guarantee is there that the patient has been truly competent to decide what is appropriate? As Veatch observes: 'There really are circumstances where we know what is in the patient's interest better than the patient does himself.'[63]

Until legislation clarifies the issues, negotiated deaths will continue as an inevitable and, some argue, sole alternative to a long-suffering deathbed, desired by no one. If medical ethics and the law have progressed since Karen Ann Quinlan lapsed into her fatal coma in 1975, there is still a long way to go.[64]

# CHAPTER EIGHT

# *Compassionate Crimes*

The public acceptance of voluntary euthanasia in Britain suffered a severe setback in 1981–2 with the prison sentences imposed on Nicholas Reed, the general secretary of EXIT, and Mark Lyons, a long time volunteer worker. Such ignominy upon the oldest voluntary euthanasia society in the world, formed in 1935 by such luminaries as Havelock Ellis, Julian Huxley, Harold Laski, and Lord Listowel (still 50 years later its president), was largely ill-deserved; the organization's record for attempting change in right-to-die laws and attitudes was exemplary and unequalled. (See pages 45, 55, 84 and 97.)

To a degree, however, it was this persistent failure to achieve reform through constitutional channels that frustrated a few more radical members of the organization, prompting them to circumvent the law in helping people to die. This change of strategy was never approved by the executive committee, which controls the organization, although there is reason to believe that a few members of the executive board were aware that such help with dying existed on a small scale and that they tolerated it so long as it was, they felt, discreet and justified on humanitarian grounds.

Nicholas Reed, an Oxford classics graduate, worked with the euthanasia society for some ten years as member, press officer, and assistant general secretary, before becoming general secretary in 1978. A dynamic crusader with considerable powers of persuasion, things soon began to hum at the Voluntary Euthanasia Society with his leadership. First, the group's plain name was changed to the more pithy EXIT—'for the sake of modernity'[1]—in 1979. (It reverted to its original name three years later.)

The same year the leadership discussed the idea of publishing a 'do-it-yourself' manual for terminal patients as a temporary expedient until Parliament could be persuaded to change the law to permit physician aid-in-dying or de-criminalize assisted suicide. Legal opinions were gathered about whether such a book was lawful, and most views conflicted. The opinion holding greatest sway was that of Professor Glanville Williams, author of the celebrated law book, *The Sanctity of Life and the Criminal Law*, who felt that a suitably worded pamphlet would be 'reasonably safe'; however, Williams stressed that such a publication should offer no encouragement to suicide but serve only those who had already decided to end their lives, enabling them to choose a manner not distressing for themselves nor for relatives.[2] Williams emphasized that the manner of the introductory wording was crucial in influencing the Director of Public Prosecutions.

Publicity about the name change and the planned suicide manual catapaulted EXIT into the public mind as a 'suicide club'. Only a minority of people realized that its true aim was to assist the terminally ill in a graceful self-determination. Still, membership shot up from 2,000 to 11,000 inside a year; a group which for forty years had seemed the brainchild of a handful of idealists and intellectuals was rapidly becoming a populist bandwagon.

Increasingly people were contacting EXIT for help with death, and not all of them were dying of a physical ailment. Many unhappy or disturbed people sought help as well. 'Distress calls doubled and trebled,' said Reed.[3] During the preparation of the booklet and its delayed publication (some of the old guard in the movement were against it, preferring to continue to fight for legal euthanasia through traditional methods), Reed received many frantic calls for active assistance with dying, and to some he responded.

Long before Reed took over, there had been a regular volunteer in the office named Mark Lyons. Reed's predecessor as general secretary, Charles Sweetingham, had occasionally sent Lyons with drugs to help members who were dying in a painful manner, but this rarely happened and when it did, was carried out with complete discretion.[4] In many ways Lyons was the ideal choice as 'the angel of death' as he was later dubbed by the press; he had no guilty feelings about helping people to die. As a spiritualist he viewed death as merely a transition from one psychic state to another. As the distress calls poured in to the now famous EXIT, with its leaders interviewed on radio and television almost daily, Reed began to send Lyons to these people—but merely 'to counsel' them, as he later claimed in court. Yet quite a few (it was never conclusively proved how many) were found dead after Lyons had called. All had died from an overdose, and some were found with a plastic bag over their heads, sealed airtight with an elastic band.

In April, 1981, Reed and Lyons were sent for trial at the Old Bailey on eight cases involving assisting people to commit suicide and conspiracy to assist suicide, while Lyons faced a further charge of technical murder of one person. If convicted of the murder, Lyons faced a mandatory sentence of life imprisonment. On the other charges, he and Reed faced up to fourteen years imprisonment.

A key factor in uncovering the full details of the case was Reed's passion for publicity—particularly publicity favourable to the euthanasia cause. He had taken quite a hammering from media critics, so when a team from 'TV Eye' convinced him that they wanted to do a sympathetic documentary, Reed passed along names of recently deceased members. When interviewing families of the deceased, the journalists found that the name Mark Lyons repeatedly surfaced, and eventually they shared this discovery with the police. The families had spoken of a strange old man, partly blind, wearing a woollen hat, who carried a 'suicide kit' of Tuinal tablets, brandy, plastic bags and elastic bands. Shortly afterwards police arrested Lyons and raided his home. This raid frustrated Lyons's agreement to help James Haig die. (See pages 152–4.)

Not only did the police find stocks of Tuinal and thousands of other drugs, but a set of diaries. Lyons was in the habit of keeping a journal in which he painstakingly recorded every single detail of his life, even down to the detailed content of every meal, which bus he caught and when. Inevitably, the requests from Nicholas Reed asking him to visit certain people— later found dead—were logged in Lyons's prodigious diary and this information was directly helpful to the detectives. For instance, after visiting a woman named Sheila, there was a diary entry: 'S. went home. 12.15.'[5] From such a plentiful source, detectives traced many deaths and were able to select a sample of eight in which the evidence was clearest. At the end of the magistrates' court hearing, Reed's lawyer Geoff Robertson argued that just because people telephoned EXIT it did not follow that the society would necessarily administer euthanasia. To which the magistrate countered: 'If I telephone a fishmonger and ask him to send a man, I expect fish. If I telephone the voluntary euthanasia society and ask them to send a man, I expect euthanasia.'[6]

At their trial at the Old Bailey in October 1981, both men pleaded not guilty. They were a contrasting pair: Reed, 33, bearded, intellectual, consistently denying that he knew Lyons was helping people to die. 'I was run off my feet,' Reed testified. 'Lyons liked talking to people . . . on the death bed people can get a lot of comfort from talking . . . I told him by telephone about some people who needed counselling, others he heard about in the office. . . . If I had known about Lyons's actions I would have been shocked. He had no authority to help people to die . . .'[7]

Lyons was defended by John Mortimer, QC, also a writer of some prominence, who described the case as one of the most unusual ever to be tried at the Old Bailey, adding that his client was a strange and outlandish figure and undoubtedly he was someone about whom to use the word eccentric 'was the understatement of the year.'[8] The seventy-year-old

Lyons has an obsession with cold and wears bundles of woollen clothes at all times of the year, indoors and out. His bizarre conduct and statements in the witness box perplexed the public and outraged the judge, particularly when Lyons asked permission in court to consult his spirit medium. It was refused! While he admitted giving people pills and using plastic bags, he at no time directly admitted helping people to die. In out-of-court conversations, it became clear that he had no concept of death as it is commonly known. The words 'dying', 'terminal', and 'death' were not in his vocabulary.

At the trial's end, Reed was found guilty on four counts of assisted suicide and conspiracy to assist and sentenced to two and a half years immediate imprisonment. Lyons was acquitted of the murder charge, but found guilty on six other counts. The judge took into consideration that Lyons had been in prison awaiting trial (while Reed had not) for nearly a year, and he was released on a two-year suspended sentence. Reed's appeal the following year against his conviction was rejected but his sentence was reduced by a year to eighteen months, all of which he served in an open prison. He resigned his position at EXIT and was susbsequently expelled from membership by the annual meeting.

Some of the people helped in their dying were desperately and distressingly ill and while it was legally wrong to have helped them, the moral rightness for doing so was strong. However, the disturbing feature of the Reed–Lyons case was that some of those helped, or offered help, were mentally ill, depressive, or alcoholics. Treatment and cure were possibilities. The EXIT organization's legal reform plans have never embraced the concept of euthanasia for unhappy people; thus the enormous damage that the Reed/Lyons misbehaviour and subsequent trial did was to brand the organization in the public's mind as a 'suicide club' for any and all reasons. However much EXIT's executive committee protested that the occurrences were not only unknown to them but completely unauthorized, the lay person's perception of EXIT was too often that of a place where anyone could obtain the 'magic pill' to leave this life. As a witness in the case said: 'I expected a suicide pill at the EXIT office. That's the basis on which I thought EXIT worked. Suicide pills for anyone who cared to drop in. It was my own mind which gave me that impression ... Yes, I only caught part of the programme on the radio, never the full story.'[9]

There was no criminal motive in Reed's actions, nor did he gain financially from his involvement. His fault lay in his zealous desire to help people and, if necessary, to reform the law by a *cause célèbre*. Had he chosen to plead guilty to the charges, arguing that he had acted on humanitarian grounds, the case would have lasted minutes and the publicity considerably less, certainly not as damaging to the movement as it was.

As a rule, the Director of Public Prosecutions has not shown any desire to punish assisted suicide when it came to his notice so long as it involved a terminally ill person, the helper was a close family member, and the motive for helping was obviously a compassionate one. This practice was underscored at Reed's appeal when one of the judges remarked that cases of assisted suicide within the family were not appropriate in the courts— although they are technically illegal. On the other hand, it was the 'call-out' nature of the Reed-Lyons service which upset the police and the prosecutor's office and provoked prosecution.

While Reed and Lyons were awaiting trial, the controversial booklet, *A Guide to Self Deliverance*, appeared, but a good deal of its thunder had been stolen the year before by a similar publication in Scotland, *How to Die With Dignity*, by George B. Mair, a retired physician. Mair's book was printed in Scotland because of the internal quarrel in EXIT in London about the rightness of publishing a suicide manual. EXIT's fight evolved into a lawsuit which delayed publication of the London book for a year.

Frustrated at the failure to publish in England, Miss Sheila Little, a part-time worker at EXIT's office, had gone to Scotland and, in concert with Dr Mair and others, formed a breakaway group, Scottish EXIT, with the intention of bringing out the booklet that appeared. In Scotland, which has its own legal system, assisted suicide is not a crime, therefore a suicide manual was safer to publish there. With his long experience, Dr Mair knew how to write such a guidebook and had considerable fame in the field of euthanasia. In 1974 he had published an autobiography, *Confessions of a Surgeon*, in which he related how during his medical career he had helped terminally ill patients to die. After the publication of *Confessions of a Surgeon* there were calls for his prosecution but as he had revealed no details of the incidents, this would have been impossible—even if the authorities had wished to do so.

*How to Die With Dignity* was sold only to members of Scottish EXIT, but there was no waiting period nor was there any age limitation. The booklet was concise: only three of its thirty-one pages gave specific information on lethal drugs and how to use them. A purchaser was told that the contents should 'be kept confidential and not divulged to anyone.' Thousands of copies were sold, in large measure to people not in the British Isles because demand in England and Wales was met from 1981 onwards by the London EXIT booklet.

*A Guide to Self-Deliverance* had attracted so much advance attention that, when it was available, it might have sold hundreds of thousands of copies had EXIT not restricted sales to members of three months standing who were over twenty-five years of age. Every copy was numbered so that its purchaser later could be traced if necessary. Requests by the media and academics for review copies were sharply rejected.

Adding to its celebrity was the preface by writer Arthur Koestler, who referred to euthanasia being 'a means of reconciling individuals with their destiny.'[10] The first words inside the thirty-two-page pamphlet were: 'Before considering self-deliverance, have you rung the Samaritans? Their number is in your local phone book.' While this exhortation would most likely be ignored by a terminally ill person, it was an attempt to deter emotional suicides. After Koestler's brief preface, there followed ten pages of discussion on whether it was necessary in every case to commit suicide, asking on page nine, 'Could yours be a temporary crisis?'

The substance of the booklet so far as the dying were concerned was three pages listing lethal doses of drugs. However, these proved difficult for the lay person to comprehend, and in some instances figures were incorrect, so within a few months a four-page supplement was issued. During this time, EXIT was besieged with inquiries for the booklet, for which they charged six pounds. Combined with the condition that a purchaser also become a member, it was hoped young people would not be deterred by expense.

Suicide prevention groups protested that the booklet had possibilities for abuse, and as some examples appeared, they were eagerly reported in the media. The most prominent case occurred when a twenty-two-year old music student took a room in Claridge's, invited all his friends to dinner, and later committed suicide with an overdose. Beside him was EXIT's booklet and a note to the management of Claridge's thanking them for 'the best terminal care facilities in Europe.' At the inquest it was revealed that the young man had had an obsession with violent death from an early age. His mother said that he had tried to commit suicide previously in similar circumstances.[11] After the police inquiry, the Director of Public Prosecutions decided not to charge anybody at EXIT, but the Attorney-General warned the group that he was applying for an injunction to prevent further distribution of the book and all remaining copies. EXIT responded that they welcomed the opportunity to put their case before the courts and get a legal ruling in what has been a very grey area of the law.

Also in 1981, the Hemlock Society in the USA published a suicide manual of considerable length. The Society turned down the opportunity to publish the English or Scottish booklet, comparing them to recipe-books. 'They would be unacceptable here because of their bleakness and insufficient consideration of the social, psychological and familial factors which go with self-deliverance,' said Hemlock's board of directors. In contrast, the 134-page Hemlock guide, *Let Me Die Before I Wake*, gave the lethal drug dosages within the context of true stories of suicides by terminally ill people—which enabled other considerations to be aired. The book's legal indemnity lay in two features: It is not unlawful to report true stories, and under the First Amendment of the American Constitution, the right to free speech is paramount. But these cannot be the only factors leading to the acceptance of the book: It has sold in bookstores for several years in Canada, where the laws are virtually the same as in Britain. If society wants it, then society tolerates it.

Hemlock was aware that the book, like its UK counterparts, was subject to abuse, but in its first five years, after selling 62,000 copies and having been maintained in most public lending libraries, not one instance of misuse was reported. A partial explanation for this may be that 64.3 per cent American men and 40.7 per cent of women who commit suicide shoot themselves.[12] Firearms are not commonly owned in the United Kingdom.

Support for EXIT came from an unlikely quarter, the medical profession's journal *The Lancet*, which observed in a leading article on suicide that it was time to recognize the increasing number of rational individuals with no recognizable or treatable mental illness who may wish to terminate their lives when their future seemed likely to be irredeemably marred by physical or dementing disease. 'The interest attracted by EXIT suggests that debates on euthanasia may be to the 1980s what our agonizing about abortion was to the 1960s,' the article concluded.[13]

When Mr Justice Woolf delivered his judgment on the publication of EXIT's booklet, it was neither a victory nor a defeat for EXIT. The court stated, in effect, that a bookstore could sell *A Guide to Self Deliverance* because the vendor had no knowledge of what his books were going to be used for. However, if a euthanasia society sold the booklet, they were likely to have foreknowledge of how the book was to be used (similar to the 'fish argument' made by the Hendon magistrate).

'The intention of the individual would normally be inferred from the fact surrounding the particular supply. As a matter of principle, as long as there was the necessary intent to assist those who were contemplating suicide, it did not matter that the supplier did not know the state of mind of the actual individual.'

Mr Justice Woolf denied the Attorney-General a declaration that the booklet was, in specified circumstances, an offence under Section 2 (1) of the Suicide Act, 1961, since that would amount to declaring that future conduct was criminal when that conduct was not clearly in contravention and when in each case the jury would have to decide whether the necessary facts were proved.[14] The Judge added that the law on aiding suicides needed clarification and if this could not be done in the courts, then Parliament should provide the answer.

EXIT could have appealed but decided against it, and ceased publication of the booklet. Some 9,000 copies had been sold. Several commercial publishers showed interest in issuing it, but when their lawyers and marketing staffs advised against publication they soon lost their enthusiasm.

Barbara Smoker, EXIT's chairman for 1980 to 1985, summarized in her 1984 annual report the group's position:

> If we were to re-publish the Guide ourselves, or were to act as a selling agency (or even a referral agency) for similar publications from other countries, we would revive our close association with an enterprise on the edge of the criminal law and would increase the risk we already face of civil court cases being brought against the Society by bereaved relatives. This would almost inevitably entail sensationalized newspaper coverage, thus delaying still further any foreseeable chance of our Bill being introduced in either House, let alone its being successful in bringing about a change in the law which has always been our primary aim.[15]

In addition, the group—by now having reverted back to the more respectable name, Voluntary Euthanasia Society—put out feelers about introducing legislation. However, they were met with a disappointing response and, anticipating another defeat, pigeon-holed any efforts to change the law.[16]

The unevenness of the administration of the law in euthanasia cases was never more clearly demonstrated than in the nine month prison sentence imposed upon Helen Charlotte Hough at the Old Bailey in 1984. As reported earlier in this chapter, there has been a reluctance to charge family members who helped a terminally ill loved one to die: for example, Norman and Janet Houghton, who were found guilty the following year of manslaughter of their quadriplegic son, received probation (see page 166, The Handicapped and Euthanasia). Yet Charlotte Hough received a harsh sentence for a 60-year-old woman of unblemished character.

The woman she helped to die, Anita Harding, aged 83, had no family to turn to for help. She was arthritic, suffered from chronic back pain, had difficulty in breathing, and was going deaf and blind. Her few real friends had preceded her to the grave. Miss Harding had foreseen the day when her declining health would be an intolerable burden to her and joined the Voluntary Euthanasia Society in 1978, also purchasing the suicide manual when it first appeared.

In 1983 Miss Harding was ready to die and approached her only friend, Mrs Hough, who had come to know her as a visiting voluntary social worker. She asked Mrs Hough to get her the pills and bring the plastic bag, and she also extracted a promise that she would not be allowed to survive. Mrs Hough brought the materials and sat with the old lady while she took her life. Before doing so, Miss Harding wrote a suicide note: 'I have decided to take my own life. This is a decision taken in a normal state of mind and is fully considered.'

Miss Harding took the overdose, but as she was still breathing four hours later, Mrs Hough—according to their agreement—put the plastic bag over her friend's head and drew the red ribbon tight around her neck. When she was dead she removed the bag, as Miss Harding had requested, and left. The death was considered a suicide. Unwisely for her own good, Mrs Hough talked about what she had done to colleagues in the Samaritans in Canterbury who subsequently told the police.

Mrs Hough appeared at the Old Bailey charged with murder although two days into the trial she agreed to plead guilty to attempted murder. Passing the sentence, Judge Tom Pigot, QC, said that he recognized that Mrs Hough was a caring, sympathetic, and compassionate woman who had acted out of the best Christian principles. He added: 'The law exists to protect the sanctity of life, even if that life is a person in a coma on the verge of death. What you did was to accelerate death, which was probably inevitable in a very short time. I have no desire to punish you but I must bear in mind public policy. I must have in mind the need to deter others less altruistic than you who wish to accelerate death in different circumstances.'[17]

Some saw contradictions in his statements. For instance, the law is supposed to be based on 'good Christian principles' so if Mrs Hough was caring and compassionate, why did she deserve prison? There had been sufficient flexibility in her case at one stage or another to have treated her more mercifully. It appears that Mrs Hough was made to pay a stiff penalty because she was 'not family', the court ignoring the reality that Miss Harding had none. Similarly, the appeal judges held it against the defendant because she provided the pills and the plastic bag. '... Too ready to play an active part in the provision or using of the paraphernalia of death,' they said, dismissing her appeal.[18] How else was this sick old lady to get the means to end her life but from another person?

Perhaps remembering the scandal of the Reed–Lyons case, Mrs Hough made it known that she did not support the Voluntary Euthanasia Society and did not want the law in this area changed.

Alone in the media, *The Sunday Times* criticized the sentence on Mrs Hough, remarking that as committing suicide had not been a criminal act since 1961, today it seemed strange that it ever was. Prosecutions for assistance in suicide were rare, said the newspaper, and when proceeded with the guilty were treated with great sympathy and leniency. The leading article continued:

What is often morally right in this sensitive area remains legally incorrect because, as a nation, we tend to sweep discussion of death under the carpet. In 1976 Baroness Wootten introduced a bill into the House of Lords which would have brought a modicum of good sense and regulation to the subject of euthanasia. But it was not supported. As a result, uncounted numbers of people, kept alive by medical science, often die without dignity unless a sympathetic doctor, moved by private pleas, helps them. Mrs Hough's crime was compassion and it served to underline once more the need for better legislation governing voluntary euthanasia and the dangers of being without it.[19]

This leading article was the first time a major British journal had come out in favour of legalized voluntary euthanasia.

By the end of 1985 the Voluntary Euthanasia Society felt that the climate had improved sufficiently to try for a modest reform of the law. With five of their officers (Lord Listowel, Lord Jenkins, Lord Soper, Baroness Wootton and Lord Beaumont) having seats in the House of Lords, they were in a strong position to get a bill tabled and test the water.

Accordingly, one of their vice-presidents, Lord Jenkins, introduced the Suicide Act 1961 (Amendment) Bill on December 11, 1985, remarking that in order to decriminalize suicide a quarter of a century ago, it had been politically necessary to introduce a completely new offence—that of aiding, abetting, counselling and procuring the suicide of another, which carried a penalty of up to fourteen years imprisonment. As there was no provision for any defence, it became a new crime to assist in bringing about what was no longer a crime.

Lord Jenkins claimed that his bill did only two things: give the Director of Public Prosecutions a reason not to subject a compassionate assister to the trials of prosecution and sentence if he judged that the defence provided for in the Bill would succeed. Second, give a compassionate judge and jury the justification to refrain from convicting in a case in which they might otherwise have no alternative under the present statute.

Lord Jenkins wished to add to the Act the words: 'It shall be a defence to any charge under this Act that the accused acted on behalf of the person who committed suicide and in so acting behaved reasonably and with compassion and in good faith.'

Lord Jenkins told the Lords that he had no complaint about the way the existing law had been administered, for court cases had been few and sentences usually took into account precisely the considerations which his bill wanted taken into account. But legislation was needed to give the Attorney-General and the Director of Public Prosecutions, judges, and juries the support of the law in what they were already doing and bring the law into line with existing practice. The time, said Lord Jenkins, when more substantial changes were necessary and acceptable might not be too far distant. He concluded: 'It simply provides a defence for one who has done what many of us hope we might have the courage to do if we were answering the plea of a friend or relative. It also means that if we were in the position of asking for that assistance, we could do so without feeling that we were subjecting our reliever to a risk of up to fourteen years imprisonment.'

Objections in the debate came from the Earl of Cork and Orrery, who outlined the hypothetical scenario of an unmarried daughter in her thirties caring for a sick, demanding, and housebound mother, who was tired of the burden. The daughter could switch more potent pills into a bottle of aspirin, wait for the old lady to take them, then call the police and say: 'I assisted her to commit suicide. I killed her, with her help.' The Earl described the bill as about the most deadly ever introduced into Parliament.

Baroness Macleod of Borve called the bill 'a licence to kill to anyone and everyone who wishes to see the particular person out of the way.' Such a murder could be for personal gain, for money, revenge or for many other reasons.

Lord Denning, who had supported the original Suicide Act in 1961, was probably the bill's most effective critic, pointing out that under recent legislation the Director of Public Prosecutions had to report to the Attorney-General and the Minister as to the public guidelines on the policy which he adopts in regard to prosecutions. Lord Denning went on: 'He would not prosecute in the ordinary case of mercy killing, and I hope he will not ... A policy will be evolved from case to case which he can report and from which it can be clear, and clear to the public, that, in cases such as Lord Jenkins has mentioned, which really ought not to be regarded as criminal and certainly ought not to be prosecuted at all, there will be no prosecution.'

Among the many pro and con arguments, Lord Paget of Northampton revealed that for years he had had a pact with a friend to come and give assistance to the other if requested. 'Whether or not this law is in being will not make the slightest difference to me in that pact,' he declared. The bill was rejected by forty-eight votes to fifteen.[20]

The failure to take Lord Jenkins's modest bill any further than one debate underlined the weakened state of the pro-euthanasia movement in Britain. Most observers blamed the Reed–Lyons scandal, for it showed how abuse might creep in, even with well-motivated people. Others argued that it was precisely the lack of carefully-constructed laws on euthanasia which caused this and other abuses; people tended to ignore an outdated law. Also, the precise meaning of the laws on assisted suicide remained as ambiguous as Mr Justice Woolf described them. It was a Catch 22 situation: The Director of Public Prosecutions was not anxious to indict in cases of assisted suicide—and few would want him to do so on humanitarian grounds—yet the lack of a suitable case with which to test the law all the way to the House of Lords meant that it remained uncertain.

The American euthanasia movement had in the 1930s and 1940s taken its leadership and style from the London group, its British counterpart. Many Americans believe today that British attitudes and laws on the subject are the most progressive in the world: This erroneous view is derived from the abundance of news about euthanasia that has emanated from Britain over the years, and the constant reporting, in books and journals, of the four attempts at legislative change in Britain; there is a presumption that these must have eventually succeeded. Now the leadership had switched: The three American groups report legislative progress (36 states had accepted Living Wills by 1985), rising public interest demonstrated in public opinion polls and attendance at meetings, and the unhindered publication of a suicide manual for the terminally ill.

Despite the set-backs of the early 1980s, leaders of the euthanasia movement in Britain saw more hopeful signs for progress in the second half of the decade. A 1985 National Opinion Poll showed that 72 per cent of the public favoured physician aid-in-dying for the terminally ill who requested it, and the medical profession began to take a serious interest in the subject. For example, the British Medical Association's ethics committee began a long-term study of euthanasia, including sending representatives to the Netherlands to study how it was handled there, and writing up their observations sympathetically, if cautiously, in the BMA News Review.[21] The news media, which had taken a perverse delight in EXIT's travails in 1980–81, began to follow the *Sunday Times* lead and write more responsibly on the subject, as their American counterparts had always done.

'We are finding a wider and more intelligent interest in euthanasia,' said Mrs Jean Davies, a veteran leader in the movement who became chairman of the Voluntary Euthanasia Society in 1985. 'Members, some of them influential in politics and the church, who left us during our troubles have rejoined. New minds have come in. I believe it to be just a question of a lot of education and time before law reform comes. Of course, the conservative wing of the medical profession will always oppose change but I estimate that about a third of the profession, particularly younger doctors, will be supportive of justified and lawful euthanasia.'[22]

# CHAPTER NINE

## *An Upsurge in Mercy Killing and Double Suicide*

Jim K. Collums was lying in a hospital bed at the end of 1981, suffering from Alzheimer's disease. His brain cells had seriously deteriorated, he was unable to speak or care for himself, and he was being kept alive by nutrients flowing through a tube into his nose and stomach. A retired army lieutenant colonel who had fought in the Korean War, Collums was now seventy-two. All members of his family accepted that his death was merely a matter of time.

A frequent visitor to the hospital was Woodrow Collums, Jim's younger brother by three years. The two had been close all their lives, beginning with the Depression years on the family cotton farm without a father. Not long after he left the army, Jim contracted the disease which led gradually to helplessness and senility, and eventually would cause his death. Well before the illness was advanced, Jim had written a letter to his doctor, saying that if they couldn't do something to help his brain, to please put him to sleep forever. Given the legal difficulties and the moral climate, it was a great deal to ask the doctor.

Woodrow paid another visit to his brother, who could say nothing comprehensible but did make grotesque mouth movements as if trying to say something. A few minutes later Woodrow went out to his car. After pausing briefly, he took the thirty-eight-calibre pistol that he kept in the vehicle, returned to the bedside, and fired three shots in rapid succession through his brother's head and two more through his stomach. Calmly, Woodrow put the gun down on the feeding tray and waited for the police to arrive.

Collums was booked for first-degree murder and subsequently set free on a ten-thousand-dollar bond.[1] The day after his release, he wrote a letter to his neighbours in the little town of Poteet, Texas, explaining, in script wavering over three pages, why he had done it. It said, in part:

> I feel no regrets about my act. I feel only happiness that he is out of his misery. He had suffered long enough. I could not stand to see him suffer

any longer. My brother knocked loose one of the many tubes running through his body. She [a nurse] fussed at him a bit like she was talking to a six-month-old baby. She then jammed the tube back through his nose and throat as I supposed she had to; he flinched from head to his toes. I knew then he had all his feeling.[2]

Nurses told the police immediately after the shooting that Woodrow had said: 'If you would have taken the tube out of his nose he would have starved to death and I wouldn't have to do this. I've killed horses, cows and dogs that were suffering. He's suffered long enough.' To the police, he denied his act was murder, 'because I feel like he's been dead since he's been in this condition.'[3]

A lengthy process of plea bargaining began, with the aim of avoiding a prison sentence. Both prosecution and defence were nervous of what the outcome might be if the case went before a jury. Eventually they arrived at a curious solution. The district attorney asked for a five year sentence, which the defence accepted; then the judge postponed passing the sentence for another ten years. Calling it 'ten years probation', he added that Woodrow must do ten hours' work a week as a volunteer in a senior citizens' centre. The judge remarked afterwards: 'No better person ever walked through the door [of my court] charged with murder. This was a murder with no justification but an awful lot of mitigation.'[4]

Jim Collums's widow said that she thanked God her husband was out of his misery. 'I hate to think it had to be done the way it was done,' she said, 'but I understand it. I couldn't ever have shot him. I could have asked for the life-supports to be taken away because I don't believe in life-supports. I just think it's cruelty for someone who's terminally ill to stuff a tube down his nose from May to November. That's agony and cruelty.' Other members of the family said they could not find it in their hearts to criticize Woodrow. In court they expressed satisfaction with the unusual judicial solution.

The Collums story is only one of many similar tragedies that began increasingly to happen in the 1980s as people took the law into their own hands.

The earliest recorded prosecution for euthanasia in any form in America was that of Frank Roberts, who in 1920 received life imprisonment for assisting his wife's suicide when she was terminally ill (*see* Chapter 1). From that time until November 1985, there have been 134 recorded euthanasia cases.* Seventy per cent of them occurred between 1980 and 1985. In no other decade is there a comparable death toll.

* In this instance, we take euthanasia to mean mercy killing, mercy killing followed by autoeuthanasia, double suicide, assisted suicide, and autoeuthanasia incidents that came to the attention of law enforcers.

Slightly more than half of the mercy killings (the taking of a loved one's life to relieve suffering) since 1920 have occurred in the 1980s, while a quarter of all cases were in 1985 alone. This gives a 300 per cent increase from any prior year. The extraordinary number of mercy killings (eighteen) in 1985 exceeds the total (eleven) for the ten-year period 1950–9. Mercy killing–autoeuthanasia cases, in which one person kills another (almost always a husband or wife) and then kills himself or herself, increased from four known between 1920 to 1979 to thirty-three so far in the 1980s. Double suicides, in which two people commit suicide together because of illness, rose from three to seventeen.

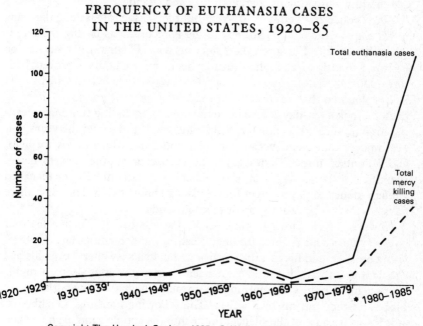

FREQUENCY OF EUTHANASIA CASES
IN THE UNITED STATES, 1920–85

Copyright The Hemlock Society, 1985   S. Waller 9/27/85

The Hemlock Society, the sole organization compiling such statistics, does not claim that they are completely accurate, because of the difficulties in researching incidents going back sixty-five years.* (Researchers have used newspaper, journal, and book accounts, the best available sources.) However, allowing for some errors of omission, the figures display a disturbing trend.

Not surprisingly, the majority of people involved in euthanasia cases are the elderly. Sixty-four per cent were over sixty years old, while fifty-one

* Needless to say, no one can speculate accurately on the number of unreported incidents, but experts claim that there is a significant number concealed from the public to prevent further family grief and embarrassment.

per cent were over seventy. The reported euthanasia cases involve, in order of prevalence: cancer, Alzheimer's disease, stroke, and heart disease. In more than eighty per cent of the cases, the dominant figure is the male partner, and the method most commonly used is firearms. The second most common means of self-destruction is drugs, but this method is likely to be heavily underreported because autopsies are rarely considered necessary on the terminally ill.

The lack of supportive care for the terminally ill person, and—just as important, if not more so—for the caregiver, who often has to spend twenty-four hours a day with the problem, has been a crucial factor in understanding a great many mercy killings and suicides.

When police arrested sixty-six-year-old Joe Wilson for slashing the veins of his eighty-year-old comatose wife, he is recorded as having muttered: 'No help. I did it.' For seven years since his wife, Thelma, had a stroke, Joe had meticulously cared for her, turning her every two hours to prevent bedsores. During that time she had not talked, walked, or fed herself. In 1978 he had doubted that he could handle the situation but, pressed to do so by doctors, took a ten-day course in home nursing, including training in feeding his wife through a catheter. Stroke followed stroke over the years, but death never came. His money gone, Joe could not afford to pay for help, and volunteer nurses' aides gave one excuse or another not to come. Eventually, when it was clear he would collapse without help, he managed enough money to pay a helper four dollars an hour, two hours a day, three days a week, so he could shop or talk to friends.

However, even with part-time relief, Joe was tied to Thelma for four constant days and nights, feeding, cleaning, and turning her. To meet rising bills, he sold his car, the television, Thelma's jewellery, even his bed (he slept in a chair). Eventually financial worries plus four sleepless nights overwhelmed him. One morning he opened Thelma's veins with a razor blade and then cut his own wrists. The following morning, neighbours, suspicious because of the silence, broke into the couple's mobile home and found them lying unconscious in pools of blood. Joe recovered, but Thelma died two weeks later from pneumonia brought on by weakness from loss of blood. Sitting in the county jail, facing a long prison sentence, Joe calmly told his state-appointed attorney, 'I should get what I deserve.'[5]

Joe sold the home in Valley Mobile Home Park, in Beaumont, California, to pay his wife's medical bills. When bailed out, he moved into rented accommodation. Behind the scenes, lawyers plea-bargained, and it was eventually agreed that Joe could plead guilty to attempted murder. He was given three years probation and 250 hours of community service. The judge commented: 'I don't see how this court can punish Mr Wilson any more than he's already punished himself.'[6]

*

A mercy killing followed by a suicide in Alexandria, Virginia, in 1985 was almost entirely due to lack of money for medical care. Cory Watts, twenty-two, had crashed his motorcycle in 1982, sustaining severe injuries that left him with brain damage and partial paralysis. His care was costing his family about $18,000 a month. Already the family debts amounted to some $500,000.

Claiming that the crash helmet worn by Cory was defective because it snapped just above the nape of his neck, the family paid a lawyer $30,000 in advance to bring a $10 million suit against the manufacturer, trusting that the settlement would resolve their financial problems. However, after a three-day trial the jury decided in favour of the helmet company, leaving Mr and Mrs Watts in deeper debt. Two hours after the court decision, Mrs Watts shot her son with a revolver; minutes later she killed herself with the same gun. Neighbours told reporters that the constant worry that someday soon there might not be enough money to give Cory basic medical care overwhelmed the family.[7]

Similarly, many of the elderly who take their lives have been apprehensive about their mounting medical bills; some are already in debt, others have a foreboding of the debts that may overwhelm them as their health further declines. The anger and dread that some old people feel was expressed in the suicide letter Lois Neese Martin, seventy-three, of Torrance, California, wrote just before she and her husband took their lives with an overdose of drugs. Noting that all their money was spent on medical care, she went on to say:

> It will soon run out and then we'll be at the mercy of the convalescent hospitals where the patients are treated like those confined to 'snake pits' of the nineteenth century. We are not a humane society. Our old people are discards and yet we're not allowed to make our own decisions. We are captive of our own people. A concentration camp in war could not be any more cruel or less caring for the dignity of the individual than our physicians and lawmakers are of the terminally ill.[8]

The anger expressed in this letter came from a retired school psychologist, who, despite her ailments, was well able to organize her thoughts. Mrs Martin's husband, Paul, eighty, a former college president, was also extremely ill from numerous complaints, and after much thought the couple agreed to end their lives on a certain day. They informed their daughter of their plans. Reluctant at first, she eventually agreed, while their son, a physician living in another town, disagreed but did not interfere. Mr and Mrs Martin laid careful plans for their deaths, pinning warning notes to doors and lying on plastic sheets to prevent soiling of the bedclothes. They then swallowed one hundred Valium each, shared a bottle of bourbon, and went to bed for the last time.

143

Although their financial position was strained, the Martins were managing. It was the worry that things might get worse which troubled them, as it did many others. Their daughter, Diane, said afterwards: 'My mother agonized over the cost of her medical care, and spoke of being a burden to me, to my brother, to Medicare, to Social Security. I tried to reassure them, to tell them they had earned these rights—they who had retired with their sick leave intact and unused, they who had cared for me and for my brother.'[9]

The Martins' worries were not atypical. Along with fears of becoming a burden, dread of nursing homes is endemic in the American elderly. The troubling accounts of the poor quality of care in many has given almost all of them a bad name, not entirely deserved. Few people seem to appreciate that health care in America is not a 'right' but a business, for 85 per cent of American nursing homes are run for profit. Professor Stephen Blum, of the University of California, Berkeley, one of the foremost authorities on nursing homes, says that the popular epithet 'houses of death' is factually incorrect because only 4 per cent of residents die in them, the majority spending their final hours in an acute care hospital, often in the intensive care unit. Blum argues that the time has come for alternatives to nursing homes, such as hospices or palliative care units, almost anything to avoid the typical nursing home, which, by the nature of its business, must care for the average elderly person with the average medical problems. 'Everyone requires something different because we are individuals,' says Blum. 'We need other 'houses of death', or nursing homes where there will be no transfer at the last minute.'[10]

However, some people are so ill or have such special problems that nursing homes do not want them. For example, extremely heavy people who are paralyzed from strokes, and need constant turning, are anathema to a nursing home staff. Also, some elderly ill are difficult to handle psychologically, such as ninety-year-old Walter Healy, of La Jolla, California, who not only was bedridden with emphysema, arteriosclerosis, and the effects of strokes, but had severe hallucinations that he was being attacked by birds. Even if a nursing home had agreed to take him, he was adamant that he would not enter one, despite the fact that his strokes recurred for ten years, by which time he was deaf and in constant pain.

In March 1983, his wife, Dorothy, who had nursed him valiantly, collapsed under the strain and strangled her husband of forty-eight years with a nylon stocking. She later told police: 'Walter would thank me. Walter would appreciate what I did.'

Once again the law connived with itself to give mercy to Mrs Healy, seventy-one, without the ordeal of a trial. It was agreed by prosecution and defence to allow her to plead guilty to voluntary manslaughter (which in itself could have earned her eleven years in jail); however, the judge said that he saw 'moral and ethical reasons for her actions', and ordered five years probation, a ten-thousand-dollar fine, and a thousand hours of community service work.[11]

In court, the prosecutor dutifully requested a prison sentence of one year for Mrs Healy, telling the judge: 'We are dealing with homicide. It's important to recognize that there is no legal, moral or ethical justification for this kind of act.' Outside the court, however, the prosecutor told newspaper reporters: 'Obviously, it's a special case, a seventy-one-year-old woman with no prior record. I don't know if this was exactly a mercy killing or not. But our problem is that we don't want to come right out and justify euthanasia. Sometimes we'll just wink at it, like we did today.'[12]

Before his retirement, George Hoffman delivered food to nursing homes. Later he would say that what he saw so disillusioned him that when his wife developed severe medical problems in old age, neither he nor she would even consider her being cared for other than at home. Mrs Hoffman, seventy-nine, was bedridden and weighed two hundred pounds. Visiting nurses helped George, eighty, with her care, but after several years of sleepless nights he was thin, nervous, and shaky—in his words, 'a walking zombie'. Contributing to the wearing-down process were his wife's cries for help, day and night, her hallucinations, and a subsequent refusal of aid. Nurses and neighbours described him as 'kindly and helpful'. George purchased a gun; a month later, in June 1978, he fired three bullets into his wife's head as she slept.

In court, a psychiatrist observed two things about George: he was the product of an aristocratic turn-of-the-century German culture that believed a husband had absolute authority to make this type of decision; and the delay between purchase and use of the gun was not unusual for such an organized, methodical man. 'Sometimes very bright people deliberate much longer before making decisions,' the court heard. Once again, the authorities accepted a plea bargain, the first-degree-murder charge being reduced to manslaughter, and a penalty of fifteen years probation imposed.[13]

As was the case with George Hoffman (who in 1983, at the age of eighty-five and in failing health, shot himself and died instantly), mercy killings are usually the result of a combination of reasons, although in some instances there is one dominating motive. In the cases just discussed, shortage of money and fear of nursing homes appeared to have been the catalyst. However, the overwhelming number of such killings are carried out in the belief that the dying person will be saved further suffering, which, in the eye of the caregiver, is unbearable. A point is sometimes made by prosecutors that the accused person was primarily intent on relieving his or her own suffering, the horror and drudgery of what he or she daily had to see and deal with, and sought escape. Undoubtedly there is an element of this in most mercy killings. A more compassionate view is that the killer believes he or she is relieving the intolerable suffering of the loved one, which is, more often than not, objectively the case.

Twenty-seven-year-old Martin Stephenson, for example, had a history of mental problems when he doused himself with gasoline and ignited it in 1982. Burns covered 62 per cent of his body, but he did not die. For nearly seven months he lived in a severely injured condition. When he was due to have further reconstructive surgery on his head and neck, he had told the surgeons he did not want it. The night before the scheduled operation, his father, a retired army officer, shot him with one bullet from a nine-millimetre Luger pistol. Martin died later the next day.[14]

A nurse subsequently told the court that the young man 'frequently stated he wanted to die, and that he regretted failing in his attempt.' The tearful father, expressing regret to the doctors and nurses who had cared for his son so well for so long, testified: 'Now Marty's gone, and he existed with integrity and went with integrity.' The judge noted that Colonel Stephenson had sat with his son in the hospital for more than two hundred days as he lay deaf and almost immobile. 'I'm satisfied that there is no punishment I can impose that's more severe than what you have already suffered with the death of your son,' he commented, accepting a reduction of charge from second-degree murder to manslaughter. Stephenson pleaded guilty; his prison sentence of five to fifteen years was suspended as long as he performed a hundred hours of community service a month for the next five years.[15]

In another case, death from cancer of the throat was only days away when Jeremiah Stephens's daughter, Patricia, visited him in Howard University Hospital, Washington, D.C., in May 1979. Stephens's throat was completely blocked, and he was supplied air from a respirator and food through a tube. The sixty-five-year old man had also suffered several heart attacks, was in a coma, and his five-foot-ten-inch frame was emaciated. Patricia, unable to bear the sight of her father's suffering, waited for the nurses to leave the room, took a pair of scissors out of her purse, and snipped all the tubes connected to her father's body. She then unplugged the electrical outlet to the artificial respirator. When nurses returned, they found Patricia sitting quietly at the bedside. As her father took his final breath, she stood and made the sign of the cross over his body.

In a statement made specifically to remove responsibility from the hospital, Patricia, a sociologist working in London, said her only desire was to see her father die in peace. The police did not feel they needed to arrest her, but turned the case over to the grand jury when the medical examiner classified the case as both euthanasia and homicide. The members of the grand jury were sympathetic, and declined to bring any charges against her.[16]

In fact, Patricia had only done what many physicians do: discontinue treatment. She had taken the timing of her father's death into her own hands. Still, caution was apparent in the comments of Leroy Walters, director of the Center for Bioethics of the Kennedy Institute of Ethics at Georgetown University, Washington: 'I don't think one would want to condone the general practice of having relatives disconnect life support systems. Since it's so difficult to determine motives, one wouldn't want to open the door . . . because some people might want to hasten the death of a relative for less than honourable reasons.'[17]

Of course, when a physician sees a friend undergoing great suffering, he may find himself under a special moral obligation to help, not only because he has the skill and experience to assess how sick the patient is, but because he has the means to end life. This was the case with Dr John Kraai—and it ended in a double tragedy.

In late August 1985, the elderly physician in a small New York town was arrested and charged with the second-degree murder of his patient and old friend Frederick C. Wagner. Mr Wagner, who was eighty-one, had suffered from Alzheimer's disease for five years and had also developed gangrene in one foot as a result of ulcerous sores. He was a patient at Penfield Nursing Home. Staff members said that he was in pain and that he no longer recognized anyone.

On the morning of Mr Wagner's death, Dr Kraai, alone with the patient, injected three large doses of insulin into the right side of Wagner's chest cavity. He then indicated to a nurse that the injection was a vitamin $B_{12}$ shot. However, several hours later, as Wagner's condition worsened, staff members became alarmed. By midafternoon, when it was apparent that Wagner was dying, a nurse called the state Health Department Patient Abuse hot line. At 5:30 P.M. Dr Kraai returned to the nursing home and pronounced Wagner dead. By this time, the nursing home staff had notified the state attorney general's office, the medical examiner's office, and the state health department. Sheriff's deputies began their investigation, and within forty-eight hours Dr Kraai was arrested and charged with murder. Later the sheriff told reporters: 'Dr Kraai was overwhelmed with emotion at the deteriorating condition of his patient.'[18]

Less than a week later, Dr Kraai was released on a fifteen-thousand-dollar property bond. After minor prostate surgery, he waited at home to hear the prosecutor's decision, which would be evaluated after consultation with Wagner's widow. 'There's no doubt the case will be prosecuted,' the county district attorney said. 'The question is how.' However, two weeks later, apparently despondent over 'mounting pressures' and failing eyesight, Dr Kraai got up early one morning and injected himself in the leg with a lethal dose of Demerol. At 6:45 A.M. his wife found him lying face down in the driveway. When paramedics arrived, they pronounced him dead.

Shortly after Dr Kraai's arrest, the sheriff had commented: 'This is the saddest kind of thing. I know of Dr Kraai. He was the type of doctor who still made house calls.' Support for the doctor in Fairport—a town with fewer than seven thousand residents—had been overwhelming. Friends and neighbours had universally praised Kraai, who had practised medicine for fifty years. Twice he had received Fairport's Citizen of the Year Award. 'Dr Kraai would take care of anybody in this village,' the mayor said. 'You were more than his patient, you were his friend.'[19]

Still, community support and the belief that he had acted humanely had not been enough, apparently, to keep Dr Kraai from killing himself. Prosecution, a lengthy trial, and possible imprisonment may well have been more than a seventy-six-year-old man felt he could endure, especially a man in deteriorating health. As well, the knowledge that another seventy-six-year-old man, Roswell Gilbert, had earlier in the year been found guilty in Florida of first-degree murder for shooting his wife (suffering from Alzheimer's and a painful physical ailment) may have been discouraging. Perhaps Dr Kraai feared the same treatment.

The president-elect of the medical society in Dr Kraai's county commented, after the suicide: 'As professionals, we have all been very sympathetic. . . . It was not Dr Kraai's sole burden.' A rabbi wrote of Dr Kraai: 'The very descriptions of [him] reveal vulnerability and decency. He made house calls and was not always particular about receiving payment. He carried food in his car to leave with the destitute hungry. . . . [He] rushed to relieve pain and [was] devastated by the suffering of others. He cared too much. He is a tragic figure like Prometheus. But like Prometheus he is also a giant.'[20]

Yet the law could not help him.

The rise in double suicides in the 1980s was just as significant as that of mercy killings—and an even greater enigma. Some saw it as a sign of love and devotion that one mate with a still useful life to live would choose to die with the partner who was doomed; psychiatrists tended to blame the phenomenon on male dominance of the weaker partner; others saw it as a further weakening of the principle of the sanctity of life and God's hold over man. Disagreeing with the final point is Dr John D. Arras, philosopher in residence at Montefiore Medical Center, in the Bronx, New York, who advises doctors on issues of medical ethics. He asserts: 'I don't know why believers can't have the view of God as a compassionate innkeeper, who gives his residents the right to check out whenever they want to.'[21]

A couple who reflected this thought were Reverend and Mrs Tod Ewald, of Corte Madera, California, who were in their seventies. Mrs Ewald had terminal cancer, and friends knew how depressed the couple had been over the prognosis. Mr Ewald, described as a 'high churchman', who had been in the Episcopal ministry all his adult life, was not known to be sick. Without warning, both were found in their closed garage, with the engine of the car running. The dean of the Episcopal church in Marin County, where Mr Ewald lived in retirement, described him as 'a good priest who will be sorely missed.'[22]

A more controversial double suicide was that of the writer Arthur Koestler and his wife, Cynthia, in 1983. Koestler was a vice-president of the Voluntary Euthanasia Society in London, where he lived; he had written an essay for the society's booklet *A Guide to Self-Deliverance*. He was dying, and he had made known his intentions with a suicide note. But Cynthia, fifty-five, was in good health. Koestler's suicide note, written ten months earlier, had referred to Cynthia's living after him.

Best known for his powerful anti-Stalinist novel, *Darkness at Noon*, Koestler at seventy-seven was suffering from Parkinson's disease and leukemia. His doctor had detected a swelling in the groin which he suspected was a metastasis of the cancer. It did not come as any surprise to his friends that he had taken his life, but Cynthia's death was an unexpected and obviously a late decision, perhaps made shortly before. The only clue to the timing is that on the morning of the day she died, she had had their pet dog, David, destroyed by a vet.[23]

On March 3, 1983, the Koestlers' maid arrived for work and found a note pinned to the door in Cynthia's handwriting: 'Please do not go upstairs. Ring the police and tell them to come to the house.' Police found them sitting in their usual places, Arthur in the armchair, with an empty brandy glass in his hand; Cynthia to his left, on the sofa. They had been dead about thirty-six hours, from an overdose of barbiturates. Half a glass of whiskey and two empty wineglasses with a residue of white powder were in front of them on a coffee table.[24]

Koestler had written his suicide note in June 1982:

To Whom It May Concern.

The purpose of this note is to make it unmistakably clear that I intend to commit suicide by taking an overdose of drugs without the knowledge or aid of any other person. The drugs have been legally obtained and hoarded over a considerable period. Trying to commit suicide is a gamble the outcome of which will be known to the gambler only if the attempt fails, but not if it succeeds. Should this attempt fail and I survive it in a physically or mentally impaired state, in which I can no longer control what is done to me, or communicate my wishes, I hereby request that I be allowed to die in my own home and not be resuscitated or kept alive by artificial means. I further request that my wife, or physician, or any friend present, should invoke habeas corpus against any attempt to remove me forcibly from my house to hospital.

My reasons for deciding to put an end to my life are simple and compelling: Parkinson's Disease and the slow-killing variety of leukemia (CCL). I kept the latter a secret even from intimate friends to save them distress. After a more or less steady physical decline over the last years, the process has now reached an acute state with added complications which make it advisable to seek self-deliverance now, before I become incapable of making the necessary arrangements.

I wish my friends to know that I am leaving their company in a peaceful frame of mind, with some timid hopes for a de-personalised after-life beyond due confines of space, time and matter and beyond the limits of our comprehension. This 'oceanic feeling' has often sustained me at difficult moments, and does so now, while I am writing this. What makes it nevertheless hard to take this final step is the reflection of the pain it is bound to inflict on my few surviving friends, above all my wife Cynthia. It is to her that I owe the relative peace and happiness that I enjoyed in the last period of my life—and never before.[25]

Cynthia had typed her own footnote to this: 'I should have liked to finish my account of working for Arthur—a story which began when our paths happened to cross in 1949. However, I cannot live without Arthur, despite certain inner resources.'[26]

Koestler's obituaries lauded his literary works, and he was described as one of the century's foremost intellectuals, but even his adherents questioned the logic of his wife's suicide. Psychiatrists and suicidologists postulated that such a powerful personality as Koestler's must have been an overpowering influence. 'One wonders if his wife arrived at that conclusion independently and without undue influence,' observed Dr Richard Seiden, an expert on suicide.[27] Feminists were quick to say it was part of patriarchal bias in our culture. 'The life and death of Cynthia Koestler reflect the colonization of women's minds throughout society,' wrote one in a letter to a newspaper.[28] Did the fact that the Koestlers were seated in separate chairs suggest a certain distancing at the end, or intellectual and bodily self-respect?

One of their closest friends, fellow Hungarian-born writer George Mikes, says that no one knows or will ever know what exactly happened between the couple. But everyone who knew them well could see the inevitable logic of her act, and Mike feels that Cynthia's footnote to Koestler's suicide note is the clearest possible statement of her free will. He said, 'She was not the type to become the rich widow. She was not to be

Cerberus, guarding her great husband's memory and legal rights. She was an intelligent and lovable woman who had dedicated herself to a man. And a strong personality, because only a very strong person could come to her decision and execute it with such dignity and self-discipline.'[29]

Unusual though the Koestlers' double suicide was, it is nevertheless fairly rare for the healthy spouse, especially one so young, to self-destruct. Many, if not most, consider dying with their mate but eventually do not do so. The other cases in this chapter are typical of the overall pattern, and experts fear that mercy killing and double suicides of ailing partners will increase in the second half of this decade. Euthanasia societies use the statistics showing the increase as ammunition for their case for the legalization of physician aid-in-dying. Many health professionals are worried that the rising number of cases of AIDS (Acquired Immune Deficiency Syndrome) will provoke more mercy killings and suicides, especially as the nature of the ravages of the disease becomes more widely known. In October 1985, two AIDS victims tied themselves together with a drapery sash and jumped from the window of their thirty-fifth-floor apartment in New York City. Police declared it a double suicide.[30] Euthanasia groups report many approaches from AIDS sufferers who wish to know how to terminate their lives later on, if they feel it necessary. A few AIDS patients have spoken of considerable sympathy from the medical profession when they've asked for help with euthanasia.[31]

# CHAPTER TEN

# *The Handicapped and Euthanasia*

Active euthanasia—as the rational action of a mature adult—is at its most controversial in the cases of paraplegics and quadriplegics who wish to have help with dying. Is their death wish created by a desire to escape their appallingly handicapped physical state with all its humiliations? Is this route justified? Are they giving up too easily? Would their accelerated death send other seriously handicapped people a message that struggling against the odds is pointless? Such rationalizations and questions—most of them emotionally tinged—arise when a severely handicapped person elects suicide.

In Britain and America, there have been four well-publicized cases of requests for euthanasia by paraplegics in recent years: James Haig of Oxford, England; Kenneth Wright of Connecticut; Elizabeth Bouvia of California; and Robert Houghton of Kent, England.

These four people are real-life exemplars of the protagonist—Ken Harrison—of the celebrated 1978 stage play and 1982 movie *Whose Life Is It Anyway?* The play and movie clearly demonstrate the empathy occasioned by the vicarious experiencing of another's shattered life.

James Haig was twenty years old when his motorcycle collided with a car as he was riding home from his night-shift job. When he recovered consciousness many weeks later in Stoke Mandeville Hospital, Oxfordshire, he found that he was a quadriplegic. He could talk, blink, gulp food and drink, swivel his head, and use the fingers of his right hand—nothing more. His brain was unscathed. Someone else's traffic error had sentenced him to full mental alertness and complete physical inertness: Except for his five fingers, he was totally paralyzed from the neck down. Before the accident he had been a two-hundred-pound centre for the Marathon Rugby Football Club in Oxford; after the accident, Haig's weight dropped to eighty-five pounds. He was so light that it required little effort for nurses to lift him into the wheelchair that would be his sole subsequent transport.

Haig spent several years, on and off, in Stoke Mandeville Hospital, which specializes in the care of people with broken backs or necks. He received physical therapy, psychological counselling, and job retraining. Not long before the accident, he had married. Six months after the tragedy, a daughter, Emma, was born. He was now a man with family responsibilities.

After two years, Haig began to feel suicidal. The desire to die certainly did not come from shortage of money—there had been a generous cash settlement from the insurance company of the driver at fault—nor from lack of love: His wife, Ruth, stood nobly by him. It was Haig's own desires, plus his feelings that he was depriving his wife and daughter of a proper life, that disturbed him.

'He used to get very upset because he could never hold Emma. He could be her father only with his voice,' said Ruth Haig. 'It depressed him not being able to do anything for her. James had wanted a large family, but, of course, after the accident that was impossible.'[1]

Haig tried to work in a telephone exchange, but he was dissatisfied with the work. He had excellent educational qualifications and now found himself doing work far below the level of his expertise. To raise his spirits he bought a used Rolls-Royce, but rode in it only a few times before storing it in a garage. Finally, Haig realized he could not bear life at home with his wife and child, so after a few months he moved back into the hospital, telling Ruth to forget him. He started divorce proceedings.

'My sexual desires are just as strong as before the accident,' Haig told an acquaintance. 'I cannot bear to look at my wife—or any woman—knowing I cannot touch her. Along with the inability to work, this has made my existence unbearable.'[2]

He made plans to take his own life. His first attempt was by starvation. When he found this too difficult, he drove his electric wheelchair into the Thames. But as the machine left the banks of the river, the wheels stuck in the mud and the chair toppled over. Haig was ignominiously pulled out of the mess.

'He couldn't accept being paralyzed and was constantly wanting to kill himself. He joined EXIT, the voluntary-euthanasia society, and talked about it all the time,' Ruth recalled.[3]

Haig talked to a volunteer worker at EXIT, Mark Lyons, who agreed to bring drugs to a motel room in Oxford. Such assistance would, of course, be a crime punishable by one to fourteen years imprisonment (under Section Two of the Suicide Act, 1961). As it happened, Lyons was arrested for other offences by police before he could meet with Haig; he was later sent to prison for helping others to die.

In September 1980, Haig, still determined, heard that the World Federation of Right to Die Societies chanced to be holding its third biennial conference at Oxford University, and he persuaded friends to take him to the meeting. Delegates from euthanasia groups throughout the world gave

Haig an audience for his moving plea to be helped to die. 'Life for me is intolerable,' he said. 'It's my right to end my life, and have help if I can't do it myself.' Everyone left the meeting deeply moved by Haig's sincerity.

However, it was an appeal they did not dare heed. The previous year, Mrs Berit Hedeby, leader of the Swedish Euthanasia Society, had been sentenced to six months imprisonment for helping a young man suffering from advanced multiple sclerosis to die. Further, Nicholas Reed, general secretary of EXIT, London, and the volunteer worker, Mark Lyons, were then under police investigation for assisting suicides. Unfortunately for Haig, the mood among delegates was one of caution.

The majority of conference delegates was critical of Reed's willingness to help Haig die without first investigating his state of mind and whether there were alternatives. To remedy this, EXIT chairman Larry Hill befriended Haig and met him on three occasions.

'On none of the occasions when I saw Haig did we talk about suicide or voluntary euthanasia,' Hill said later. 'We discussed his interest in football on one occasion, but primarily we talked about politics, on which he held quite strong views, and I found myself largely in agreement with him. We also discussed his taking further 'A' level exams, and he certainly appeared to have quite some interest in undertaking the necessary studies. At this stage I gained the impression—wrongly, it transpired—that he no longer intended suicide.'[4]

Four years after his motorcycle accident, Haig succeeded in killing himself, in a solitary and gruesome manner: He burned himself to death. With only the limited movement of his right hand, he used a cigarette lighter to set fire to a sofa in his living room. He then drove his wheelchair up against it. In what must have been a slow and painful death, Haig was so badly burned that, later, he could be identified only by the sores on his feet, a condition characteristic of quadriplegics.

At the legal hearing to determine cause of death, the Oxford coroner described Haig as a 'brave man' and brought in a suicide verdict.[5]

His newfound friend, Larry Hill, said: 'I think it's awful that society should make him choose a terrible death like this. A mature person like James who had given it due consideration should be able to go into a hospital and be helped to die.'[6]

Views critical to Haig's suicide may well have been voiced but were not published.

In 1980, a twenty-five-year-old Connecticut paraplegic found two friends willing to help him commit suicide, and they narrowly escaped going to prison for assisting him. Kenneth Wright, injured in 1978 in a freak wrestling accident during an informal match with a friend, had been left paralyzed from the waist down and in a good deal of pain.

'He couldn't cope. He was an athlete,' his mother said.[7]

Wright talked of suicide to William R. King and Brian Taylor, asking them to saw off the barrel of a twelve-gauge shotgun so that he could easily turn it on himself.

Not wanting to shock his mother and make a mess of the mobile home he shared with his parents, Wright persuaded his friends to wheel him to a clearing in the woods. They said their final goodbyes and walked away, later telephoning the police, who found the young man dead from a self-inflicted gunshot wound.

Taylor and King were charged with second-degree manslaughter, a Class C felony in Connecticut, for 'intentionally causing or aiding another person, other than by force, duress or deception, to commit suicide.'

Law enforcement officials' sympathetic remarks were quoted in local newspapers and the accused were released on small bonds. Initially they pleaded not guilty, asking for a jury trial, but later they plea-bargained with the prosecutor; in return for guilty pleas, it was agreed not to send them to prison.

The *Hartford Courant* commented:

The two accomplices to a sad story, both in their twenties, can stand accused of being misguided, but they are not felons deserving of years in prison.

Laws require not only the putting of pen to paper, but also the support of a society that recognizes them as fair, and accurately reflecting a societal consensus on justice. The law demands that William King and Brian Taylor face judicial scrutiny for their participation in the death of a fellow human being—and that is both necessary and just. That judgment should be lenient; the crime and its aftermath have already taken their toll, and extracted their punishment, on the two young men who thought they were helping a friend.[8]

Mrs Phyllis Wright, the dead man's mother, told the state's attorney that she did not want King and Taylor to go to prison. She added that she wished they had never been prosecuted.

In their final court appearance, the men were given suspended sentences and told by the judge:

Rather than dissuade your friend from his suicide you appear to have helped him. You will have to live with that. He was your friend. That's a severe punishment. It is only because of the unique circumstances that there has been no condition imposed [on the sentences]. You have had to deal with the publicity in this case, the stigma of the arrest, and you will have to live with a felony conviction.[9]

In 1984, international attention was focused on the request by Elizabeth

Bouvia to be allowed to remain in a hospital while she starved herself to death. It would be mistaken to think that there are hundreds of people in her medical condition wishing to commit suicide, and similarly handicapped people seem divided in assessing whether she was justified. The facts of her case are fairly unique, not least of all because she pursued her request for help in dying with litigation.

Unlike the two young men just discussed, who became suddenly handicapped after twenty years of active life, Elizabeth was born a quadriplegic. She suffered from cerebral palsy since birth, having virtually no motor control in any of her limbs or skeletal muscles. Like James Haig, she had limited control over the movement of her right hand, enabling her to operate the controls of an electric wheelchair. She can eat and drink as long as someone puts food in her mouth. She can brush her teeth and smoke a cigarette.

Elizabeth's parents were divorced when she was five. Her mother remarried, and when she became pregnant again, she put Elizabeth into a children's home in Desert Hot Springs, California. Over the next eight years, mother and daughter saw each other only twice. Elizabeth left the home at eighteen and spent some time with her father in Seattle, but she was determined to make plans for her own life, independent of either parent.

Initially Elizabeth enrolled at Riverside State College, California, but later she transferred to San Diego State University, where she completed a B.S. degree in social work. During this time she needed twenty-four-hour home care and a secretary to take dictation. She made plans to start on her master's degree.

In 1983 and 1984, Elizabeth, now twenty-six, ran into personal difficulties. Interrupting her plans for graduate work, she married Richard Bouvia, a machinist, whom she came to know while corresponding with him as he served a prison sentence for robbery.[10] After their marriage, they went to live with his parents in Iowa. There were tensions, however: her husband could not cope with her paralysis or their debts, and after a week Elizabeth returned to her father in Seattle. After a month there was a formal separation.

Her troubles multiplied. The graduate school where she had been studying refused to readmit her, and her brother was drowned in a boating accident. Not long after, Elizabeth had a miscarriage, and she learned her mother was dying of cancer.

Determined once again to be in charge of her fate, she asked her father to take her to the county hospital in Riverside, near Los Angeles (an area where she had friends), for an examination. She checked herself into the psychiatric ward and told physicians that she wanted to die by starvation. Elizabeth specifically asked that, until she died, she be looked after normally and given painkillers when her arthritis was troublesome.

The hospital staff, alarmed and startled by this request from a highly intelligent young woman of twenty-seven, refused to help her. Quite the contrary, they told her she would be force-fed if she persisted. Adamant, Elizabeth Bouvia started her fast to death in September of 1983, despite the hospital's warning. Realizing she could not handle the situation alone, she tried to hire a lawyer. Several attorneys refused to help her on ethical grounds. Also she had no money.

To draw attention to her plight, Bouvia contacted a local newspaper reporter and declared:

> You can only fight for so long. It's a struggle for a person like me to live and a struggle to die. It is more of a struggle to live than die. Death is letting go of all burdens. It is being able to be free of my physical disabilities and mental struggle to live.
>
> I know from my physical limitations, it's almost impossible. If I really could, I would go out there and kill myself. But I can't. I physically can't.
>
> It's not that I don't have the will to live. It's too much of a struggle to live within the system or depend on someone in the system. In reality, my disability is going to keep me from doing the living I want to do. I'm trapped in a useless body. Unfortunately, I have a brain. It makes it all the worse. If I were retarded or senile, I wouldn't know the difference to care.[11]

In this and in a UPI wire report next day, Bouvia appealed again for help from an attorney. Almost immediately, as the case was making national headlines, she had offers from three lawyers, all of whom were promised funding from the American Civil Liberties Union. At the same time, the hospital threatened to transfer her out of the psychiatric ward of the hospital or to a long-term care facility. Her attorneys went to court and secured an order delaying the action. The judge, however, refused to issue an order against force-feeding. He also allowed Bouvia's estranged husband to intervene in the case, as well as a group called Advocates of the Developmentally Disabled—the first indication of how widespread the controversy over Bouvia's death wish would become.[12]

Bouvia was losing weight rapidly. She was persuaded by her attorneys to accept some nourishment while litigation continued. In the weeks before the hearing to decide whether the hospital could accede to Bouvia's request—to be allowed to starve herself to death in the hospital—many groups and individuals surfaced, each presenting their own point of view.

Spokespersons for the disabled largely deplored Bouvia's decision. A twenty-eight-year-old disabled person who worked as a family planning and disability consultant said there were 'genocidal overtones' to the idea that for someone physically different, life may not be worth living.[13]

Members of Advocates for the Developmentally Disabled held candle-light vigils outside Bouvia's hospital. The group's attorney said: 'Everyone with that sort of disability contemplates suicide at some time or another. They [the Advocates for the Developmentally Disabled] are afraid if Elizabeth does it, a lot of disabled people will say: "The hell with it, I'm going to give up the fight, too."' Bouvia's lawyers responded that such intervention was 'a flagrant violation of a person's right to privacy and freedom of association.'[14]

An attorney for the Law Institute for the Disabled called the Bouvia case 'a social problem' of a disabled person who has been told she couldn't be productive. 'She needs help to learn to live with dignity,'[15] he commented.

At the court hearing, Bouvia responded by saying, in a voice tinged with anger, 'The only thing that irritates me is the media coverage, and people trying to tell me my alternatives and give me a second chance.'[6]

As promised, the A C L U provided Bouvia with attorneys. While that organization said it had no ruling on suicide, it had 'long believed that a mentally competent person has the right to refuse medical treatment. Elizabeth Bouvia is such a person. She has constitutional rights of privacy and self-determination in health care and her right to be free of unreasonable government intrusion.'[17]

Former President Richard Nixon and his wife, Pat, sent Bouvia a letter saying: 'We hope you will decide to keep fighting. But above all, whatever happens, we hope for all the best for you.'[18]

The right-to-life movement kept a low media profile on the case, but had observers at all court hearings.

When the hearing resumed on December 5, 1983, to decide whether Bouvia could prevent doctors from force-feeding her, the case was put by the Riverside County attorney, who argued that to allow her the right to refuse medical care would amount to court-sanctioned suicide. 'There can be no other definition,' the attorney told the court. 'Never can there be a right in a civilized society to tell others, over their moral objections, to assist in a suicide.'[19]

Bouvia spent two and a half hours in the witness box, stoutly defending her position. Millions watched on television as she said: 'I believe I have fully weighed the alternatives. I'm fully aware of the resources available to me. I chose not to use them. I realize the consequences of my serving this court order. Ultimately it would be death.'[20]

The chief of psychiatry at Riverside County General Hospital, Dr Donald Fisher, told the court that Bouvia had had suicidal tendencies for several years, but that this death wish occurred only when she suffered serious emotional trauma. He thought her desire to kill herself curable given time.

Bouvia's attorneys called in Lauren White, a cancer specialist on the faculty of the University of California School of Medicine in San Francisco, who said that in some cases he had recommended suicide to terminally ill cancer patients, even though he knew such advice was against the law. He argued that in cases of kidney patients refusing dialysis, knowing the consequence would be death, it was proper for the hospital to accept the patient's decision and to provide basic custodial care and try to keep the patient comfortable.

'I am of the opinion that the patient's wishes are paramount and I don't believe it's suicide,' said Dr White, a former chairman of the ethics committee of the California Medical Association. He added that staff members at Riverside Hospital, who might find Bouvia's proposal unacceptable, had to weigh their personal ethics against their responsibility to treat some people they did not necessarily feel should be treated. 'That's the most troublesome thing about this. Mrs Bouvia's First Amendment rights may hit somebody else's medical ethics right between the eyes.' But, White added, 'I feel you have given up some of these rights simply by working for a county hospital.' He admitted that had he been on the staff, he probably would have tried to 'talk her out of it.'[21]

A pro-life advocate, psychiatrist Nancy Mullen, was called as a witness by the attorney for Richard Bouvia, the estranged husband. 'In my opinion, Mrs Bouvia is not competent to make her own health-care decisions,' Mullen testified. She said she could conceive of no case in which someone could make a competent decision to take his or her own life.[22]

Nevertheless, other psychiatrists said that Bouvia was competent, and the judge eventually agreed. Medical witnesses were called in to argue about the morality of force-feeding to prevent Bouvia's self-starvation. On the whole, they maintained that she was morally right but legally wrong, while others said she was in error in involving, however indirectly, the staff in her self-destruction.

Rejecting her petition to be cared for while she starved herself, Judge John H. Hews ruled: 'The court has determined that the ultimate issue is whether or not a severely handicapped, mentally competent person who is otherwise physically healthy and not terminally ill has the right to end her life with the assistance of society. The court concludes that she does not.'

He added: 'Bouvia does have the fundamental right to terminate her own life, but this right has been overcome by the strong state interests in this case. Our society values life. The plaintiff is not terminal and her life will be preserved by this decision.'

Judge Hews said that he considered Mrs Bouvia's death request to be based primarily on her disability and not on her failed marriage and educational problems, as the county's attorneys had argued. He accepted that Bouvia was physically unable to take her own life.[23]

Despite losing the case, Bouvia started fasting immediately. In a week her weight dropped from ninety-five to ninety pounds. Hospital authorities returned to court to ask the judge to permit force-feeding on the grounds that her life was endangered and that the hospital was at risk from lawsuits. By now she had lost another four pounds. Permission was granted, and soon afterwards a nasogastric tube was inserted through Bouvia's nose and into her stomach.

The situation at the hospital worsened when Bouvia chewed through the feeding tube, cutting off the flow of nutrients. To prevent her manipulating the tube between her teeth, the staff placed her one good arm in a restraint. As a result, Bouvia and her attorneys threatened lawsuits for battery against the staff. Nurses took to taping over their name tags to prevent identification. Finally, doctors said that her presence was a misuse of a medical facility and even talked of putting her out in the street.

Bouvia went back to court, seeking an order barring the hospital from discharging her. She lost that case as well. A guard had to be put on her door to stop people wanting to preach to her about living. She received some two hundred Bibles in the mail. 'I deplore the media circus it has become. I, Elizabeth, have got lost in all this,' she said.[24]

The case quickly moved on appeal to the California Supreme Court. The hospital preempted any argument as to whether Bouvia could or would be discharged by saying she would not be, although so long as she stayed and refused food she would be force-fed. Hospital attorneys pointed out that they knew of no state or federal programme that financed or subsidized suicide, and Bouvia's treatment had cost the county more than $65,000.

Bouvia lost at the supreme court level without the benefit of any oral arguments. All seven justices voted to deny her petition and refused to interfere with Judge Hews's ruling.[25]

In the weeks that followed, Bouvia ripped out the feeding tubes from her nose three times. At the first forcible reinsertion, she screamed as staff held her down. For several hours, restraints were placed on her arms.[26]

Seven months and three court cases after checking herself into Riverside Hospital, Bouvia quietly discharged herself and went with friends to an address that was kept secret. More than a hundred people and organizations had offered her sanctuary, but all withdrew their offers when they learned that she wanted her prospective host to help her to die.[27]

A few weeks later, Bouvia turned up in a hospital in Tijuana, Mexico, which she had entered for treatment for an infection. She asked doctors there to help her to die and when they, too, refused, she checked into a motel. Within a month of her leaving Riverside Hospital, it was reported that she had changed her mind and decided to live, although the ACLU issued a statement that it was merely a postponement until she could find a better way to die without asking for collaboration.[28]

Rumour persisted that Bouvia had changed her mind completely. However, fourteen months after her original decision, her attorneys issued a statement that she was in failing health and was still waiting for a better opportunity to carry out her death wish.[29]

Two years after her first announcement of her death wish, Bouvia was still bringing law-suits against physicians asking to be left alone. The California Appeal Court in May, 1986, told her physicians they must remove the tube by which they were force-feeding her and the Supreme Court refused to hear a further appeal by the physicians. By invoking her constitutional right to privacy, and the laws of informed consent to treatment, Bouvia won handsomely. Ironically, she then resumed normal eating.

Feelings remained divided and unresolved. The ACLU board of directors meeting on March 21, 1984, was, in its own words, 'what may have been the most extraordinary meeting in the history of the ACLU of southern California.'[30] Members of the community of the disabled vented their anger, disappointment, and frustration over the organization's decision to represent Bouvia.

Dr Carol J. Gill, herself confined to a wheelchair, and a licensed clinical psychologist, told the directors: 'The ACLU has accepted the judgment of a handful of medical experts who assert that Bouvia was competent when she made the decision to starve herself.' Dr Gill said that, in her work, she frequently dealt with suicidal, disabled persons and that 'crisis counselling was more appropriate than the ACLU helping Bouvia commit suicide.'[31]

The ACLU, which had spent some $18,000 on the case (five lawyers and a law student had donated their time), supported its decision to represent Bouvia on the grounds that consent to treatment was a basic civil liberty. Nevertheless, a representative said that the organization had decided to review its policies on euthanasia in the light of this chastening experience.[32]

Just as the Bouvia case was at its height, the controversy was intensified by the case of an eighty-five-year-old man in Syracuse, New York, who was permitted by the state supreme court to achieve death by fasting. Was it acceptable for an octogenarian to kill himself this way but not a twenty-seven-year-old?

G. Ross Henninger, a former president of the Ohio College of Applied Science, was a patient at the Plaza Health and Rehabilitative Center for nine months after suffering a stroke. Depressed about the poor state of his health, Henninger decided to starve himself to death. The nursing home, unsure how it stood legally, went to court for clarification. Which was paramount: the patient's right to refuse treatment and care, or the nursing home's responsibility to provide it?

Henninger's doctor told the court his patient was, after forty-five days of fasting, malnourished and dehydrated. The physician favoured continuing medication and nourishment, but he disapproved of force-feeding, which would involve tying Henninger to the bed. Since his patient was responsive and intelligent, the physician said Henninger knew exactly what he was doing. Mr Henninger was estimated to have only one or two more weeks to live unless he took nourishment.

'He tells me he has nothing to live for and he knows if he does not eat he will die,' said his doctor.[33]

Ruling that there was no obligation to force-feed, Supreme Court Justice Donald H. Miller said:

> The court is heavily burdened by these questions and although personally does not lend approval or approbation to the termination of life . . . will not order this 85-year-old person to be force-fed or operated on or restrained for the rest of his natural life. The individual in question was competent at the time he elected to cease eating in December 1983. He willingly made that decision knowing the consequences: a hastened death. Well over 40 days have passed since he made his decision. The immediate family is supportive of his right to make his own decision and of his competency.[34]

Henninger died late the next day.

In the debate that followed, the different rulings—for Henninger and against Bouvia—provoked the following comments from syndicated columnist Ellen Goodman:

> these cases are so provocative that I, like many, agree with both these opposite decisions. Having written in disapproval of Bouvia's legal plea, I nevertheless approve the ruling in Henninger's case. We are so often told that our attitudes should remain consistent about issues, that we may easily forget the details of the human life at its centre. It occurs to me now that our apparent inconsistencies may say the most about these questions of life and death. They remind us that we're dealing with individual lives.[35]

The strength of Henninger's case lay in his advanced age and his extremely poor and deteriorating health. The weakness of Bouvia's case was her youth. There remained, for many, the suspicion that she was depressed as much by the current calamities in her life as by her physical handicaps. The different decisions were a victory for those ethicists who argued, like Fletcher, that each case must be judged on its facts: that there cannot be a 'national standard' or prescribed formula for allowing to die. The right-to life movement's argument posed in the question 'Where do you draw the line?' was therefore answered by: 'You don't draw lines: you assess need.'

One of the few people to side publicly with Bouvia was columnist Arthur Hoppe, who wrote:

I had the feeling that the judge, the doctor, and the hospital had found Elizabeth Bouvia guilty—guilty of not playing the game. It was as though the Easter Seal Child had looked into the cameras and said being crippled was a lousy deal and certainly nothing to smile about.

The handicapped are supposed to suffer in silence, preferably invisibly. When they make a fuss, they come to our attention. They make us uneasy. We feel guilty that we are physically better off than they. But Elizabeth Bouvia said the hell with playing the game. She said she opted out. And I think it must take courage to say that.

I don't know whether Elizabeth Bouvia should take her own life. I am generally opposed to suicide. It limits your options. But it's not my life. I do know it's also not the judge's life nor the doctor's life nor the hospital's life. I felt it was Elizabeth Bouvia's life, to do with what she would in a free society.[36]

John Arras, philosopher in residence at New York's Montefiore Medical Center, said in reference to Bouvia's physical inability to take her own life. 'She's claiming the classic liberal right of self-determination but, tragically, she's not self-determined.'[37]

The right-to-life movement disagreed with Bouvia's wish to die but issued no statement of their arguments for this. On the other hand, the quarterly newsletter of the Hemlock Society backed Bouvia's right to die while disagreeing with her approach:

Hemlock's view in similar cases is that a person terminally ill, or severely handicapped and deteriorating, has the individual right to end it all, after careful consideration of the circumstances and options.

But it is a very private action, certainly inappropriate at this stage in a hospital because both current law and medical ethics forbids assistance. Hemlock believes that if you have a loved one or close friend who is willing to help upon request, if needed, then that is your business.

The integrity of the decision, planning and absolute discretion are the only way to justified euthanasia.[38]

The Bouvia case had so many dimensions that most philosophers and ethicists were reluctant to pass judgment. As well, there was always the chance that Bouvia could change her mind. Conflicting reports of her intentions had surfaced. Her physical mobility deteriorated and she also received constant morphine intravenously for pain.

Still, while much of the public debate had subsided, in the spring of 1984 Bouvia was far from a forgotten case. The interest of lawyer and ethicist George J. Annas remained strong because of his longtime opposition to force-feeding as an invasion of an individual's privacy. However, Annas was not oblivious of the ramifications of the Bouvia saga. He wrote:

> Society is simply no match for this woman, and we know it. Unable to respond with either reason or compassion, we resort to slogans. Perhaps the courts cannot help Ms Bouvia. Perhaps we cannot do better than respond with the full force of the state while claiming to be on the side of 'life'. The stakes are high for either publicly condemning or approving Ms Bouvia's actions.

Professor Annas attacked administrative and legal authorities who made it clear that they did not care whether she lived or died, 'as long as she did not die in Riverside General Hospital and put them at risk of legal liability.' He pointed out that steps had been taken to try to transfer her to another type of health care facility. These had failed because society has failed to provide reasonable alternative settings for quadriplegics.

Annas was nothing if not forthright in his condemnation of force-feeding, stressing that patients' rights must come before physicians' rights because of patients' trust that their doctors will do right:

> Competent adults should have the right to refuse any medical interventions. Their physicians have a legal and moral duty to honour their refusals, because the physical and psychological impact of the physical invasion on the patient is greater than the psychological impact on the doctor and because of the fiduciary qualities inherent in the doctor–patient relationship.[39]

Why, asked Annas, did society always presume that someone who wanted to commit suicide was incompetent? If we see a person about to leap off a parapet, then we are right to suspect, given that fleeting situation, that the person may be temporarily deranged. Again, we are probably right in trying to stop it, even though attempted suicide is not a crime. In that sense, it was right of the staff at Riverside General to try to prevent the suicide of someone who said she wanted this, but where do reasonable and required steps end, and unreasonable and unconscionable actions begin? The judge had ruled Bouvia competent, adding that her decision was rational and sincere.[40]

How long, Annas went on to say, was it reasonable to force-feed such a person in the hope that the person will eat voluntarily? He suggests this is never justified: Only efforts at persuading the individual to take nourishment can be permitted. If hospitals are to avoid becoming torture chambers, some reasonable limits must be placed on treatment, he continued, pointing out that California law permitted the authorities to hold an attempted suicide for no longer than thirty days, whereas Bouvia's force-feeding had received the blessing of the court to continue endlessly.

Annas bitingly referred to

the full weight of the medical establishment and state brought to bear on an almost completely paralyzed young woman, [and] that continuing it brutalizes us all. Four or more 'attendants' wrestle her from her bed in the morning and restrain her while a nasogastric tube is rudely forced through her nose and into her stomach.

Is such brutal behaviour required by medical ethics? Where are nursing and medical students schooled in the martial arts of restraint, forced treatment, intimidation, and violence? If we will not refrain from force-feeding Ms Bouvia because we do not believe she has a 'right to die', we should refrain from that action because it perverts the very meaning of care and treatment. Medical care must be consensual or it loses its legitimacy.

We can all grieve for Ms Bouvia and express sorrow at her plight without adding further violent injury to her.[41]

Some doctors took strong exception to Annas's claim that patients' rights had superior status to their own. Such a view was held by Dr Joanne Lynn, assistant clinical professor of health care services (geriatrics) at George Washington University Medical Center, Washington, D.C., who said that if involved, she would have pulled out of the case.

Although I have incomplete information, I believe that I would have found it personally unacceptable to support Ms Bouvia's intent to starve to death by continuing to provide for her comfort as she died (though I would contend that her choice should be legal) and I would have found it unacceptable to force-feed her. I could neither encourage her death nor brutalize us both. Therefore, the only alternative left to me would be to withdraw from her care. Even if, after investigating, I could find no one who would accept transfer of her care, the same claim that warrants respect for her value judgements also warrants respect for mine.[42]

In any case, the crippled young woman dependent on public financial support for her care was heavily outflanked by the authority, experience, and financial power of medical and administrative people able to call on unlimited legal resources. If Elizabeth Bouvia had been wealthy—and had shrewdly used the independence money brings—she would have been able to decide her medical treatment herself. For instance, multimillionaire Howard Hughes used his wealth to make physicians and nurses his servants as he followed his eccentric lifestyle, even unto his death in an air ambulance.

Had Bouvia taken her life by starvation in the guarded circumstances of an affluent recluse, it probably would have been termed a 'normal death'. It would be doubtful if the word 'suicide' would be attached, since the matter would have been handled discreetly. In theory, the law exists to protect the rights of the poor and the needy, but in Bouvia's case, the ethics of the more powerful faction clearly won.

The prosecutor in the case concerning the murder of Robert Houghton, a twenty-two-year-old quadriplegic, told the court: '[Houghton's] desire to die was an obsession, but his physical condition was such that he could not commit suicide.'[43]

Before the court, charged with their son's murder, were his parents, Norman and Janet Houghton. In 1985, the court in Maidstone, Kent, England, was told that Robert was injured in a car crash five years earlier, which left him almost totally paralyzed and with impaired speech. Previously he had been a motorcycle enthusiast and a fisherman. His parents devoted their lives to caring for him, and in addition to the emotional and physical strain there were financial difficulties. Only a small amount of insurance was collectible on the accident, so Robert's father sold his fishing tackle business to raise money for care.

The parents' dilemma was described by the father: 'We were devastated when our son first asked us to take his life because it was something unthinkable. But we were driven to it by his constant suffering. He kept appealing to us to end it all.'[44]

At times Robert tried living in an institution to relieve his parents of the twenty-four-hour-a-day care, but he was unhappy there. Not long after his parents brought him home for the last time, they agreed to do something about his wish to die, since all attempts to persuade him to change his mind had failed.

Finally Robert was given a combination of drugs. Four hours later he was still alive, begging his parents to try again. This time he was given three sleeping tablets, and a plastic bag was placed over his head. Within fifteen minutes, he died of asphyxiation, while his parents watched. Later Mrs Houghton said, 'In the end, we were just driven to it.'[45]

Law enforcement authorities refused to accept the Houghtons' plea of guilty to manslaughter on the grounds of diminished responsibility, and the case went to trial by jury on a murder charge. Psychiatrists called by the defence described the almost intolerable degree of stress to which Mr and Mrs Houghton were subjected by Robert's constant requests to die. They claimed this was a factor that would substantially diminish a person's sense of responsibility. The superhuman efforts the parents had made to cope were not challenged in court.

The jury, dismissing the murder charge, found the couple guilty of manslaughter. Equally tolerant and understanding, the judge placed the

Houghtons on two years probation, saying:

> To take the life of another human being is a dreadful thing and one which
> in virtually every case is visited by a sentence of imprisonment according
> to the degree of homicide in question. But in the light of the verdict and
> all the circumstances, the public interest does not require you to receive
> any further punishment.[46]

The Houghton case might have been forgotten in one day of headlines
but for a remarkable outburst ten days later by Dr Christiaan Barnard, the
heart transplant pioneer. Barnard expressed his horror at the failure of the
medical profession to discuss the rights of those people who want to die and
have the justification for doing so. Visiting the Houghtons in their home,
Barnard explained that he was moved to apologize for his profession's failure to help them. He then went into print with some harsh criticism:

> I point the finger of blame at my colleagues—their young son's
> doctors—who shelved their responsibility. Five years ago, after a ter-
> rible road accident, they should have allowed Robert to die. I know that
> what I write may shock people. Where there is life there is hope, as they
> say. But I know this is not true.

Barnard argued that the goal should be not to prolong life but to improve
the quality of it. At times, he held, a doctor may have to decide, however
reluctantly, that death is the best option. He went on to say:

> But doctors do not like 'letting people die'. The temptation, especially in
> the last decade since the invention of hundreds of life-supporting drugs
> and devices, has been to fight off death at all cost. There is an unspoken
> law to maintain life. Against this tide, it has taken me my entire career to
> face up to writing a book in open support of euthanasia. Most of my col-
> leagues prefer not even thinking about it. . . . If you live in a house that
> no longer pleases you, you have the right to leave it. But if that house is
> your own body, the individual is by today's medical standards con-
> demned to it almost interminably.
>
> Dying is the only way to leave—and many doctors believe that their
> job is preventing death at all costs. To me this attitude is a great short-
> coming in our attitude to human life.[47]

In speeches throughout the world, Barnard has consistently argued in
favour of asking persons admitted to hospitals to sign a form—like the consent to a postmortem they already sign—saying they would like doctors to
end their life if they become terminally ill. Barnard believes that doctors
should use their compassion together with sound clinical judgment to end
some lives when written advance permission has been given. The decision
and the timing, he believes, should be arrived at jointly between patient

and doctor. There are no medical miracles that can save quadriplegics, argues Barnard, but it takes courage by doctors to admit it.

# CHAPTER ELEVEN

## *The Right-to-Life Viewpoint*

The right-to-life movement developed in the 1960s out of Roman Catholic opposition to abortion. Alarmed by the growing demand of many women to have abortion made legal, the Church acted. 'The only reason we have a pro-life movement in this country is because of the Catholic people and the Catholic Church,' Roy White commented in 1975 when he was executive director of the National Right to Life Committee.[1]

With papal edicts as guides, the Church provided the ideology, the resources, and the manpower for the right-to-life movement, in European countries as well as America. Without Church funds as seed money, the movement would never have got off to a strong start. The Church refrained from political involvement, however. In the late 1960s, as bills legalizing abortion came before the Congress and state legislatures, there was the traditional and legal division of church and state in the United States. Additionally, the Church did not want to jeopardize its tax-exempt status by lobbying. In 1973, the National Right to Life Committee, a political campaigning group, was created as an offshoot of the Family Life Division of the National Conference of Catholic Bishops. From then on, though separate organizations, they continued to be extremely supportive of each other.[2]

David Mall, executive director of Americans United for Life, has written about the necessity for a variety of spokespersons to make a stronger impact in pluralistic America: 'It is no secret that non-Catholic spokesmen, too numerous to mention, have assumed highly visible positions in the American pro-life movement and that this visibility has been promoted and encouraged.'[3]

When the US Supreme Court made its 1973 decision on *Roe* v. *Wade*— a woman is entitled to an abortion on demand—that might have been the end of the argument. Similar decisions in European countries had settled the controversies there. But Justice Harry Blackmun's pronouncement, instead of dwelling on principles of human conduct and the law affecting this, laid down a formula stating when abortions were or were not permissible. Rather than clarifying the law, as an appeal court should, the decision seemed to make law, which is properly the task of the legislature.

As it was, the Supreme Court opinion read more like a set of rules for doctors than a legal definition. It also failed to specify the point at which a foetus becomes a person and has rights—which was, and still is, a matter of fierce controversy debated by scientists, ethicists, and others. Overall, the opinion left the right-to-life movement with a great deal more to fight for. The movement has fought hard to get the Blackmun decision overturned, but in 1983, the Supreme Court issued a ruling upholding its original decision. The Reagan administration has continually threatened to have a constitutional amendment introduced to nullify the Court's decisions, but has lacked enough political clout in Congress to succeed.

Euthanasia was an issue only rarely addressed by the pro-lifers; their campaign against abortion absorbed them. As right-to-die groups grew more powerful and vocal in the late 1970s and early 1980s, they were surprised at the relatively light counterattack from their opponents. The popularity of the anti-abortion stance, with its financial benefits, was obviously a rewarding fight for the right-to-life wing. Before 1985, when several court decisions, such as Conroy and Bartling, supported euthanasia, criticism by pro-lifers was minimal.

By this time, however, the right-to-life movement had slowly begun to broaden its base, perhaps fearing that the right-to-die issue would be a serious challenge. Euthanasia is one of the last serious moral issues for modern society to decide upon, if not the last. Simplified divorce, birth control, homosexual rights, and abortion were issues that already had been largely resolved by more liberal factions. Intellectuals in the pro-life movement feared that the acceptance of euthanasia would mean a total breakdown of family values. As Steven Valentine, writing in *National Right to Life News*, said: 'The great fear of the "pro-life" movement is that the legalization of some form of involuntary euthanasia against the helpless old will be the next domino to fall in the onward march of a utilitarian ideology about human life at its edges.'[4]

In the 1970s the pro-life movement fought hard against Living Will legislation. Relying on the sympathy for Karen Ann Quinlan from 1976 onwards, the Living Will had made giant progress. In the 1980s, however, the pro-lifers' attack became more muted as the reality of the problems of modern medical technology became better understood. And by the end of 1985, some forty states had approved Living Wills.

To counter this, Valentine urged pro-lifers to support a more reasonable policy, one that would 'recognize both the inalienable right to life and the vital distinction between killing and letting die.'[5]

After 1980, the right-to-life movement had powerful supporters in the Reagan administration. Appointed to the position of surgeon-general in 1981, C. Everett Koop (a pediatric surgeon who gained fame in 1974 for successfully separating Siamese baby twin girls at Children's Hospital in Philadelphia) was a staunch ally. He saw abortion and the right to die as twin evils. In his paperback book, *The Right to Live, The Right to Die*, Koop reiterated what has become a traditional stance:

> Once any group of human beings is considered fair game in the arena of the right to life, where does it stop? If the mongoloid is chosen as the first to be deprived of his right to live, what about the blind and the deaf? If the hopeless cripple confined to a wheelchair and considered to be a burden on society is chosen first, what about the frail, the retarded, and the senile? It does not take a fanciful imagination to extend this to include certain categories of disease such as cystic fibrosis, diabetes, and a variety of neurologic disorders.[6]

Koop went on to say that euthanasia allows the opportunity for fraud, deception, and deceit, with people hastening the death of elderly relatives to avoid the burden of maintaining them, or to get at a legacy.[7]

Koop maintained that more important than the quality of life was the sanctity of human life, as upheld by the Judeo-Christian tradition. Respected by nonreligious as well as religious people, such a code 'makes it possible for us to live day by day in the relative security of the obviously imperfect, poorly defined parameters of decision-making concerning death and dying in medicine.[8]

The sanctity-of-life argument also holds to a form of vitalism: Even if a person does not believe in life after death, a poor existence is better than none. On the question of feeling that someone we love might be better off dead, a pro-life pamphlet says:

> Is it because the loved one is suffering or because we are suffering when we watch him? Handicapped people, for instance, feel normal, even if they don't look that way. Senile people are seldom as aware of their confusion as onlookers are. To judge whether someone's life is worth living, we need a degree of wisdom never attained by ordinary mortals.[9]

Little of the pro-life literature makes mention of religion as the guiding moral factor in the anti-euthanasia position. The implication is that the code is so all-embracing that it hardly needs to be stated. Yet the rights of people of other religions, or nonbelievers—members of nontheistic societies and agnostics and atheists—are not acknowledged in pro-life arguments.

Malcolm Muggeridge is the leader of the British right-to-life movement, known as the Festival of Light. He is a well-known critic and a highly articulate, intellectual spokesman of the cause. His opposition to abortion and euthanasia has an essentially spiritual base:

> If there was no God, nor any transcendental purpose in the experience of living in this world, then a human being's life [would be] no more intrinsically sacred than is that of a broiler-house chicken, which, if it stops laying eggs, or is otherwise incapacitated, no longer rates its allowance of chicken feed and has its neck wrung.[10]

For Muggeridge, life is something that deserves our infinite respect; under no circumstance are we in a position to judge its quality or its necessity. 'Life is sacred because it is created by God for a purpose,' he maintains, 'and that purpose comes to an end when you die. It's not for you to choose the moment at which to die.'[11]

In a televised discussion in London with Archbishop Anthony Bloom of the Russian Orthodox Church, Muggeridge described the necessity of pain as a primary source of ennoblement.

> *Muggeridge:* I think this horror of pain is a rather low instinct and if I think of human beings I've known and of my own life, such as it is, I can't recall any case of pain which didn't, on the whole, enrich life.
>
> *Bloom:* I think it always does enrich life, and people who try to escape it from cowardice miss something extremely precious.[12]

Pro-lifers with a less religious view of mankind prefer to stress the value of the hospice movement, with its considerable skills in reducing pain. Dame Cicely Saunders, founder of the modern hospice movement, has shown that 90 per cent of terminal pain can be controlled through the use of narcotics and the famous Brompton mixture. 'Double effect', or stepping up drug medication to relieve pain—even to the extent that the patient's life is shortened—has been accepted by even the most conservative Catholics for nearly three decades now. As Joseph J. Piccione, a philosopher working for the conservative Child and Family Protection Institute, explains: 'A direct act, such as a narcotics overdose, to *intentionally* cause death is wrong. However, the palliative use of narcotics for pain reducing reasons may have a side effect of shortening life; as an indirect effect of an act serving the good of pain control use of these drugs is not wrong.'[13]

The Moral Majority, the fundamentalist religious group founded in 1979 by Jerry Falwell, finds its richest appeal in fighting abortion and rarely strays into discussing euthanasia. When it does, the argument is invariably linked to abortion, reasserting the sanctity of life. But the movement takes a tolerant if dismissive attitude towards Living Wills, regarding them as inadequate because they lack legal standing.

Asked for his position on the right to die, Falwell stressed that he and others should do all they can to encourage people to find meaning in life: 'it is true that depression and despondency are very real problems in the case of terminal illness. But I believe that we should be committed to helping people to learn how to live rather than allowing them to opt for death. I would approach the "right-to-die" matter with great caution. We should be life-oriented.'[14]

The most outspoken wing of the American pro-life movement is the Human Life Alliance, based in Minnesota. In contrast to supporters in the rest of the country, its leaders there have considered euthanasia to be far more insidious than other arms of the movement, and its statements are pointed and critical. Mary Senander, president of the Alliance, has condemned Living Wills in no uncertain terms, maintaining that right-to-die legislation favours death as the ultimate and only solution to difficult human problems. Such legislation, she has argued, ignores the individual circumstances that should determine the nature of terminal care. It promotes attitudes that the elderly and infirm are financial and emotional burdens on society; it removes dying, disability, and death from the context of love, life, and meaning.

Senander refers to euthanasia supporters as 'death promoters', equating them with murderers or destroyers of life. 'The unspoken purpose of the Living Will is to hasten or encourage death, directly or indirectly,' she says.[15]

Whatever their differences, virtually all pro-lifers believe that the Nazi experience has powerful lessons for modern society. Noting that planning for the wartime extermination movement began as early as the 1920s in Germany, they also hold that Hitler was not solely responsible. As one pamphlet pointed out:

It was respected psychiatrists and pediatricians—not Nazi thugs—who killed seventy-five per cent of the chronically ill in Germany. It began by killing German, non-Jewish persons suffering serious defects. As time passed the reasons for killing became slighter—for example 'badly modelled ears', bed-wetters and 'difficult to educate'. An estimated 275,000 persons who had been in nursing homes, hospitals and asylums were killed.[16]

For these facts, the pamphlet depends on *A Sign for Cain*, a book by Frederic Wertham, M.D., published in 1966. Yet other historians, writing more recently, have put the death toll at around 100,000 Germans between 1939 and 1941, with several thousand more (mostly children) killed during the remainder of the war. The pamphlet ignores the unpalatable truth that British and American 'thinkers' and 'scientists' in the 1920s and 1930s propounded similar theories of eugenics. (See Chapter 1.) Fortunately for mankind, there was no subsequent Nazi-like regime to put them into practice in those countries.

Elaborating on the Nazi atrocity against Germany's mentally handicapped, some pro-lifers have produced 'death selection' or 'managerial euthanasia' theories of the future. A past president of Minnesota Citizens Concerned for Life, Thomas St Martin, has written that this kind of strategy promotes killing anyone who is a burden, and therefore no longer socially useful. At the root of such a system is a hard-core utilitarianism,

> which sees no value beyond social utility; [thus] managerial euthanasia poses a threat to a wide range of people: the 'habitual' criminal, the aged, the seriously mentally ill, the retarded, etc. In the death selection scenario, people become 'human resources' to be manipulated in the accomplishment of 'planned' social objectives and to be discarded when no longer useful. At the moment, managerial euthanasia is the 'sleeper' in the euthanasia debate.[17]

St Martin and most others in the pro-life movement view the prospect of euthanasia as an Orwellian nightmare which logically follows the 'denigration of life' by permitting abortion on demand.

The most extreme wing of the right-to-life movement is represented by the Club of Life, the brainchild of Lyndon LaRouche, a man who has swung politically from left to right, and in 1984 unsuccessfully ran for President of the United States. The club gets much of its public visibility from stationing members at airport entrances, where they ask, 'Are you against Jane Fonda?' or 'Don't you think America needs nuclear industry?' Their most recent airport gambit has been to campaign for laser defence technology. These tactics seem to be aimed more at drawing attention to themselves than at advancing an argument.

Club of Life supporters claim that wealthy people such as Armand Hammer and Hugh Hefner, and various banks, are supplying funds to the Hemlock Society in order to reduce the population, bringing about a return to feudalism that will lead to greater security and power for the wealthy. Hemlock says that it has received no money from big business; its accounts show only gifts of small sums from individuals.

Another of LaRouche's foundlings is the Schiller Institute, which publishes a journal called *Executive Intelligence Review*. Most of its articles deal with world problems. On the euthanasia issue, it has referred to the Hemlock Society as composed of 'fanatic death worshippers' and commenting on the right to choose, holds that 'This Jesuitical conception of free will, which asserts that suicide is the ultimate freedom to dispose of oneself, is precisely the state of mind of a concentration camp victim who willingly walks into the gas oven.'[18]

However, the bulk of the right-to-life movement, far less radical, realizes that the extreme language and abuse practised by the Club of Life will be counterproductive in what is a serious sanctity-of-life versus quality-of-life debate.

Certainly there has been plenty of scope for analysis and dissent in the decision of the New Jersey Supreme Court in January 1985 in the Claire Conroy case. While that decision showed a greater tolerance for the right to die, and conceded that extraordinary life supports were not always appropriate, pro-lifers were forced to deal with another dimension: whether food artificially supplied (either by intravenous infusion or by nasogastric tube) was an artificial life support. Their spokesmen argued that this was merely normal nursing care, not treatment; that food was a gift of God which every human was entitled to—regardless of whether it was put into the system naturally or through a tube. They concluded that to deprive a patient of food was tantamount to murder.

However, the New Jersey Court in the Conroy case, in ruling that artificial feeding *was* a life-support method, maintained that where a patient had expressed a desire not to be so nourished and was frail and elderly, the removal of feeding tubes was therefore a lawful procedure. The court said it was the patient's response to the treatment, however simple, not the technological complexity, that was important.[19]

In 1983 the California Court of Appeal made a similar finding in the Clarence Herbert case. Mr Herbert was in a coma from which he was not expected to recover. With the consent of the family, the two treating doctors disconnected the artificial feeding devices and the patient starved to death. The doctors were charged with murder, but were acquitted on appeal. The appeal judges pointed out that 'the prosecution would have us draw a distinction between the use of mechanical devices such as breathing tubes. The distinction urged seems to be based more on the emotional symbolism of providing food and water for those incapable of providing for themselves rather than on any rational difference in cases such as the one at bench.'[20]

Such decision-making shifted the pro-lifers' attention from the abortion issue to euthanasia for the first time. Edward Grant, executive director and legal counsel for Americans United for Life, was quoted in *Human Life Report* as saying: 'Food and water are needed for "caring" for the patient, not the "treating" of the patient. Withdrawing food and water is allowing the doctor, not the illness, to introduce death.'[21] Dr Jack Wilke, president of the National Right to Life Committee, said that the New Jersey decision was far-reaching, 'changing all rules which protected your life and mine.'[22]

For many pro-lifers, the Conroy decision was a confirmation of all their worst fears on 'death selection'. Adolf Shimpf, president of the New Jersey

Right to Life Committee, called it 'one step further to conditioning society to accept the elimination of all inconvenient persons.'[23]

Pro-life leaders were further shaken by public opinion, particularly the finding of a Gallup poll that 81 per cent of Americans approved of the New Jersey ruling on Conroy. Asking for people's religious denominations, the poll revealed that almost as many Catholics backed the decision (77 per cent) as did Protestants (80 per cent).

Right-to-life philosopher Joseph Piccione conceded: 'The courts do not strike from the blue. They try to read public opinion, examine polls, and watch election returns. There has been a long road already just to get to the Conroy decision, and in it a corner has been turned to the journey towards a fundamental reappraisal of human life. It is a milestone on the same path that began with *Roe* v. *Wade*.'[24]

At the National Right to Life Convention held in Washington, D.C., in July 1985, Dr Koop warned pro-lifers about what he termed 'the juggernáut of euthanasia' and advised them to prepare their arguments much more carefully than hitherto. The surgeon-general also suggested that the movement not insist on a 100 per cent victory in euthanasia, as they had in the abortion issue, but to accept some minor defeats so long as the main goal of continuing to ban euthanasia was achieved.[25]

# CHAPTER TWELVE

# *Euthanasia in the Netherlands*

The most radical acceptance of euthanasia in the world is found in the Netherlands. There, a physician who meets strict criteria can give a lethal injection to a dying person who has requested death, and the physician will not be punished. Rather than legalize mercy killing by a bill placed before Parliament—which risks becoming a schismatic political issue—the Dutch, in a series of judicial steps since 1973, have permitted doctors conforming to rules to go unpunished. The hundred-year-old Article 293 of the criminal code says it is a crime for anyone to assist a suicide or take a life, but the Dutch have circumvented the problem by adding, step by step, exemption clauses for the medical profession only.

The Dutch have had firm ideas about euthanasia for several decades, especially during World War II when the country was occupied by Nazi invaders. The German leadership, which wanted to continue its extermination and sterilization of the mentally handicapped and Jews in occupied France and the Low Countries, realized that subtle tactics were called for. Physicians in newly occupied countries had not been subjected to the years of brainwashing their German counterparts had undergone. Therefore, direct orders to kill or deport would probably be rejected.

To get around this, the Third Reich's commander for the Occupied Netherlands Territories, Arthur Seyss-Inquart, issued an order on December 19, 1941, which read: 'It is the duty of the doctor, through advice and effort conscientiously and to his best ability, to assit as helper the person entrusted to his care in the maintenance, improvement and re-establishment of his vitality, physical efficiency and health.'[1]

The document seemed harmless enough. However, Dutch physicians interpreted it as the first step in ordering them to help the Nazis carry out sterilization, euthanasia, and deportation. As a group, they decided that any concession—especially the first—would be disastrous; they would alter their normal ethics for no one. Without hesitation, they refused to honour the directive.

When Seyss-Inquart heard their decision, he threatened to strip them of permission to practise medicine, whereupon hundreds of doctors sent him their licences and removed their names from brass plates and shingles. They stopped signing certificates of birth and death, yet secretly they continued seeing patients who needed treatment.

When further efforts by Seyss-Inquart failed, he arrested approximately one hundred physicians and dispatched them to concentration camps. Even this tactic did not persuade the doctors, who refused to cooperate with the Nazis for four more years. As a result, non-therapeutic sterilization and involuntary euthanasia were never carried out in the Netherlands.

Leo Alexander, M.D., first reported this struggle in his 1949 *New England Journal of Medicine* article, 'Medical Science Under Dictatorship' cited earlier:

> [The Dutch] had the foresight to resist before the first step was taken, and they acted unanimously and won out in the end. It is obvious that if the medical profession of a small nation under the conqueror's heel could resist so effectively, the German medical profession could likewise have resisted had they not taken the first fatal step. It is the first seemingly innocent step away from principle that frequently decides a career of crime. Corrosion begins in microscopic proportions.[2]

Seyss-Inquart, who had been a lawyer in Vienna before the war and was a diligent Roman Catholic, was ultimately branded 'The Butcher of Holland'. He was executed in 1946 after his trial at Nuremberg for his war crimes.[3]

The Dutch attitude towards euthanasia—recognition of its abuses and its proper use—remained constant. Thirty years later, in 1973, a mercy-killing case was brought to trial which eventually led to the acceptance of medically induced voluntary euthanasia for the terminally ill. In October of 1971, Dr Geertruida Postma, a general practitioner, injected two hundred milligrams of morphine into her mother's veins. Dr Postma's mother, a patient in a nursing home, had had a cerebral hemorrhage, she was partly paralyzed and had trouble speaking, and she had pneumonia and was deaf. As Dr Postma later testified, 'Again and again she had told me "I want to leave this life. Please help." She had tried to commit suicide, but she didn't succeed.'[4]

One day when Dr Postma visited her mother in the nursing home, she found her propped in a chair, tied to the arms. 'When I watched my mother,' she said, 'a human wreck, hanging in that chair, I couldn't stand it any more.' The next day she injected the lethal dose, then went to the director of the nursing home and explained what had happened, asking him to sign the death certificate. Instead, he called the police. Dr Postma was charged with mercy killing, which carried a penalty of up to twelve years.

At her trial, which appeared to hinge on whether her mother's suffering was unbearable, Dr Postma candidly stated: 'No, it was not unbearable. Her physical suffering was serious, no more. But the mental suffering became unbearable.... Now, after all these months, I am convinced I should have done it much earlier.'[5] Dr Postma was found guilty by the court, but she was given a one-week suspended sentence and a year's probation. Outside the courtroom, friends handed her a single flower in sympathy. Other doctors had signed an open letter to the Netherlands minister of justice, stating they had committed the same crime at least once.

During her trial, the people in Dr Postma's village had banded together under the local social worker and his wife, Jaap and Klazien Sybrandy. Together they formed the Society for Voluntary Euthanasia, with only a handful of members; within a few years, this tiny parochial group became the largest euthanasia society in the world, a status it still holds. At the same time, a group of academics under the leadership of a lawyer, Adrienne Van Till, started a 'think tank' organization in The Hague, the Foundation for Voluntary Euthanasia, to study the question in depth.

After several years, the Sybrandys left the Society because of policy disagreements—chiefly about the speed at which reform was being pushed through—and set up a more activist group, the Information Centre for Voluntary Euthanasia. The split was of the type faced by many humanitarian groups: Mrs Sybrandy wished to offer practical and immediate help to the dying, whereas the Society argued for a more cautious approach until the law was changed. By 1976, a country with a population of less than fifteen million had three pro-euthanasia groups.

Just as their attitude towards Nazi abuses of euthanasia was clear and purposeful, the Dutch were never afraid to tackle the issue of euthanasia as it might be properly applied. The Dutch Institute of Family Practitioners, in cooperation with the country's inspector of public health, questioned doctors about how many times they were being asked for voluntary euthanasia. Fifteen thousand times a year, came the staggering answer,[6] although this did not mean such requests were necessarily met. A few years later, the Institute of Family Practitioners pursued the question, asking members how much euthanasia was *actually* being practised. Approximately five thousand cases yearly, it found. These figures, of course, included passive and active euthanasia, although most were passive cases. The Society for Voluntary Euthanasia in 1985 estimated that around two thousand incidents of active euthanasia via injection took place each year.[7]

By then the oldest group, the Society, had grown to 25,000 members, and the Foundation closed down, considering its goals accomplished. The Society flourished largely because it had a powerful grassroots base that helped people come to grips with the queston of euthanasia in their daily lives. In contrast, those who administered the law in North America, Britain, and Australia continued to frown on public acceptance of euthanasia and to prosecute whenever possible, right into the 1980s. The Dutch authorities, on the other hand, permitted the Society to establish—as early as 1975—a members' aid service staffed by volunteers (something groups like Hemlock in the US and the British Voluntary Euthanasia Society dare not do).

Since its inception, the Dutch euthanasia aid service has had two objectives:

1.   To help those members who, while not necessarily considering euthanasia in the near future, still want to examine their ideas on the subject. (Discussions with peers are often difficult because of existing taboos.) Most of these members are elderly and often lonely.
2.   To help those members who want euthanasia because of physical or mental suffering brought on by an incurable disease or infirmity. They may either want it urgently or, because of a deteriorating condition, want to ensure that their wishes will be met later.[8]

A member wanting help contacts the society through telephone listings in its newsletter; the nearest volunteer visits to talk with the person. Distributing lethal pills or giving any physical help in dying is strictly forbidden during the visit. Since many of the inquirers have been refused help by their doctors (or are reluctant to mention the matter to them), the volunteer acts as mediator between patient and physician. The Society provides 'Euthanasia Statements' (or Living Wills) for the patient to sign, as instructions for the doctor. A press release from the Society indicates how, in some instances, accelerating death is accommodated:

> In a few cases a slowly dying patient announced that he would apply active euthanasia upon himself with the aid of a large overdose of barbiturates which he had been saving. After satisfying ourselves that his condition was really hopeless, we supplied him with all the necessary information available in scientific literature so that he could carry out his intention.[9]

The Dutch idea of providing scientific literature already in the public domain to help a dying person carry out autoeuthanasia surfaced in a few years in the Society's booklet, 'Justifiable Euthanasia: A Guide to the Medical Profession'. At the same time, London EXIT's pamphlet 'A Guide to Self-Deliverance' and Hemlock's book *Let Me Die Before I Wake* had appeared. Such writings were met with enormous public controversy initially—mainly instigated by the media—but it quickly subsided, at least in the Netherlands and the US as the publications became more widely accepted. Hemlock's lengthier, more comprehensive book soon became a heavily borrowed item in public libraries.

The Dutch Society learned as much from its aid service as did the recipients. Quickness in getting to the caller was essential to relieve stress and worry. Invariably, once the caller knew the options, there was time to make calmer decisions. Volunteers became especially skilled in helping callers work through their distress and sadness (and, perhaps, anger) before they could discuss coolly the specifics of euthanasia.

In 1980 the Society printed 'Justifiable Euthanasia', an eleven-page tract advising physicians of the most suitable drugs to be used in euthanasia and their administration, which was sent to 19,000 doctors and 2,100 pharmacists. More than 10,000 lay people bought the document. By 1985, volunteers of the Dutch Society were seeing more than a thousand people a year.

Such activity depended as much on discretion by the three groups as it did on tolerance by law enforcement authorities. The closest any of the euthanasia workers came to prosecution was in 1981, when the Ministry of Justice considered charging Klazien Sybrandy with providing a couple with information on where drugs could be obtained in France. The couple, acting on the information, had ended their lives.

The Dutch criminal code, Article 293, states that someone who takes someone else's life upon that person's explicit and sincere demand is punishable with a maximum of twelve years imprisonment.

But was passing information a crime? A. G. Bosch, chief officer of the Ministry of Justice, announced in January 1981 that he considered that this was not the case, since it was unproved that Mrs Sybrandy had induced the couple to commit suicide. She had not helped them in the act, nor had she given them the means.

On the contrary, she had spent some time trying to dissuade them. The only point that could be substantiated was that Mrs Sybrandy had provided information in rather general terms, and the criminal code required more than the giving of this information, said Bosch.[10]

The investigation of Mrs Sybrandy appears to have started because of certain hostile newspaper coverage. The Ministry of Justice clearly wanted to avoid prosecution if at all possible, because it was known that Mrs Sybrandy had at other times gone much further in helping people to die and did not disguise this. 'I didn't even know these people [the subject of the judicial investigation],' she wrote to a friend. 'I told the investigator that I gave six persons the means and they all died. All six were terminally ill.'[11]

The Sybrandy incident troubled the two other euthanasia groups, both of which disapproved of people taking the law into their own hands—although in 1978, the Society's own Advisory Commission on Legislation, when pressing for political action, conceded that 'Self-killing cannot be ruled out in some instances.'[12] The two groups preferred the route of education and law reform.

★

The Dutch are extremely sensitive to the notion that they have 'legalized euthanasia'. They hasten to point out that 'it goes unpunished', which they argue is different from legalization—a point some observers find moot. They are also sensitive because of the Nazi 'euthanasia' atrocities. Semantics aside, their progress towards justified euthanasia shows the willingness of legal authorities to respond to the complexities of the issue. In the 1973 case against Dr Postma, the judge rejected the defence of 'euthanasia', refused to suspend the criminal code, yet went to considerable trouble to spell out conditions under which euthanasia could be unpunished.

Eugene Sutorius, chief counsel to the Society for Voluntary Euthanasia, explained the transitions:

These attempts on the part of the criminal judiciary to give the medical profession a yardstick constituted the bases for further rulings in 1981, 1983, and 1984. The district courts in question, with the sole exception of Alkmaar Court (which ultimately went to the supreme court), in all euthanasia cases submitted to them, decided to convict the person rendering humanitarian aid, but at the same time volunteered a specification of conditions under which he or she would have escaped conviction. Surely a rather unusual, but laudable, activity for courts in a civil law system as we have.[13]

The Dutch legal system derives from Roman law and is chiefly a civil-law-oriented system. There is no trial by jury. Justice is administered by professional judges, appointed for life by the Queen, and their independence is guaranteed by the constitution. The judges enjoy considerable social prestige and their long record of evenhanded use of their independence and powers has gained them much respect. Never having to face elections, the judges feel confident enough to make many unpopular decisions.

In fact, Dutch legal procedures do not have precedent law ('common law'). The laws are written by the Crown and Parliament, and there is very little latitude for interpretation. The flexibility in the system is provided instead by the public prosecutor's office, which handles all cases of penal offences. It possesses a discretionary freedom which would be the envy of many prosecuting officers in other countries. In the Netherlands, the prosecutor's office comes under the aegis of the Ministry of Justice, which can intervene only for constitutional reasons. The office can, quite autonomously, drop criminal cases if the public prosecutor considers it in the public interest, and indeed, in about 80 per cent of cases it takes no action. These offences are dealt with in other ways. As Anka Sutorius, a Dutch judge, noted:

This regard to such socially sensitive issues as euthanasia is shown when the prosecutor's office, confronted with several judgments in lower courts, decided on a concentral coordination of them. All euthanasia cases are referred to its top officers and in special cases even to the Ministry of Justice. They together decided that the prosecution policy should no longer run counter to the conditions of impunity developed in the administration of justice by the lower courts.[14]

Between 1982 and 1984, the prosecutor's office considered thirty-six euthanasia cases, but they immediately dropped twenty-eight of them and dismissed a further five after judicial inquiry. Four of the thirty-six cases were of such political sensitivity that they were discussed personally with the Minister of Justice.[15] It has been estimated that some two thousand Dutch doctors (out of seventeen thousand)[16] practise various degrees of euthanasia, but the handful of cases—thirty-six—that have come to official notice indicates that most keep their actions a secret.

The Dutch also try to keep euthanasia cases out of the courts—while still retaining control over the criteria for aid-in-dying—by allowing the prosecutor's office to enter into agreements with the Office of Medical Inspectors, which controls the quality of health care.

A landmark case in the evolution of Dutch euthanasia occurred in 1981 when the criminal court in Rotterdam set standards for noncriminal aid-in-dying and laid out these ten rules:

1. There must be physical or mental suffering which the sufferer finds unbearable.

2. The suffering and the desire to die must be lasting (i.e., not temporary).

3. The decision to die must be the voluntary decision of an informed patient.

4. The person must have a correct and clear understanding of his condition and of other possibilities (the results of this or that treatment and of no treatment); he must be capable of weighing these options and must have done so.

5. There is no other reasonable (i.e., acceptable for the patient) solution to improve the situation.

6. The [time and manner of] death will not cause avoidable misery to others (i.e., if possible, the next of kind should be informed beforehand).

7. The decision to give aid-in-dying should not be a one-person decision. Consulting another professional (medical doctor, psychologist, social worker, according to the circumstances of the case) is obligatory.

8. A medical doctor must be involved in the decision to prescribe the correct drugs.

9. The decision process and the actual aid must be done with the utmost care.

10. The person receiving aid-in-dying need not be a dying person. Paraplegics can request and get aid-in-dying. (Point 10 is out of a former court decision and has now been endorsed by the Netherlands Medical Association).[17]

Recently another case went all the way to the supreme court. A ninety-five-year-old woman, who repeatedly asked her doctor about euthanasia over the five years he had treated her for poor health, fractured her hip in a fall and was bedridden, unable to sit up. She was catheterized and totally dependent on the nursing staff for all care. Feeling that her life no longer had value, the woman redoubled her requests to her doctor for euthanasia. She had signed a Euthanasia Statement five years earlier.

At this stage, when she could no longer drink or take solid food and had difficulty in speaking, the patient enlisted her son's help in pleading with the doctors for help in dying. After a conference with the woman, her son, and another doctor, the attending physician agreed to help. The patient made arrangements for her cremation and sent goodbye messages to friends. After a private farewell with her son and daughter-in-law, she received three injections: barbiturates to induce sleep, additional barbiturates eight minutes later to send her into a coma, and curare five minutes after that, which brought about fatal respiratory arrest.

The doctor who administered the lethal injections, believing that euthanasia is better practised openly, wrote on the death certificate that this was an 'unnatural death' and proceeded to inform the police of his actions. At his trial, in Alkmaar, he was acquitted on the grounds that his conduct—judged from a legal point of view—could not be termed undesirable and that he had satisfied the highest standards of conscience. (His colleague who had participated in the decision-making was not prosecuted because he had not taken any direct action.)

This was the first time that a lower court had acquitted a physician; the prosecutor's office decided to appeal the verdict. The Amsterdam Court of Appeal found the doctor guilty because, it argued, there was not a sufficiently mature body of opinion to sustain a view of euthanasia in direct opposition to Section 293 of the criminal code.

The Society for Voluntary Euthanasia helped the doctor take the case to the supreme court. While the senior judges were still deliberating, a significant announcement was made by the Royal Dutch Medical Society in August 1984, giving its standpoint on euthanasia, which can hardly have failed to escape the jurists' attention.

If in 1973 the Medical Society had a firm stand against any form of aid-in-dying, now, eleven years later, they wanted to set up regional advisory

boards where doctors could get the legal standards explained. The physicians' group said a doctor need not perform euthanasia, *but he was then
obligated to help the patient find another doctor who would*. The Medical
Society acknowledged that euthanasia took place; they ruled that it was
preferable for its legality to be clarified quickly.

In November 1984, the supreme court sent the case back to the court of
appeal for reconsideration. They took the view that the appeal court had
neglected to investigate whether from the standpoint of medical standards
and ethics, the doctor on trial for helping the ninety-five-year-old woman
to die had any alternatives. A supreme court is not permitted to judge the
facts or assess the merits of the case, so it is limited to passing judgment
purely on the law. In an unusual move, the court incorporated in its judgment a reference to the conflicting duties a physician faces in dealing with
his own ethical and legal situation. The judges ruled that the primary judgment should rest in the medical world, while the second judgment—that of
law—remains the duty of society. Where there was a conflict of facts in a
case, they ruled that the criminal courts should decide the issue of whether
the physician had made a justified choice.

The supreme court provided the lower court with a few further points to
consider:

1. Was the progressive degradation of the person of the ninety-five-
year-old woman, and the disintegration of her personality, to be expected?
And would there be further deterioration? The judges wanted both physical and mental suffering considered.

2. Could it be reasonably foreseen that she would soon no longer be able
to die in a dignified way?

3 Were there still any alternative ways acceptable to the patient to alleviate her suffering?

In effect, the court ruled that voluntary active euthanasia performed by
physicians may be justified by medical, ethical, and legal standards—even
without amendment of the criminal code.

'Our judges did not follow the road of compassion,' observed Eugene
Sutorius, attorney for the physician in the supreme court case, 'but chose a
more structural solution, the medical exception. Like the surgeon who, in
the exercise of his profession, has to harm his patient with a scalpel on purpose but is not prosecuted for battery, so will voluntary euthanasia as a final
part of medical practice remain unpunished under the very, very strict conditions to be set up by the medical profession itself.'[18]

By 1985, the debate on voluntary euthanasia in the Netherlands was
rapidly changing in favour of parliamentary legislation to put the decisions
and policies of the law courts into statute form. A government commission

that spent three years studying ways to deal with the euthanasia question recommended in August 1985 that it would be preferable that euthanasia now be legalized under certain conditions.[19]

With polls suggesting that more than three-quarters of the Dutch population supports euthanasia, and an estimated seven thousand people dying by euthanasia each year,[20] the political parties agreed to tackle the question but not until after the 1986 general elections. The Christian Democratic party has made known its opposition to euthanasia, but it was (prior to the 1986 election) outnumbered in Parliament by the Liberal and other parties, which tend to support euthanasia. 'Although the Christian Democrats will probably form part of the next government, they are unlikely to be able to prevent liberalization of the euthanasia law,' reported *The Economist*.[21]

Why the Netherlands has made such an advance towards acceptance of aid-in-dying compared to the relative inactivity in other Western countries is an enigma that even few Dutchmen try to explain. Other countries have had similar numbers of highly publicized 'mercy-killing' cases; there were pro-euthanasia groups in the US and Britain well before those in the Netherlands. In the last few decades, a reorientation on life, illness, dying, and death has been taking place in Dutch society (as in others), in which the right to abortion and self-determination in death have been paramount. One factor appears to be that in addition to no single church playing a dominant part in the Netherlands, some 27 per cent of the population says it has no religious denomination.[22] 37 per cent of the population is Roman Catholic, but Dutch Catholics are renowned for their aversion to the dogmas of Rome. 'The Netherlands is almost unique in the degree to which its Catholics have "democratized" the Church and de-emphasized the hierarchical structure,' said the *New York Times* in May 1985, when reporting the demonstrations, jocular send-ups, and absence of admiring crowds in the Netherlands during Pope John Paul's tour.

Dutch people are extremely proud of their personal liberty. No wartime resistance movement was more courageous against the German occupiers in World War II. They are, in the main, solid, down-to-earth people with an honest approach to life's problems. Thus when the euthanasia issue surfaced in the 1970s, ordinary people, academics, physicians, and lawyers all joined forces to tackle the problem in a workmanlike manner. They did not refer the issue to the politicians to settle. Indeed, by the time the matter reaches lawmakers, the codes of conduct on aid-in-dying, which the majority of the nation appears to want, will already have been settled.

# CHAPTER THIRTEEN

# Euthanasia and Hospice

The contemporary euthanasia movement has grown up in tandem with modern hospice. Both movements have deep historical roots—euthanasia in ancient Greece, hospice (the word is derived from the Latin *hospitium*, 'hospitality') in the Middle Ages—but both have received wide popular support only since the 1960s. And since then, there has been a controversy centred on whether hospice cancels out the need for euthanasia.

Euthanasia supporters argue that both options are important for a terminally ill adult. While almost all euthanasists would probably resist the idea of dying in a hospice, none would seek to prevent this style of palliative care for others. In fact, the membership rolls of both movements overlap considerably.

Hospice leaders, however, often argue that euthanasia is unnecessary now that they have perfected techniques of pain control through sophisticated administration of the wide variety of drugs available. The Roman Catholic Church, in particular, has thrown its weight behind the hospice movement, largely out of its traditional practice of caring for the needy, but also—judging from public statements by Catholic theologians and priests—as a practical answer to growing interest in euthanasia.

Hospice removes the pain and the loneliness from dying. Its supporters contend that if these two factors are removed, no rational person would wish autoeuthanasia or active euthanasia, because he can live out his final days comfortably. It is not that simple, reply the euthanasists, because pain is by no means the sole consideration of a person contemplating euthanasia. Anguish caused by distressing symptoms such as incontinence, vomiting, haemorrhaging, physical weakness, and loss of sight is crucial to many people; while a hospice can do much to alleviate these symptoms, it cannot eliminate their psychological effects. One person may have a greater tolerance of distressing symptoms than another. Concerns about pride, modesty, and self-control frequently intrude.

On the pain-control question, the debate centres around side effects of drugs, usually narcotics such as morphine, cocaine, or heroin. Modern hospice claims that a shrewdly mixed 'cocktail' of painkilling drugs, adapted to the individual, reduces drowsiness to a minimum. Nevertheless, medical literature on hospice tends to avoid discussing whether uncomfortable symptoms or side effects are provoked by the illness or by the drugs administered.

For instance, in a lengthy article, 'Hospice Care: Redressing the Balance in Medicine', Dr Robert Twycross, a world authority on pain control, stated: 'In addition to obviously pressing symptoms such as pain, vomiting and dyspnoea [difficulty in breathing], patients may experience discomfort from a variety of other symptoms such as dry mouth, altered taste, anorexia, constipation, pruritus, insomnia.'

In his extensive review, Dr Twycross does not discuss whether any of these problems are, or are not, side effects of drug medication. However, clearly some are. Dr Twycross goes on: 'It is generally possible to relieve the patient's symptoms either completely *or to a considerable extent.*'[1] (Emphasis added.)

Still, being in a hospice is a far more acceptable alternative than many others. For instance, although acute care hospitals, undoubtedly influenced by the fame of the hospice movement, have considerably improved their methods of caring for the dying, it is more beneficial to be in a hospice during a painful terminal illness. A study by a team at UCLA School of Medicine, published in *The Lancet* in 1984, showed that the pain patients suffered did not differ significantly whether they were in hospital or hospice, but hospice patients expressed much greater satisfaction with the quality of care. The reason for this appeared to be treatment coming from a special team, with heavier staffing ratios.[2]

Can everyone be admitted to hospice? Obviously not. Statistics show that only one-fourth of all the people dying from cancer in the United States each year will gain access to a hospice programme, either hospital based or home based. And what of those dying of other painful chronic diseases?[3]

In 1985, according to the National Hospice Organization, the vast majority of the nine hundred and thirty-five fully operational hospice programmes in the United States were home hospices. The average American hospice caters to no more than fifteen patients a month.[4] In Britain, there are fifty-three independent hospices, while another forty-seven have access to inpatient facilities in hospitals. The rest of the patients may seek home hospice care, where visiting doctors, nurses, and helpers give aid, although studies[5] show that the pain control is not quite as effective as at an inpatient hospice. Because of the enormous US population, great distances between hospitals, and the high cost of medical care, the average American will have little choice but home hospice, and even that is available only to a minority.

Interestingly, Scandinavian countries have no hospices and see no need for them, because all health care practitioners are trained in palliative care. Additionally, hospital administrators argue that hospice care would deplete their nursing staffs and might damage a well-organized medical system. Perhaps, then, with pain control mastered, a hospice system is not always the preferred alternative for the suffering terminal patient.

Hospice, as much as being a facility, is a philosophy of caregiving. The National Hospice Organization describes its philosophy in the following manner:

> Hospice affirms life. Hospice exists to provide support and care for persons in the last phases of incurable disease so that they might die as fully and comfortably as possible. Hospice recognizes dying as a normal process whether or not resulting from disease. Hospice neither hastens nor postpones death. Hospice exists in the hope and belief that, through appropriate care and the promotion of a caring community sensitive to their needs, patients and families may be free to attain a degree of mental and spiritual preparation for death that is satisfactory to them.[6]

The major elements of the programme are: the family as the unit of care, symptom control, interdisciplinary team care, home care services, staff support, and avoidance of inappropriate treatment. The patient and family are central figures in the determination of a care plan. Spouses, children, or parents of the patient serve as primary caregivers as well as receiving care and support. In both hospital-based and home care hospice, family members or 'primary care people' are encouraged to aid in caregiving.

Families are made aware that help is available as needed. Staff members are on call twenty-four hours daily and respite care is provided so that caretakers in the family may sleep. Volunteers offer supportive aid. Visiting hours and age limits are flexible, and room is provided for family members to stay in inpatient facilities. This enables them to be present to participate and offer emotional support to the patient as much as possible. The staff is supportive and therefore recognizes and counsels family and patients as needed.

Another component of hospice care is the avoidance of inappropriate treatment. The aim is not to preserve life but to make whatever life remains meaningful. In 'Hospice Care', Dr Twycross pointed out:

> Cardiac resuscitation, artificial respiration, intravenous infusions, nasogastric tubes, and antibiotics are all primary supportive measures for use in acute or acute-on-chronic illnesses to assist a patient through the initial period towards recovery to health. To use such measures in the

terminally ill, with no expectancy of a return to health, is generally inappropriate and is, therefore, bad medicine by definition.[7]

He contends that treatment is a continuum, with cure at one end, palliation in the centre, and symptom control at the other end.

However, some oncologists object to hospice's concept of treatment. One physician stated that some patients

> did not choose palliative care, but rather terminal care.... Once this course is decided on, the implied limitation is usually insured by death-hastening narcotic (morphine) therapy.... To designate this as 'bravery' is sheer nonsense. To avoid patient abuse and premature demise, I would suggest a 'second opinion' for all patients being considered for hospice terminal care.[8]

Another oncologist feels that patients at every stage of illness should have well-organized laboratory services and consultations from oncologists to ensure that all avenues of anticancer therapy have been explored before care is based on symptom control.[9] Still others would like to see hospice patients given the opportunity to participate in experiments with new agents or treatments, as long as risks/benefits are acceptable to the informed patient and family.[10]

As a response, some hospices are providing more than palliative care. For example, Calvary Hospice in New York City initiates active therapeutic measures, such as chemotherapy, in instances where curative possibilities have been overlooked, though no heroic measures are taken to prolong life.[11] This intervention seems to contradict the hospice principles. Some critics argue that perhaps patients should be given these options before they are admitted to the hospice, thus making the interventions unnecessary.

There is additional criticism that many hospices confine admissions to cancer patients; in fact, 95 per cent of the people who die in hospice suffer from that disease. People dying of A.L.S. (amyotrophic lateral sclerosis), heart disease, respiratory ailments, and other illnesses are unlikely to gain admission. Surveying these facts, euthanasia supporters argue that it is unreal, and raises false hopes, to claim that hospice is the ultimate—and only—solution for the dying.

Is hospice, with its philosophical acceptance of death and extensive use of narcotic drugs, itself a subtle form of euthanasia? Some have maintained that it is very similar to passive aid in dying. Hospice proponents counter that it cannot be passive euthanasia because that term applies to the discontinuance of artificial means of life support. However, is a death that takes place under the influence of painkilling drugs not part of the 'double effect' phenomenon likely in this type of terminal care? A nurturing technique that depends largely on heavy drug dosages runs the risk of oversedation, which is euthanasia.

Dame Cicely Saunders, the English doctor who is the founder of modern hospice, has responded spiritedly that hospice, 'rather than being a "foot in the door" for euthanasia ... can be a powerful force for undercutting a movement for active euthanasia.'[12]

Not all hospice staff share Dame Cicely's abhorrence of euthanasia. The medical chief of a major American city's hospice said: 'I have no trouble with helping patients to die if requested and if it is justified. I give a lethal injection and sit with them as it takes effect.'[13]

The arguments for and against hospice, then, tend to centre on an individual's view of life, spiritual rewards, and responsibilities. Dame Cicely describes her approach to the dying in the following manner:

> Let us be with [those who are dying] so we can learn what their needs are. We can't run from them, for the more you run, the worse their death appears. ... Although we do not hope to cure, we look at our patients as vital persons in distress and therefore concentrate on giving them relief: relief that leads to an ability to enjoy family, friends and food and drink and all the activity they can.[14]

The euthanasists' response to her credo weighs the factors of personal independence—chiefly the patient's and family's control and choice of the manner of death, not being overly dependent on medical staff, and not permitting medical staff to make ethical and legal decisions for them. Dame Cicely leans heavily on the case for family and friends being present at the deathbed: nevertheless, it is distressing to some patients to have loved ones witness the strain of their dying, while to others, dying is an event to be shared. What is appropriate for some is unsuitable for others.

The classic euthanasia view is expressed in a booklet issued in 1985 by the West Australia Voluntary Euthanasia Society:

> The whole matter of dying is so fraught with complications that it is quite unjustifiable overconfidence to assume that any single method of dealing with it will suit everybody. Even in considering terminal cancer, which has often been stated (usually by people who happen not to be suffering from it at the time) to be 'quite manageable', we must conclude that Hospice Care is most unlikely to be universally acceptable. When the whole range of 'incurable' conditions is contemplated, with their whole range of symptoms that can devastate as disastrously as can pain, the likelihood of some people seeing VE [voluntary euthanasia] as the desirable alternative becomes plain. Furthermore, it seems that at present Hospice Care, whether in hospital or at home, is available only to terminal cancer cases (and not all of those as yet), where the expected time

of care is of the order of six weeks. There are, unfortunately, many 'incurable' diseases which, whether 'successfully' treated or not, can cause long-term distress from which some people would wish to escape.[15]

Two of the most trenchant opponents of euthanasia are hospice pioneer Dame Cicely, and Dr Elisabeth Kübler-Ross, its spiritual leader in America. Both women have made enormous contributions to world understanding and practical care of the dying. However, their narrowly focused, unqualified dismissal of euthanasia seems to some observers to stem from their insistence that they have found in their own professional skills the perfect answer to the problems of dying and will countenance no variations.

Whether a hospice stalwart is hostile or sympathetic to the concept of euthanasia depends, to a large degree, on whether his or her motivation for work is based on religious faith or service to humanity. On the West Coast of America, where the major religions are less entrenched than in more conservative or orthodox areas, hospice organizations tend to be more receptive to euthanasia groups, exchanging speakers at conferences and referring patients to each other. In quite a few instances, area leaders of the hospice movement will also be active members of the Hemlock Society. East Coast hospice groups tend to be less cooperative, while British hospice is disapproving of all euthanasia societies.

Dame Cicely, who normally refers to any assistant in a euthanasia as a 'killer'[16] and who believes pain control makes euthanasia unnecessary, is a deeply religious woman, a recent convert to fundamentalist Christianity.[17] Any suffering over and above physical pain, she feels, is a normal part of religious experience and makes faith more meaningful.

The authors asked several experienced hospice workers to estimate how many of their colleagues might also be sympathetic to euthanasia. Their response put the support at one-third. 'For me it is a fundamental point of individual choice,' said a hospice chairman of long standing. 'If I were terminally ill I would wish to make use of hospice but also I would not like to shut the avenue to euthanasia in case that became what I wanted. I don't buy the total denial of voluntary euthanasia by Dame Cicely and others. If I were suffering, the knowledge that I could eventually opt out through euthanasia would be of great comfort to me.'[18]

Dr Gary A. Jacobsen, who chaired the National Hospice Organization's first bylaws and membership committee, and was formerly medical director of the Oregon Comprehensive Cancer Programme, has said: 'Hospice is not for every dying person. Hospice is an additional option for patients. Choice will depend upon individual lifestyles, beliefs, and value systems.'[19]

# CHAPTER FOURTEEN

# *High Technology:*
# *A Mixed Blessing*

It is incontrovertible that fear of dying in the cold clutches of modern technology has given a major boost to public acceptance of voluntary euthanasia. In the days when physicians and nurses practised the 'healing arts' without the benefits of modern medicine, euthanasia was rarely requested because death came naturally and at home. When aid-in-dying was appropriate, the privacy of the domestic bedroom shielded a doctor who deliberately oversedated.

Today's doctors might correctly be defined as 'body technicians'. As we tend to die in health care facilities, the treating physician is likely to be one of many caring for the patient. There may well be someone of an opposite ethical viewpoint, such as a pro-life nurse, who would report a deliberate overdose (as has been done), however much that action was requested and was administered out of compassion.*

As well, many patients are connected to alarm systems which report fluctuations in body functions. Resuscitation efforts are ceaseless, and when the hapless patient dies, it is to the accompaniment of buzzers and bells.

Public education about medical treatment is so thoroughly and explicitly reported in the media that today few people are unaware of what hospital care entails. The middle-aged and the elderly, who frequently visit dying parents and loved ones in the hospital, are particularly sensitized to the process of excessive, and not always desired, treatment. The phrase most often heard by euthanasia societies is: 'I have a dreadful fear of being trapped and out of self-control like my mother/father was.'

It's hardly surprising, then, that one writer concluded that euthanasia is a phenomenon 'created or intensified by recent advances in medical science

---

* As reported earlier, this was the case with Dr Vincent Montemarano, for example, who was charged with murdering a patient in 1973. In 1981 a nurse reported Drs Barber and Nedjl, who were subsequently charged with murder and wrongful termination of life in California. In August 1985 a nurse called a patient abuse hot line when she became suspicious about a patient's sudden decline. Later, the physician, John Kraai, was charged with murder.

and technology.'[1] While many medical advances in diagnosis and treatment have happily saved lives and reduced suffering, in other instances they have had appalling consequences. For many patients, suffering has been prolonged by lifesaving techniques often called 'heroic'. Yet what is heroic about the results? Medical critic Richard Taylor described an intensive care unit he had observed:

> Rows of physiological preparations (also known as human beings) lie surrounded by an astounding array of mechanical gadgetry. A tube or catheter of some description violates every natural orifice, and perforations in various parts of the body are made especially for the placement of others. Multicoloured fluid is pumped in, similar fluid drains out, respirators sigh, dialysers hum, monitors twitch, oxygen bubbles through humidifiers. The unfortunate hostages, mercifully unresponsive to their environment (either through natural causes or drugs) lie silent while their ritual desecration takes place.[2]

For lives saved by such aggressive technology, for lives whose usefulness is restored, unquestionably the pain and discomfort are worthwhile. But why should those people with no chance of recovery be subjected to such treatment? When is it appropriate to refuse aggressive measures? When is it appropriate to withdraw such 'heroic' efforts?

Before the twentieth century, little was written about the care of the dying. The absence of antibiotics, chemotherapeutic agents, and sophisticated medical procedures made illness more likely to be deadly than it is today. Certainly, death then was more swift. Yet in just a few decades, technological advances in medicine have dramatically transformed this situation. Infectious diseases, once life-threatening, have become reversible, while degenerative and chronic diseases have become the predominant causes of death.

By the 1950s, technological wizardry had come to the forefront with stunning results. In that decade, for example, an artificial breathing technique was developed for polio victims, as well as the cardiopulmonary bypass machine and coronary angiography. Such breakthroughs were considered miraculous by most people, both lay and medical. The 1960s saw even greater medical progress: Renal dialysis, organ transplants, cardiac valve prostheses, external cardiac massage, coronary care units, and nonsurgical life supports were all in use. Computerized axial tomography (CAT) scanners were developed in the 1970s.

A decade later, CAT's successor, the Nuclear Magnetic Resonance Imager, and the artificial heart made their way into medical use.[3] Such developments have influenced the care of the sick and dying and saved many lives. In cases in which they have not been able to prevent death, they have changed the manner in which it occurs—for better or, in some instances, worse.

Medical technology has been defined by the Office of Technological Assessment as: 'The drugs, devices and medical surgical procedures used in medical care, and the organizational and supportive systems within which such care is provided.'[4] This definition includes diagnostic therapies (e.g., the CAT scan), preventive measures such as polio vaccines, therapeutic treatments (chemotherapy), administrative aids (computers), and supportive or ancillary technologies like more effective hospital beds.

In fact, there is a kind of hierarchy of technologies, depending upon their relative effectiveness. Physician and writer Lewis Thomas categorized each of these by the degree of understanding medical science has of the disease process. His categories fit on a continuum, from having little understanding of the disease to having a complete understanding—and thus the ability to deal effectively with it. For instance, 'high' technologies, such as antibiotics and vaccines, fall into the latter category. On the other hand, nontechnological procedures are generally regarded as supportive care or reassurance. In essence, they are not technology as such but a part of patient care, the kind that doctors give patients with intractable cancer—supportive therapies and other soothing techniques that help patients endure the course of their disease until they die.

'Halfway' technologies are efforts to compensate for the incapacitating effects of certain diseases whose course the physician is unable to do very much about. As Thomas explained, their purpose is to 'make up for disease, or to postpone death.'[5] Examples of halfway technologies are artificial organs, such as hemodialysis and the artificial heart, transplanted organs, and chemotherapy. Such measures are used when there is limited information about the ailment. The main objective is to ease discomfort and to keep the patient functioning, rather than to necessarily arrest the disease.

Yet it is the halfway technologies that are often the most debatable, since in some instances they lead to an undesired level of functioning. In the 1950s, for example, polio could be treated only with an iron lung. Fortunately, polio today is understood and controllable with a vaccine, an example of high technology. But questions remain, like those raised by Gertrude Morrow, a victim of polio in 1952. She must live her life as she has done for the last thirty-three years, dependent on a respirator and a motorized wheelchair. While she manages to lead an active life, she is sure that, should she suffer a heart attack or stroke, she does not want to be resuscitated. 'Living a life more limited would be very difficult,' she says.[6]

Still, Gertrude Morrow has adjusted fairly well to her life, depending on a halfway technology. Others are not as fortunate. A case in point is hemodialysis, which purifies blood passing through kidneys that no longer function properly. There are many advantages to this treatment, but patients are constantly reminded of their disease and their dependence on a machine. They often have physiological complaints. On top of that, they must adhere to a strict diet, treatments may be uncomfortable, and there is the inconvenience of the dialysis appointments—four hours, three times a week. For many, the treatment and discomfort are unendurable. As one patient said, when he ripped out the tubes and left the treatment room, 'It's just not worth it.' He was dead a week later.[7] Notably dialysis patients have a suicide rate seven times higher than the national average.[8]

Should these patients have a right to refuse treatment?

Peter Clinque, who won the right to halt his dialysis, was blind, incapacitated, and in pain as a result of kidney disease. Treatment did nothing to relieve his suffering, and he decided to halt it. However, his case was argued in court. The acting plaintiff was the hospital, which refused to abide by Clinque's wishes.

Deciding in favour of the defendant, Justice Arthur Spatt held that Mr Clinque had the right to terminate his extraordinary means of life support, dialysis, because his decision was based on a desire to escape the 'constant and severe pain caused by his multiple debilitating, irreversible and terminal conditions.'[9] Clinque died within one hour of the ruling.

Certainly technology creates some problems, particularly for the terminally ill patient if the technological imperative takes precedence over the individual's values. By the 1950s, those techniques that had been developed to serve human interests, and which often did so brilliantly, began, in a moral sense, to override and even displace human priorities. Since then, though some therapies have eased pain and suffering, in other instances they have been used inappropriately and overzealously.

As David Thomasma of the Chicago Medical Center observed: 'The direction of medicine towards life prolongation leads to an increasingly positivistic view of man as a biological functioning machine. . . . Our political system no longer preserves life in its fuller dimensions, but enhances only the biological quality of life.'[10]

Such an attitude has often led to the overutilization of intensive care units. Initially these units were designed to treat trauma and some postoperative cases, not the hopelessly ill. Yet intensive care units are now full of the elderly, those with underlying untreatable diseases (such as cancer), those who could have been managed successfully on ordinary wards, and patients with loss of cerebral function.[11] Such people will not benefit from the high concentration of medical techniques available in these units, nor would many of them approve of the procedures—ones that limit their freedom and dignity—if they were capable of choosing.

Thomasma believed that the use of such artificial devices to prolong life will lead to a vision of man as a technological product.[12] If we depend on biological functioning, he argued, we may lose sight of those social aspects that are so important in living and interacting; we have come to perceive of medicine as a powerful force that can control nature.

As one philosopher stated, such power over nature then becomes an abstraction and an ideal, with knowledge as the sole, manipulating instrument.[13] Death is regarded as a failure, and the terminally ill as embodiments of such failure.

In their zeal to fashion new and better technologies, many doctors have promoted measures that have unintended consequences. These efforts have provoked a certain backlash of disapproval, such as growing resistance to cardiopulmonary resuscitation (CPR)—a technique that has greatly increased survival from cardiac arrest, but has not yet found a way to deal with the brain damage resulting from diminished oxygen supply during the arrest.

Side effects from other techniques have been criticized. Researcher D. S. Kornfeld found that patients recovering from open-heart surgery were immobilized by catheters and tubes, and disturbed by the lights and sounds of monitoring machinery. As a result, they showed signs of sensory monotony and sleep deprivation.[14] Observing similar circumstances, one sociologist concluded: 'The technological environments themselves have dehumanizing effects that may be counter to the intentions of the developer.'[15]

The artificial heart has had similar drawbacks. After surgery, the recipient faces an existence radically different from what even the most sedentary person has known. Typically, he is constrained by a six-foot-long air hose which is attached to a 375-pound cart of equipment. Dr William Parmley, chief of cardiology at the University of California, San Francisco, said: 'If it were me, I don't think I'd be too excited about it, if it meant being tethered to an external air source.'[16] An official at Humana Heart Institute said that the artificial heart 'is not a success so far because it has substituted mechanical problems for disease.'[17]

Is the risk worth the end result? Millions of Americans watched, horrified, as news flashes showed the mental and physical deterioration of heart-transplant recipient William Schroeder. Even Schroeder's wife expressed her doubts. 'If he had anticipated the hardship,' she said, 'he might not have done it. Bill thought he'd either die or be better.'[18] The article quoting her pointed out that Schroeder was 'suspended in a twilight zone between life and death—a guinea pig in an unfinished experiment, a patient whose treatment had gone sour.'

Such examples illustrate our society's infatuation with technology. Faith in the power of such solutions to medical problems gives rise to expectations of omnipotence—expectations shared, to some degree, by patients and doctors alike. We tend to be so awed at what medical progress can do that we often lose sight of the fact that there can be unbearable consequences. Technology is helpful, but its applications must be controlled. Observers in hospitals have sometimes noticed that technology is often being used because it is there, not because its use is justified by patient need.

How can this imbalance be explained? One writer suggests: 'Technological emphasis on medical care in the United States is not happenstance; rather, it is the natural extension of producers' and consumers' efforts to harness science and technology.'[19]

Once this technology is harnessed without consideration given to the ethics of treatment, it has a tendency to be used excessively or inappropriately. Such overuse is prompted by physicians' training—which places great value on scientific achievement—as well as by malpractice fears, methods of reimbursement, national priorities, and fear of death.

Consumer demands also promote the use of technology in medicine. The public's perceived needs or wants, at times manipulated by the media, are not always realistic. More often than not, these wants are created by the desire to understand or control the unknown.

For instance, feared diseases such as AIDS or herpes create a need, sometimes excessive, for services and additional information. Ivan Illich, the philosopher and writer, feels the public fascination with high-technology care and death in cases like this can be understood as a 'deep-seated need for the engineering of miracles.'[20]

In other words, technology offers the possibility of cure to patient and family, promising eternal hope. The yearning for highly specialized techniques and procedures turns into expectations which, however unreal, are then translated into demands. In turn, hospitals often bow to such pressures and acquire excess equipment and gadgetry to quell these consumer demands. And once the skilled procedures are secured, they must be utilized to meet the costs of use and maintenance.

The physician is subjected to similar pressures. Striving to live up to patient expectations, he often provides care beyond what is necessary and, in some cases, desired. This is particularly true with the terminally ill. There is no question that these patients will die, but more often than not, only after aggressive medical intervention. When the occasional therapeutic attempt is successful and there is, say, a miraculous remission, the physician and his team are heralded by their colleagues and the press, fuelling the public's expectations even more—despite the fact that these cases reflect a tiny minority.

National priorities, too, influence the proliferation of new technologies through research and development grants. Again, the desire for never-ending cures accounts for much of the funding. As one observer noted: 'The technological explosion of the late 1960s encouraged the myth that technology could rescue patients from the consequences of the major diseases affecting the population.'[21]

As a result, the government has continued to invest more money in finding new and better cures. In 1983, for example, $6 billion was spent on health research alone. This is expected to increase to $10 billion in 1990.[22]

Dr William Knaus, director of intensive care research at George Washington University Medical Center, commenting on the funding, said: 'We believe in the power of science to correct our problems, so we have invested a great deal of confidence and money in these life-support systems. . . . The machines are useful, but not in making miracles.'[23] Yet the belief that more is better predominates over the practical issues of assessing the use and application of these technologies in diagnosis and therapy.

How does all this affect the dying? While many life-support systems and techniques *are* beneficial, too often they are used simply because they are there, and because they reinforce the notion that death can be eluded indefinitely. Studies have shown that many terminal patients are isolated from others and receive less personal attention from the staff than recovering patients.[24] Insofar as the physician believes that 'to care for' means 'to cure', he is as helpless to act in the face of suffering as the terminal patient is. Thus, not only are many dying patients secluded, they are also overtreated—but by machines and therapies, rather than by personal contact. Any acknowledgment of death is avoided.

The physician's fear of death is also apparent in his reluctance to tell a terminal patient the truth about his illness, even though, according to the law of informed consent, he is supposed to.* To compound the problem, many patients' families fail to discuss among themselves the appropriateness of a life-prolonging procedure because of the same fear.

Too, skilled techniques and sophisticated therapies—all dubbed 'life-saving'—postpone decision-making. As one medical health writer noted, the use of such artificial life supports 'demonstrates how the medical profession, by and large, has shrunk from coping with new dilemmas, and how inaction has allowed medical technology to dictate its actions.'[25]

Thus the dying patient, if he is conscious, lies isolated, bewildered,

---

* The doctrine of informed consent establishes a dual responsibility for physicians: (1) a duty to disclose to the patient the nature and ramifications of available treatments, and (2) a duty to obtain the patient's consent to any treatment prior to its administration. Recent judicial decisions have established the responsibility of a physician to inform his patient adequately of treatment alternatives as an integral protection of the informed consent doctrine.

betubed, and monitored not by human contact but by the marvels of scientific progress, the almighty life-support system.

In 1949, 50 per cent of the population died in institutions—hospitals, medical centres, or nursing homes. In 1958, the figure was 61 per cent. Two decades later, the number had risen 10 per cent. Finally, in the 1980s, 80 per cent of the chronically ill died in institutions.[26]

To the dying person in particular, hospitals tend to be intimidating and impersonal. Typically, the terminal patient is a captive to his life-lines— monitors, tubes, and other mechanical gadgets carrying life-sustaining nutrients and fluids. Privacy is limited as the medical staff, looking for any significant change, observe the patient. Family contact is often restricted by a rigid schedule for visiting hours. The ubiquitous machinery surrounding the patient resembles an intricate obstacle course, defying even minimal physical contact.[27] One woman who wanted to lie with her dying husband in his final moments dislodged an intravenous tube. She retreated, horrified. No one can experience a peaceful, dignified death in such an alienating atmosphere.

While the dying still cling to life, the question remains: At what point should the terminal patient refuse further treatment, insisting that enough is enough? Pope Pius XII's statement in 1957 differentiating ordinary from extraordinary means has been used as a benchmark by many people in deciding what is appropriate treatment. Catholic thinkers such as Gerald Kelly have struggled to define these terms more explicitly so that they can have meaning for a patient, especially one who is Catholic and wants to adhere to Church policy.

Kelly defines ordinary means as all medicines, treatments and operations 'which offer a reasonable hope of benefit for the patient and which can be obtained and used without excessive expense, pain or other inconvenience.' Extraordinary measures, on the other hand, are those which 'cannot be obtained or used without excessive expense, pain or other inconvenience, or which, if used, would not offer a reasonable hope of benefit.'[28]

However, as admirable as these attempts to define different forms of treatment are, they are open to a great deal of interpretation. Clearly, what is painful, inconvenient, or expensive to one patient may not be to another. Also, what is ordinary treatment for one patient may be extraordinary for someone else. For instance, in the case of Claire Conroy in New Jersey, nasogastric nutrition was ruled by the court to be an extraordinary means of treatment and was discontinued. Not surprisingly, many people disagreed with the court's ruling, arguing that food and water are essential elements for life and are therefore part of ordinary care.

Thus the complexities of new and innovative techniques demonstrate how technology has confounded the issue of which treatments are suitable for which patients, especially for those who are dying. In many ways, there are no fixed guidelines to decide what is suitable. One can only ask: Who is to decide? And, as happened in the Conroy case, is litigation inevitable when the question can't be answered? Most people find this possibility appalling.

Further confounding the options available for a hopelessly ill patient is when death can and should be declared. Many people in the early stages of a terminal illness fear, more than anything, being kept alive in a state that can only be described as vegetative. David Lygre, in *Life Manipulation*, illustrated how machines can keep a patient 'hovering between life and death ... even mask [ing] death.' He went on to say: 'For as long as [the machines] circulate, oxygenate, and cleanse the patient's blood, his organs will continue many of their normal functions.'[29] With the aid of such medical intervention, people can exist in a comatose state for years. Karen Ann Quinlan, for example, died after being in a coma for ten years, in a state no one could describe as living. Instead, it was prolonged dying.

Although the point of death has been redefined in the last few decades, it has been confined to a strictly biological point of view, much to the horror of ethicists and others. There is more to a person than organs and brain-stem functioning. Even with the most recent proposal for a definition of death—the Uniform Determination of Death Act—personality, memory, and emotions are not considered relevant factors in deciding whether a person is technically dead and whether any quality of life remains or could remain.

To rely on technology to define the state of life and of death is to deny those parts of man that give his life substance. Medical decisions based solely on biological functions disregard the social and spiritual aspects of life which make it truly fulfilling and unique.

Why *are* hospitals so dependent on technology?

If there are drawbacks for the terminally ill, who may be overtreated to death, there are unmistakable advantages for the hospital, advantages that take precedence over more humane considerations.

Certainly, if a hospital prides itself on its sophisticated procedures and equipment, it will attract talented and superbly qualified physicians. It will also attract more patients, who respond to the reputation of the skilled medical staff. The word spreads. A first-rate staff and richly endowed resources ensure success, success that is often defined in terms of a bank statement.

Humana, Inc., illustrates this point. Administrators there were able to attract William DeVries, the prominent heart surgeon, to Louisville to perform artificial-heart operations. As the magazine *Business Week* observed, this, administrators felt, was the 'shrewdest move to date ...

[which] has already paid off in spades.'[30] As a result, they plan to capitalize on free publicity generated by the success of the artificial-heart operations and to turn Humana into a 'national brand of health care.'[31] Chairman and chief executive David Jones was heard referring to patients as 'customers'; he is said to be concentrating on the profits of artificial-heart implants, rather than weighing the relative benefits and harm generated by this new and startling technology.*

Much of this philosophy, more fiscal than humanitarian, is camouflaged by the insistence that all such procedures are lifesaving and therefore to be applauded. In this respect, hospitals are categorically dedicated to the principle that they improve life since such procedures prolong it. Little mention is made of whether the patient approves of such procedures, if, indeed, he has a choice, or whether quality of life is enhanced in the process. As the director of Beth Israel Hospital in Boston said: 'The hospital must be pro-life. When you see someone who looks as if he is dying, you don't question whether it is moral or ethical to save him, you just go.'[32]

Such a one-dimensional attitude also means that fewer decisions have to be made. The assistant chief of medicine at Stanford Medical School in California commented that, even with the hopelessly ill, 'it is much less complex and stressful to place such a patient on a breathing machine and send him to ICU [intensive care unit] than to decide that he has almost no chance to regain good quality of life and therefore should not be placed on extraordinary life support.'[33]

A frequently mentioned example of patient abuse is cardiopulmonary resuscitation, which has saved the lives of many otherwise healthy patients but has prolonged the suffering of the terminally ill. The *New England Journal of Medicine* reported a study in which only 14 per cent of all patients who were resuscitated lived to leave the hospital.[34] The procedure is violent; the family must stand by, aware that with someone who is hopelessly ill, CPR only ensures a more protracted deathbed. Yet a hospital could boast that it had revived and saved the lives of certain patients, without mentioning that those who left the hospital and returned to a meaningful existence were in an extremely small minority.

How can patients counter this?

In some hospitals, ethics committees serve as a sounding board for decision-making. The American Society of Law and Medicine describes these committees as: functioning to review treatment decisions on behalf of

---

* On the September 25, 1985, radio show *Morning Edition*, Michael Harrington noted: 'Medicine is developing more and more on the corporate model. There are merger discussions under way for profit hospitals and medical suppliers, which would create new entities yielding more than $5 billion a year in sales. Indeed, the Republic Health Corporation is now trying to figure out the costs and profitability of performing tonsillectomies or coronary bypasses. The poor, needless to say, are shunted over into the public sector.'

the patient; reviewing medical decisions having ethical implications; providing social, psychological, spiritual, or other counselling where necessary; establishing treatment and administrative guidelines; and providing education to the public about ethical questions in the health care field.[35]

However, the committees are purely advisory, and they are not intended to replace traditional methods of decision-making between doctor and patient. And as Leonard Glanz, from the Boston University School of Public Health and Medicine, warns: 'We must be very careful [with ethics committees]. We don't want just another layer of bureaucratic decision-making to bog down our health care system more.' Nor does he want ethics committees to diffuse the responsibility on sensitive issues, although he does foresee such committees as making real progress in teaching that 'sometimes less treatment is better treatment.'[36]

In some hospitals, to avoid overtreatment and CPR abuses, do-not-resuscitate orders are honoured for those patients who would be otherwise hopelessly revived. For instance, the Minnesota Task Force on the Affordability of New Technology and Specialized Care defines DNR orders as an explicit policy that 'preempts the emergency summoning of a resuscitation team if the patient suffers a cardiac arrest.'[37] Such a policy is decided on by the attending staff—which weighs medical and ethical criteria, as well as the wishes of the patient and the patient's family. In short, a DNR decision is upheld when it is agreed that the patient's best interests would not be served.

The Critical Care Committee of Massachusetts General Hospital has gone even further, recommending a system of classification for treatment decisions. The system consists of a ranking of conditions from A to D, with category D explicitly addressed to those patients for whom resuscitation would be futile.

Class A: Maximal therapeutic effort without reservation.

Class B: Maximal therapeutic effort without reservation, but with daily evaluations because possibility of survival is questionable. This enables the physician to obtain further consultation and promotes communication between the doctor, the hospital staff, and the patient.

Class C: Selective limitation of therapeutic measures. At this time certain procedures may cease to be justifiable and then become contraindicated, i.e., resuscitation limiting full CPR; inappropriate admission to Intensive Care Unit. The patient must be given full general supportive care.

Class D: All therapy can be discontinued. Any measures which are indicated to insure maximum comfort to the patient may be continued or instituted. Turning off the life support systems is to be performed by the physician only after consultation with and concurrence of family members and hospital committees.[38]

★

This system emphasizes consensus among physician, patient, family, hospital staff, and hospital director.

However, problems do arise, especially when the patient's wishes are not specified beforehand. A Living Will has not been signed, for example, or the patient has not made his priorities clear to his family. To avoid this confusion, patients and the medical staff, whenever possible, should discuss in advance the treatment anticipated and how far it should be carried out.

Still, in spite of advances made in this area, many physicians resist the DNR order, no matter how explicit a patient has been. In many instances, 'no code' instructions—do not resuscitate—are not prominently displayed on a patient's chart; when someone whose heart has stopped is brought into emergency, nurses work to revive the patient (something that is almost reflexive), before taking the time to read the chart.

As a kind of compromise, a measure called 'slow code' (loosely defined as responding to a code slowly or not using every available lifesaving measure) is practised in some hospitals. Here attempts are made to revive the patient, but only after a delay, usually long enough to ensure that the patient won't respond. In this way, the patient's wishes—or so the physicians can claim—have been honoured, while the hospital is protected from possible litigation. However, as one nurse noted, resuscitation, even when delayed, is rarely done for the patient's benefit: 'Resuscitation is more for the benefit of the living than helpful to the dead or dying patient. The family can say they tried everything, but [the loved one] was too far gone to bring him back, and the act of resuscitation makes the professional staff look efficient.'[39]

Because of the lack of consistent standards, more accurate ways of assessing the patient's needs should be installed in all hospitals, using the kind of criteria adopted by Massachusetts General Hospital, for example. As well, ethics committees to back up such decision-making help secure the best and most fitting treatment.

Until that time, an absence of such measures—or compromise techniques such as slow codes—only ensures that many patients will be treated in ways they would not have wished. They will be resuscitated and subjected to an abundance of diagnostic and therapeutic procedures that are senseless, costly, and, ultimately, undignified. The patient lies, either comatose or with his mental and physical capacities severely diminished, a hostage to a system that too often believes that lives should be saved, whatever the cost.

Physicians collude in the pattern of overtreatment for a variety of reasons. Certainly, medical schools emphasize technological progress and sophisticated therapies, concentrating on attacking the disease without necessarily weighing the ethics of such treatment. After medical school, most doctors specialize. This means that, unlike the old-fashioned doctor–patient relationship in which patient and disease were treated as a whole, today the doctor tends to the specific area that interests him: the organ or body function that is his particular speciality.

The pattern is further compounded, the responsibility further diffused. Often, in the process of treating one patient, several physicians are called in, thus diluting decision-making as well as personal rapport. For instance, a patient suffering from breast cancer may first be diagnosed by her gynaecologist. If she has surgery, which is likely, she will be treated subsequently by an oncology surgeon and an anaesthesiologist, not to mention chemotherapy specialists, laboratory technicians, oncology nurses, a pharmacist, a social worker, and other health care workers. Coordinating information—not to mention crucial decisions that have to be made—is complicated even more. Responsibility for the patient is spread over a team of specialists, not all of whom have equal input about the patient's welfare. Nor do they necessarily have equal say or equal interest.

In many cases, the physician in charge continues to use his expertise to press for intensifying treatment, even when the patient is in the final throes of a fatal illness. The doctor justifies his efforts by claiming that such undertakings combat the disease and prolong the life of the patient, considered by many to be the sole objective. As Ivan Illich noted:

> Not only does the medicalization of terminal care ritualize macabre dreams and enlarge professional licence for obscene endeavours; the escalation of terminal treatments removes from the physician all need to prove the technical effectiveness of those resources he commands. There are no limits to his power to demand more and more.[40]

Ultimately he can say he has done everything possible to help the patient. The family will thank him profusely, and the rest of the medical staff will nod approvingly.

In the process, the doctor has become little more than a body technician, isolating himself from the organism as a whole—the patient. As Illich said: 'The doctor's refusal to recognize the point where he has ceased to be useful as a healer, and to withdraw when death shows on his patient's face, has made him into an agent of evasion or outright dissimulation.'[41] And, sadly, the patient's inability to die on his own terms makes him pathetically dependent, painfully helpless.

If technology is a mixed blessing, then, it is because it has been developed and incorporated into hospital and medical practices at such a rapid rate that decisions on how to use it appropriately have lagged behind. Melissa Spears, a nurse, commented in an article in the *Washington Post*: 'I think we have a real gap between our technology and our ethics.'[42] Typically, medical decisions have emphasized the mechanistic or qauntifiable aspects of treatment, while corporate decisions—such as those arrived at by hospital boards—concentrate on cost effectiveness and population impact. Ethics committees and other counter-measures have been slow to arrive on the scene. By the end of 1985, only 30 per cent of hospitals had ethics committees, according to an American Hospital Association survey.

Laurence Tancredi, associate professor of law and psychiatry at New York University, has suggested ways in which technology can be employed usefully but in more humane ways. Utmost in Tancredi's philosophy is the ability to assess the efficiency of a particular technology—say, accelerated chemotherapy—in direct relation to a patient's personal evaluation of how such a treatment will affect his or her quality of life.

Tancredi's factors include: the ability to return to baseline function, the degree of relief from expected symptoms, the requirements of treatment and how well the patient can adapt to them, the psychological effects of the procedure, the impact of such a treatment on the patient's self-image (e.g., loss of hair), the cost of the procedure, and finally, the quality of death.[43] Another law professor, John Robitscher, defining the latter, spoke of 'a death that saves us from a meaningless prolongation of a painful existence or maintenance of some body process in the absence of consciousness and the hope of regaining consciousness.'[44] The ultimate goal is to prolong a patient's life only when a sense of wholeness, of self-determination, and of freedom remains intact.

Such a sense of wholeness can be made clear only if a patient has indicated his wishes beforehand to his physician and family. Informed consent is crucial in giving the patient the power to signal to the medical team the extent to which he or she wants treatment—ordinary, extraordinary, or otherwise.

Even today, many people are unaware of the fact that everyone has the right to refuse treatment. If it is administered against a patient's will, the physician is guilty of technical battery, based on a patient's constitutional right of privacy. Tancredi has defined the goal of informed consent as to 'shift, whenever possible, the decision-making power onto the patient, and to incorporate the patient's values in dealing with the social, psychological, economic, and medical issues involved in his or her treatment.'[45]

Karen Ann Quinlan and Claire Conroy have become symbols of the fight against technological death. In both cases, they were unable to make medical decisions for themselves, but their 'proxies' held that it was in the patients' best interest to have their life-support systems removed. As Associate Justice Sidney M. Schreiber said in the Conroy case: 'A competent patient has the right to decline any medical treatment, including artificial feeding, and should retain that right when and if he becomes incompetent.'[46]

Reviewing the matter, one journalist pointed out that 'medical technology has its benefits, but it also has its limits, and it is [the court] that is measuring what those limits are.'[47] Although such litigation has been costly and time-consuming—as well as painful for the plaintiffs' families—it has at least upheld what many ethicists and others have insisted on for so long: that we do indeed have the right to die. Once technology is inalienably linked to that right, as many recent court decisions have confirmed, innovative techniques and bold new medical procedures can be used ethically and humanely, and very much to the patient's advantage.

Medicine is not solely a technical profession. Neither are physicians simply monitors of electrolytes or brain-stem functions, or dispensers of drugs. They are healers of human beings. Assessing the place of technology at the patient's bedside, one writer concluded that it is useful only inasmuch as it helps people 'feel the rich fabric of life'. He went on to say: 'We should respect a patient's decision to decline further treatment when life has become burdensome. . . . We must learn how to make death a decent and humane experience, not something bitterly contested to the last gasp.'[48]

# CHAPTER FIFTEEN

# *Mercy Killing and the Law*

The arrest of Dr John Kraai in August 1985 galvanized the local press and much of the nation. As noted (pp. 147–8) Kraai had injected three large doses of insulin into the chest cavity of longtime friend and patient Frederick C. Wagner, who lay in a nursing home, suffering from Alzheimer's disease and gangrene. To many, his act was one of compassion and courage. To the authorities, it was cold-blooded murder. (Three weeks after his arrest, Kraai committed suicide.)

The fact that Dr Kraai acted humanely and that the patient's condition made death appear a more welcome option than life would have been irrelevant in a court of law. Traditionally, criminal law in the United States disregards humane motive as a factor in mercy-killing cases, as it does the terminal condition of the patient. Judeo-Christian tradition has always held life sacred, and the law in America has reflected this belief. For instance, in 1946 the Virginia Supreme Court of Appeals reiterated that 'The right of life and to personal security is not only sacred ... but is inalienable.'[1] Twenty years later, in *People* v. *Conley*, a California court declared: 'One who commits euthanasia bears no ill will towards his victim and believes his act is morally justified, but he nonetheless acts with malice if he is able to comprehend that *society prohibits his act regardless of his personal belief.*' (Emphasis added.)[2]

It's possible that Dr Kraai, seventy-six years old and in poor health, was aware of the law's emphasis on sanctity of life and was equally aware of what lay ahead of him; it's possible that suicide was preferable to the stigma of prosecution and possible imprisonment. For anyone charged with a mercy killing, the chances were extremely high that there would be a trial. Of the fifty-six mercy-killing cases reported between 1920 and 1985 in which there were criminal charges (and a trial), ten defendants were found guilty of criminal homicide and imprisoned.

There was leniency in forty-six cases: twenty suspended sentences or probations, fifteen acquittals, and six cases dismissed. (Five defendants were not brought to trial.) However, each of these forty-six defendants had to endure a preliminary hearing and a trial, invariably a lengthy, costly, and emotionally draining experience. Also, with the rise of mercy-killing cases in the 1980s, some of the trials and defendants gained a certain notoriety, most notably Roswell Gilbert, found guilty of first-degree murder in the slaying of his ailing wife. At the time of Dr Kraai's suicide, several defendants were awaiting trial, some in prison.

For medical ethicists and others, the Kraai tragedy embodies the intricacies and quandaries of dying with dignity. Here was a patient with no directive or Living Will, who was suffering and incompetent, and who was incapable of giving his physician any kind of informed consent. Here was a physician, emotionally vulnerable, who regarded his patient as a friend: they had known each other forty years. The relationship between the two men was also somewhat isolated. There had been, to all appearances, no dialogue between Kraai and Wagner's wife as to the appropriateness of further treatment, and the nursing home had no ethics committee which could have functioned in an advisory capacity.

As well, the potentially adversarial nurse–physician relationship was dramatized by the telephone call made by one of the attending nurses. Apprehensive over Wagner's sudden decline, the nurse reported to a patient abuse hot line what appeared to be suspicious circumstances. Was such an action inappropriate? Only four years earlier, two physicians in Los Angeles had been charged with murder for the removal of life-sustaining machines from a dying patient. Would a nurse who ignored what appeared to be a more direct attempt to end a patient's life be regarded by the courts as an accessory to murder?

Traditionally, murder (which was the label applied to Kraai's act) is distinguished from homicide in law. The former is a less neutral term, implying 'malice' and the absence of any factors that might justify or excuse the killing, such as self-defence or insanity. In some jurisdictions, the judge or jury must decide whether, under the circumstances, a 'reasonable person' would have entertained thoughts of killing, especially when the killing was thought to be in some way provoked. However, in mercy-killing cases like Kraai's and Gilbert's, sympathy, love or compasson are not considered adequate provocation. Malice is implicit in the charges laid, inasmuch as there is no question that there has been premeditation and deliberation. Kraai and Gilbert (and others) thought about and planned what they were about to do, and they acknowledged as much.*

* Other defendants in mercy-killing cases have been charged with lesser degrees of criminal homicide. The law distinguishes between first-degree murder (wilful, deliberate, and premeditated) and second-degree murder (the unlawful killing of another but without deliberation and premeditation). Voluntary manslaughter is an intentional killing committed under circumstances that mitigate the homicide while not justifying it. The crime of manslaughter

Regardless of overwhelming support for Kraai from the community, the district attorney's office was determined to prosecute. The pattern was the same as most other mercy killing cases; a conviction would be sought. Knowing this, what assurances did Dr Kraai have that a court would consider a humane motive? While in a significant number of mercy-killing cases prosecutors had displayed leniency by charging defendants with lesser degrees of homicide, Kraai had no certainty that this would apply to him. Indeed, notwithstanding the clemency shown to many defendants, the fate of Roswell Gilbert, convicted of first-degree murder and imprisoned for twenty-five years, looked ominously.

Until there are standards defining the propriety and legality of euthanasia, and clear procedures for dealing with criminal charges in mercy-killing cases, physicians like Dr Kraai and family members like Roswell Gilbert will continue to make life-and-death decisions without the backdrop of laws that supervise, regulate, and protect. Until then, physician, family member, and patient are defenceless. The courts, rather than protect, only confuse the issue.

Up to and including the 1950s, despite the defining of mercy killings as first-degree murder, substantial clemency for defendants was common. Of the fifteen cases that were tried between 1920 and the mid-1950s, only three defendants were found guilty of murder or manslaughter and were imprisoned: one of them for life, one for six years, and one for four. There were two probations, nine acquittals (four for temporary insanity), and one refusal to indict.

As reviewed earlier, sentences varied. Frank Roberts, who had assisted his terminally ill wife to die, received a life sentence and hard labour; Harold Mohr, who had helped his blind, cancer-stricken brother, served six years. In both cases, their assistance had been requested.

It's interesting to note that the acts of those acquitted for temporary insanity were often carried out in a more brutal fashion than the others, although as one juror noted, the circumstances in each case had been 'heart-wrenching'. In every instance the victim was terminal or chronically ill (often mentally); each defendant dealt with the desperation in a different way, from strangling to suffocation to shooting to drowning. In four cases (those noted earlier: Blazer, Braunsdorf, Greenfield, Repouille) children were involved, and there was no question in the courts that the act was one of involuntary euthanasia. Such inconsistency prompted one attorney, commenting on Otto Werner's case—he was found guilty of manslaughter and then freed—to declare: 'This is just another in the expanding galaxy of examples of apparent disrespect for the law in euthanasia cases.'[3]

was developed as an alternative to murder and its attendant death penalty for homicides that were not as extreme and that were explainable.

In 1954, Harvard Law School research associate Helen Silving published an eloquent article, 'Euthanasia: A Study in Comparative Criminal Law.' Reviewing mercy-killing cases of the previous fifty years, she concluded that the American Strategy in such cases has been to leave the law intact (a law which proclaims that premeditation and deliberation necessarily mean that the taking of another's life is first-degree murder), and to rely instead on the discretion of the prosecutor, judge, and jury to show sympathy, often in defiance of the law as it stands. As a result, Silving claimed, the law has been unequally and unfairly applied, leaving people with the impression that 'not all law means what it says.'[4]

Silving further noted that through a shifting of issues—allowing defendants to claim temporary insanity or lack of causation (i.e., that the deceased had already died before the alleged criminal act), there has been no uniformity of treatment.* Stressing the need for law reform, she contrasted the European tradition with the American. In the former, a humane motive is of great consequence, while premeditation and deliberation decrease in importance or disappear entirely. For instance, in Switzerland, Article 63 of the Penal Code of 1937 states: 'The judge shall mete out punishment in accordance with the guilt of the actor; he shall consider the motives, the prior life, and the personal circumstances of the guilty person.' Norway stipulates that punishment is not applied when the victim has consented, 'or where an actor motivated by mercy takes the life of a hopelessly ill person.' Similarly, Uruguayan law punishes no one motivated by compassion, as induced by repeated requests of the victim.[5]

Following the example of these codes, Silving recommended a specific statutory reduction of penalty for mercy killing in America. 'The examples of euthanasia,' she wrote, 'show that where there is a close relationship in fact between the various forms of acts, it is desirable that they be treated as a class . . . suggesting a penal code conceived as a 'system' of criminal law rather than a loose collection of incoherent criminal provisions.' She concluded: 'Similarity of motive should be considered systematically as a factor uniting the pertinent provisions.'[6]

In 1969 law professor Anton Pestalozzi-Henggeler of Zurich University extended and updated Silving's thesis in 'Euthanasia Under the Swiss Penal Code'. Emphasizing the condition of the patient at the time of death, Pestalozzi-Henggeler pointed out that if the person killed is a sufferer, this

---

* Indeed, any observer would be puzzled by the inconsistency of the courts' decisions. For example, of five cases, somewhat similar, in which a hopelessly ill person pleaded to die, there was: (1) a refusal to indict in an asphyxiation killing (Johnson); (2) an acquittal by lack of causation in a beating death (Allie Stephens's nephew); (3) two acquittals by reason of temporary insanity in shooting deaths (Paight, Waskin); (4) one conviction of homicide with six years imprisonment in a slaying (Mohr); and (5) one dismissal in a strangling death (Werner).

will affect the degree of punishment. While Section 114 of the Penal Code states: 'He who kills a person upon his serious and urgent request is punishable by imprisonment,' the judge will consider whether the patient was terminal, whether he requested death, and whether the defendant acted for 'noble' reasons.[7]

When there has been no known request from the patient, especially where a doctor is concerned, the particular circumstances and motive are weighed. 'Such an act *per se* does not evince a reprehensible motive or extreme dangerousness,' Pestalozzi-Henggeler said, adding that mitigating circumstances are always considered. Where medical treatment has been omitted, the nature of the contract between doctor and patient becomes a major factor in evaluating the seriousness of the case.[8]

Naturally, there have been physicians and attorneys who have argued that it is better to leave things the way the are. Responding to Silving's article, for example, law professor Yale Kamisar, in an exhaustive review of mercy-killing cases, concluded that the flexibility of juries—even if they depart from the strict letter of the law—is still the best way to evaluate a defendant's behaviour. 'The Law in Action is as malleable as the Law on the Books is uncompromising,' he declared. Motive is notoriously difficult to establish, and any changes in legislation would be too open to abuse, most notably in cases of patients 'euthanatized' against their will.[9]

In the same vein, in 1969, attorney Joseph Sanders, in 'Euthanasia: None Dare Call It Murder', held that neither the consent of the victim, the extremity of suffering, nor the imminence of death could be proper defences to homicide. In a statement endorsed by many physicians, Sanders pointed out: 'The medical profession generally seems willing to permit the status quo to remain, partly because it permits a great deal of discretion . . . and partly because physicians do not wish to accept the extra burdens a statute might impose on them.'[10] While deploring the present laws in mercy-killing cases, Sanders would not recommend any specific changes, saying, like Kamisar, that it was better to leave things the way they were. Yet he added in a final ironic note that those most affected by a change in the law—the dying—were in no position to argue one way or the other.

By 1970 the Living Will had been introduced,[11] and it would soon be widely distributed by the Euthanasia Education Council. Such a patient directive could significantly diminish the possibility of patient abuse feared by Kamisar and others. Acknowledging this, two attorneys, abhorring unwanted, last-gasp measures often inflicted on dying patients, proposed voluntary-euthanasia bills that would allow a physician to administer a lethal dose to a terminal patient—*if the patient had previously signed a Living Will declaration.*[12]

Obviously this would relieve a desperate friend or relative of the burden of having to act on his own. And in fact, between 1954 and 1970, of the nine mercy killings reported, responses varied, as indicated earlier: Two men (Sell, Nagle) were declared not guilty in the shooting of their handicapped children; a father (Collins) was sentenced to life imprisonment for the shooting of his mentally defective son; another (Petyo) was charged with manslaughter and jailed for slaying his terminally ill wife, who had pleaded with him to kill her; William Jones was imprisoned for a year for electrocuting his ailing wife; one woman (Margaret Cannon), who shot her ill husband, was committed to a state hospital for the insane; Anne Eldridge, who gave her ailing sister sleeping pills, stood trial for murder, during which time charges were dismissed; an eighty-four-year-old man, William Reinecke, accused of murder, was placed on probation after strangling his cancer-stricken wife; and Robert Waskin, a college student, also charged with murder, was declared not guilty by reason of temporary insanity for the shooting of his terminally ill mother, who had pleaded to die and had made attempts to take her own life.

'The agonizing aspect of some deaths,' one of the attorneys wrote, 'requires that the sanctity of life be weighed against the competing values of compassion, liberty, and human dignity. . . . A voluntary euthanasia statute constitutes a significant step on the path towards human dignity and a more humane justice.'[13]

Other writers in the 1970s echoed such sentiments. The contradiction between the actual laws and the verdicts the courts handed down was noted, and the inadequacy of existing statutes deplored. 'Is the law shirking a responsibility by failing to provide more easily discernible guidelines?' one lawyer asked. 'Our system of justice might give more serious consideration to allowing "motive" to enter the substantive law.'[14] Another attorney observing the high rate of acquittals pointed out that despite evidence of a felony, 'an indictment frequently is not even sought, perhaps because the elected prosecutor perceives a community sanction for some form of mercy killing.'[15]

Yet another attorney concluded that with cases such as these, which consistently revealed a public sentiment that looked askance at a particular law, the time had come for legislators to take heed.

From the foregoing [cases], it becomes apparent that juries have taken it upon themselves to rewrite the criminal law so that it lends greater recognition to motive. It is reputedly an essential requirement of a system of criminal jurisprudence that uniformity of treatment be accorded to those convicted of an offence. Yet how can such uniformity be assured, in spite of the nature of the substantive law with regard to euthanasia, where jury sentiments have dictated verdicts as diverse as those indicated?[16]

However, during the 1970s there was a virtual silence from attorneys who only a decade earlier had proclaimed the need for a change in mercy-killing laws. It's possible that much of the silence reflected growing confidence in the Living Will. The Karen Ann Quinlan case fuelled the debate even more, with the result that dozens of right-to-die laws (inspired by the Living Will) were introduced into state legislatures. Such bills emphasized the importance of a patient's wishes and stripped of its substance Sanders's observation that the dying are in no position to argue. Those on the cusp of death would no longer be voiceless, powerless beings—at least not in theory.

As death-with-dignity legislation was adopted by more and more states, however, the incidence of reported mercy killings increased at an alarming rate. The majority of them occurred in states with right-to-die legislation. Seven of the fifteen cases reported between 1976 (post-Quinlan) and 1981 took place in such states; twenty out of twenty-six from 1981 to 1983, when thirteen more states had adopted such legislation; and thirty-two out of thirty-eight from 1983 to mid-1985 (some still pending), when a total of thirty-six states had enacted right-to-die laws.

Typically, these cases were unevenly tried. Of those brought to court, approximately one-fifth of the defendants were found guilty of murder or manslaughter and were imprisoned, one-third received suspended sentences or probation, one-quarter were acquitted, and one-sixth either had their case dismissed or were not brought to trial. Perhaps it's not surprising, then, that the sole article to appear during this time, 'Euthanasia: A Comparison of Criminal Laws of Germany, Switzerland, and the United States,' published in 1983, was a virtual repeat (albeit updated) of Helen Silving's 1953 article. Thirty years later, very little had changed.

The author, Mustafa Sayid, reiterated that despite euthanasia's status as wilful homicide, it is a continued practice, especially among physicians. This, in turn, creates a problem for the American criminal justice system. His solution, like that of Silving and Pestalozzi-Henggeler, was to incorporate German and Swiss penal code concepts into the criminal law system, making humane motive a significant factor in weighing culpability for a crime.

Sayid's recent review of the German Penal Code reveals that it has abandoned the premeditation and deliberation test in defining murder and manslaughter. Instead, the presence or absence of a 'base motive' (committing a crime out of greed, lust for killing, or satisfying a sexual urge) determines which charge shall be imposed. Further, Section 213 of the Code provides for a reduction of penalty if there are extenuating circumstances indicative of honourable motives.[17]

Although the Swiss Penal Code considers premeditation significant, it functions only to evaluate the actor's dangerousness or perverse mentality. As in Germany, motive is a vital factor; anyone who has acted honourably towards the deceased—although convicted of a criminal offence—may receive a reduced sentence or avoid punishment entirely. In both Switzerland and Germany, a judge may mitigate the sentence of an individual who has committed a homicide at the request of the deceased.[18]

Attorneys assessing American laws that deal with accused mercy killers criticize their inadequacies almost unanimously. If humane motives, as well as the terminal condition of the deceased, remain irrelevant, courts will continue to produce inconsistent results, as they have in the last sixty-five years. The outcome of every case may well depend, as it often has, on factors that are hardly pertinent. Neither rapport between defendant, judge, and jury, nor contrition (no matter how apparently sincere), nor ability to communicate the desperation of the act, should have significant effect, even though remorse and emotionalism have proved to be highly effective in swaying a jury (as have suicide attempts following a mercy killing).

In the majority of cases, juries have taken it upon themselves to reinterpret the law, ignoring its obvious mandate. Regardless of instructions to the contrary, they have queried the underlying causes of the defendant's conduct. However, instead of motive being openly acknowledged, it has been obliquely incorporated into decision-making and camouflaged: Temporary insanity pleas, often patently contrived, are put forth; lack-of-causation defences dodge the real issue; the lesser degrees of homicide are sanctioned, regardless of the deliberate and wilful (albeit compassionate) taking of another's life. These are fictions which do nothing to enhance the prestige of the courts. In fact, they are blatant abuses of the law.

The verdicts in these cases seem to depend on numerous factors, often subjective and difficult to pinpoint—like judicial discretion, the rapport between the defendant, judge, and jury, or such extraneous factors as pretrial publicity, the personality and clothing of the defendant, and the weather. For example, in 1983, Hans Florian was not even indicted for the shooting of his ailing, Alzheimer's-stricken wife. Two years later, in the same Florida county, Roswell Gilbert—who shot his wife under strikingly similar circumstances—was convicted of first-degree murder.

History suggests that some mercy killings, especially those in which there have been no indictments, are legally and morally sanctioned. The police, the prosecutors, judges, and juries simply ignore clearly established facts. As Helen Silving said in 1953: '[Such] acquittals tend to give laymen the impression that the law is a magic formula rather than an honest tool of meting out justice.'[19]

In mercy-killing cases, little has changed. As a result, the public is bewildered, defence attorneys are encouraged to use ploys that shift rather than confront the issue, and critics ridicule the law's archaic formulas for dealing with such cases. Not least important, defendants suffer the consequences of an arbitrary and capricious legal system, some more unhappily than others. Severe sentences such as Gilbert's are regarded as a rigorous application of the law, especially where a defendant shows no remorse or emotion. One attorney's explanation for the excessiveness of Gilbert's sentence was this: 'The jury was overworked. They were tired. Gilbert wouldn't cry. The weather was real bad too.'[20]

The United Kingdom has also wrestled with these issues. Typically, since 1957, defendants in mercy-killing cases have pleaded guilty to a lesser charge of homicide (manslaughter), with diminished responsibility as their defence. More than 90 per cent of the defendants have been placed on probation, with the court frequently offering them condolences.[21]

Significantly, after 1957, 'compassionate killing' was no longer strictly regarded as murder and thus subject to the death penalty. A review of such cases by the Royal Commission on Capital Punishment produced a less rigid approach. (In evidence to the Commission, the Home Office explained jury recommendations of mercy in the past: 1,071 cases reported between 1900 and 1949 could be attributed to 'pitiable circumstances'. The Commission accepted the suggestion that a high proportion of these cases were mercy killings; commutation of the death sentence to life was frequently followed by an early release.)[22]

Although the Commission failed to recommend any specific changes in the laws relating to mercy killings, the diminished-responsibility defence was incorporated into section 2 of the Homicide Act of 1957. However, this has been criticized as inadequate in dealing with the scope and realities of the cases. Not only, as one critic pointed out, is it possible to find any number of psychiatrists willing to testify to a defendant's diminished responsibility 'once their sympathies are engaged'. In addition, as Baroness Wooton observed, 'The terms of section 2 are stretched to a point where the offender, far from suffering from any diminution of responsibility, appears to have acted from excessively responsible motives.'[23]

In 1976 a Working Paper on Offences Against a Person recommended a shift away from the accused's state of mind in mercy-killing cases to the circumstances and related motives. The proposed offence (subject to a maximum of two years imprisonment) would apply to a person who from compassion unlawfully killed another 'where the accused with reasonable cause believed that the victim was (i) permanently subject to great bodily pain or suffering, or (ii) subject to rapid and incurable bodily or mental deterioration.'[24]

However, the proposal was dropped on the grounds that it was 'too controversial', leaving the courts with the amorphous 'diminished responsibility' as the sole mitigating device, a strategy subject to abuse and misapplication. One judge commented on the 'vagueness' and 'woolliness' of such a tactic: 'Lawyers retained to defend in a "mercy killing" case quickly appreciate the use which [can] be made of diminished responsibility.'[25] Another critic noted:

> Mercy killers are not all alike: they occupy a continuum that stretches from the mother, so deranged by constant reminders of her child's suffering that she cannot control her desire to end the child's misery, to the parents, who, having rationally weighed up all factors, consider that it is their responsibility to the child to end their suffering. The former clearly falls within the terms of [diminished responsibility], the latter . . . does not.[26]

Like their American counterparts these critics call for a general statutory provision which recognizes mercy killing as a special and separate crime subject to different criteria than those applied to murder. On whichever side of the Atlantic, present laws are clearly deficient: the dangers of judicial discretion lead to unequal and unpredictable treatment of defendants; devices such as diminished responsibility and temporary insanity are often inappropriate and subject to abuse; and statutes that categorically deny a humane motive and circumstance force juries to wink at existing laws and boldly defy them if they wish to behave humanely.

However, a system like the German or Swiss ensures that no homicide, whatever the reasons, is a matter of indifference to society. It can, instead, be properly weighed and measured in a court of law without straining the credulity and imaginative resources of judge, jury, and defence attorney. Moreover, such a change reinforces what can be inferred from the majority of decisions in mercy-killing cases: that the taking of another's life, while not permissible in the eyes of the law, can be noble.

Unlike John Kraai, one need not be a doomed Prometheus to extend a final, compassionate gesture.

# CHAPTER SIXTEEN

# *Is There a Constitutional*
# *Right to Die?*

What of individuals who refuse treatment and risk death? Do the laws ensure that a person is free to choose his fate, even if in choosing, he or she rejects lifesaving procedures and medication?

The right to determine what shall be done with one's own body is by no means a novel judicial concept. American common law and the Constitution have long recognized individual freedom from bodily invasion or interference. As early as 1891, supporting a plaintiff's refusal to submit to a pretrial medical examination, the United States Supreme Court commented:

> No right is held more sacred, or is more carefully guarded by the common law, than the right of every individual to the possession and control of his own person, free from all restraint or interference by others, unless by clear and unquestionable authority of law.[1]

Moreover, a patient's right to bodily control has been demonstrated for some time in the tort* doctrine of informed consent.[2] Except in emergencies, no medical procedure can be performed without a patient's explicit permission. Although this principle is well established (dating back to the eighteenth century[3]), court rulings have depended largely on the jurisdiction. In most cases, its breach has led only to civil liability, but some courts have considered it a criminal battery. *Mohr* v. *Williams*,[4] in 1905, appears to be the first precedent for tort liability of a doctor exceeding his patient's consent. It was followed in 1914 by *Schloendorff* v. *Society of New York Hospital*, in which Justice Benjamin Cardozo, confirming a person's right to self-determination, said: 'a surgeon who performs an operation without his patient's consent commits an assault, for which he is liable in damages.'[5]

---

* A tort is a civil action in which an injured plaintiff seeks money damages from a wrong-doing defendant. It differs from a criminal action brought by the state against a criminally wrong-doing defendant.

A long, slow metamorphosis preceded the significant development of informed consent in the decades of the 1960s and 1970s. Its principles were debated and tested in a spate of cases, with conflicting and often puzzling results. An apparently uncomplicated idea has proved more elusive in the courtroom.

In 1965, in a dispute over birth control information and the use of contraceptives, the United States Supreme Court, in *Griswold* v. *Connecticut*,[6] first recognized the right to privacy as a fundamental constitutional guarantee,* one that would figure prominently in subsequent right-to-die cases. Such a right shielded an individual from invasion of protected freedoms and from state interference — so long as the state's public interests were not betrayed.

Typical of the common law and of constitutional litigation, the court in *Griswold* left the ultimate boundaries of privacy to be determined on a case-by-case basis. Thus, in every ensuing euthanasia case, one of the most pervasive themes in constitutional law was debated: the individual right to privacy balanced against society's interests. The issue was whether the state had a sufficient interest to justify preventing individual autonomy, when such autonomy resulted in a person's death.

To determine whether euthanasia can in fact derive constitutional validity from the right to privacy, the question remains: Is the right to die truly private? Certainly it is private inasmuch as it involves control over one's self, or, as Justice Louis Brandeis commented in 1928, 'the right to be left alone'.[8]

Yet the public may have an interest in its potential to undermine the traditional value placed on human life by religious and moral thought in America. The state might also have an interest in regulating the cooperation of others (i.e., physician, family member, or friend), so frequently required by terminal patients desiring death. Thus self-determination is balanced in court against society's claims to maintain morals and to control the conduct of others. In order for the state to overrule the individual, it must establish that the private right is restricted by considerations of public welfare.

What are the state interests that justify interference with individual liberties? It has been urged that the state must concern itself with:

1. Preservation of society. The state has a legitimate interest in promoting a thriving and productive population. Concern, therefore, to avoid the

* Justice William O. Douglas, in a much-quoted statement, explained that 'specific guarantees in the Bill of Rights have penumbras formed by emanations from those guarantees that help give them life and substance. . . . Various guarantees create zones of privacy.'[7]

corrosive effect of any challenge of the cheapening of life's significance is to be expected.

2. Sanctity of life, the foundation of a free society. Closely related to the former consideration is the state's interest in the preservation of life. By denying the patient an opportunity to choose death, a court may be promoting general respect for life.

3. Public morals. Rejection of life-prolonging treatment is a form of suicide, traditionally anathema in Judeo-Christian culture.

4. Protection of an individual against himself. The state may function to protect someone from his or her own imprudence, despite the individual's reluctance to be safeguarded (e.g., if a court were convinced that the patient did desire lifesaving treatment but could not freely and openly consent due to religious scruples). Also, if a patient is *in extremis* (at the point of death) and incompetent to make a decision regarding medical treatment, the intervention of a court guardian may be deemed necessary.

5. Protection of third parties. The state should: (a) protect the interests of surviving adults, traumatized by the death of a loved one; (b) avoid distraction of physicians and hospital staff, as well as disruption of hospital procedure (by withholding treatment, not only may the physician be acting against his best professional judgment, but he also risks civil and criminal liability); and (c) where there are surviving minors, safeguard a child's welfare through the doctrine of *parens patriae* (the state's assuming the protective role of parent or guardian), overriding a parent's objection to medical treatment.[9]

### PRE-QUINLAN COURT CASES

Not surprisingly, right-to-refuse-treatment cases in the 1960s and early 1970s reflected much of the tension between state and individual rights. Not only was a person's right to self-determination pitted against the state's concern with protecting life; in some instances the Constitution's First Amendment right of religious freedom was held to be justification for rejecting lifesaving procedures. What distinguished these trials (and this would hold true in the late 1970s and early 1980s) was the diversity of the courts' decisions. Also, rarely was the constitutional issue squarely confronted.

In a number of cases, religious objections to blood transfusions were overridden by the state's paternalistic interests, as embodied in *parens patriae*. For example, in *Application of President and Directors of Georgetown College*,[10] the Court of Appeals for the District of Columbia upheld a court order requiring a twenty-five-year-old woman to submit to a blood transfusion. The woman, a Jehovah's Witness and the mother of a seven-month-old child, refused (with her husband) to authorize a transfusion, despite a severely ruptured ulcer. Circuit Judge J. Skelly Wright based the court's decision on a number of factors: The patient, it was argued, was not competent when rejecting the transfusion, thus permitting the court to compare her condition to that of a minor; since the patient had minor children, the court could further invoke *parens patriae* and prevent, through the mother's death, an act of 'ultimate abandonment'; and finally, Judge Wright held that to let the patient die ran counter to the professional judgment and skills of the hospital and physicians, and might expose them to criminal liability.[11]*

In a similar case in Connecticut the following year, *United States* v. *George*,[13] a district court, relying heavily on the *Georgetown* opinion, insisted that a father of four minor children submit to a blood transfusion, despite the man's opposition on religious grounds. Here the patient's competency was not questioned. Instead, the court maintained that the state had an interest in upholding respect for the doctor's conscience and professional oath, and therefore must not require physicians to forego doing what their responsibility requires.[14]

Another case in which the state prevailed over a patient was *Raleigh Fitkin-Paul Morgan Memorial Hospital* v. *Anderson*.[15] Here a woman, refusing treatment for religious reasons, was in her eighth month of pregnancy. The Supreme Court of New Jersey ordered a transfusion since 'the welfare of the child and of the mother are so intertwined and inseparable that it would be impracticable to attempt to distinguish between them.'[16] Since the welfare of the child was the deciding factor, once again the patient's right to die for religious reasons (a constitutional issue) was avoided.

And in *Powell* v. *Columbia Presbyterian Medical Center* in 1965,[17] a postoperative Caesarian-section patient refused—again, on religious grounds—to authorize a blood transfusion. Here the court avoided the constitutional issue by deciding the case not on any theory of law but on its own emotional intuition that the patient actually did want the transfusion she had refused to authorize. As the judge stated:

Never before had my judicial robe weighed so heavily on my shoulders. . . . . How legalistic-minded our society has become, and what an ultra-legalistic maze we have created to the extent that society and the individual have become enmeshed and paralyzed by unrealistic entanglements!

* In a dissenting opinion, Circuit Judge (now Chief Justice) Warren Burger rejected the argument that a legal right grew out of an affirmative moral duty of a hospital towards its patient, by stressing that the subject was clearly not fit for judicial determination since it so saliently involved 'great moral, religious, and philosophical issues'. He added that, despite the motive of the state or the foolishness of refusing lifesaving medical care, the individual has the 'right to be left alone'.[12]

I was reminded of 'The Fall' by Camus, and I knew that no release—
no legalistic absolution—would absolve me or the Court from responsibility if I, speaking for the Court, answered 'No' to the question
'Am I my brother's keeper?' This woman wanted to live. I could not let
her die![18]

The extent and unreasonable degree to which the courts could impose
the doctrine of *parens patriae* was further demonstrated in the 1971 case
*John F. Kennedy Memorial Hospital* v. *Heston*.[19] Delores Heston, twenty-
two years old and unmarried, was admitted to the hospital after suffering
severe injuries in an automobile accident. Doctors concluded that Miss
Heston would die without surgery, which would require a blood transfusion. Miss Heston and her mother, both Jehovah's Witnesses, refused to
give their consent. (The hospital chose to overlook the fact that for six years
the patient had carried a card specifying her choices.) On behalf of her
daughter, Jane Heston executed a release for the hospital and medical staff,
freeing them from any liability arising from Miss Heston's refusal of treatment. Still, the hospital applied to a superior court for a temporary guardian for the patient, with the authority to consent to transfusions. The order
was granted. Blood was administered during surgery, and Delores Heston
lived.

After Miss Heston recovered, she and her mother asked the court to
vacate (annul) the order on the grounds that her religious freedom as
guaranteed by the First Amendment had been violated. However, the
Supreme Court of New Jersey, despite the controversy being 'moot', accepted the issue because 'the public interest warrants a solution.' In a 6–0
decision, the high court upheld the lower court decision. Chief Justice
Joseph Weintraub's written opinion stated that there was no constitutional
right to die. He cited the fact that attempted suicide was a common-law
crime in New Jersey.[20]* He concluded: 'Nor is constitutional right established by adding that one's religious faith ordains his death. Religious beliefs are absolute, but conduct in pursuance of religious beliefs is not
wholly immune from governmental restraint.'[21]

In 1972, in a case that revolved solely around a patient's competency, the
New York Supreme Court authorized the implantation of a new battery in
the pacemaker that maintained the heartbeat of seventy-nine-year-old
Clarence A. Bettman.[22] The surgery, a relatively simple fifteen-minute
procedure, was resisted by Bettman's wife on the grounds that her husband
was unaware of his condition and incapable of making a decision. Court
authorization for the surgery was requested because Mr Bettman, according to hospital sources, was 'factually incompetent'.

* Since that time, all legislative prohibitions of attempted suicide have been repealed in
New Jersey.

State Supreme Court Justice Gerald P. Culkin, in his ruling, ordered the hospital to 'perform whatever medical and surgical procedures are necessary to protect or sustain the health or life of Mr Bettman.' Distressed by the court order, Mrs Bettman responded: 'What has [my husband] got to live for? Nothing. He knows nothing, he has no memory whatsoever. He is turning into a vegetable. Isn't death better?'[23]

As the cases involving patient competency, blood transfusions, and religious beliefs demonstrated, the most compelling state interest for overruling an individual's wishes was preserving the sanctity of life—whatever the reasons. Such an interest also reflected the concern of several courts for the criminal and civil liability of doctors and the well-being of patients unable to give their consent to treatment.

However, during this time judicial sentiment was by no means unanimous in favour of court-ordered treatment. Between 1962 and 1974, there were eight cases in which courts upheld the right of an individual to refuse lifesaving procedures. For instance, despite the state's interest in preserving in 1962, in *Erickson* v. *Dilgard*,[24] a New York superior court refused to equate a patient's rejection of blood transfusions with suicide. Despite a 'very great chance' that the patient would die without a transfusion, the court ruled emphatically in favour of self-determination:

> It is the individual who is the subject of a medical decision who has the final say and . . . this must necessarily be so in a system of government which gives the greatest possible protection to the individual in the furtherance of his own desires.[25]

In this case, the patient was acknowledged to be competent, and religious objections were not considered an issue.

Three years later, in Illinois, the most articulate statement to date was made for another patient who resisted transfusions, in *In re Brooks*.[26] Bernice Brooks, suffering from a peptic ulcer, was a Jehovah's Witness, had no minor children, and was competent at the time of her decision to refuse blood. She had repeatedly told her personal physician that her religious convictions prevented her from having transfusions. Moreover, she had signed a release which absolved the hospital and her doctor from liability.

Still, the lower court appointed a conservator for the patient, and blood was subsequently transferred. However, on appeal, the reviewing court dismissed the lower court's petition and nullified all orders in the conservatorship proceeding, stating that they violated the patient's right to free exercise of religion. The higher court—refusing to invoke *parens patriae*, and rejecting the hospital's argument that the statutory proscription against suicide was being violated—met the issue squarely. It upheld the patient's refusal of a transfusion:

Applying the constitutional guarantees and the interpretation thereof
. . . to the facts before us, we find a competent adult who has steadfastly
maintained her belief that acceptance of a blood transfusion is a violation
of the law of God. Knowing full well the hazards involved, she has firmly
opposed acceptance of such transfusions, notifying the doctor and hospital of her convictions and desires, and executing documents releasing
both the doctor and hospital from any civil liability which might be
thought to result from a failure on the part of either to administer such
transfusions. No minor children are involved. No overt or affirmative
act of the appellant offers any clear and present danger to society—we
have only a governmental agency compelling conduct offensive to appellant's religious beliefs. Even though we may consider appellant's beliefs
unwise, foolish or ridiculous, in the absence of an overriding danger to
society, we may not permit interference therewith in the form of a conservatorship established in the waning hours of her life for the sole purpose of compelling her to accept medical treatment forbidden by her
religious principles. . . . In the final analysis, what has happened here
involves a judicial attempt to decide what course of action is best for a
particular individual, notwithstanding that individual's contrary views
based on religious convictions. Such action cannot be constitutionally
countenanced.[27]

In the same manner, in Dade County, Florida, in 1971, a dying woman,
Carmen Martinez, won the right to halt further treatment. Afflicted with a
fatal form of haemolytic anaemia, Mrs Martinez, the hospital maintained,
would die without surgical removal of her spleen and additional transfusions that had to be forced into her withered veins by painful surgical
incisions. Mrs Martinez begged to have all forms of treatment discontinued, saying she preferred death. 'Please don't torture me any more,'
she pleaded.[28]
Her doctor brought the case to court, fearing he would be charged with
assisting a suicide if he granted Mrs Martinez's requests on the one hand,
or treating a patient against her will on the other. Circuit Court Judge
David Popper, while acknowledging that the law clearly opposes suicide,
also observed that 'Mrs Martinez's treatment seems as bad as her disease.'
Ultimately, he held, the sanctity of life is not seriously endangered when
dying patients choose a peaceful death over a prolonged life of physical pain
and mental anguish. Thus the state was not justified in invading a patient's
right to privacy. 'I can't decide whether she should live or die; that's up to
God,' Potter said. 'But a person has a right not to suffer pain. A person has
the right to die in dignity.' He concluded that it was not in the interest of
justice for a court to order a patient to be kept alive against her will.[29] Mrs

Martinez died twenty-four hours after the court ruling, 'quietly and without pain'.[30]

A New York court the same year, in *Winters* v. *Miller*,[31] supported the beliefs held by a fifty-nine-year-old woman and ruled that such beliefs must be respected by the hospital, despite charges of incompetency. Rejecting *parens patriae*, the court defended the patient's right to refuse medication, noting that any incompetence during hospitalization in no way altered previously held religious views. Weighing the state's interest against Miss Winters's, the court ruled that no clear interest of society would be substantially affected by the patient's exercise of the First Amendment right to religious freedom.[32]

Mrs Gertrude Raasch of Milwaukee also won a legal battle concerning refusal of treatment.[33] Having spent seventeen years in and out of hospitals and nursing homes, she had undergone two major operations for gangrene of the leg. When doctors insisted that amputation was necessary for survival, Mrs Raasch withheld her consent, claiming that she would rather die.

The hospital, applying for a court-appointed guardian, argued that Mrs Raasch was mentally incompetent and therefore incapable of deciding whether surgery was appropriate. However, Judge Michael T. Sullivan, hearing testimony from her hospital bed, ruled that Mrs Raasch had the right to refuse the operation, even though it meant death from gangrene. 'There is absolutely no evidence of incompetence,' he said. 'Mrs Raasch knew what was being asked and she did not want the operation. . . . It is not the prerogative of this court to make decisions for adult, competent citizens, even decisions relating to life or death.'

Also in Milwaukee in 1972, the nephew of Delores Phelps, applying for guardianship, asked that the court recognize the hospital's right to administer blood transfusions to his aunt, despite her apparent opposition. At a hearing at the bedside of the comatose and terminal patient, a judge heard evidence of Mrs Phelps's earlier assertion to the staff that, as a Jehovah's Witness, she would not consent to transfusions. She had also signed a 'release for refusal to permit procedure.'

Mrs Phelps's adult son testified that he and his father were in agreement with the refusal. The court concluded that no evidence of mental illness had been presented; that Mrs Phelps was sincere in her religious beliefs; and that while the court itself preferred to order the transfusion, it 'cannot use a guardian device in order to foist its own personal opinions upon an adult competent citizen.'[34] Mrs Phelps's nephew's petition was thus denied. Mrs Phelps died the following day of massive gastrointestinal bleeding. She was forty-one years old.

In Pennsylvania in 1973, in an intriguing decision, the court upheld sixty-year-old Maida Yetter's right to refuse surgery, defending the decision of a 'mature, competent adult', despite the fact that Mrs Yetter was a patient at Allentown State Hospital, suffering from schizophrenia.[35] She refused surgery for breast cancer, claiming that her aunt had died of similar surgery. In a seven-page opinion, Northampton County Judge Alfred T. Williams said:

> the constitutional right to privacy includes the right of a mature, competent adult to refuse to accept medical recommendations that may prolong one's life and which, to a third person at least, appear to be in his best interests; in short, that the right of privacy includes a right to die with which the state should not interfere where there are no minor or unborn children and no clear and present danger to public health, welfare, or morals. [Emphasis added.][36]

In an equally intriguing case, in Washington, D.C., the following year, a superior court upheld a woman's right to refuse a blood transfusion, even though the woman was nine months pregnant. Thirty-year-old Patricia Bently requested that her seven-days-overdue baby be delivered by caesarian section, but doctors at Washington, D.C., General Hospital refused to perform the operation when Miss Bently would not consent to blood transfusions. Refusing to invoke parens patriae, Judge Alfred Burke ruled, after eight hours of medical and legal testimony: 'The court finds, with great sorrow, that the mother does have a right to die.'[37] Happily, Miss Bently gave birth by caesarian section the following day and there were no complications.

AN ANALYSIS

The preceding cases demonstrate the courts' efforts to weigh and balance states' interests against individual liberties. The doctrine of informed consent, reflecting profound legal concern for bodily integrity and self-determination, has not been impervious to judicial intervention, as shown. Between 1962 and 1974, there was widespread support for such intervention when the patient had minor or unborn children (Bently being the notable exception); the state had an important, overriding interest both in avoiding an economic burden and in protecting the physical and emotional well-being of a youngster.

However, beyond that, attitudes towards compelled treatment varied greatly. On the one hand, some sources regarded the state's interests in preserving life as too chimerical to justify interference with an adult's private choices. Other courts regarded imposition of lifesaving measures as not only permissible but desirable. According to this view, the state's interest in preserving life—even by overriding private choice—is real and compelling.

For instance, in *Georgetown College*, the court concluded that the patient did express a desire to live—despite refusal of blood—because she had submitted herself to the hospital's care. It further feared that a refusal to order transfusions would expose the medical staff to liability.

However, the court failed to acknowledge that the patient's submission to treatment was conditional and explicitly so; Releases *had* been given to the hospital and its staff. The sole factor not in dispute was the woman's duty to her minor child. More judicial consideration should have been given (as the *Phelps* case demonstrated) to subordination of the desire for treatment and life to religious convictions.* Although Judge Wright conceded that 'Death to Mrs Jones was not a religiously-commanded goal, but an unwanted side-effect of a religious scruple,' such an observation led to his conclusion that, above all, 'Mrs Jones wanted to live.'[39]

In *Kennedy Hospital* v. *Heston*, the New Jersey Supreme Court went even further, arguing that there is no difference between suicide and passive submission to death. The flaw, of course, is that (as in *Georgetown*) a Jehovah's Witness, in passively allowing death by refusing a transfusion, lacks the intent to die; death is not the objective but instead an unwanted consequence of refusal. Furthermore, the law generally treats nonfeasance (passive acceptance) differently from misfeasance (active causing of a reprehended result). Nonfeasance engages no liability normally, and it frequently arises where there is no duty to act otherwise, and where death is not an inevitable consequence at any rate.[40]

Prior to *Heston*, the courts upheld statutes against such religious practices as polygamy and snake handling (a religious ritual), invoking the police power of the state to protect public health, welfare, or morals.[41] However, the state supreme court in *Heston*, in going beyond the public defence concept, was specifically concerned with protecting an individual from her own *in*action. Religious beliefs were subjected to governmental restriction, with essentially no real showing of governmental interest. Invocation of *parens patriae* hardly substitutes for reason in preserving life at the expense of religious freedom.[42] (As stated, for six years, Delores Heston carried in her wallet a card that explicitly spelled out her desire not to receive blood. This fact, together with the affidavits of her mother, her minister, and herself, left little doubt that she had completely and competently withheld her consent prior to the accident.[43])

In contrast, in *In re Brooks*, the court displayed a more reasonable approach by determining the competency of the patient *at the time the consent was initially withheld*, not at the time the transfusion was to be made.

---

* Notably, the case, which influenced so many other decisions, was not decided on by a majority of the court. The order was granted by a circuit judge on oral petition. The petition for hearing *en banc* was simply denied. The United States Supreme Court also refused to hear the case.[38]

Like Mrs Martinez, Mrs Brooks was elderly. In both cases the courts maintained that the sanctity of life is not challenged by a dying patient's choice of a peaceful death over a prolonged life of physical pain or mental anguish. As the Illinois court observed in *Brooks*: 'Courts may decide whether the public welfare is jeopardized by acts done or omitted because of religious beliefs; but they have nothing to do with determining the reasonableness of that belief.'[44] Their conclusion? That a competent adult may refuse to act for religious reasons as long as the 'refusal to act is not directly harmful to society.'[45] Thus the *Brooks* decision (like *Winters*) dealt directly with the First Amendment infringement, which *Heston* failed to do, resorting instead to the shibboleth of *parens patriae*.

*Heston* is factually similar to *Phelps*, but diametrically opposed in its holding. The New Jersey court rejected claims of Miss Heston's competency despite substantial evidence confirming and validating her choice, while the Wisconsin court inferred from Mrs Phelps's previous statements and a signed release that her decision to refuse treatment was the product of a sound mind. As in *Brooks*, the patient's religious beliefs were honoured. In the same vein, the judge in *Raasch* took pains to determine the patient's previous wishes, ultimately rejecting incompetency and defending Mrs Raasch's right to refuse further treatment.

Similarly, the *Yetter* and *Bettman* cases are factually alike—as are the *Bently* and *Anderson*—yet contradictory in their holdings. Because Clarence Bettman was declared incompetent, the New York court insisted on protecting his life; with Maida Yetter, despite a clinical diagnosis of schizophrenia, a Pennsylvania court defended her ability to make a 'competent' choice.

In the most startling contrast, Mrs Anderson, eight months pregnant, was forced to undergo a blood transfusion despite religious objections because of the state's compelling interest in the welfare of her unborn child. Patricia Bently, on the other hand, gave birth without transfusions, the court insisting on her right to refuse treatment—even at the risk of death, and regardless of risks to the baby.

Such confusion of case law underscored the need for guidelines, since the courts provided no guidance about individual autonomy regarding one's own life. Contradictions only confounded the issue of when a person can refuse lifesaving treatment. Would the courts force an individual to live or allow him to die? The answer to this critical question awaited each new case. The role of the physician was hardly enviable, either: Should he choose to end a life (even by request), he was not protected. Should he insist on continuing treatment without consent, he was, at least theoretically, equally liable. As shown in the above cases, some courts stressed the importance of protecting the physician by asserting an overriding state interest, while others zealously defended the right of self-determination even if it resulted in death.

Such a conflict—weighing an individual's rights against those of society—would persist. With every case potentially dealing with the issue of whether a constitutional right to die existed, the United States Supreme Court denied 'certiorari', the right to review a case in the country's highest court, thus denying society a binding standard that lower courts would follow.

## QUINLAN AND AFTER

## 1975–76

It all started simply enough. In mid-April 1975, Karen Ann Quinlan, twenty-one, took drugs and alcohol on an empty stomach. As reviewed earlier, within hours she lapsed into a coma, from which she would never recover. Her condition was described as a 'chronic persistent vegetative state', meaning that the brain stem and the lower parts of her brain were still functional, but the 'sapient' functions—the cerebral lobes and cortex—were irreversibly damaged. Because she did not meet the Harvard criteria for brain death, the question was whether she could be taken off the ventilator—even though there was no question of her meeting requirements for death either legally or according to existing ethical standards.

A lawsuit arose in which Joseph Quinlan, Karen's father, asked to be appointed his daughter's guardian so that the court would grant him 'the expressed power of authorizing the discontinuance of all extraordinary means of sustaining the vital processes of his daughter, Karen Ann Quinlan.'[46] However, Judge Robert Muir of the Morristown, New Jersey, Superior Court, refused Mr Quinlan's request on the grounds that:

1. The judicial power to act in the incompetent's best interest in this instance selects continued life and to do so is not violative of a constitutional right.

2. There is a duty to continue the life-assisting apparatus, if within the treating physician's opinion, it should be done.

3. There is no constitutional right to die that can be asserted by a parent for his incompetent adult child.

4. Continuation of medical treatment, in whatever form, where its goal is the sustenance of life, is not something degrading, arbitrarily inflicted, unacceptable to contemporary society or unnecessary.

5. The court does not consider the 'extraordinary' versus 'ordinary' discussion viable legal distinctions.

6. Humanitarian motives cannot justify the taking of a human life.

7. The fact that the victim is on the threshold of death or in terminal condition is no defence to a homicide charge.

8. A patient is placed, or places himself, in the care of a physician with the expectation that he (the physician) will do everything in his power, everything that is known to modern medicine, to protect the patient's life. He will do all within his human power to favour life against death.

9. The precedential effect on future litigation of granting the Quinlans' request would be legally detrimental.[47]

The case was then appealed to the New Jersey Supreme Court in 1976.[48] The main argument was based on Karen Quinlan's right to privacy, asserted on her behalf by her guardian. Opposition—represented by her doctors, the hospital, the Morris County prosecutor, the State of New Jersey, and her guardian *ad litem*—held that removal from the respirator would not conform to the customary medical standards and practices that guide physicians.

Part of the argument for removal of therapy was that if Karen Quinlan were miraculously lucid for a time and aware of her condition she would decide to discontinue the therapy, even if it meant death. The argument also included the point that continuation of treatment represented a judicial intrusion into the personal decision-making of the patient. Further, the attorney for Mr Quinlan emphasized the difference between this case and previous ones, in which the state had intervened in order to compel patients to receive blood transfusions against their will. In those cases, he argued, the procedure constituted only a 'minimal bodily invasion' and the chances of recovery were 'very good'; however, in the Quinlan case, there was much more pronounced bodily invasion and a dimmer prognosis. Hence, the individual's right to privacy was greater.[49]

Chief Justice C. E. Hughes, rejecting the arguments that First Amendment rights and Eighth Amendment protection against cruel and unusual punishment were impinged upon, ruled that the constitutional right to privacy *did* include the right to refuse treatment, thus overturning the lower court decision. Drawing on a 1965 case, he stated:

> The Court in *Griswold* found the unwritten constitutional right to privacy to exist in the penumbra of specific guarantees of the Bill of Rights formed by emanations from those guarantees. . . . We have concluded that Karen's right of privacy may be asserted on her behalf by her guardian under the peculiar circumstances here present. . . . One would have to think that the use of the same respirator or like support could be considered 'ordinary' in the context of the forced sustaining by cardio-respiratory processes of an irreversibly-doomed patient. . . . [Furthermore] there is a real and in this case determinative distinction between the unlawful taking of the life of another and the ending of artificial life-support systems as a matter of self-determination. . . . Upon

the concurrence of the guardian and family of Karen, should the responsible attending physicians conclude that there is no reasonable possibility of Karen's ever emerging from her present comatose condition to a cognitive, sapient state and that the life-support apparatus now being administered to Karen should be discontinued, they shall consult with the hospital 'Ethics Committee' or like body of the institution in which Karen is then hospitalized.[50]

Thus *Quinlan* is significant for: (1) extending the constitutional right to privacy to include the decision to end life-sustaining medical care, in this case through proxy consent; (2) indicating a judicial willingness to alter traditional concepts of compelling state interest in preserving life; (3) recognizing the quality and visibility of life in the context of rejecting treatment; (4) distinguishing between suicide and the passive withdrawal of life supports; and (5) extending the concept of immunity to the doctors treating Karen Quinlan. Where the patient's family and doctors concur, the court held, application to the courts to confirm such decisions—'impossibly cumbersome'—should not generally be made; such a decision necessarily involves the physician's expertise, and the patient-family-doctor relationship is grounded in tradition and the expectations of the patient. However, the court emphasized the importance of hospital ethics committees to oversee such decision-making.

In Massachusetts the Supreme Judicial Court dealt with a legally incompetent patient who was terminally ill and for whom there was a possibility of providing life-prolonging treatment.[51] Joseph Saikewicz was a sixty-seven-year-old mentally retarded man who was able to communicate only through gestures and physical contact. He had an IQ of ten and a mental age of two years and eight months. Afflicted with acute myeloblastic leukemia, Saikewicz would live, according to doctors, only weeks or months and probably without great pain or suffering. With chemotherapy, there was a 30 to 50 per cent chance of remission for two to fifteen months, although such a treatment would have produced considerable suffering and side effects. Furthermore, Saikewicz would be unlikely to understand the nature of the treatment and it was speculated that it would be difficult for him to cooperate.

The Massachusetts probate court, taking all this into consideration, had recommended that such treatment would not be in Saikewicz's interest, ruling that an individual's right to privacy, even if not exercised by the patient, was more important than the state's interest in protecting life. In its decision, the court also noted the patient's age, the pain, the low likelihood of remission, and the quality of life available to Mr Saikewicz even if the treatment was successful.

On appeal, the supreme court supported the lower court's decision not to treat, but rejected the notion of quality of life as a basis for decision-making, stating that the value of life under law has no relation to intelligence or social position.* Instead, the court based its decision on a balance of prospective benefit against pain and suffering, and the belief that it was in the patient's best interests and preferences not to treat. Like the *Quinlan* case, emphasis was on patient autonomy, with decision-making based on the needs and wants of the person involved—or substituted judgment. Thus the question of what a reasonable person (or the majority of people) would do in these circumstances was not considered, but rather what this *particular person* would do, if he or she were aware of living in the particular situation.

The *Saikewicz* decision departed from the *Quinlan* in its insistence that the ultimate authority in such matters should be the courts.

> such questions of life and death seem to us to require the process of detached but passionate investigation and decision that forms the ideal on which the judicial branch of government was created. Achieving this ideal is our responsibility and that of the lower court, and is not to be entrusted to any other group purporting to represent the 'morality and conscious of our society,' no matter how highly motivated or impressively constituted.[52]

Unlike *Quinlan*, whatever the family of a patient wanted or what an ethics committee recommended would have to be judicially weighed.

## 1977

In three cases in 1977, courts allowed patients to be disconnected from life-support systems. In Tennessee, a lower (chancery) court judge, saying that Della Dockery, 'may be in a state worse than death', ruled that her doctors could legally remove her from life-sustaining devices that had kept her alive for months.[53] The forty-six-year-old patient had been in a coma for nearly a year after suffering a heart attack and massive brain damage. Her family had filed suit seeking legal permission to disconnect Mrs Dockery from her respirator, claiming that for all practical purposes she was dead.[54]

In Wisconsin, an eighteen-year-old brain-damaged patient at University Hospital in Madison was allowed to die after a court order permitted doctors to remove mechanical life supports.[55] The judge maintained that although Wisconsin had no statutory definition of death, he would not apply the common-law standard that defined death only as the point at which all circulation and respiration had ended. 'I will accept and adopt

---

* The court promised a fuller opinion at a later date. Two months later Saikewicz died, apparently without pain or discomfort. A year and two months after his death, the court issued its full opinion.

total and irreversible cessation of brain activity as death,' he said, noting that with the patient, there had been no brain activity. The youth, who had suffered severe brain damage after a heart attack, was pronounced dead hours after the court's decision.

And in Massachusetts, citing the *Saikewicz* Supreme Court ruling, a probate court judge ruled that Mrs Esther Piotrowicz, who had been in a coma for nearly two years, could be removed from her respirator.[56] On the testimony of doctors who said there was no chance the woman would recover, Judge Henry Mayo gave Mrs Piotrowicz's husband, Walter, permission to have the life-support system disconnected. 'If my wife were sitting here now,' Piotrowicz said, 'I wouldn't want her to be going through what I'm going through. She looked out for me, I looked out for her.' Mrs Piotrowicz died one day after doctors, complying with the court order, disconnected her from her life-support equipment.[57]

# 1978

In 1978 in Florida, Abe Perlmutter, a competent seventy-year-old retired cabdriver, tried to remove the respirator sustaining him. As he suffered from A.L.S., or amyotrophic lateral scelerosis (Lou Gehrig's disease), Perlmutter's doctors did not expect him to live more than a few hours without the respirator—although his life expectancy with it was two years. Even though his family supported his decision, the Florida Medical Center—which monitored Perlmutter's respirator with an alarm system— refused to honour his wishes. As a result, Perlmutter petitioned the circuit court for an order restraining the hospital from continuing his life-sustaining treatment.[58]

In deciding the case, the circuit judge issued the restraining order by declaring the patient competent and defending his constitutional right to privacy: 'It is ordered and adjudged that Abe Perlmutter, in exercise of his right to privacy, may remain in defendant hospital or leave said hospital, free of the mechanical respirator now attached to his body, and all defendants and their staffs are refrained from interfering with plaintiff's decision.'[59]

Affirming the court order, the Fourth District Court of Appeal ruled that a competent patient has a constitutional right of privacy to refuse life-prolonging treatment after the prognosis of an agonizing terminal illness.[60] 'It is all very convenient,' the court noted, 'to insist on continuing Mr Perlmutter's life so that there can be no question of foul play, no resulting civil liability and no possible trespass on medical ethics. However ... such a course of conduct invades that patient's constitutional right of privacy, removes his freedom of choice, and invades his right to self-determine.'[61] Perlmutter died on October 6, 1978, with his family and his lawyer at his bedside. When the respirator was disconnected and an alarm sounded, Perlmutter's son turned the alarm off. Twenty-four hours later, the patient died.

A year after Perlmutter's death, the Supreme Court of Florida, in a 6–0 ruling, adopted the opinion of the district court.[62] Equating the act (disconnecting the respirator) with a passive act of refusing surgery, the court held that only intentional death invokes the state's interest in preventing suicide.

In Massachusetts, *In re Dinnerstein*[63] shed some light on the question the *Saikewicz* case had raised: Which cases had to be submitted to courts for review, and which fell within the competence of the medical profession? Although *Dinnerstein* was not reviewed by the state supreme court (as *Saikewicz* was), the Appeals Court of Massachusetts ruled that cases like *Dinnerstein* fell within the realm of physicians and the discretion of the attending medical staff. Shirley Dinnerstein, a sixty-seven-year-old woman suffering from Alzheimer's disease and the effects of a massive stroke, was in an essentially vegetative state: immobile, speechless, unable to swallow without choking, and unable to cough. Both her son (a physician) and her daughter arued that if a cardiac or respiratory arrest occurred, no resuscitation efforts should be made. Thus the family, attending physician, and hospital joined in filing a suit to determine whether such a decision required the prior approval of the court.

The appeals court, noting an absence of any treatment capable of curing or relieving the illness (unlike *Saikewicz*, although the chemotherapy was rejected there), concluded that such cases did not need to be presented to the court. The circumstances surrounding Shirley Dinnerstein's treatment were entirely within the competence of the medical profession, to take 'measures [that] are appropriate to ease the imminent passing of an irreversibly, terminally-ill patient in light of the patient's history and condition and the wishes of her family.[64]

Also in Massachusetts, in a case reminiscent of Carmen Martinez's, the court of appeals held that an elderly woman, Rosaria Candura, did not have to have her gangrenous leg amputated, though doctors said she would die otherwise:[65] 'We hold that, on the evidence and findings on this case, Mrs Candura has not been shown to be legally incompetent and that her leg may not be amputated unless she herself can consent to the operation.'[66]

And in a case in Minnesota involving a brain-dead battered child, the supreme court upheld a lower court's decision to disconnect the child's respirator. District Judge Archie L. Gringold ruled that the hospital 'remains under no further obligation' to continue life support; after the supreme court's decision, the respirator was discontinued and the child was pronounced dead.[67]

## 1979–80

In August 1979, Brother Charles Fox, eighty-three, a member of the Catholic Order of the Society of Mary, suffered a hernia while gardening. During surgery at Nassau Hospital on Long Island, New York, he had a cardiorespiratory arrest and suffered brain-stem anoxia. He was placed on a respirator in an intensive care unit. Father Philip Eichner, a close friend of Brother Fox's, requested that the respirator be removed.

Despite two neurosurgeons' testimony that Brother Fox would never regain consciousness, the hospital refused to remove him from his life support. Consequently, Father Eichner, like Joseph Quinlan, went to court to seek appointment as representative or guardian of his friend in order to authorize removal of the respirator.[68] He predicated his petition on Fox's constitutional right to privacy.

The trial court, accepting testimony that Brother Fox would never regain 'cognitive functioning', granted Father Eichner's petition. It ruled that, were Fox competent, he would order the respirator disconnected.* It found that Brother Fox was entitled to have the life supports discontinued on the common law right of bodily self-determination, and that Father Eichner, as his committee, could exercise that right for him. The court also echoed the *Saikewicz* standard, stating that enlightened decisions favoured significant judicial involvement. The lower court found no constitutional right of bodily self-determination.

However, the district attorney, Dennis Dillon, appealed the case, and while the appeal was being considered, on January 24, 1980, Brother Fox died of congestive heart failure. The appellate division of the state supreme court refused to rule the case moot or find lack of jurisdiction, since Father Eichner sought relief, and the court held that this type of case was likely to recur.[70] Under Justice Milton Moller, the court asserted the right of a comatose, terminally ill patient to stop life-support systems; unlike the lower court, it found 'sufficient State action to invoke the right to privacy embodied in the Fourteenth Amendment,'[71] thereby upholding the constitutional right to privacy: 'This constitutional right coexists with the common law right of bodily self-determination and even though the rights afforded by each are distinct, they produce the same results.'[72] Using the principle of substituted judgment, the court upheld decision-making by the patient's guardian, based on the patient's 'actual interests and preferences', and an assumption that 'the patient would have wanted it that way.'[73]

---

* Eichner stated that Fox had previously expressed the wish that if his brain were incapable of rational, sapient thought, life supports should be discontinued and nature allowed to take its course.[69]

However, the New York Court of Appeals, the state's highest court, disagreed with much of the appellate division's ruling.[74] Instead of accepting the constitutional right to privacy and substituted judgment, the court of appeals argued that the right to refuse treatment was a common law right, and could be exercised by incompetents only if there was clear and convincing proof of the patient's previous wishes—as there was in Fox's case. Unlike the lower court, the higher court reserved judgment about the extent or wisdom of judicial intervention, insisting instead that 'if it is desirable to enlarge the role of the courts in [such] cases ... by establishing ... a mandatory procedure of successive approvals by physicians, hospital personnel, relatives, and the courts, the change should come from the Legislature.'[75]

In 1980, in *Leach* v. *Akron General Medical Center*,[76] the court continued the trend of allowing the removal of life supports from an incompetent, terminally ill person. Afflicted with A.L.S., Lou Gehrig's disease, seventy-year-old Edna Marie Leach suffered a cardiac arrest at Akron General Medical Center and fell into a semicomatose, chronic vegetative state. Her husband petitioned the court for guardianship, requesting that Mrs Leach be taken off her respirator. The court, relying on the *Quinlan* and *Eichner* decisions, upheld Mr Leach's request on the basis of the constitutional right to privacy. Recognizing that the patient (like Karen Quinlan) was not brain-dead, the court commented that 'the basic question is how long will society require Mrs Leach and others similarly situated to remain on the threshold of certain death suspended and sustained there by artificial life-supports.'[77]

Differing from *Quinlan*, however, the court did not rely on substituted judgment. Instead, it felt it had sufficiently established that Mrs Leach, while competent, expressed her preferences as to medical treatment; therefore, self-determination was promoted by allowing the guardian to implement her wishes.[78] Ignoring the issue of whether a judicial intervention was necessary, the court recommended procedures to be followed before life supports can be disconnected: physician's certification of the patient's continuing vegetative state; forty-eight-hour notice of the doctor's examination to coroner and prosecutor; and forty-eight-hour notice, after the examination, of the act of discontinuation, also to coroner and prosecutor.[79] Moreover, the court maintained, to ensure that a patient's wishes were absolutely in favour of discontinuing treatment, the evidence reflecting these wishes must be 'clear and convincing'.[80]

In a subsequent case, described as 'see-saw', three Massachusetts courts debated the fate of Earle N. Spring, a seventy-eight-year-old senile patient dependent on haemodialysis to keep him alive. Although dialysis stabilized Spring's end-stage kidney disease, his dementia worsened until he could no longer recognize his family and began resisting medical care. (Doctors controlled his hostile behaviour with sedatives.) Spring's wife and his son (who became his father's temporary guardian) petitioned the probate court to end dialysis.[81] Although attending doctors said that the patient would die without these treatments, Mrs Spring and her son argued that were he competent, Spring would want no more dialysis even if it meant death. In opposition, a court-appointed guardian *ad litem* argued that there was no evidence to support the inference that Spring wanted dialysis continued.*

Relying in part on the *Saikewicz* decision, Franklin County Probate Court Judge Sanford Keedy reaffirmed that the right of competent persons to refuse medical treatment in appropriate circumstances (based on the constitutional right to privacy) can be equally extended to incompetent persons in Massachusetts.[82] Also, citing the court's ability to 'don the mental mantle of the incompetent', Keedy invoked the doctrine of substituted judgment, especially as influenced by the family and the doctor: 'The decision of the family, particularly where that decision is in accord with the recommendation of the attending physician, is of particular importance ... as evidence of the decision the patient himself would make in the circumstances.'[83]

On appeal (initiated by the guardian *ad litem*), the intermediate appellate court upheld the lower court's ruling, reaffirming that the probate judge had acted in Spring's interest by delegating the treatment decision to the patient's family, physician, and guardian.[84] However, the supreme judicial court reversed, stressing: 'We disapprove shifting of the ultimate decision-making responsibility away from the duly-established courts of proper jurisdiction'; the guardian *ad litem*'s contention that Spring had *not* been evaluated incompetent prompted the court to order a thorough examination of the patient's competence.[85] Unlike Quinlan, Saikewicz, and others, Spring was conscious and able to communicate. However, shortly after dialysis was resumed, in April 1980, Earle Spring died of cardiorespiratory failure.

Although the supreme court addressed the need for a court order in such cases, it took pains to list circumstances taken into account when deciding whether application for a court order is necessary before discontinuing treatment for incompetent patients—thus implying that not all cases need to be presented for judicial review:

The extent of impairment of the patient's mental faculties, whether the patient is in custody of a State institution, the prognosis without the pro-

---

* In cases like *Spring*, the probate court appoints temporary guardians in emergency situations to avoid a particular harm to an incompetent's person or property, whereas the court appoints guardians *ad litem* to enforce or defend the legal rights of an incompetent in court proceedings.

posed treatment, the prognosis with the proposed treatment, the complexity, risk and novelty of the proposed treatment, its possible side effects, the patient's level of understanding and probable reaction, the urgency of decision, the consent of the patient, spouse, or guardian, the good faith of those who participate in the decision, the clarity of professional opinion as to what is good medical practice, the interest of third persons, and the administrative requirements of any institution involved.[86]

While noting that action taken without prior judicial approval may be subject to criminal or civil liability, the court went on to say that the absence of judicial approval does not necessarily result in automatic liability. Without eliminating this risk altogether, the court did acknowledge the value of private decision-making. Specifically, when family, guardian, and physician agree that the patient would refuse treatment if competent, the courts should expressly empower physicians to end treatment without 'antecedent judicial authorization', thus expediting the exercise of the incompetent's right to refuse medical care.[87]

In a similar ruling, which stressed the importance of judicial review, the Delaware Supreme Court ruled that a chancery (lower) court has the power to authorize disconnecting life supports for a comatose, incompetent patient—although it pointed out that there is no legislation that clearly addresses the matter.[88] In 1980, Mary Severns, who suffered massive brain damage in an automobile accident, lay in a coma. As in the Leach case, the patient's husband, William Severns, petitioned the lower court for guardianship so that he could consent to discontinuing his wife's life-support systems. Both the hospital and a guardian *ad litem* for Mrs Severns opposed that petition. At the request of all three parties, the chancery court asked the state supreme court to hear the evidence and decide whose jurisdiction was appropriate.

Relying primarily on *Quinlan*, *Spring*, and *Eichner*, the supreme court ruled that until the legislature had provided more specific guidelines, the lower (in this case, chancery) court not only had the right to appoint a guardian for Mrs Severns, but also could empower the guardian to withdraw lifesaving treatment: 'We are satisfied that the Court of Chancery has the power, indeed, it has the duty, to grant appropriate relief based on the invocation and establishment of constitutional rights.' Moreover, decision-making should not be based on the 'stipulation of the parties'; instead, there must be a 'full evidentiary hearing.'[89]

## 1981

In a case reminiscent of *Saikewicz*, the New York Court of Appeals considered whether a profoundly retarded terminally ill patient—incapable of giving consent—should submit to medical procedures that might prolong but not save his life.[90] (The court examined the case together with that of Brother Fox and the two became companion pieces, although, significantly, each proceeded from separate principles and led to different results.) John Storar, fifty-two, a resident of the Newark Development Center, was diagnosed as having cancer of the bladder. Unlike Saikewicz, Storar had a mother, who, as his legal guardian, gave doctors permission to administer blood transfusions to replace blood loss related to the bladder cancer.

However, a month later, Mrs Storar asked that the transfusions be discontinued. The director of the medical centre refused, petitioning the court for authorization to continue treatment. At the hearing, it was established (and not disputed) that: John Storar found the transfusions disagreeable (he had to be sedated and restrained before treatment), he could not understand what was happening to him, and even with the transfusions, he would live only three to six months. Without the transfusions, he would eventually bleed to death. Mrs Storar argued that she believed her son would want the transfusions stopped. The lower court, upholding her right to decide for her son, sanctioned the withholding of further transfusions. The appellate division also upheld Mrs Storar's right to decide, reasoning that application of the substituted judgment standard permitted her to exercise the right to end treatment on her son's behalf.

However, the New York Court of Appeals reversed, insisting that the transfusions be administered in spite of Mrs Storar's objections.[91] Although the court noted that an incompetent person has the right to refuse medical procedures, it maintained that the common-law right to decline treatment presented several analytical difficulties. Arguing that such a right could be honoured only if there was proof of such a belief *prior* to incompetency,* the court found the self-determination principles applied in *Eichner* not relevant. Since, as it reasoned, Storar had always possessed the mentality of an infant, the court concluded that it was therefore unrealistic to try to determine what he would have wanted. With infant status, while a parent had the right to consent to or refuse treatment, the state, as *parens patriae*, can impose limitations on that right in protecting the health and welfare of children.[92] Further, although Storar's bladder cancer was incurable, the blood transfusion could counteract loss of blood, and therefore was 'necessary to prevent death'.[93] The court would not address the question of whether suffering induced by the treatments would change or affect the results: 'Whether the presence or absence of excessive pain would be determinative with respect to the continuation of a life-sustaining measure need not be reached under the facts of this case.'[94]

* Not unlike *Leach*, the court ruled that the appropriate burden of proof is shown by clear and convincing evidence, i.e., a decision to end treatment made *before* becoming incompetent.

In a subsequent case in California, on the other hand, the wishes of a competent patient who wanted no further treatment were honoured.[95] Here there was clear and convincing proof of the patient's wishes. William Foster, suffering from A.L.S., Lou Gehrig's disease, asked the hospital to disconnect his life-support system so that he could die naturally. The hospital refused to take any action until ordered to do so by a federal court. Before that could occur, however, Foster suffered a heart attack and lapsed into a coma. As a matter of law, the court concluded that the plaintiff's last wishes as a competent adult should be upheld. Acknowledging that further application of extraordinary treatment constituted an invasion of Foster's constitutional rights of self-dignity, privacy, and liberty, the court also observed that any guardian *ad litem* appointed would have to argue for disconnecting the respirator, since he would be bound to make a substitute decision for the plaintiff 'consistent with his wishes'.[96]

# 1981–83

In a far more intricate case, also in California, two physicians were charged with murder for discontinuing mechanical ventilation and intravenous fluids for a patient.[97] Clarence Herbert, a fifty-five-year-old security guard, had an ileostomy in May 1981, to correct an intestinal obstruction. In the recovery room, he suffered cardiopulmonary arrest and never regained consciousness. Three days later, Herbert's physicians judged his condition 'hopeless'; the patient remained comatose, unable to move and with impaired brain-stem function. His wife and eight children indicated that they wanted all machines taken off that were sustaining life, wishes consistent with Herbert's previous statement that he did not want to be kept alive by artificial life supports. When the respirator was removed, Herbert remained comatose although he continued to breathe. Five days after the arrest, the family agreed with doctors that intravenous fluids be discontinued. Herbert died six days later.

Subsequently, Herbert's two attending physicians—Robert Nedjl and Neil Barber—were charged with murder for taking a severely brain-damaged comatose patient off a respirator and cutting off intravenous feeding. The prosecution alleged that the physicians murdered the patient to disguise malpractice and to save money for a prepaid health plan. Nedjl and Barber claimed that they were following the wishes of a family in a case of irreversible coma.

After a preliminary pretrial hearing, a magistrate dismissed the charges in March 1983. On May 5, a superior court reinstated them. In October, the court of appeals dismissed the charges and the prosecution decided not to appeal. Refusing to distinguish between the use of a respirator and intravenous feeding tubes (and citing the President's Commission Report), the court argued that the distinction between mechanical life supports and intravenous nutrition in such cases 'seems to be based more on the emotional symbolism of providing food and water to those incapable of providing for themselves rather than on any rational difference.... *Medical* nutrition and hydration may not always provide net benefits to patients.'[98] Nedjl and Barber, it held, had participated in withdrawing 'heroic' life supports, which constituted not an affirmative act but an omission of further treatment, considered useless by the physicians, who in turn were guided by Herbert's previous wishes and those of his surrogate: 'There was evidence that Mr Herbert had, prior to his incapacitation, expressed to his wife his feeling that he would not want to be kept alive by machines.... The family made its decision together ... after consultation with the doctors.'[99]

Echoing the *Quinlan* decision that judicial intervention can be 'impossibly cumbersome', the court noted the absence of legislative guidance in such matters, or 'the gap between the statutory law and recent medical developments.'[100] With such a gap, it concluded, physicians and patients' families are called upon to make uniquely painful and personal decisions in an area that provokes an uneasy challenge, as observed in *Severns*.

> Now ... we are on the threshold of a new terrain—the penumbra where death begins but life, in some form, continues. We have been led to it by the medical miracles which now compel us to distinguish between 'death', as we have known it, and death in which the body lives in some fashion but the brain (or a significant part of it) does not.[101]

## 1983–84

In two thoughtful decisions in 1983 and 1984, the state of Washington Supreme Court ruled in the cases of two patients, one formerly competent and one severely retarded.[102] In *Welfare of Colyer*, the court allowed the patient's guardian/husband to assert Bertha Colyer's right to refuse life-sustaining treatment. Mrs Colyer had been admitted to the hospital with a cardiopulmonary arrest; three weeks later, in a special *en banc* hearing, the supreme court (with two judges assenting)* sustained the trial court in allowing her life supports to be removed. (The patient was diagnosed as irreversibly comatose and unable to breathe on her own.) Mrs Colyer died shortly after.

In an opinion subsequent to the court order, the supreme court reaffirmed Mrs Colyer's right to refuse life-sustaining treatment based on her common-law right to be free from bodily invasion and her constitutional right to privacy. Balancing a patient's right to refuse treatment with countervailing state interests, the court (citing *Quinlan* and *Saikewicz*) held that

* Dissenting Judge Dore pointed out that the whole question was decided too precipitously, arguing that a minimum of 120 days should elapse before treatment is withdrawn.[103]

judicial intervention is unnecessary when physicians agree on the patient's prognosis and a close family member as guardian asserts the rights of the incompetent patient. Yet, departing from *Quinlan*, the supreme court rejected the suggestion that a hospital ethics committee oversee the accuracy of diagnosis, noting specifically: 'the concept of an ethics committee has been criticized for its amorphous character, for its use of nonmedical personnel to reach a medical decision, and for its bureaucratic intermeddling.'[104] (The dissenting judge disagreed here, preferring the diverse membership of an ethics committee.) Instead, the court recommended the unanimous confirmation of a prognosis board (consisting of the patient's physician and two others).

Where there has been disagreement among those physicians or among family members as to the patient's wishes, the court ruled that judicial intervention is necessary—as it is when there is no family member to serve as guardian, when motives counter to the patient's best interest surface, or when the patient has always been incompetent and his wishes cannot be ascertained from any previous behaviour.[105] Thus *Colyer* avoided the extreme position that court approval had to be sought in every case involving the cessation of treatment for incompetents.

Shortly after *Colyer*, the Washington Supreme Court was confronted with a case that required the 'detached opinion of the judiciary.'[106] In *In re Hamlin*, a treatment decision was required for a severely retarded blind man in a vegetative state. Like *Saikewicz*, the patient had always been incompetent, and there was no immediate family to serve as guardian. Following their reasoning in the previous case, the court ruled that judicial involvement, if partial, may indeed be adequate to prevent abuses: (1) Since a court must be involved in the appointment of a guardian in this type of case, it 'need not always be involved in the actual substantive decision,' and (2) if the attending physicians, prognosis committee, and guardian agree that life supports should be withheld or withdrawn, no court order is necessary unless there has been a conflict in the decision-making process.[107]

## 1984

In a similarly straightforward case—*John F. Kennedy Memorial Hospital* v. *Bludworth*—in which *Colyer* and the prognosis panel concept were cited, the Florida Supreme Court upheld the right of a formerly competent patient to refuse life supports.[108] At the time of his admission to the hospital, Francis Landy was permanently brain-damaged and unable to speak. However, several years earlier, Landy had signed a Living Will. His wife, who delivered the directive to hospital physicians, asked that all extraordinary means of treatment be discontinued. Subsequently, the hospital filed suit for a declaratory judgment, asking the court to assess its rights and liabilities in complying with Mrs Landy's request.

Relying heavily on *Perlmutter*, the court declared that requiring judicial approval for this type of case 'is too burdensome, is not necessary to protect the state's interests or the interests of the patient, and could render the right of the incompetent a nullity.'[109] Arguing that a Living Will is persuasive evidence of an incompetent patient's intention and should be given great weight by those who substitute their judgment for others, the Florida court, in a significant step, gave unqualified approval to removing the decision-making from the courts. A concept similar to the *Colyer* prognosis panel was recommended, the court requiring certification by the attending physician and two other doctors, which, together with the family's decision, would be sufficient to justify withdrawal of life supports. Such a move reflected a developing trend towards reducing restrictions in right-to-refuse-treatment cases. The decision was one of the first that expressly allowed consenting family members to exercise the patient's right on his behalf, without court appointment of a guardian.

In a case that set a life-support precedent in Minnesota, the state supreme court authorized the Hennepin County Medical Center in Minneapolis to disconnect Rudolfo Torres's respirator and allow him to die.[110] Torres, who had been hospitalized for injuries suffered in a fall, was severely brain-damaged when a restraining strap on his hospital bed choked him. On the advice of two ethics committees from outside hospitals,* the court decided to discontinue treatment. Traditionally such committees have served only to set guidelines about ending treatment for patients, or to provide guidance to them and their families when faced with such a dilemma. 'This is the first time in the United States where ethics committees have submitted an opinon in writing to the court,' commented Dr Ronald E. Cranford, co-chairman of the medical centre's biomedical ethics committee. 'This is the role that some of us envision for these committees in the future—to actively cooperate with the courts in difficult decisions.'[111] Although the court maintained that in this particular case a court order was necessary, it added, in a final footnote, that in more common cases, such orders may not be required:

At oral argument it was disclosed that on an average about ten life-support systems are disconnected weekly in Minnesota. This follows consultation between the attending doctor and the family with the approval of the hospital ethics committee. It is not intended by this opinion that a court order is required in such situation.[112]

---

* Because the hospital was negligent in the accident, a conflict of interest existed for its biomedical ethics committee; hence the need for two external committees.

And in Massachusetts, Mary Hier was a ninety-two-year-old mentally ill woman who had lived in a psychiatric hospital for fifty-seven years. Because of a hiatal hernia and a cervical diverticulum, she was unable to take food orally. Then years earlier she had had a gastrotomy, but she repeatedly removed the feeding tube, which finally necessitated another gastrotomy. The nursing home therefore applied to the court for authorization to administer psychotropic drugs (Thorazine) and to perform the needed operation, then to replace the feeding tube that Mrs Hier dislodged.[113]

The probate judge, confirming the patient's incompetence, authorized administration of Thorazine, but would not authorize the operation, arguing on the basis of substituted judgment. He concluded that were she competent, Mrs Hier would consent to the drugs but not the operation: She had already indicated her opposition, and her prognosis was poor, irrespective of whether the gastrotomy was performed or not.

The appeals court affirmed, observing that although the patient's expressions of opposition could not be given legal effect because of her incompetency, they were nevertheless taken into account.[114] Further, the court differentiated between supplying nutritional support with 'only modest intrusiveness and supplying it through the use of the highly intrusive surgical procedures' that were proposed. (Notably, a month after the appellate decision, on new medical evidence a gastrotomy was performed.)

In a poignant case in California in 1984, William Bartling, who was competent and wanted to be removed from a ventilator, died before his case was settled.[115] Unlike Francis Landy in *Bludworth*, whose wishes were honoured, Bartling experienced resistance to his preferences by the hospital and a lower court.

Afflicted with a minimum of four potentially fatal diseases (among them lung cancer), seventy-year-old Bartling was placed on a respirator after the collapse of a lung when a biopsy was performed. However, the respirator caused the patient discomfort and distress; he repeatedly asked to have it taken away, and several times removed it himself. As a result, his hands were tied to the sides of his bed.

Consequently, the hospital and Bartling became involved in litigation in which the hospital actively opposed following the patient's wishes. Despite lawyers' mention of similar cases (*Quinlan, Saikewicz*)—those in which courts authorized withdrawal of treatment for patients who were not terminal, comatose, or brain-dead—Superior Court Judge Lawrence Waddington supported the hospital's contention that Mr Bartling should remain on the respirator. Although Bartling's legal competency was not challenged, the doctors questioned his ability to make a meaningful decision because he reportedly vacillated between wanting to live and wanting to die. And because Bartling's physicians would not certify him terminally ill, he could not come within the coverage of the Natural Death Act.* His hands remained tied to the bedside.

The case was appealed.[116] Presiding Justice J. Hastings, overturning the lower court decision, later wrote that, exercising his constitutional right to privacy, Bartling 'wanted to live but preferred death to his intolerable life on the ventilator.' The fact that the patient periodically wavered, he observed, did not justify the conclusion of the hospital and his treating physicians that his ability to make such a decision was 'impaired to the point of legal incompetence.'[117] On balance, Bartling's right to refuse unwanted medical treatment outweighed the hospital's and doctor's concern about the preservation of life, the prevention of suicide, and the maintenance of the medical profession's ethics.

Still, the decision was too late for William Bartling, who died on November 6. 'He had to serve a life sentence on the ventilator,' his attorney said. 'He had to live another four and a half months in great discomfort, in what he regarded as degrading circumstances.'[118]

In another case in which a patient died before the case was resolved, the nephew (also the legal guardian) of eighty-four-year-old Claire Conroy petitioned a New Jersey superior court to have his aunt's nasogastric tubes removed.[119] There was no question that Miss Conroy was terminal. Her condition was remarkably similar, if not identical, to the stupor Karen Quinlan had lapsed into. However, Miss Conroy's physician refused to honour the request, and her nephew sought judicial sanction for removal.

Reviewing the testimony of physicians, nursing home administrators, and a priest (and personally observing Miss Conroy), Judge Reginald Stanton concluded that nature should take its course and that the patient's right to privacy—her right to refuse medical treatment—could be exercised on her behalf by her nephew.

However, the superior court's decision was appealed by Miss Conroy's court-appointed lawyer, who objected to the removal of the tube.[120] Although the tube was never taken away and all medications were continued, Miss Conroy died thirteen days after Judge Stanton's decision. Still, the appellate division refused to dismiss the case. Its conclusion— that removal of a feeding tube from a mentally incompetent, gravely ill woman constituted homicide and violated a fundamental medical principle to do no harm—rejected the former holding of the New Jersey Supreme Court in the matter of Karen Ann Quinlan.† 'In our view,' the appellate court argued, reviewing the Stanton decision, 'we regard it as the authorization of euthanasia.'[121] Characterizing the tube as ordinary nursing

---

* Bartling had executed a nonstatutory Living Will, a California Durable Power of Attorney for Health Care (appointing his wife), and an additional statement specifying his wishes.

† The *Quinlan* court held that it is the patient's condition, not the removal of medical treatment, that causes death.

care and food, the court found that, as such, it has to be kept intact.

Reversing the ruling in January 1985, the Supreme Court of New Jersey found no legal difference between artificial feeding and other intrusive artificial life-support systems.[122] Approving the withdrawing or withholding of life-sustaining measures from incompetent nursing home patients when certain conditions are met, the court stipulated the following situations:

1. Patients who have made it clear that they would refuse treatment under the present circumstances, and who are 'elderly, incompetent, nursing-home resident[s] with severe and permanent mental and physical impairments and a life expectancy of approximately one year or less.' The patients' wishes can be embodied in a Living Will, an oral directive, or a durable power of attorney.

2. Patients who have given some indication of their wishes, but who have not unequivocally expressed their desires, when the treatment at issue would 'merely prolong suffering'.

3. Patients who have not indicated their wishes, if the treatment 'clearly and markedly outweigh[s] the benefits the patient derives from life,' and the 'recurring, unavoidable and severe pain of the patient's life with the treatment should be such that the effect of administering life-sustaining treatment would be inhumane.'[123]

The court further stated the necessity of contacting the Office of Ombudsman for the Institutionalized Elderly before treatment might be withdrawn in any of the three circumstances.

Finally, in a ruling similar to the appellate court's in *Conroy*, a Massachusetts probate judge in October 1985 denied a family's request to withdraw food and water from a comatose patient. Forty-eight-year-old Paul E. Brophy, a firefighter, was considered in 'robust health' in March 1983, when a blood vessel in his brain swelled, threatening to burst. Surgery for the aneurysm was performed, but Brophy lapsed into a 'persistent vegetative state'.[124]

Brophy's wife, Patricia, asked the hospital to withdraw all life supports in November 1984, but the hospital, citing medical and ethical standards, refused. In February 1985, she filed suit. Although expert witnesses agreed that the prognosis for Brophy was hopeless and that his vegetative state was worse than a coma, they also said that he was not suffering from any particular illness that threatened his life.* The judge, David H. Kopelman, had to consider whether to honour Mr Brophy's frequently stated wish to die swiftly if he was afflicted with a serious, disabling illness. He was also asked to decide if Mrs Brophy's wishes could be honoured as the substituted judgment for her comatose husband.

* Such reluctance is reminiscent of *Bartling*, in which, despite acknowledging nearly a half-dozen potentially lethal ailments, doctors would not label his condition terminal.

As well, Judge Kopelman had to consider a request to bring about a death by starvation. If the patient was deprived of food and water, doctors disagreed whether the cause of death should be properly listed as starvation or brain damage. Kopelman's response: 'It is ethically inappropriate to cause the preventable death of Brophy by the deliberate denial of food and water, which can be provided to him in a noninvasive, nonintrusive manner which causes no pain and suffering, irrespective of the substituted judgment of the patient.'

Patricia Brophy said she would probably appeal the case. She was backed in her lawsuit by her four children, her husband's seven brothers and sisters, and his ninety-one-year-old mother.

## AN OVERVIEW: CONFUSION

The one uncontested area in cases after *Quinlan* has been the competent patient's right to refuse life-sustaining treatment. Generally, courts have had no difficulty recognizing that such a right is based on the constitutional right to privacy, or the right to bodily integrity recognized at common law.[125]

However, in upholding that right, courts have found it less easy to identify and formulate substantive principles on which to base their decision-making. Should the same principles apply to a competent patient as to one who is brain-dead, in a persistent vegetative state, or severely or irreversibly demented? And what of those who are 'pleasantly senile', who, before some medical emergency, appear to be enjoying their moderately restricted lives? Should all life-sustaining measures be taken (or, conversely, cut off), especially when there is no previous indication of the patient's wishes, and no family to indicate what the wishes might have been?

Yet despite no easily formulated answers, courts have had to attempt to resolve these life-and-death dilemmas. Not only have they had to adjudicate, they have had to indicate why they acted as they did. A review of cases since *Quinlan* shows, above all, the disparity of judicial interpretation, much of which stems from the courts' nervousness in applying quality-of-life standards. The result has been confusion. While some courts have emphasized the need for judicial involvement, others have criticized such involvement (echoing *Quinlan*) as cumbersome and unnecessary. Also, if there has been no patient directive, should the more subjective substituted judgment test be used, or the more objective 'best interests' test?* In some instances, ethics and prognosis committees have been advocated as ideal

---

* 'Best interests' is measured by the President's Commission as the relief of suffering, the preservation or restoration of functioning, and the quality as well as extent of life sustained. Substituted judgment is used to determine whether a particular person would or would not decide to discontinue treatment if he or she could be substituted into (and were competent in) the present situation. Either test is recommended in the decision-making process for surrogates.[126]

vehicles for weighing what is best for the patient, while other courts have emphasized the need for more specific legislative guidelines. Certainly, physicians have been (and continue to be) uncertain about the need for a court order to permit them to end treatment, just as many lawyers have been equally uncertain about what criteria a court will base its decision on.

## Who Decides?
## Court Involvement Versus Individual Decision-Making

The *Quinlan* court mentioned aspects of best interests *and* substituted judgment, while in the case of Joseph Saikewicz, the court used the substituted judgment test for a person who had never been competent. However, notwithstanding the common use of the more subjective test, there were dramatic differences between the cases. Karen Quinlan had been an intelligent person of sufficient judgment before lapsing into a coma. It was presumed by the courts (as her parents testified) that were she to have had a few miraculous moments of lucidity, she would have been able to arrive at a reasonable decision about preferred treatment.

In contrast, Joseph Saikewicz had always been mentally retarded. The problem in applying substituted judgment here is that, ordinarily, one must have in mind some model of the more rational and competent person making the decision. Saikewicz had never been either. Thus a legal fiction was created in the court's presumption that the substituted judgment test could be applied by imagining someone like Saikewicz suddenly sufficiently capable of arriving at an enlightened decision—which, of course, was not Saikewicz at all. Still, the court's reasoning was that decisions in such cases 'should be that which would be made by the competent person, but taking into account the present and future incompetency of the individual.'[127]

The *Saikewicz* court departed further from *Quinlan* in its insistence on judicial involvement in right-to-refuse-treatment cases. According to the Massachusetts Supreme Court, such involvement is absolutely necessary in such life-and-death matters—even when there is no dispute among the patient's representatives (guardian, family, physician, ethics committee). On the other hand, the *Quinlan* court specifically entrusted decision-making to the patient's surrogate/guardian, family, and physicians, to be confirmed by consultation with a hospital ethics committee.[128]

Not surprisingly, the *Saikewicz* decision was criticized on a number of levels. As the New Jersey Supreme Court observed in *Quinlan*, judicial procedure can indeed be cumbersome. Such delays rarely, in fact, benefit the patient, but instead ensure that treatment is continued until otherwise authorized by a court order. The necessity of judicial intervention could also encourage doctors to use only the most rigorous life-prolonging measures until otherwise directed. As one Massachusetts attorney noted:

[This case] can be construed as requiring Massachusetts physicians to apply to a probate court in *any* circumstance in which it is believed that *potentially* life-prolonging treatment should be withheld from a person *incapable* of making his own decision. Also implicit in the . . . decision is the notion that doctors must always opt for life-saving treatment pending a court decision. . . . An ultimate consequence of the *Saikewicz* ruling . . . is the potential 'return to the closet' by physicians who are frustrated by the legal process.[129]

Moreover, the proposal that all decision-making (even that unanimously arrived at beforehand) be made in a courtroom setting presumes that a group decision made by the patient's family and medical staff cannot ever be reasonable or trustworthy. Such a presumption is highly questionable, as other courts have observed. Nor does such a position necessarily ensure that the prescribed adversarial process (involving, in theory, two opposing points of view) will yield arguments both for and against continuing treatment: While the appointment of a guardian *ad litem* presupposes that all reasonable arguments will be made in favour of administering treatment to prolong life, there is no mention that balancing arguments for suspending treatment will as a matter of course be included. One critic pointed out: 'There may well be as much need for a court-appointed advocate for death-with-dignity as there is for a guardian *ad litem*.'[130]

Like *Saikewicz*, the Delaware Supreme Court in *Severns* emphasized the necessity of a full evidentiary hearing: 'A decision of this magnitude cannot be based on the stipulation of the parties.'[131] Also, the Supreme Judicial Court of Massachusetts, in *Spring*, reversed a lower court's ruling that the patient's physician, wife, and son could decide on the appropriateness of further treatment. 'We disapprove of shifting the ultimate decision-making away from the duly established course of proper jurisdiction,' the higher court held.[132] However, acknowledging the financial and emotional burdens of such lengthy proceedings, the court went on to recommend prompt probate procedures to appoint guardians and expedite appeals; it also encouraged physicians to initiate treatment decisions on their own, adding that courts will evaluate physicians' conduct under the same 'good faith' and 'reasonable medical practice' negligence standards applied to all medical decisions.[133] Mention was made of the concurrence of qualified consultants and the value of prognosis panels and medical consultants. Thus, the court concluded that once a Massachusetts court was presented with a case, it had to decide it, but (unlike *Saikewicz*) not all cases necessarily had to be judicially reviewed.

Yet the court's specific refusal to state what combination of circumstances would require (or not require) prior judicial approval was a major drawback. Despite attempts to recognize the value of private decision-

making, the court's vagueness underscored the potential for liability—
since it established no clear guidelines by which hospitals and physicians
could decide whether or not to seek court approval for discontinuing treatment. Also, no distinction was made between cases in which all parties
unanimously agreed, and those in which a patient's wishes were unclear.*

Questions about the wisdom of unqualified judicial intervention in
*Spring* and elsewhere were more boldly and explicitly posed in other cases,
most of which reflected an increasing awareness of the importance of individual decision-making. For instance, if the attending physicians and the
patient's family agree that the patient will never recover (as, say, in *Quinlan*) 'cognitive, sapient functioning', and that the patient, if competent,
would absolutely reject further medical procedures, is a court order necessary?

As noted, Chief Justice Hughes, in deciding the case of Karen Quinlan,
recommended that a medical prognosis criterion be applied by the patient's
guardian, family, and physician; and that this, in turn, be confirmed by a
hospital ethics committee.[136] Similarly, in 1978 the Appeals Court of Massachusetts, in *Dinnerstein*, maintained that in the absence of any treatment
capable of curing or relieving the illness, whatever measures were suitable
for the patient could be decided by the attending physicians.[137] Also, Judge
Jones, dissenting in *In re Storar*, explained why he thought courts were not
the proper place to resolve such cases:

> The methodology and techniques for our classic adversarial system are
> not best suited to the resolution of the issues presented. The courts can
> claim no particular competence to reach the difficult ultimate decision,
> depending as it necessarily must not only on medical data, but on theo-
> logical tenets and perceptions of human values which defy classification
> and calibration.[138]

In 1983 the Washington Supreme Court, in *Colyer*, reviewing *Quinlan*
and *Saikewicz*, indicated its affinity with the former in holding that judicial
intervention in every treatment decision is not required. Where there is a
dispute among the decision-makers, evidence of wrongful motives or malpractice, absence of a family member or guardian, or where the patient has

---

* The New York Court of Appeals in *Storar*, while behaving in a paternalistic fashion in
reducing the patient to the status of an infant and insisting on treatment, did not profess to
reach beyond the facts of the case. The majority opinion was notable for its restraint in, for
example, reserving the question of whether the presence of excessive pain from transfusions
would change the result.[134] Also, in *Eichner*, the higher court (contradicting the lower court's
concern with adjudication) seemed unwilling to encourage or discourage such intervention,
stressing instead the need for legislation.[135]

always been incompetent, judicial review is necessary.[139] In its subsequent ruling in *Hamlin* (the case of a retarded, incompetent patient), the same court ruled that when the court-appointed guardian, physicians, and prognosis committee agree, a court order is unrequired.[140]

The Florida Supreme Court in *Bludworth* also noted the 'burdensome' nature of prior court approval in such cases. Again, emphasis was on a lack of dispute between the patient's family and a prognosis committee. The court further stipulated that guardians were not always necessary:

> The decision whether to end the dying process is a personal one for family members or those who bear a legal responsibility for the patient. . . . While the courts are always available to protect the rights of the individual, the condition of this individual is such that the decision is one to be made by the family and the medical community.[141]

As observed in the case of Rudolfo Torres, although the court ruled that intervention was appropriate in that particular instance, treatment could be withheld where the patient's family, doctors, and the hospital ethics committee agreed.[142] And in *Conroy*, the Supreme Court of New Jersey indicated that a court order is not always necessary, since (quoting *Bludworth*) 'Doctors, in consultation with close family members, are in the best position to make these decisions.'[143]

Three other courts questioned the wisdom of ubiquitous court intervention while pointing to the specific need for legislative guidelines. In the case of Brother Fox (*Eichner*), the New York Court of Appeals claimed, on the one hand, that it was not inappropriate for the surrogate to apply to the court for a ruling. On the other, it emphasized that such a procedure is optional, since 'Neither the common law nor existing statutes require persons generally to seek prior court assessment of conduct which may subject them to civil and criminal liability.'[144] Further, if the role of the courts in such cases would be enlarged, any changes should come from the legislature.[145]

More strongly, the Delaware Supreme Court, in reviewing Mary Severns's case, concluded that courts *must* decide all right-to-refuse-treatment cases when there has been no legislation to address the issue. Noting that the legislature had been either silent or ambiguous on the subject, it inferred that the problem was 'too profound to imply legislative approval.'[146] In the meantime, without any guidelines, both lower and higher courts would have to preside. Similarly, the California Supreme Court in *Barber* observed the absence of legislative guidelines. However, like *Eichner*, it argued that judicial arbitration in all such cases was unnecessary and unwise, following the *Quinlan* opinion that such arbitration can be inappropriate and cumbersome.[147]

## HOW TO DECIDE? WHICH TEST?

In the cases of brain-dead patients, even without revised definitions of death in the concerned states, there was little hesitancy on the part of the courts to discontinue treatment. Where patients petitioned courts themselves—*Perlmutter, Candura, Foster*, and *Bartling*—in three of the four cases (*Perlmutter, Candura* and *Foster*) the courts consistently upheld the patients' competency as well as their right to refuse further medical care. In the case of William Foster, the court, typically reflecting positive attitudes towards patient's rights, argued that the plaintiff's wishes as a competent adult should be respected since he had been 'fully and meaningfully informed of the likely consequences of declining further . . . treatment and other life-sustaining measures.' The continued application of extraordinary treatment 'constituted an invasion . . . of the plaintiff's constitutional rights of self-dignity, privacy, and liberty as guaranteed by the penumbra of specific guarantees of the Bill of Rights.'[148]

However, the California Superior Court in the matter of William Bartling ruled that because the patient was neither terminally ill (despite emphysema, hardening of the arteries, arteriosclerosis, an aneurysm, and lung cancer) nor brain-dead, he could not be removed from the respirator. Judge Lawrence Waddington based his conclusion on the argument that injunctions such as Bartling's were disfavoured under California law, and he could find no case from any jurisdiction where a person applying for similar relief was not terminally ill, or in a comatose, vegetative, or brain-dead state. He did not question Bartling's competence. As lawyer/ethicist George Annas has observed, the judge,

> instead of seeing his role as protector of the liberty of an individual who was being held and treated against his will . . . seemed to see himself as making a medical decision. . . . [He] seems also to have redefined the legal issue of competence in the case into a medical one so that he would not have to take personal responsibility for a decision that might result in Mr Bartling's death.[149]

Although a higher court would overturn the superior court's ruling, it did not do so until after Mr Bartling's death, when he was still on a respirator.

In the remaining cases in which patients were incompetent and a surrogate was used, not only did rulings differ, but the criteria varied as well as their interpretation. To reach a decision, the tests of either substituted judgment or best interests were generally used (either explicitly or by inference), as the President's Commission had recommended:

> The Commission believes that, when possible, decision-making for incapacitated patients should be guided by the principle of substituted judg-

ment which promotes the underlying values of self-determination and well-being better than the best interests standard does. When a patient's likely decision is unknown, however, a surrogate decision-maker should use the best interests standard and choose a course that will promote the patient's well-being as it would probably be conceived by a reasonable person in the person's circumstances.[150]

Most courts have employed the substituted-judgment test. Quality-of-life decisions inherent in the best interests test have, it seems, made judges uncomfortable.

In *Saikewicz*, for example, the higher court rejected the lower court's use of quality of life as a determining factor. As a result, a fiction—a discerning, mentally sound patient—was created, stretching credulity beyond reason. In the matter of Brother Fox, three different courts offered their interpretations, each adding a new dimension. Both the lower and the intermediate courts upheld the patient's constitutional right to privacy and the common-law right of self-determination, arguing that there was no rational reason to discriminate between competent and incompetent individuals in exercising these rights. They further pointed out that the means for exercising these rights was through substituted judgment, with Father Eichner as Fox's principal representative.[151]

Yet the highest court (the New York Court of Appeals), emphasizing the common-law right to refuse medical care, held that such a right extends only to 'persons of adult years and sound mind'.[152] This requirement could only be met if, prior to incompetency, the patient had expressed a desire not to be maintained by life-prolonging procedures if he became debilitated. Thus the court's extension of the common law to uphold Brother Fox's right to refuse treatment was based, not on substituted judgment, but on the fact that in an earlier conversation with Eichner, before becoming ill, Fox had specifically expressed such a wish. Such 'clear and convincing evidence' was, the court found, sufficient to justify removal of life supports.

The main problem with the higher court is emphasis on clear and convincing proof—and its dismissal of substituted judgment—is, as one critic stated, a process that 'disenfranchised a whole class of people: those without a living will or its equivalent.'[153] Under such a standard, the vast majority of people who had never expressed any kind of opinion on the rights of the dying would necessarily have to undergo life-sustaining treatment, since there had been no 'solemn pronouncement' that would satisfy the burden of proof. Further, what, in fact, constitutes 'clear and convincing evidence': a written directive, a proxy voucher, an oral declaration, a casual conversation, a notarized statement? None of this was made clear.

In the case of Edna Leach, the patient's right to self-determination was the decisive factor. The Ohio court based its conclusion on Mrs Leach's

'specific intent', or the fact that while still competent she had unequivocally expressed a desire not to have her life sustained by artificial means.
Aligning itself closely with the high court decision in *Eichner*, *Leach* adopted the highest possible standard of proof—clear and convincing evidence,
without setting any specific procedures beyond those that applied to Edna
Leach.[154]

In contrast, with Earle Spring there was absolutely no proof that before
he became ill, Spring had any views at all on the subject. Therefore the
courts could not rely on clear and convincing evidence which in turn would
support (as it had with Edna Leach and Brother Fox) the patient's right to
self-determination. As in *Eichner*, the lower court defended the rights of
both the competent and the incompetent to refuse treatment, but in this
case turned to substituted judgment to uphold that freedom:

> Where the person is incompetent, the law intervenes, not to displace the
> traditional role of the family and the attending physician in weighing that
> question, but to protect the rights of the incompetent person by deter-
> mining, as best it can, what his wish would be.[155]

Relying on Spring's family and doctor, the lower court thus accepted the
petition of the guardian (Spring's son) to end dialysis treatment. An intermediate court agreed with this ruling.

Although the Massachusetts Supreme Judicial Court reversed, it did not
necessarily dismiss substituted judgment. As the court argued, the conclusion that Mr Spring would, 'if competent, choose not to receive the life-
prolonging treatment' was 'not clearly erroneous'.[156] Such an observation
prompted one critic to comment that 'Mr Spring himself ... had *never*
stated any preference regarding medical treatment he might require after
he became incompetent, and the relevant evidence provided by the family
members is virtually nonexistent.'[157] Instead, emphasis in court was on the
patient's irreversible mental condition (senility), which, despite dialysis,
would never again be restored to a 'normal, cognitive, integrated, functioning existence.'[158] This, in turn, seems uncomfortably close to a quality-of-
life assessment and reflects little, if anything, about substituted judgment.
As Annas noted:

> [Such a] statement, rephrased, reads, 'If one is not and cannot be
> returned to a normal, cognitive, integrated, functioning existence, but
> can simply be kept alive, it is not required that one be kept alive.' ... It
> argues that only life which is 'normal' (however that is defined) and
> involved 'integrated functioning' (however that is defined) is worthy of
> legal protection.
>
> Phrased another way, there are some categories of people who are so
> abnormal or ill-functioning that the state has no interest in seeing to it
> that their lives are preserved.[159]

Despite the President's Commission's emphasis on the importance of *reliable* evidence to invoke substituted judgment,[160] there appears to have been none at all in the *Spring* case. The courts got around this by calling attention to the close family ties and lack of financial motives. Unlike *Bludworth*—in which a Living Will was deemed 'persuasive evidence' to justify substituted judgment—a complete absence of such proof in cases like Earle Spring's risks the substitution of the surrogate's subjective judgment for that of the incompetent. As well, quality-of-life considerations are camouflaged under the guise of this criterion, without the accompanying standards (and context) of the best interests test recommended by the President's Commission: as noted, relief of suffering, preservation or restoration of functioning, and the quality as well as the extent of life sustained.[161]

Deciding whether to withhold transfusions from John Storar was even more intricate, since Storar (like Joseph Saikewicz) had been retarded his entire life. At first the lower and intermediate courts used substituted judgment, reasoning that Storar's mother could exercise her son's right to refuse treatment. Yet the highest court, the New York Court of Appeals, reversed, reducing Storar to infant status and invoking *parens patriae*. Like the high court *Eichner* ruling, such a decision has been criticized as a serious barrier to the rights of incompetents to refuse treatment.[162]

Yet the court of appeals' decision to dismiss the substituted judgment test in *Storar* can indeed be applauded. It noted that since Storar was always 'totally incapable of understanding or making a reasoned decision about medical treatment . . . it is unrealistic to attempt to determine whether he would want to continue potentially life-prolonging treatment if he were competent.'[163] Thus the fiction created in *Saikewicz* was avoided. As the high court observed, although there seems to be a desire to 'treat incompetents and competents alike . . . the inescapable problem is that they are in fact unlike in respect of the capacity relevant to the right—the physical ability to make an informed choice.'[164]

Unfortunately, it went no further in its analysis, reverting to paternalism instead of the best interests alternative. Although it could be argued that the high court opinion implied such an approach—evidence of the effects of transfusions on the patient was considered—such evidence (as in *Spring*) was not weighed in the broader context of best interests as a whole, such as the severity of the patient's pain (with and without the transfusions), the degree of salvageable existence, and alternative treatments.

In contrast, decisions in *Colyer* and *Hamlin*, dealing implicitly with substituted judgment (and best interests), deliberately moved away from such paternalism: if the patient's court-appointed guardian, his family, physician, and the prognosis committee agreed, judicial involvement would be unnecessary. Specific guidelines recommended were:

- A unanimous concurrence by a prognosis board . . . that the patient's condition is incurable and there is no reasonable medical probability of returning to a cognitive, sapient state;
- Court appointment of a guardian for the incompetent person . . . including the appointment of a guardian ad litem *to represent the best interests of the incompetent in that proceeding*;
- Exercise of the patient's right of privacy and freedom from bodily invasion by the guardian, *if it is the guardian's best judgment that the patient, if competent to make the decision, would choose to have the life-sustaining equipment removed*;
- If required, a court determination of the rights and wishes of the incompetent, with a guardian ad litem appointed to represent the incompetent patient and to present all relevant facts to the court. [Emphasis added.][165]

The *Hamlin* decision (Hamlin, like Saikewicz and Storar, was severely retarded) modified *Colyer* by diminishing the importance of a court-appointed guardian, stressing instead agreement among family members, attending physicians, and a prognosis committee in deciding the patient's best interests.[166] Here the notion of substituted judgment appears to have vanished altogether.

However, in the case of Mary Hier, the pendulum swung back again. Long a psychiatric patient (fifty-seven years), ninety-two-year-old Mrs Hier was obviously incapable of making the necessary decisions about her medical treatment. Donning the 'mental mantle' of the incompetent, the probate judge resorted to substituted judgment and concluded that, were the patient capable of making a decision, she would accept the medication recommended (Thorazine) but reject another gastrotomy. (There were no family members to testify.) The appellate court agreed with the lower court's use of substituted judgment, pointing out that the patient's obvious and persistent refusals were significant factors in considering further surgery; it stated that Mrs Hier's actions 'all may be seen as a plea for privacy and personal dignity.'[167] Both courts also observed various alternatives for nourishing Mrs Hier, the benefits and burdens of surgery, and the state's interest in preserving life. Several physicians testified to the appropriateness (or inappropriateness) of a gastrotomy.

Needless to say, the flaw in using substituted judgment at all here is that, on the one hand, the patient's incompetency was acknowledged by the courts while, on the other, her incoherent, incompetent statements and actions were used as a pretext for ruling against treatment—or the behaviour of an incompetent patient was interpreted as a competently held belief. Like *Saikewicz* and *Spring*, mental retardation and senility were factors ultimately held against the patient, which could, as one observer noted, be used as gross discrimination against all such patients:

> Because [the Hier court] reads *Saikewicz* as saying we don't have to give older, mentally retarded patients chemotherapy because they can't understand it, and *Spring* as saying that we don't have to give disruptive, senile nursing home patients dialysis because they don't like it, it concludes that it is simply following past precedents by ruling that we don't have to feed senile, mentally ill nursing-home patients who pull out their feeding tubes because they don't want to be fed that way.[168]

The decision in *Hier* underscores the need for more extensive use of the best interests test, especially with incompetents. Certainly, the Supreme Court of New Jersey, in deciding Claire Conroy's case, made an attempt to provide more realistic guidelines for decision-making in the cases of incompetent patients, recommending two objective best-interests tests: the limited objective and the pure objective, which may be used only in terms of pain, suffering, and possible enjoyment of life.[169]* Pain was a major criterion primarily because the court was apprehensive about the consequences of authorizing surrogates to make quality-of-life decisions for others:

> We expressly decline to authorize decision-making based on assessments of the personal worth and social utility of another's life, or the value of that life to others. We do not believe that it would be appropriate for a court to designate a person with the authority to determine that someone else's life is not worth living simply because, to that person, the patient's 'quality of life' or value to society seems negligible. The mere fact that a patient's functioning is limited or his prognosis dim does not mean that he is not enjoying what remains of his life or that it is in his best interests to die.[170]

However, the court would not adopt the best interests criteria recommended by the President's Commission, and it conceded that despite its emphasis on pain as a criterion, using this as a sole test 'may transmute the best interests determination into an exercise of avoidance and nullification rather than confrontation and fulfilment.'[171] Still, such a criterion is not entirely inappropriate when the court is concerned (as it was in *Conroy*) with the plight of aged nursing home patients, many of whom are mentally impaired, suffering, and not expected to live long. While the supreme court was reluctant to enlarge on more comprehensive quality-of-life stan-

---

* It allowed for a subjective test, but only in cases where there is clear and reliable evidence (such as a Living Will) that indicates what the patient would have chosen were he or she competent.

dards, it is possible that, in a broader sense, the 'suffering and enjoyment of life' referred to might be used to embrace the fundamental notions of personal privacy and bodily integrity, while avoiding 'social worth' value judgments. Still, each case would have to be reviewed and evaluated on its own merits:

> Each case—such as that of the severely deformed newborn, of the never-competent adult suffering from a painful and debilitating illness, and of the mentally alert quadriplegic who has given up on life—poses its own unique difficulties. We do not deem it advisable to resolve all such human dilemmas in the context of this case. It is preferable . . . . to move slowly and to gain experience in this highly sensitive field. As we noted previously, the Legislature is better equipped than we to develop and frame a comprehensive plan for resolving these problems.[172]

Whether or not, as the *Conroy* court suggested, the legislature is the more suitable place for developing guidelines, there are several factors to consider, none of which are easy to resolve. The extent of judicial involvement and the necessity of appointing a legal guardian have to be weighed against the importance of individual decision-making. The merits of substituted judgment versus the more objective best-interests test must also be assessed; implicit in this consideration are questions about quality of life and the role of advanced age in decision-making. Not least important, the role of nourishment cannot be avoided. In which cases should feeding be regarded as noninvasive and therefore part of ordinary (and required) treatment, and when should it be regarded (as it was in *Conroy*) as artificial? As difficult as it might be for the legislatures and the courts to unscramble these issues, without such guidance, decisions will continue to be made solely on a case-by-case basis, with a variety of interpretations and outcomes, often at the expense of the dying patient.

Some courts have offered more specific definitions and guidelines, but admirable as that attempt might be, one drawback is that such far-reaching criteria cannot properly allow for the uniqueness and idiosyncracies of each individual case. Also, as George Annas notes in 'When Procedures Limit Rights: From *Quinlan* to *Conroy*', such a method can lead to a 'Catch-22 approach to treatment refusals, in which incompetent patients are given a substantive right to refuse treatment that must be procedurally exercised in such a way that it will never be exercised, or can be exercised in a way inconsistent with their wishes.'[173] In contrast, in states where courts have ruled vaguely (as in the *Spring* case\*) or reserved judgment, physicians and surrogates will probably seek court orders more often, not only because of

---

\* Here the court concluded by saying: 'We are not called upon to decide what combination of circumstances makes prior court approval necessary or desirable, even on the facts of the case before us. Moreover, since the scientific underpinnings of medical practice and opinion are in a constant state of development, our opinion as to that particular set of facts may not be a reliable guide to the proper solution of a future medical problem.'[174]

the absence of guidelines and standards, but also to protect themselves from liability.

Equally debatable is whether the family member acting as surrogate for the incompetent patient should be appointed by the court. When there has been no disagreement over the patient's welfare, some courts (e.g. *Bludworth* and *Barber*) have held that judicial guardianship proceedings are not absolutely necessary. As the Florida *Bludworth* court observed: 'If there are close family members such as the patient's spouse, adult children, or parents, who are willing to exercise that right on behalf of the patient, there is no requirement that a guardian should be judicially appointed.'[175] Certainly, this makes sense in that such a strategy avoids the 'cumbersome, burdensome' nature of court proceedings which may result in unwanted and impractical delays.

Yet guardianship procedures provide a safeguard that should not be dismissed. With more ad hoc decision-making, there is always the risk that hasty decisions will be made that are not in the patient's best interests, and that the guardian may be acting with motives that would be questioned by a court. Indeed, some guardianship proceedings require that a guardian *ad litem* be appointed to ensure that the proposed surrogate is not motivated in an untoward way.[176]

In addition, despite recent rulings that a court order is not always necessary in right-to-refuse-treatment cases (whether for a guardian or a ruling), many hospitals nonetheless apply for them anyway, to protect themselves from liability. Not only did the *Barber* case (in which two physicians were charged with murder) instil fear in the medical community; many lawyers and physicians working in this area are insufficiently educated to be clear about what the best and most appropriate action is. Too often, to appease their fears, they choose to err on the side of caution. Annas, in reviewing the *Quinlan* and *Saikewicz* cases, observed that many lawyers, such as the ones advising Massachusetts hospitals,

> lack experience and training in health law and have little familiarity with either medical practice or hospital procedures. This has resulted in [continuing and unnecessary litigation] ... primarily because hospital administrators have asked their legal counsel how the hospital can be protected from *any* liability. ... Physicians should know at least enough law to be able to tell when the advice their lawyers are giving them is so incredible that it is most likely wrong. ... Finally, physicians should realize that there are no 100 per cent guarantees in law any more than in life, and that part of being a professional is taking responsibility for decisions within one's own professional competence.[177]

In deciding whether to discontinue life supports for an incompetent, the doctrine of substituted judgment has proved to be problem-ridden. In theory, such a doctrine arises out of the desire to accord the incompetent the dignity that society believes every human being is entitled to. In this respect, the form of substituted judgment may be pleasing, appearing as it does to place competent and incompetent individuals on the same level with the same rights.

However, such a device has been criticized, not only because it creates a falsehood, but because it can lead to quality-of-life considerations that are erroneous and unfair to the patient. Specifically, the guardian or surrogate may confuse a quality-of-life evaluation with his own standards rather than those of the incompetent's, probably because he has little else to go on. So, too, if the decision-maker is unaware of the basis on which he is deciding, he cannot take the necessary precautions to limit his assessment to dimensions he might be familiar with (such as pain) and to disregard factors with which he has had little experience, such as severe retardation.

As things stand, quality-of-life decisions are constantly being made, but they are camouflaged or disguised, primarily because the public and the courts are uneasy with the idea that the senile and retarded are categorically different from patients who are 'normal' and might therefore be subject to different criteria. However, even if quality-of-life judgments about incompetents make people uncomfortable (reminiscent, perhaps, of the Nazi concept of 'useless eaters'), and even if they are potentially more dangerous and open to abuse, an effort must be made to incorporate these decisions into a structured and safeguarding context. Perhaps Beth Rubin, associate editor of the *Columbia Journal of Law & Social Problems*, expresses it best when she observes that the courts simply must do better:

> We must develop standards to meet the new questions raised by the machines and other life-sustaining devices which are keeping patients alive for increasingly long periods of time. Moreover, we need to develop principles for dealing with senile persons and other persons with diminished incompetence who are often subjected to such treatments.... Instead of ignoring the fact that quality of life considerations are inherently involved in antidysthanasia [the failure to take positive steps to prolong the life of an incurable patient, or the removal of life-sustaining equipment] decisions, we should safeguard and refashion the decision-making process.[178]

Still, there have been advances. Certainly, the efforts of the courts to uphold a patient's right to refuse treatment and to distinguish between the removal of life supports and suicide have significantly clarified the issue. Similarly, in the case of Clarence Herbert, Claire Conroy, and Mary Hier, the question of whether it is ever justifiable to withhold nutrition from dying patients was addressed.[179] On the whole, the dominant legal trend has been to view nutritional supports as part of medical treatment procedures. In this way, when a patient's ailments are painful to endure and are irreversible, with death imminent, efforts to feed have not been considered mandatory, just as antibiotics and resuscitation are not considered appropriate for a patient in the final stages of a terminal illness. Thus courts are most likely to sanction removal of nutrition supports for patients whose death is close at hand and who have lost consciousness.

Not all questions regarding nourishment have been answered, however. Thorny issues remain, such as the difficulty of balancing the behaviour of a persistently refusing incompetent patient like Mary Hier against the state's protective interests, and how to evaluate such behaviour. As well, will courts be more disposed to authorize withdrawal of nourishment from the elderly? And how will such nourishment be categorized? Given the differing costs and complexities of nutritional supports, will courts distinguish between a gastrotomy tube, such as that in the Hier case, and a nasogastric tube or a peripheral intravenous line?[180] These and other problems remain, some of them almost impossibly difficult to resolve.

What, then, is the answer? Should future changes which better ensure the rights of the dying be sought primarily in the courts or in the legislatures? Which would be more effective?

While courts exist to serve and protect, reliance on adjudication to defend the rights of the terminally ill has been deplored as unwieldy, inconvenient, and burdensome. It is true that the safeguards provided by our legal system are absolutely necessary to provide the 'detached but passionate investigation and decision' advocated by the *Saikewicz* court. But such legal imperialism, as it has been dubbed, undermines the value of private decision-making. Moreover, the courts, in their concern for the vulnerable and defenceless patient, often recommend intricate and impractical procedures that must be surmounted before a patient's rights can be properly exercised. In more than one case, a patient has died during litigation.

On the other hand, legislation—invaluable in providing uniform standards and guidelines—has drawbacks too. In the process of passing an act of legislation such as the Living Will, for example, too often changes are made along the way which prove to be deleterious and contrary to the bill's initial objectives. Similar problems are anticipated with the model legislation drafted by the legal advisers of Concern for Dying, the Right to Refuse Treatment Act.[181] While such an act would clear up many of the problems with Durable Powers of Attorney by making them uniformly applicable to health care decisions, George Annas (himself a legal adviser to Concern) points to some of the difficulties: '[Such a bill] might imply to some that these rights do not currently exist,' and would not exist if the legislation was not enacted.'[182]

One proposed alternative has been to strengthen the role of ethics committees in the decision-making process. Dr Ronald E. Cranford, quoted in the *Torres* decision, maintained that while the movement is still in its infancy, 'within five years, virtually every American hospital will have an ethics committee of some sort.'[183] Not only can ethics committees advise patients, their families, and physicians; they can develop hospital guidelines for treating the dying as well as educate health care workers and administrators in ethical and moral issues. Equally important, such committees can decide which cases would be most appropriately settled by the courts. They could also minimize the chances of hospital liability, since such panels can confirm that whatever medical decision is undertaken is consistent with acceptable medical practice.

Ideally, an ethics committee is interdisciplinary, consisting of physicians, nurses, social workers, hospital administrators, lawyers, bioethicists, laymen, and the clergy. Medical ethicist Robert Veatch has pointed out that a state legislature could ultimately shift reviewing away from the courts to such committees, thus alleviating the courts' burdens while speeding up the decision-making process. However, he adds that such a shift is undesirable 'unless the committee becomes a public body functioning as an agent of society with public review of appointments, due process, and other protections to ensure that it does not represent a hospital's idiosyncratic prospective.'[184]

Although many of the dilemmas concerning ethics committees remain unsolved,* there are merits that are unmistakable, not least of which is surrogate appointment. Rubin, in 'Refusal of Life-Sustaining Treatment for Terminally-Ill Incompetent Patients', argues:

> Ethics committees, by developing and applying guidelines for questioning surrogates' motives, can also provide a solution to the choice of surrogate problem. In the past, some courts required guardians to be judicially appointed. Judicial guardianship proceedings often included the appointment of a guardian ad litem, whose function was to question the motives of the proposed surrogate. Ethics committees may be in a better position to provide this same important safeguard of questioning the surrogate's motives and recommending judicial intervention if a dispute arises between relatives, or if evidence of ill motives exists. By avoiding judicial intervention in every case, the whole decision-making process can be expedited.[186]

Whatever the method, whatever the alternative, there *are* hard choices ahead, most of which revolve around quality-of-life criteria. Both the courts and the legislatures must attempt to deal squarely with these issues,

---

* The President's Commission points out some of those problems: patient confidentiality, hospital liability, excessively bureaucratic hospital structure, membership committee appointments, diffusion of responsibility, escalation of medical care costs, and legal liability of committee members.[185]

regardless of their intricacies. Above all, what we must aim for are laws that continue to preserve the rights of the dying, and defend and protect from abuse those who are unable to speak for themselves. What we can insist on is a judicial system that effects these rights. Specifically, legislation and the courts should affirm: the right of competent patients to refuse treatment, even if that refusal includes artificial feeding; the honouring and enforcement of a person's treatment decisions (reflected in a Living Will or oral declaration); and, in the case of incompetent patients who have never indicated their wishes, the ability of a legal guardian or surrogate to decide whether treatment should be discontinued (including artificial feeding), assessed only after a painstaking scrutiny of the burdens of treatment balanced against prospective benefits.

With or without the aid of appropriate laws, right-to-refuse-treatment cases will still be argued as courts interpret, modify, and refine whatever statutes exist, each case mirroring, to varying degrees, personal autonomy balanced against the state's interests. Without the wisdom of the U.S. Supreme Court, which has so far refused to adjudicate in any such cases, there remains the absence of a binding standard and the absence of a constitutionally recognized right to die. In the meantime, lower, intermediate, and higher state courts will continue to apply the letter of the law within the context of existing mores. As Dr Samuel Johnson said, observing the inextricable nature of our legal system and morality, 'The law is the last result of human wisdom acting upon human experience for the benefit of the public.'

# CHAPTER SEVENTEEN

# *Defining Death*

For centuries, death was measured by a physician feeling the pulse and putting a mirror under the patient's mouth. If there were no signs of life—no pulse, no breath—death was certified. In the last few decades, however, a physician's duty has not been so simple. More intricate scientific tests may be called for, and the law defining the point at which life ends is not so easy to formulate.

Two factors in recent years have made a widely accepted definition of death crucial: organ transplants and life-support machinery. For what historically had always been considered a fairly straightforward issue, the path towards a clear definition of death has been arduous and controversial. Even now, not everybody is satisfied with what medical science has come up with.

As early as the eighteenth century, relying on a patient's circulatory and respiratory signs to determine death was flawed, since there are numerous accounts of premature burial. Jean Bruhier, a Paris physician, collected the histories of fifty-two people allegedly buried alive and seventy-two cases mistakenly certified as dead, while in the nineteenth century, forty-six cases of people who recovered while awaiting inhumation were recorded.[1]

As a result, physicians strove to develop criteria that would diagnose death beyond any doubt. Besides checking respiration and circulation, they observed whether rigor mortis had set in or whether a body left in 'waiting mortuaries' was decomposing. There was even a signal device: a bell attached to a pole that rested on the chest of the buried person, whose movement, if he was alive, could trigger the bell to summon rescuers.

Technological innovations in the nineteenth century helped; the stethoscope enabled heartbeats to be detected with greater sensitivity. Yet vague definitions of death still persisted, such as the one written in the 1891 *Principles of Forensic Medicine:* [Death] is the cessation of the phenomena with which we are so especially familiar—the phenomena of life.'[2]

In the 1950s and 1960s, despite the use of the electrocardiograph, so

264

responsive to cardiac activity, sophisticated life-support equipment and technologies made people question if and when death had occurred. In the past, if the heart stopped, a patient was assumed to be dead. Now resuscitation teams, guided by mechanical monitors, could restart vital functions (their efforts were dubbed 'heroic' measures).

The increase in type and number of organ transplants also confounded the issue. The Uniform Anatomical Gift Act of 1968 authorized the gift of all or part of a human body for specified purposes after death. Yet in Section 7 of the act, the Commission on Uniform State Laws failed to give an updated definition of death, but declared: 'The time of death shall be determined by a physician who tends the donor at his death, or, if none, the physician who certifies the death.'[3] As a result, many critics feared that doctors would have a vested interest in declaring a donor dead before all resuscitation efforts had been made. (For a successful organ transplant, the organs must be removed at the earliest possible moment. If heart activity is prolonged mechanically for a lengthy period of time in, for example, a brain-damaged donor, organs may deteriorate beyond benefit to a recipient.)

In Britain in 1961, the Human Tissue Act had not provided any satisfactory definition of death,[4] nor had the World Health Organization seven years later, with its definition 'permanent disappearance of life with no possibility of resuscitation.'[5] Both definitions avoided mention of brain death (identified by French neurophysiologists in 1959 as *coma dépassé*) or the precise moment of death.

However, by the late 1960s, the impetus for developing brain death criteria had become so pronounced that the Twenty-second World Medical Assembly, which met in Sydney, Australia in 1968, published guidelines for physicians. They stated: Death is a gradual process at the cellular level with tissues varying in their ability to withstand deprivation of oxygen supply. The assembly listed four criteria:

1. Total lack of response to external stimuli.
2. No muscular movement, especially breathing. If the patient is on a mechanical respirator, it may be turned off for three minutes to establish if the patient is breathing on his own. No reflexes.
3. Fall in blood pressure.
4. Flat electroencephalogram (EEG).[6]

The same year, the Ad Hoc Committee of the Harvard Medical School to Examine the Definition of Brain Death defined four characteristics of a permanently nonfunctioning brain, the first three of which can satisfactorily diagnose death, with the fourth, the EEG, as confirmatory data.

1. Unreceptivity and unresponsivity—total unawareness to externally applied stimuli and inner need and complete unresponsiveness.

2. No movement or breathing—observation for one hour of spontaneous muscular movements, respiration, or response to stimuli. If patient is on a mechanical respirator, absence of spontaneous breathing may be established by turning off respirator for three minutes and observing.

3. No reflexes—fixed and dilated pupils, no ocular movement or blinking, no postural activity; no contraction of muscles due to stimulation.

4. Flat EEG—ten minutes per recording.[7]

The above tests are executed twice, twenty-four hours apart. Death is declared before the respirator is turned off, an action taken by physicians-in-charge in consultation with one or more doctors involved in the case. Disconnection after determination of death protects physicians from accusations of causing the death if they have discontinued life supports for a person who is legally alive.

Useful as the Harvard criteria have been, researchers have pointed out that a flat EEG reading by itself is not conclusive proof of death. According to one medical researcher, an EEG is an effective tool for diagnosis of death if it is used in conjunction with other findings.[8] Notable exceptions to the flat EEG as a reliable indication of death are cases of drug intoxication and hypothermia. Dr Peter Black, in the Collaborative Study of Brain Death, studied Harvard's criteria and compared them to outcomes of death. He found that 'the Harvard criteria accurately predict cardiovascular collapse and somatic death within several days despite supportive therapy.'[9]

Meanwhile, legislators tried to find legal solutions to the problem. In 1970, Kansas became the first state to formalize a definition of death into law. Attorney William Curran observed that 'the new Kansas law eliminates this macabre limbo of law and medicine.'[10] He felt it was commendable that the statute did not require two physicians nor did it spell out detailed clinical procedures (left to the medical profession). The statute stated:

A person will be considered medically and legally dead, if in the opinion of a physician ... there is the absence of spontaneous respiration and cardiac function ... or,

A person will be considered medically and legally dead if ... there is the absence of spontaneous brain function.... Death is to be pronounced before the artificial respiratory and circulatory functions are terminated and before any vital organ is removed for purpose of transplantation.[11]

Two years later, Alexander Capron and Leon Kass, in an article resulting from the work of a research group from the Institute of Society, Ethics and the Life Sciences proposed model legislation. The basis of their recommendations was that 'Death is not a technical matter nor one susceptible to empirical verification.'[12] They advised that public bodies undertake to formulate a set of officially recognized standards. The Kansas statute, they felt, implied two concepts of death. To avoid confusion—one doctor confirming death with one definition, with which another physician might not agree—Capron and Kass both defined death traditionally and invoked brain death in respect to the use of mechanical life support:

A person will be considered dead if in the announced opinion of a physician, based on ordinary standards of medical practice, he has experienced an irreversible cessation of spontaneous respiration and circulatory functions. In the event that artificial means of support preclude a determination that these functions have ceased, a person will be considered dead if in the announced opinion of a physician, based on ordinary standards of medical practice, he has experienced an irreversible cessation of spontaneous brain functions. Death will have occurred at the time when the relevant functions ceased.[13]

In 1975 the American Bar Association offered its definition: 'For all legal purposes, a human body with irreversible cessation of total brain function, according to usual and customary standards of medical practice, shall be considered dead.'[14] The advantages of such a definition were delineated by Dennis Horan, a critic of brain death definitions, who felt this one permitted judicial and medical determination of facts of death, while avoiding any religious determinants. While avoiding the prescribing of medical criteria, it advocated changing medical factors to correspond with current practices (incorporating heartbeat, brain, and respiration tests). Further, it avoided any mention of euthanasia—active and passive—while appeasing both the medical and the legal professions by covering death as a process (medical preferences) and as a point in time (legal preferences).[15]

Using slightly different emphases, the Royal Medical Colleges and their faculties in Britain since 1976 have stressed physical examination and brain-stem reflexes but have required neither an EEG nor any tests of cerebral circulation. They consider the history of the disorder and carbon dioxide levels in testing for spontaneous respiration.

Brain death is diagnosed only if the patient is deeply comatose, and the coma is not due to depressant drugs, hypothermia, or metabolic disturbances. The tests used to confirm brain death are: absent brain-stem reflexes, fixed and nonresponsive pupils, no vestibular-ocular reflexes, no motor response elicited by stimuli, no gag reflex, and no respiratory movements when the patient is disconnected from the respirator for a period of time. This testing should be repeated within twenty-four hours. A consultant should be called in to help make the decision to disconnect the life-support system.[16]

The Minnesota Medical Association in 1976 placed more emphasis on clinical tests than Harvard had and did not require EEG or cerebral circulation findings. They recommended that physicians observe whether there is movement and breathing when the respirator is turned off for four minutes, and if there is an absence of brain-stem reflexes for twelve hours.[17]

The December 1979 interim meeting of the American Medical Association offered this definition of death:

> An individual who has sustained either (1) irreversible cessation of circulatory and respiratory functions, or (2) irreversible cessation of all functions of the entire brain, shall be considered dead. A determination of death shall be made in accordance with accepted medical standards.[18]

Further, the definition removed the threat of liability from a physician who is acting properly while determining death.

The President's Commission for the Study of Ethical Problems in Medicine and Biomedical and Behavioural Research felt the question of an accepted standard of death warranted its attention. In 1980 the Commission proposed the Uniform Determination of Death Act, which was endorsed by the National Commission on Uniform State Laws, the American Medical Association, and the American Bar Association, superseding all existing 'model bills'. The Commission recommended the adoption of the following statute in all jurisdictions in the United States:

> An individual who has sustained either (1) irreversible cessation of circulatory and respiratory functions, or (2) irreversible cessation of all functions of the entire brain, including the brain stem, is dead. A determination must be made in accordance with accepted medical standards.[19]

Physician and author A. Earl Walker noted two flaws in his model, which do not, however, detract from its general purpose. First, the act provides two standards of death without explanation of their relationship and the conditions under which each is applicable. Moreover, it is impossible to assess 'all functions of the entire brain'.[20] Walker concedes that all statutes have similar inconsistencies.

As model bills were devised, more states began to introduce brain death legislation, thus making determination of death a legal as well as medical decision. Kansas had taken the first step in 1970, and by 1984, thirty-eight states had enacted statutes in various forms. Three states (Indiana, New York, and Washington) had a legal definition of death based on case law.[21]

Legally, death is susceptible to three definitions: The first is a nonphysical definition, such as the declaration of death of a missing person after an unexplained absence of five to seven years. Because nonphysical evidence is presented in the form of legal rules, there is no dispute. The second definition is a physical one that does not involve the person's prospects of recovery—for instance, declaring a patient dead in order to allow recovery of insurance proceeds to survivors. Declaration of death in this case does not deny the very slight chance that life remains. The second definition is used, too, in determining death as a prerequisite in a homicide prosecution. The third definition applies to organ transplants, autopsy, and burial.[22] A physical definition, it leads to decisions to take irreversible action that will end the patient's existence.

Of the thirty-eight states that had enacted statutes, thirty changed their laws to conform with the Uniform Determination of Death Act proposed by the President's Commission;[23] the other eight states continued to base their proposals on recommendations made by the American Medical Association, the American Bar Association, Capron and Kass's model, the Kansas statute, or a nonstandard proposal. In Arizona, Kentucky, Massachusetts, Minnesota, Maine, New Hampshire, North Dakota, South Dakota, South Carolina, and Utah, where there is no legislation, physicians use their own definitions for what they feel constitutes death.

In the past, courts became involved in such matters solely to determine issues of survivorship and inheritance. *Black's Law Dictionary* was frequently used to determine the common-law definition of when a person's life ended. In the 1959 edition of *Black's*, death was defined as:

> The cessation of life; the ceasing to exist; defined by physicians as a total stoppage of the circulation of the blood, and a cessation of the animal and vital functions consequent thereon, such as respiration, pulsation, etc.

By the 1970s, however, as legal and medical experts debated definitions that only judges could rule on, disputes invariably revolved around patients on life-support systems. Often families wanted them discontinued because they considered the matter hopeless. Moreover, as technology progressed and organs were successfully transplanted, several physicians were accused of murder by families and representatives of the donors.

As a result, three states adopted a definition of death based on case law: Indiana, New York, and Washington. New York's highest court, the Court of Appeals, as one example, ruled on October 31, 1984:

> Ordinarily, death will be determined according to the traditional criteria of irreversible cardiorespiratory repose.
>
> When, however, the respirator and circulatory functions are maintained by mechanical means . . . death may nevertheless be deemed to occur when, according to accepted medical practice, it is determined that the entire brain's functions has irreversibly ceased.[24]

The presiding judge cited the Harvard criteria as a standard.

Criminal prosecutions of physicians accused of murder when a transplant organ has been removed are frequently rejected by the judiciary, based on 'proximate cause of death', and/or 'cause-in-fact'. Proximate cause cases determine that a criminal act (e.g., a gunshot wound in the head) is the cause of death. For example, an Arizona court in 1979, in *State v. Fierro*, ruled that the criminal defendant (a man who shot the patient but accused the doctor of murder for removing an organ while there were still vital signs) 'is liable for the natural consequences of his act.'[25] Cause-in-fact rulings accept a physician's conclusions about the occurrence of death as matters of fact.[26]

Two cases that typify the court's intervention and subsequent determination of the definition of death are *Tucker* v. *Lower* in Richmond, Virginia, 1972, and the Lyons case in Oakland, California, 1974, both of which point up the gap between law, medicine, and ethics.[27]

In 1968, Bruce Tucker, unconscious from a massive head injury, was admitted to a Richmond hospital. The next day he was pronounced dead. The hospital searched for relatives to claim his body, but found none. Because his body was unclaimed, he became an involuntary donor of the heart transplant programme at the hospital. (His heart was transplanted into a donee who died one week later.) Later, Bruce's brother, William, appeared and charged the hospital and the fourteen physicians involved in the transplant with wrongful death. Asking for $100,000 in damages, he argued that because his brother's heart was beating—he had respiration, blood pressure, and body temperature—he was alive at the time of the transplant, which William claimed was the cause of death.

Because the trial judge broadened the definition of death to include medical or neurological criteria as well as the statute definition, testimony was heard from medical experts, in particular neurologists. It took the jury fifty minutes to rule in favour of the physician: Bruce Tucker had died when his brain ceased to function.

The second case involved Andrew Lyons in northern California. Samuel Allen, Jr. (a.k.a. Samuel Moore), and Andrew Lyons were having an argument at the latter's house when Lyons pulled a gun and shot Allen in the head. Allen was later pronounced dead, and Lyons was charged with homicide. Because only Allen's brain had been damaged, his body was kept alive with artificial life supports until (like Tucker) his heart was removed for transplanting. Lyons then brought a lawsuit, charging that Allen was killed by the doctors who removed his heart, not by the bullet in his brain.

At the time, because California had no legal definition of death, the state accepted the attending physician's decision. Expert witnesses were called to testify that the best definition of death is irreversible cessation of brain activity. The judge, William J. Hayes, in his instructions to the jury, defined death as 'the cessation of life. A person may be pronounced dead if, based on usual and customary standards of medical practice, it is determined that the person has suffered an irreversible cessation of brain function.'[28] Lyons was found guilty of manslaughter.

Several cases have demonstrated problems with the statutes. A 1979 Maryland case, *State* v. *Robaczynski*,[29] challenged a statute similar to Kansas's original legislation. A Baltimore nurse was tried for murder after she disconnected the respirator of a forty-eight-year-old comatose patient. A mistrial was declared because the jury had difficulty interpreting the word 'spontaneous' as 'irreversible cessation of spontaneous brain function.' Did the legal meaning apply (i.e., inherent versus artificially maintained), or did the medical definition (manifested without intervention versus apparent only upon stimulation)?

A second problem presented itself in the court case of *Bacchiochi* v. *Johnson Memorial Hospital* in 1981.[30] Connecticut was one of two states that had incorporated their statute on death into their organ transplantation law. This caused difficulty when Mrs Bacchiochi's family—after the doctor declared her brain-dead—indicated that they wanted her removed from the respirator. Not surprisingly, the doctor refused to disconnect her unless he was granted immunity from prosecution. He feared that he would be accused of murder even though the state had adopted the brain death provision, because that applied only to potential donors. Because Mrs Bacchiochi was not a donor, the law did not apply to her.

Cases such as these demonstrate the flaws and intricacies in brain death legislation. As Peter S. Janzen declared in the *Hamline Law Review*: 'In order to compensate for the inadequacies that still exist, patients and their guardians are increasingly being forced to assert their right to die.'[31]

Many nations have brain death criteria. The statement on brain death made by the Conference of Royal Colleges and Faculties of the United Kingdom are assumed to be the accepted criteria for determination of death in Britain, even though they are not law. They do not use an EEG or cerebral activity as signs of brain-stem functions. West Germany's definition states: 'An individual with irreversible cessation of all functions of the entire brain, including the brain stem, is dead.'[32]

In A. Earl Walker's book, *Cerebral Death*, a table sets forth the medical and legal standards of brain death in different nations. Out of thirty-nine countries, thirty-five had medical concepts of brain death, while only thirteen had legally accepted standards.[33] Australia had an accepted medical and legal concept of brain death, as did Canada.

Different medical practices affect the need for brain death statutes. In China, for instance, 'brain death' is known only in academic circles, probably because pronouncing a person dead on the basis of brain function is infrequent. Resuscitative techniques are not commonly used, so if a patient does not recover normal respiratory functions, the case is abandoned.[34]

Reaction to medical and legal definitions of death varies, not only among nations but also among people and professions. The most controversial issue involved in brain death is what precisely constitutes cerebral death.

Many agree that death is not an event but a continuing process. Each part of the body dies at a different rate. For example, the brain is more vulnerable to oxygen depletion than the heart. Because of this, no single clinical factor is considered sufficient evidence of death.

The brain also dies in stages. The first part to die is the cerebral cortex (reponsible for higher thought processes). The midbrain dies next, and then the brain stem (responsible for reflexive functions). Walker defines brain death as 'an iatrogenic state resulting from advances in resuscitative techniques. Consequently, it occurs more frequently in major medical institutions with active emergency rooms and neurological and neurosurgical services.'[35]

Moreover, there is often confusion regarding what brain death refers to. To some, it means the entire brain has died, including the brain stem, whereas cerebral death is partial death of the brain. Which should be used to define death?

Under the entire-brain-death definition, Karen Ann Quinlan was alive for ten years. However, her neocortical functions were irreversibly damaged. Though she could breathe and circulate oxygen on her own, she could not communicate, think, experience, or feel. A person with a destroyed cerebral cortex and a functional brain stem can maintain life with cardiorespiratory functions for long periods of time. Upper-brain destruction, with a functional subcortex region, leaves a person in a 'persistent vegetative state'.

Are such definitions adequate? Ethicist Joseph Fletcher criticizes the brain death standard because the 'death of the individual is the irreversible loss of whatever component in his biological system holds the essence of the person, and that component is the cerebrum in the brain, not the whole brain.'[36] Similarly, Dr S. D. Olinger, director of neurology, the stroke unit, and the EEG department at Baylor University in Texas, concurs with Fletcher, pointing out that the whole-brain-death theory does 'not recognize the cerebral quality of human life [since] the cerebrum might be totally destroyed without hope of recovery, although circulation and respiration could persist or be supported indefinitely.'[37]

Opponents of cerebral death believe that a partial-brain-death definition presupposes that life has no intrinsic value, only an instrumental value. Dennis Horan, cited earlier, chairman of the Americans United for Life Legal Defense Fund in Chicago, described his opposition:

A physician is authorized under the standards of medical practice to discontinue a form of therapy which in his medical judgment is use-less. . . . By hopeless is meant that the prognosis for life (not meaningful life) is very poor. The fact that someone may or may not return to 'sapient or cognitive life' may or may not fulfil the requirement depend-ing upon other medical factors, but in and of itself it does not. . . . Brain Death is a condition of impending bodily or somatic death as well as one of massive brain destruction.[38]

He feels that such a definition is not to be confused with a permanent unre-sponsive state, such as Karen Quinlan's—except for those who consider broadening the criteria beyond what is accepted today.

Besides cerebral death, there is the problem of the 'locked-in-syndrome', in which a person has damage to the upper brain stem, causing paralysis in all extremities while the lower part of the brain is intact and respiration and blood pressure are maintained. The individual receives stimuli from the environment but may only be able to respond with eye movements. Current law offers no answer for this situation.

States without any formalized definition of death also face dilemmas. For instance, a fourteen-year-old girl in Massachusetts was found to meet all brain death criteria. Her organs were in good condition, and her parents authorized their removal for transplantation, but because there was no law recognizing brain death, a superior court judge was petitioned to sanction ventilator removal.[39] However, such judicial intervention is questionable inasmuch as time is of the essence for the organ donee.

Many hospitals vacillate in their reaction to brain death legislation. Some see brain death as a means of decreasing the costs of terminal care borne by the government, while others, reluctant to become involved in litigation, have appointed brain death committees. Such committees are composed of internists, electroencephalographists, and neurologists, acting as consul-tants to the physician.

All physicians have a technical, legal, and ethical interest in brain death legislation, and need guidelines since they are still legally responsible for determining the point of death. However, with the threat of malpractice looming over the profession, medical institutions and doctors are cautious when making a declaration that may be contested. There is also the fear that the practice of medicine will become excessively regulated by guide-lines, which will in turn infringe upon the individual physician's judgment.

Because the largest group of comatose patients do not meet brain death criteria, many physicians must still use their own discretion. A survey con-ducted for the President's Commission indicated that fewer than 5 per cent of deaths are certified on the basis of brain death.[40] Thus, even when the standards are available, they are not always used—either because the case is not complicated or because the standards are burdensome and impractical.

# CHAPTER EIGHTEEN

# Religion and Euthanasia

Most Christian groups do not oppose passive euthanasia, and although they are less specific about it, neither do most Eastern religions. Allowing a hopelessly ill person to die by not imposing extraordinary measures is widely accepted today by the churches as being part of God's will. Only Mormons, Evangelicals, and other strict Gospel denominations are opposed to passive euthanasia in the West, while Islam is opposed in the East. Had any of these groups been asked about their position on euthanasia ten or more years ago, they probably would have been unable to give a ready answer. Public policy-making in this area has almost entirely followed the Karen Ann Quinlan case in 1976.

But active voluntary euthanasia—taking one's own life or helping another to die—is a different matter. No church hierarchy has endorsed the practice, although many would not condemn it, preferring instead to leave the matter to individual conscience and decision. Part of this lack of official policy is due to the nature of the reformed churches: They tend to eschew dogma and authoritarian figures, preferring their congregations to govern themselves according to a basic moral code. Another reason is the realization that active euthanasia is both a complex and an explosive question theologically.

The Roman Catholic Church, however, has never avoided the touchy issues of euthanasia. Its position—acceptance of passive but rejection of active—is the most clearly articulated of any faith, especially since the Vatican's 1980 Declaration on Euthanasia, which said, in part:

1. No one can make an attempt on the life of an innocent person without opposing God's love for that person, without violating a fundamental right, and therefore without committing a crime of the utmost gravity.

2. Everyone has the duty to lead his or her life in accordance with God's plan. That life is entrusted to the individual as a good that must bear fruit already here on earth, but that finds its full perfection only in eternal life.

3. Intentionally causing one's own death, or suicide, is therefore equally as wrong as murder; such an action on the part of a person is to be considered as a rejection of God's sovereignty and loving plan. Furthermore, suicide is also often a refusal of love for self, the denial of the natural instinct to live, a flight from the duties of justice and charity owed to one's neighbour, to various communities or to the whole of society—although, as is generally recognized, at times there are psychological factors present that can diminish responsibility or even completely remove it.

However, one must clearly distinguish suicide from that sacrifice of one's life whereby for a higher cause, such as God's glory, the salvation of souls or the service on one's brethren, a person offers his or her own life or puts it in danger (cf. Jn 15:14).[1]

The Jewish position is that passive euthanasia can, under carefully scrutinized conditions, be allowed. Jewish thinkers speak of 'indirect euthanasia', wherein the patient's death is merely the unpremeditated result of some medication given only to relieve pain or is a consequence of the withdrawal of treatment.[2] But as Rabbi Immanuel Jakobovits warns: 'A patient must not shrink from spiritual distress by refusing ritually forbidden services or foods if necessary for his healing; how much less may he refuse treatment to escape from physical suffering.'[3]

Because there is no possibility of repentence for self-destruction, Judaism considers suicide a sin worse than murder; therefore active euthanasia, voluntary or involuntary, is forbidden.

While Jewish law rates the mitigation of a patient's suffering, especially in the ordeal prior to death, above virtually any other consideration, if necessary even his ability to make his spiritual and temporal preparations for death, what it cannot do is purchase relief from pain and misery at the cost of life itself. This is based on Judaism's attribution of infinite value to human life. Infinity being indivisible, any fraction of life, however limited its expectancy or its health, remains equally infinite in value.[4]

Some Jewish authorities would categorize any active and deliberate hastening of death as 'sheer murder'.[5]

Yet despite the strong prohibition by Jewish thinkers, it is of interest to note that the membership roll of the Hemlock Society, for instance, contains a substantial number of people with names of Jewish origin.

Broadly speaking, Episcopalians and Anglicans are sympathetic to active euthanasia so long as there is justification for the act, as are Methodists, Unitarians and Quakers. But there have been no pronouncements from their leaderships. Hindus and Sikhs also rely on personal choice and conscience, while orthodox Buddhists condone passive but not active euthanasia.

Lutherans favour passive euthanasia but excoriate active. The followers of this church were reminded in a 1979 official report that even if a time should come when mercy killing is no longer a crime in the eyes of society, it would still be a sin in the eyes of the church.

> It is within's God's purview alone to decide on the moment when the individual is to share that life which lies beyond death in a world restored to a splendour even greater than its pristine purity. Within the context of this certain hope, mercy killing runs squarely against the grain of the will of a gracious Creator.[6]

The point at which most churches find it easy to accept passive euthanasia but must stop at active is on the question of whether one way is natural, i.e., God's, and the other, suicide, is a taboo. As reported in Chapter 1, the early Greek and Roman civilizations were tolerant, sometimes approving, of justified suicide. Their philosophers, especially Plato, discussed suicide a great deal and endorsed it within specific limitations. While today suicide for reasons of old age is a major problem, in those early civilizations life expectancy—with rare exceptions—was only into the late twenties. Suicide was usually the result of disappointment in battle or politics. Even so, it was largely restricted to the upper classes: servants and soldiers whose services were needed were not permitted to take their own lives.

The coming of Christianity changed all this. Few have put it better than Doris Portwood in *Commonsense Suicide: The Final Right*:

> The early Christians brought a new attitude towards suicide by taking a fanatic delight in the prospect of instant salvation. There was no shortage of candidates for the tortures of the arena: a martyr's death meant a reserved seat among the blessed in heaven. These suicides were, in today's language, passive rather than active. The primitive Christians did not fall on the sword or hold the hemlock cup to their lips, but they walked willingly—men, women and children—into situations (often deliberately provoked situations) that meant not only death but death of a most grim variety.[7]

This meant that the spread of Christianity was likely to be affected severely by loss of adherents. The Council of Braga in A.D. 563 condemned suicide and later councils confirmed this, citing as their authority the Sixth Commandment: 'Thou shalt not kill.' The councils decreed that self-destruction was as much a sin as homicide. The philosophical basis had been developed by St Augustine (A.D. 354–430: Life was a gift of God and not man's to give away. Many years later, St Thomas Aquinas (1225–1274) reinforced this argument, saying suicide was a mortal sin, contrary to natu-

ral law, damaging to the human community, and symbolic of humans assuming divine prerogatives concerning decisions of life and death. The
Augustine–Aquinas view has prevailed in church dogma ever since.

Contrary to popular belief, the Bible contains no condemnation of
suicide (except a literal interpretation of the Sixth Commandment) and
in its reporting of six suicides speaks of them as part of the tragedy of
life. The Greek approach to suicide clearly still influenced the Bible's
authors.

The most famous biblical suicide is, of course, that of Judas Iscariot out
of remorse for betraying Jesus Christ; the next-best-known is that of Saul,
who, together with his armour-bearer, committed suicide because he could
not bear the thought of being captured by his enemies. Abimelech,
Samson, Ahithophel, and Zimri also killed themselves, according to the
Bible. Some historians have noted that all these suicides were for selfish
and not altruistic reasons and therefore deserve scrutiny.*

It has been argued through the ages that Jesus Christ committed premeditated suicide by not leaving town when he knew his crucifixion was
imminent. 'Had he done so, it seems entirely likely that the Pharisees
would have left him alone,' writes William Rauscher, in *The Case Against
Suicide*. The church fathers Tertullian (A.D. 160–230) and Origen (A.D.
185–254) argued that his was a sacrificial suicide, and in the sixteenth century the English poet John Donne, in his famous essay on suicide, postulated the same theory.[8]

Theologians respond that the death of Jesus was intentional suffering
inflicted upon himself for others, whereas the other six biblical suicides
were for reasons of self-interest only.† Yet the Bible contains many curious
references to what appear to be suicidal thoughts, as for instance when
Jonah 'asked that he might die, and said "it is better for me to die than to
live"' (Jon. 4:8). And as Jesus prepared his disciples for his death,
'Thomas, called the Twin, said to his fellow disciples, "Let us also go that
we may die with him"' (John 11:16). The Book of Revelation has a sentence, 'And in those days men will seek death and will not find it; they will
long to die, and death flies from them' (Rev. 9:6).

Perhaps Rauscher says it best:

---

* Suicide for altruistic reasons is extremely rare. A famous case reported in the early
twentieth century was of Captain Titus Oates, whose lameness slowed Scott's Antarctic expedition as it struggled home. Oates deliberately went out into the night to die in a storm. (It
was a noble but wasted gesture, because Scott's entire expedition perished a few days later.)

† In the 1970s when several Irish Republican Army men imprisoned by the British in
Ulster starved themselves to death in protest at the continued foreign occupation of their
country, the Roman Catholic Church, of which they were members, refused to condemn their
self-destruction because it was done for a cause larger than themselves. It was, in effect, suicide justified by altruism, as noted at the end of the Vatican edict of 1980.

The ethical dilemma that we face is before us because we have not understood, been unwilling to understand, what the Bible really says about
death and suicide.... In our day the problem of suicide is a tremen-
dously complicated one. When we go to the Bible for guidance, it
appears that what we find is an insistence that intentional death must be
viewed as suffering—and not for oneself alone. It must include the kind
of redemptive suffering enacted by the death of Jesus.[9]

Theologians have argued against killing under any circumstances, stressing the sanctity of life. But has Christianity ever truly practised what it
believed? 'Just' wars have been countenanced, killing in self-defence
approved, and capital punishment sanctioned. History shows many
instances of shrewd kings and politicians using religious feelings and jea-
lousies as an excuse to wage war (this is nowhere better illustrated than in
Barbara Tuchman's historical record of the fourteenth century, *A Distant
Mirror*). In another example, God's help was trenchantly invoked during
the Civil War in Britain between the Roundheads (mostly Puritans) under
Oliver Cromwell and the Cavaliers (mostly Catholic) under King Charles.

A theologian who points out that the principle of the sanctity of life is not
as clear as it first appears is former Cambridge University academic
P. R. Baelz, now dean of Durham Cathedral. Christianity, he says, often
makes exceptions. Furthermore, if life is defined not in biological but in
personal terms, 'we shall find ourselves asking the question whether there
are stages in the development and decline of the human animal when it is
not, or no longer, a human person.... An appeal to the sanctity of human
life may mean no more than that human life ought not to be taken unless
there are morally persuasive reasons for taking it.'[10] It is also an oddity that
all Western countries are avowedly 'Christian', yet some have abolished
capital punishment (Britain, Norway, Sweden, for instance), while the
country most proud to say it is Christian, the United States, permits
judicial executions on an increasing scale.

Baelz is another critic who argues that a person cannot look to the Scrip-
tures to settle the question of suicide; in the end, in any particular situation, an individual must exercise his own conscientious judgment and
make his own moral decision.[11] Baelz also argues that if any Christian is
convinced that suicide is always a contravention of the word of God, then
even the thought of such action must be avoided. 'If, however, he is not
convinced that neither is necessarily the case, then he must attempt to
specify the conditions under which it is permissible ... limiting them to
cases in which the process of dying threatens to destroy a man's humanity
before death itself supervenes.'[12]

Gerald A. Larue, who in 1984 conducted a survey of religions' attitudes to
euthanasia,[13] concluded that leaders' responses confronted the issue from a

theological or from an academic point of view, rather than from direct contact with pain and suffering. However, he found:

> Some liberal Protestant churches, while continuing to look to the Bible for spiritual guidance, confront the issue of euthanasia for the terminally ill in intractable pain from a humane or person-oriented posture rather than simply trying to find what the Bible may or may not have recorded.[14]

Larue, professor emeritus of religion at the University of Southern California, says that behind each position lies a belief system that in traditional religions is based on mythology, a sacred story, and a religious fiction. Further, this belief system conditions responses.

> The fundamental belief is that in some special way the divine has penetrated the realm of the secular, or that the deity has broken into the sphere of human life, to reveal acceptable life patterns and legal regulations governing life and death. . . . Out of the *mythos* or sacred story emerge rules and laws to control and direct the lives and the living of true believers. The guiding principles are believed to have been supernaturally revealed and to represent the divine will for humans.[15]

In a unique survey to ascertain the beliefs of people strongly supportive of euthanasia, demographers at the University of California, Los Angeles, asked the membership of the Hemlock Society about both their religious background and their current beliefs. Out of the sample taken, 21 per cent said religion was very important to them, 36 per cent said it was somewhat important, while 43 per cent rated it not important. Almost one-third (31 per cent) believed in life after death. Fifteen per cent of Hemlock members attend church at least monthly.

The pollsters found that Hemlock members had the following religious affiliations:

## RELIGIOUS AFFILIATION OF HEMLOCK MEMBERSHIP

| | UPBRINGING | PRESENT (IN PER CENT) | U.S. POPULATION |
|---|---|---|---|
| Protestant | 61 | 27 | 54 |
| Roman Catholic | 12 | 4 | 37 |
| Jewish | 16 | 6 | 4 |
| Atheist | 2 | 17 | — |
| Agnostic | 6 | 34 | — |
| Other | 3 | 12 | 5 |

Fortunately, many churches are reexamining their attitudes to euthanasia in both its forms. The fact that there have been significant changes in certain aspects of religious orthodoxy suggests that others will be made in regard to death and dying. For instance, the Mormon Church since 1978 has accepted black people into the priesthood; some churches and synagogues have ordained women and homosexuals—an unthinkable act twenty years ago. The time may come when a scriptural basis for acceptance of active voluntary euthanasia is found.

## BELIEFS ABOUT EUTHANASIA*

| RELIGION | PASSIVE | ACTIVE |
|---|---|---|
| Assemblies of God | individual decision | individual decision |
| The Baha'is | individual decision | oppose |
| Baptist | accept | oppose |
| Buddhism | accept | oppose |
| Christian Church (Disciples of Christ) | individual decision | individual decision |
| Christian & Missionary Alliance Church | oppose | oppose |
| Christian Scientist* | individual decision | individual decision |
| Church of the Brethren* | accept | oppose |
| Church of Christ (Christian) | oppose | oppose |
| Church of the Nazarene | oppose | oppose |
| Episcopal* (Anglican) | accept | individual decision |
| Evangelical | oppose | oppose |
| Greek Orthodox | accept | oppose |
| Hindu* | individual decision | individual decision |
| Humanists | accept | accept |
| Islam* | oppose | oppose |
| Jehovah's Witnesses | accept | oppose |
| Judaism* | accept | oppose |
| Krishna* | accept | oppose |
| Lutheran | accept | oppose |
| Mennonite* | accept | oppose |
| Mormon | oppose | oppose |
| Moravian | accept | oppose |
| Quaker Religious Society | accept | individual decision |
| Reformed Church of America | oppose | oppose |
| Roman Catholic | accept | oppose |
| Russian Orthodox | accept | oppose |
| Seventh-Day Adventist* | accept | oppose |
| Sikh Dharma* | individual decision | individual decision |
| Swedenborgianism | accept | oppose |
| Theosophical Society | individual decision | individual decision |
| Unitarian Universalist | accept | individual decision |
| United Church of Christ | accept | individual decision |
| United Methodist | accept | individual decision |
| United Presbyterian | individual decision | individual decision |

---

* 'No official statement': In such cases, spokespersons form their conclusions based on religious rationale and opinion.

Where churches have no stated official position on this topic, it is assumed that the decision is one of individual choice. Individual decision usually implies a matter of concern between patient, family, and doctor.

# CHAPTER NINETEEN

# *Helping Another to Die*

Helping another to die is probably the most intensely personal test of individual conscience known to mankind. Most of us are shocked and revolted by murder, suicide or genocide, but when someone we know cries out with justification for help in dying, who among us dares to respond? If we help accelerate death in these circumstances, are we being ruthless or humane?

Putting aside matters of law, the questions one must ask onself are:

1. Do my religious and philosophical beliefs permit me to participate in this requested death?

2. Am I upholding the dying person's autonomy—his free choice in life's decisions—by helping?

Of course, there are many supplementary questions that could be added to these two: Am I playing God? What about a possible miracle cure? Does the patient have a civic duty to remain alive? What about the patient's responsibility to his family? However, the kernel of the dilemma still lies with the two main questions.

Some base their opposition to assisted suicide for the terminally ill on the belief that the assisters are primarily putting themselves out of their own misery—the agony of seeing a loved one suffer. The strongest proponent of this 'selfish' argument is Dr Elisabeth Kübler-Ross. Although she does not necessarily regard suicide as abnormal behaviour, she disapproves of advertising suicide as everyone's right. She opposes mercy killing and assisting suicide, arguing instead that giving help to live meaningfully to the end usually disposes of the need for self-deliverance. Dr Kübler-Ross acknowledges, nevertheless, those who do take control. '[They] are those who are usually not conventionally religious, but have accepted their finiteness and would rather shorten the process of dying than linger on for another few weeks or months in what they regard as useless suffering.'[1]

Still, she roundly condemns those who might see fit to help:

> To me, that is breaking absolute universal law. They will have to pay for the consequences of their behaviour. To take consciously a life is a no-no, but to prolong life with extraordinary means is also not mandatory. To kill to abbreviate the life of a cancer patient is a problem not that the patient has, but one the caregiver has. They cannot tolerate to watch the suffering or deal with whatever unfinished business in their own lives. They try to terminate a life under the disguise of mercy and that is not mercy. Today dying does not have to be a nightmare. Dying does not have to be painful.[2]

Few ethicists will openly make the plea for help with suicide, be it ever so rational, because society's taboo on suicide makes assistance an unpalatable subject for discussion. Two exceptions are Margaret Pabst Battin, a philosopher who has made a special study of suicide, and Joseph Fletcher.

Battin argues that Christianity's prohibition of suicide in the fourth century was meant to prevent self-killing for reasons of religious zealotry. It was not designed to regulate suicides due to physical or emotional suffering, old age, altruism towards others, personal or societal honour. While there was at that time a need to prevent the surfeit of martyrs' suicides, there was, she contends, no intention to dispel the Platonic case for rational suicide. She blames theologians and philosophers for the misinterpretations.

Battin has publicly argued that it is unfair for society to insist that a person be required to commit suicide in a lonely way:

> If there is a right to die (which can be exercised either in euthanasia or suicide) this means that there may also be an obligation on the part of others—though one which we do not now either morally or legally recognize—either to perform euthanasia for the individual, or to assist him in his own self-killing. If the right is a natural right, the obligations it imposes on others may be still stronger.[3]

For his part, Fletcher believes that helping to die is more a reflexive action of an individual than anything connected to philosophy. In *Humanhood: Essays in Bimedical Ethics*, he contends:

> Occasionally I hear a physician say that he could not bring himself to resort to direct euthanasia. That may be so. What anybody would do in such tragic situations is a problem in psychology, however, not in ethics. We are not asking what we would do but what we should do. Any of us who has an intimate knowledge of what happens in terminal illnesses can tell stories of rational people—both physicians and family—who were quite clear ethically about the rightness of an overdose or of 'turning off

the machine', and yet found themselves too inhibited to give the word or do the deed.[4]

For a deeply religious person, the rejection of assistance in a suicide springs automatically from total acceptance of God's moral authority over the course of human life. However, for those who do not believe in God, or who feel that a compassionate God would approve of what they plan to do, the dilemma of aiding a death must be tackled differently.

Fletcher's arguments are born out in the recollections of a woman in Arizona who helped her mother die:

> In the last few days, and especially in the last hours before I gave her the medication, a lot of what was going on with me that was so painful was really intense self-examination to see if my motives were pure. And I found out that they were pure. There were all the things I asked myself: Do I just want to get rid of this responsibility? Do I just not want to have to cope with my mother's dying days? And the answers to these questions were, yes, I don't want to put myself through this, and I want to relieve my own suffering. I said, Are you doing this to relieve your own suffering? Yes, I am. It's something that I'm going through in all areas of my life, through my middle age, and that is realizing that my motivations for doing things are never all one thing or another. They're never all good and all bad; they're never all pure nor all malicious. They are always mixed.
>
> Although I could find elements of all these things in my feelings, the overriding one was of compassion for my mother. And I knew with such a rock-hard certainty that I loved my mother as I had never loved her in all my life that I had to trust that. I could not for mean motives kill my mother when I felt such love for her. It wouldn't be possible to have those two things. If we are honest with ourselves, we can find little selfish and mean motives for everything. So it was really good to admit that they were in there because then I didn't feel like I was untrue to myself or fooling myself.[5]

A man who shot his paralyzed mother, for whom he was caring at home, said:

> I realized that if she could go through the torture of being in bed twenty-four hours a day, unable to speak, with all those tubes connected to her, then I could do the other. [Shoot her.] I opened up the drawer with the gun, and as clear as day I heard a voice say, 'Frank, take the gun and shoot your mother.' I felt calm, like I was in a play. I took the gun, I walked out, and I put it on the back of my mother's head. My hands started shaking. I couldn't do it if she was sleeping. She was too peaceful. She looked too nice to me. It had to be when she was making that funny

noise. I went back into my bedroom and waited. I tried to get some sleep. It got to about four in the morning and I walked out again. She made this horrible noise, and the gun went off. I was surprised. I had shot my mother in the back of the head.[6]

Usually the nonmedical person who is asked for help in dying has time to review the request carefully and make a decision in accordance with conscience. The decisive factor is invariably the strength of the relationship between asker and asked. No one can say for certain that he will or will not help another to die until the request has actually been made and the circumstances are considered. Some people have an instant repulsion to the merest thought of helping; others feel that it depends on the circumstances. For some couples, being together during the final moments while the terminal partner takes a deliberate overdose is important to their relationship, a final celebration of their companionship, a logical end to the fight for life which they have together waged—and inevitably lost.

Many of the assisters are fully aware that they are breaking the law but have chosen to obey only moral law (their own, of course). Should they be discovered and prosecuted, they will accept the consequences. Prosecutions for assisted suicide are relatively infrequent, especially where a terminal illness was involved and the helper a close family member. However, the act remains a crime, and there is always the risk of charges being brought by a prosecutor with a different set of moral values.

For instance, in the 1985 trial of Roswell Gilbert in Fort Lauderdale, Florida, much was made of the argument that Gilbert killed his wife to relieve himself of the seven-year burden of caring for a demented and very sick woman. This particular argument, repeatedly stressed by the state's attorney, probably served to convict Gilbert for first-degree murder more than anything else.

An observer at the trial told reporters after the hearing:

From talking to Gilbert privately as well as hearing his testimony, I heard a voice which perhaps only those of us who have been tested in helping a loved one to die can recognize. Mr Gilbert was saying, in effect, that if people have been loving companions for a great length of time, there is a fusion of minds, where one assumes the burden of the other. The suffering is mutual, as is the responsibility to do something about it.[7]

A person who believed passionately in the right to help with suicide, the late Morgan Sibbett, of Swarthmore, Pennsylvania, assisted five people in dying. Although he always made a point of reporting these actions to law enforcement authorities, he was never prosecuted. Sibbett argued that

'Even if a person is dying by their own deliberate action, there should be someone with them holding their hand as they go.'[8]

In 1980, Sibbett spoke openly on the *60 Minutes* television programme about his beliefs and his actions and received no notably hostile reactions. Reporter Mike Wallace described him as 'an angel of death'. Sibbett first helped a physician friend of his who was seventy-five and suffered from Parkinson's disease. The two had made a 'mutual assistance' pact in writing four years earlier. When the illness was in an advanced stage, the physician asked Sibbett to be with him as he took his life.

On their final evening, the two men dined together. The doctor then wrote to his wife, who knew of the intention but not the timing, and then prepared a suicide note. He and Sibbett then went to the bedroom, where the physician took forty Seconal tablets. Sibbett, whose help was more moral support than active assistance (which would have been a felony), said later: 'Coming to me under these circumstances was the natural thing, and the only thing—the only way he could do it with dignity and without the sordidness and furtiveness of being alone. This way there was no sense of desperation, no pall of gloom. He wanted those last days to be peaceful, and they were, in a measure that is difficult to imagine. It was a good death.'[9]

Publicity about Sibbett's action caused other dying people to approach him. Before his own death, in 1982, he helped four of them with drugs given him by his doctor friend. Sibbett was scrupulously careful to get to know the people he helped. When they were ready, he would take the pills to them, show how they should be ingested, and stay with them until they died. On his own deathbed, Sibbett chose not to use the lethal drugs that he always kept on a side table. Instead, he slipped into a coma and died peacefully in the presence of his wife, Joanna. Those who knew him said there was little doubt he would have taken his own life had he felt it necessary.

Accounts of how it feels to help another person die are rare. The most compassionate of crimes is also a secret crime. The three best-known statements have come from professional writers. Not only could they explain their feelings; they were resilient enough to withstand the public criticism their actions and their words provoked. All three accounts appear to bear out Fletcher's view that helping to die is more a psychological than an ethical matter. In none of the three books is there a hint of an argument or of wavering by the helper.

In *Death of a Man*, Lael Tucker Wertenbaker describes how in 1955, in France, she helped her husband, himself an author and a veteran journalist, who had advanced cancer of the bowel. 'It had to be that night, and we both knew it. We waited until very late, talking together with a kind of final serenity unmatched at any other time. He planned everything most carefully, aware that nothing was as you planned it, but with determination that however and whatever, he must die.' Unable to kill himself solely with an overdose of morphine (probably because of tolerance built up during treatment), Charles Wertenbaker was obliged to cut his wrists. Even as he did this, helped by his wife, who cut her own fingers slightly, there was close communication. She writes: 'I said, "I love you, I love you, please die," and he said that one first phrase, too, and went into the final struggle to die and did.'[10]

Derek Humphry and his wife Jean had an understanding that when her cancer became too distressing to her, she could take her life and he would help. To Jean, forty-two years old, timing was important because she was anxious not to make a mistake and die before it was necessary. In *Jean's Way*, Humphry reports a crucial conversation:

'Derek?' Jean called softly.

'Yes, darling.'

'Is this the day?'

I panicked. My mouth dried up and I could not control the tear which rushed to my eyes. It was the most awful moment of my life. However, I had to answer, 'Yes, my darling, it is.'

There followed many minutes of silence as both considered the decision we had taken. Had I done the right thing? Should she go back to the hospital for more treatment? My tormented thoughts were checked in the midst of their chaotic rambling by Jean's calm, measured voice. 'How shall it be? You promised me you would get something.'

'I have,' I answered. 'A doctor in London has mixed me a combination of drugs which are quite lethal. You have only to take them and that is the end.'[11]

Jean Humphry took her life several hours later. When *Jean's Way* appeared in London in 1978, Humphry was warned by police that they were considering prosecuting him for assisting a suicide, an offence that in Britain carries a penalty of up to fourteen years imprisonment. After an inquiry, the public prosecutor decided not to charge Humphry.

Confirmation that a decision to help a loved one die is an intuitive thing appears in Betty Rollin's best-selling book *Last Wish*. Her mother, dying of ovarian cancer, asked six times for help in dying. Betty, not knowing how to cope at first, eventually agreed but does not—despite the book's remarkable frankness in most other matters—explore her decision to obtain information on drug dosage and give moral support.

At the end, there is a striking passage as Betty describes watching her mother swallow the pills: 'I want to jump out of my stone encasement and cheer. I want to wave a flag, blow a horn, scream, weep, cry, shout. Hooray for you, Mother! You're doing it, Mother! You're doing it just right!'[12]

How often assistance in suicide is given between nonmedical people is not known, because this act is conducted in the privacy of homes and is usually followed by discretion on the part of the lawbreaker. Euthanasia societies report tolerance by police and coroners' staffs—so long as terminal illness is confirmed and there are no complaints—whenever such a death comes to their notice.

Demographers at the University of California, Los Angeles, in their 1983 survey,[13] asked the membership of the Hemlock Society how many had helped another to die—either by providing psychological support, by offering active assistance, or by making a decision about stopping treatment. Even the euthanasia society was surprised to learn that 17 per cent of its membership had already assisted in a suicide.

## PROVIDING AID IN OTHERS'S SELF-DELIVERANCE

|  | HAVE IN PAST | | WILLING TO IN FUTURE | |
| --- | --- | --- | --- | --- |
|  | YES | NO | YES | NO |
| Provide psychological support | 45% | 55% | 91% | 9% |
| Provide assistance in self-deliverance | 17% | 83% | 73% | 27% |
| Serve as a proxy in life decision | 18% | 82% | 71% | 29% |

At a conference held in New York in 1981 by Concern for Dying, with the theme 'Suicide: Is it an acceptable choice for the terminally ill?' people were given a questionnaire that asked, among other things: Are there circumstances under which you would assist someone to commit suicide? Fifty people said yes, twenty-seven said they would not, and thirty-one were uncertain.[14]

Fletcher has said that 'the truly great issue of our times is not the right to choose to die, which is practically old hat now, but the right to help those who choose to die,'[15] and while it appears that a section of the public has no trouble with the concept or the practice, the medical world is a very different story.

The question is increasingly raised: Is there a moral difference between allowing a person to die by deliberately *not* doing something, and helping them to die by actually doing something? Doctors, of course, are comfortable with the 'we'll do nothing to keep people alive unnecessarily' concept. They point out that the first instance is within the law, while the second is not. For a physician, committing a felony is double jeopardy: the likelihood of a prison sentence plus disbarment from the profession.

Yet the moral question remains.

James Rachels argued in a *New England Journal of Medicine* article that one can let a patient die by way of not giving medication, just as one may insult someone by not shaking his hand. 'But for any purpose of moral assessment, it is a type of action nonetheless,' he says. Rachels points out what few doctors will say much about: that being 'allowed to die' can be relatively slow and painful, whereas being given a lethal injection is relatively quick and painless.

Dr Christian Barnard, the pioneer heart transplant surgeon, who in his retirement has become an international advocate of euthanasia, writes:

> It seems clear to me that a deliberate act of omission, when death is the goal or purpose sought, is morally indistinguishable from a deliberate act of commission. Procedurally, there is a difference between direct and indirect euthanasia, but ethically they are the same.[17]

The Dutch, as we have reported, have more advanced knowledge and practice of euthanasia than other countries. One of the Netherlands' leading experts, Professor Pieter V. Admiraal, author of the landmark manual 'Justifiable Euthanasia: A Guide for the Medical Profession', is scornful of distinguishing between two forms of euthanasia. 'When speaking of passive euthanasia, the "passive" in my opinion refers only to the physician's attitude. There is no place for passive euthanasia alone.' Admiraal defines euthanasia as a deliberate life-shortening act administered on an incurable patient in such a patient's interest, carried out so that a quick, peaceful death ensues.[18]

Yet other doctors and thinkers believe that there is a real difference between doing nothing and doing something. Canadian ethicist and theologian Dr J. Arthur Boorman argues that Karen Ann Quinlan is a case in point: When taken off the respirator, she ought to have died but she did not. Dr Boorman says: 'There is a finality about direct euthanasia, perhaps a certain arrogance, that is not present in the passive approach.'[19]

The Catholic philosopher Daniel Maguire, author of *Death by Choice*, one of the most influential books on the subject in the past twenty years, holds that omission and commission are different realities; since morality is based on reality, a real difference could be expected to make a moral difference. Maguire points to the psychological effect of giving a fatal dose to a loved one as opposed to letting the malady take away life. Omission can be the result of being unable to decide what is best to do, and it removes the need to take responsibility.

Finally, Maguire argues that there are as many different kinds of omission as there are of commission: For example, it is a terrible omission not to steer your car away from a child, but an acceptable omission not to tackle an armed bank robber.

Good ethics makes distinctions where there are differences and there are differences here. The difference, however, is not that one is right and the other wrong. Both may be right or wrong depending on how they feature in the value equation.[20]

In the seesaw argument, Fletcher also uses practical illustrations, pointing out one of the many dichotomies between ethics and law, where it is not a crime to allow a blind man to walk off a cliff, but it is a crime to push him over. Ethically, both are reprehensible. Fletcher castigates the law's lack of morality in euthanasia and many other forms of human conduct.[21]

Those in the medical profession who are firmly opposed to active euthanasia base their opposition on the belief that there would be a massive loss of trust on the part of the patient if it were known that the doctor had the legal sanction to kill. 'Can you imagine the thoughts that would go through a patient's head as he faced a critical illness wondering whether his or her physician might decide the effort was not worth it?' said Dr Boorman.[22]

The patient must be assured that the physician will take all reasonable steps to heal, and at all times will ensure comfort, argues Dr Matthew Conolly, professor of medicine and pharmacology at the University of California, Los Angeles, Medical School. '[A] clear distinction must be made between relieving suffering in order to minimize the trauma of death, and deliberately causing death in order to end the distress of suffering. If present laws are changed to erode that distinction, how could trust survive?'[23]

Moreover, some doctors are clearly uneasy entrusting their colleagues with the power of life and death. Dr Edmund Pellegrino, professor of medicine at Yale University, says he cannot see how such decisions could be made by single individuals decreeing what ought to happen to other human beings simply because they are in a profession. To give the physician too much power is to court abuse, he feels.[24]

Dr Arthur Caplan, a medical ethicist at the Hastings Center, also worries about the integrity of physicians. He said on a *Face the Nation* television broadcast:

> I think one of the problems with legalizing mercy killing at this point in time is that there is a real gulf forming between patients and their physicians. If I thought patients and physicians trusted each other in the way that we might hope that they do, maybe I wouldn't be so worried about legalizing mercy killing, but the fact is, attitudes concerning the old, the dying, within most—much of our hospital system are not positive, and with current emphases, as they are, on cost containment, I just fear that it's not the morality of suicide that makes me hesitant about legalizing mercy killing; it's the potential for abuse. There really are biases. There really are problems out there.

*Fred Graham:* Are you—are you saying that doctors would countenance killing old people to get them out of the way?

*Dr Caplan:* I'm saying that under the present pressures to contain costs, and with the emphases in the system to try and deliver acute care and not attend chronic illness, that people do tend to lower the estimate they're willing to put on the quality of life of an older person, of a dying person, and, yes, I fear abuse may take place if we were to go the—down that road of legalizing mercy killing and putting that power in the judgment of a physician or a nurse.[25]

Christiaan Barnard contends that the right to practise euthanasia can be valid only if two experienced doctors concur with the patient and there are guidelines for them to follow. 'For centuries, society has placed trust in the medical profession to actively help the patient to recover from ill health,' he notes. 'It is simply an extension of this trust to permit the doctor to actively help the patient in the process of dying.'[26]

Dr Admiraal discusses the question of euthanasia with his patients even before they ask for it. 'It can be a great value and great comfort for many a patient,' he says. 'Not discussing euthanasia with a patient before he asks for it can cause the [medical] team to be completely taken by surprise if suddenly a patient asks for it. It may even shock the members of the team, who may be disappointed or even angry about the request, which they did not anticipate.'[27]

A contrasting view is given by R. W. Luxton, a retired British physician: 'In the seriously ill patient fear and anxiety is readily magnified. In such circumstances [lawful euthanasia], every syringe would carry a threat.'[28]

Just how many doctors believe in euthanasia—active and passive—is difficult to assess. Because active euthanasia is unlawful, many are fearful of expressing a supportive viewpoint in case others leap to the conclusion that they practise it. Still, a 1981 survey of physicians practising in two Seattle hospitals revealed that 87 per cent of the respondents (anonymously polled) approved of passive euthanasia, and 80 per cent indicated that they practise it when appropriate. 15 per cent said that they favoured active euthanasia.

To judge by the attendance of doctors at conferences debating euthanasia, and the number of requests euthanasia societies receive to provide speakers to medical groups, there is at least a probing interest in the issue among a substantial membership of the medical profession. Surveys of physicians' views taken over the years, as reported earlier in this book, have usually demonstrated that around 15 per cent would practise active euthanasia —where justified—*if it were lawful.*

Only a handful of doctors have ever publicly said that they helped patients to die through a positive action. In 1974 the retired Scottish surgeon Dr George Mair revealed in his autobiography, *Confessions of a Surgeon*, that he had carried out several mercy killings on terminally ill patients during his long career. There was a move to prosecute him, but as he did not reveal the details of the deaths there was no evidence upon which the police could act. Also in 1979 in Copenhagen, Dr Bjoern Ibsen told a radio interviewer that he had occasionally overdosed a patient on morphine if it became clear during an operation that nothing possible could be done to help him.

Barnard has said that he would on occasion have practised active euthanasia had it not been a capital offence in South Africa.[29] In 1984 five French doctors sent a manifesto to the international congress of the World Federation of Right to Die Societies, saying that not only did they support active euthanasia but they had practised it, when appropriate despite its illegality in France.

However, the action is almost invariably a secret pact between patient and doctor, and no one hears about it. Often the doctor takes it upon himself to overdose the patient covertly, as in the case of Dr Kraai, reported earlier. He was noticed, reported, and charged. But from private conversations with physicians, it is clear that the vast majority of active euthanasia cases go undetected.

Yet as physicians observe the pendulum of public opinion swinging in favour of justified euthanasia, more frankness is being shown. For instance, in an educational film made in 1985, Dr Daniel Simmons, a pulmonary specialist at the University of California, Los Angeles, Medical School, calmly talked about the time he took a patient's life.

I may be rather unique in simply disregarding the legalities of the situation. I think the ethical and moral considerations transcend that. Most physicians don't think about this the way I do.

Patients should be given the option of terminating life or even given the option of having someone else terminate for them when the situation is obviously quite hopeless. This need not necessarily be radical treatment of pain, but sometimes the terrible psychological situation that some dying patients find themselves in.

This was the case of a thirty-four-year-old woman with Hodgkin's disease, a fatal disease, who had been in our respiratory intensive care unit for about a month on a ventilator, obviously with no hope of ever leaving the unit. Not in pain, not in physical pain, but great psychological pain. Eventually she asked me and another physician to simply give her some drug intravenously to end what might be another month of intolerable life to her. And we did do that for her. I found it very disturbing for a while. On the other hand, I think it made me realize more readily after that even active euthanasia is preferable to the alternatives in many cases.

There are numerous legal blocks towards assisting patients to end their own life or actively doing it for them. On the other hand, I make a point of not being too aware of what the blocks are because I personally do not feel persuaded to end a person's or not to end that person's life for legal reasons; to me it's strictly a moral and ethical problem. In the example I told you about, ending the life of a young woman, thirty-four years old, is illegal. However, there have been no repercussions from the law. The only repercussions have been favourable ones from the family.[30]

There is a firm belief among the general public that physicians are bound by the Hippocratic Oath not to take a life. The oath is interpreted by some as forbidding the taking of a life, but it also forbids procuring an abortion, a procedure now legalized in most countries and widely conducted by many doctors.

The Hippocratic Oath is more a tradition that has guided physicians over the centuries than a literal promise to do or not do something. Many physicians have never read or sworn it, and few medical schools nowadays require its reading at graduation ceremonies. Promulgated by Hippocrates in Cos in the fourth century B.C., the oath was meant to give the profession ethical guidelines during a time when men's minds were largely ruled by superstition. As such, it was a welcome guide through the following eras of slow medical and ethical progress. Except in the broadest sense, it has little relevance today. 'A literal interpretation of the Hippocratic oath in the twentieth century would be contrary to the very principle of application of fact that was so important to Hippocrates,' writes Dr John H. Leversee. 'Time does change most things, if not all things. The passage of twenty-four centuries certainly changes the circumstances under which one must interpret facts. . . . Thus, it seems to me, we must see his principles in their broadest sense and not be bogged down by literal interpretations.'[31]

One historian has remarked that the Hippocratic Oath, far from expressing the common Greek attitude towards medicine or of the natural duties of the physician, instead reflected the opinions of a small and isolated group.[32] Dr Richard Kravitz has argued, however, that changing societal conditions make the Hippocratic imperative to strive for the good of the patient not only increasingly relevant but in desperate need of reaffirmation. 'Furthermore,' he added, 'law is the arbiter of good conduct only in good societies. When law and individual conscience conflict, ethical codes may be a guide to physicians grappling with difficult moral choices.'[33] The Hippocratic Oath in fact says nothing about preserving life, as such. It all depends on how we interpret the phrase 'so far as power and discernment shall be mine, I will carry out regimen for the benefit of the sick and will keep them from harm and wrong.'

An elderly physician in San Francisco who a few days earlier had taken the life of a dying patient with an injection of morphine said: 'I don't believe I broke my Hippocratic Oath. Part of that Oath is not to do any harm to people and try to help people. I thought I was not doing harm but good in [Blank's] case. I thought it was my colleagues who were doing harm in prolonging his pain and suffering. The Hippocratic Oath in spirit is what I was doing. It will depend on your interpretation.'[34]

Illustrating just how the Oath can be varied to suit needs was shown in a remark made by a physician who had refused to treat emergency patients without health insurance. Commenting that his hospital took only paying patients, the doctor pointed out: 'Your Hippocratic Oath often clashes with corporate policy.'[35]

Nazi horrors caused the World Medical Association to produce an improved version of the Oath in 1948. Because it was accepted by the leaders of the medical profession at a meeting in Geneva, it is often referred to as the Geneva Oath. It contains no direct reference to abortion or the taking of a life.

Here is the Geneva version of the Hippocratic Oath, in full:

Now being admitted to the profession of medicine, I solemnly pledge to consecrate my life to the services of humanity. I will give respect and gratitude to my deserving teachers. I will practise medicine with conscience and dignity. The health and life of my patient will be my first consideration. I will hold in confidence all that my patient confides in me.

I will maintain the honour and the noble traditions of the medical profession. My colleagues will be as my brothers. I will not permit consideration of race, religion, nationality, party politics or social standing to intervene between my duty and my patient. I will maintain the utmost respect for human life from the time of its conception. Even under threat I will not use my knowledge contrary to the laws of humanity.

These promises I make freely and upon my honour.

As society moves into an era when hard decisions on euthanasia policies must be taken, there will be no greater issue than: 'Can we actually take a life? Will it coarsen the fabric of our lives if it becomes commonplace?'

# CHAPTER TWENTY

# *The Path Ahead*

Perhaps one of the biggest controversies surrounding euthanasia will manifest itself in 1987–88, when efforts are made to introduce the Humane and Dignified Death Act in California. This legislation, authored by Los Angeles attorneys Robert Risley and Michael White with the assistance of the Hemlock Society, will, if passed, allow a physician not only to switch off life-support systems but to take the life of the dying patient upon a competent request.

This will be the litmus test of public opinion. How far has it moved in favour of such an act? Has the 1980s rash of mercy killings changed views? Will the medical profession go along with public endorsement of such an Act, which a 1986 Roper opinion poll showed was favoured by 62 per cent of Americans?

In their preamble, Risley and White, who were not connected with the right-to-die movement until Mr Risley's wife died in 1984 in distressing circumstances, state:

> Prolongation of life for terminally ill persons may cause a loss of dignity and unnecessary pain and suffering, while providing nothing medically necessary or beneficial to the patient. The continuation of life under conditions of severe pain and suffering against the patient's will constitutes cruelty and a total disregard for human dignity. . . .
>
> There is nothing more private or sacrosanct than the right to control the condition of one's own life. The constitutional right to privacy should include the right of a competent terminally ill adult to choose the time and manner of his or her death. . . .
>
> The *Humane and Dignified Death Act* retains the safeguards of the [California] Natural Death Act, while allowing the patient to make a voluntary, competent and informed decision to request a physician to aid in his or her death in the least active manner.

The draft legislation stipulates that two physicians must certify that the patient is terminally ill and will die within six months. The patient must be competent, or while competent have named an agent to effect the request for aid-in-dying. There are provisions built in that will prevent intervention by family members, thus eliminating the 'push Granny into the grave' argument. The act will permit physicians to exercise mercy at a patient's request without fear of civil or criminal liability.

The opponents of this act will undoubtedly be the Roman Catholic Church, the Evangelical churches, the right-to-life movement, and the conservative wing of the medical profession. They will argue, as they have, that the Judeo-Christian tradition forbids the taking of a life and that this act is no more than legally sanctioned medical killing; also, that it is a further nail in the coffin in the traditional values without which society's cohesive fabric will erode. Furthermore, they will maintain that patient confidence in doctors will be hopelessly undermined.

A long and stormy path is certain for this ground-breaking legislation. As in 1976, when California was first to pass the Natural Death Act, formalizing Living Wills, the eyes of the world will be on America's most populous state, noted for launching progressive social ideas that have a habit of spreading.

There are still legal and ethical problems connected with allowing a person to die (passive euthanasia), but the main issues in that area have been largely resolved, as shown in public opinion polls and many court cases. All sides are now agreed, in general, that it is inhumane to keep people alive when they are in a hopeless condition, when they are suffering, and when they wish to die. Today we must face the formidable ethical frontier of whether it is ever right to help a person to die, and the Humane and Dignified Death Act will be the catalyst in that controversy.

Yet with such legislation, euthanasia ought never to be a consideration based on the saving of money or resources. As Alexander Capron noted: 'It would be even worse if concern to avoid the barbaric over-treatment of dying patients were used as an excuse for rules that would deny patients helpful care, when actually impelled by bureaucratic or financial convenience.'[1] The developed countries of the West have the resources to provide appropriate medical care for the sick and dying, as the ample amounts spent on armaments illustrate. But while politicians scramble to funnel the available public money into their favourite projects, there will always be pressure to reduce the share needed to provide decent health care for the elderly. This should be resisted. One journalist, in 'Our Elderly's Fate', commented: 'American society may be heading towards a *de facto* "final solution" to the problem of a growing elderly population. This trend raises the unthinkable prospect of the elderly one day being exterminated as a matter of law.'[2]

Nevertheless, a good deal of the money spent on the dying is wasted because much of the excessive and prolonged treatment is unnecessary. Frequently the dying patient does not need such extensive testing and therapeutics, preferring to be left alone, provided there is proper medical care and community support. Much of the equipment in modern hospitals is used for reasons other than the genuine one of diagnoses aimed at cure or palliation. Moreover, uniformity of standards would help: If the laws on dying were refined to take in all modern exigencies, if directives from patients were uniform nationally and had to be obeyed by physicians or penalty be risked, then the terminally ill would be more likely to receive the sort of medical care best suited to their situation and their desires—instead of the 'heroic' and 'defensive' measures deplored by so many. It is the absence of clear laws, guidelines, and effective ethics committees that encourages doctors and medical institutions to spend money wastefully rather than appropriately, often at the patient's expense.

If physicians have their priorities right, money is not an issue. The eventual result of such a shift will be that appropriate medical care for the dying will cost less than it does currently. Equally important, if not more so, the patient will be treated as he wishes.

The widespread public fear of hospital supertechnology could be abated by the use of advance directives from the patient as to their wishes. True, many people go through life avoiding thoughts of death. Even if Living Wills are polished to legal and ethical perfection, there will be many people unwilling to confront the emotional ordeal of making out a Living Will or Durable Power of Attorney. Consideration should be given to the idea that everybody at age fifty be obliged to sign a legal directive as to their wishes on their deathbed. A penalty for failing to do so could be exclusion from health benefits paid out of the public purse. Equally, physicians who put a patient on a life-support machine in clear defiance of stated wishes should be liable to penalty—probably a fine—after review by an ethics committee.

The enormous benefits that modern medical technology offers us must not be hampered by a soured public image provoked by patients' lack of control, the inconsistent results in court cases over refusal of treatment, and doctors' consequent confusion.

Without doubt, the most complex question regarding euthanasia concerns Alzheimer's disease. Not long after its onset, the victim is legally incompetent to make a rational decision. And certainly the early years of Alzheimer's do not warrant consideration of euthanasia; it is in the final years that this option can be a valid release from insupportable suffering, including that of the caregiver.

Here again, society may need to develop the 'negotiated death' idea, for many Alzheimer's victims are given some form of artificial life support in the final days, which could be withdrawn. The Humane and Dignified Death Act, permitting physician aid-in-dying, could help in this illness, but only on the basis of the clearest advance declaration of a desire for euthanasia while the person was still competent. Good answers to the question of how we help Alzheimer's patients to die well will have to be developed gradually by society and the courts.

We must all face the question of whether the arguments of the 'slippery slope' and the 'thin end of the wedge' are genuine fears over euthanasia.

The right-to-life movement argues: If euthanasia is permitted in limited ways today, however tightly controlled by law, what is to stop groups and/ or governments in the future from taking things a step further and introducing compulsory death for, say, the burdensome, the poor, the handicapped, the sick, and the elderly? Also, they argue, the availability of euthanasia as a lawfully and socially acceptable release will inevitably make it a duty for those old people who have 'served their purpose' to die. The right to die becomes an obligation to die. Lastly, euthanasia laws could be manipulated by unscrupulous individuals to eliminate the sick/elderly who are a burden, especially if they have money to bequeath.

Countering this, right-to-die advocates claim that the rule of the law has no purpose if society cannot, by and large, enforce it. Those who misuse euthanasia laws will merit punishment as for any other crime. Where is the sense, they argue, in telling a person dying of throat cancer that euthanasia cannot be made available because Nazi Germany murdered thousands of people in the 1940s using a method labelled 'euthanasia'? The lessons of history are there to be learned, and the Nazi experience has taught society how not to let government slip into the hands of an irresponsible minority.

One thing the World War II experience did tell us: Nazis believed in far more than 'euthanasia'. They also murdered some six million Jews, started a world war in which many millions more died, and would have crushed the Western world under a hateful tyranny had they succeeded. So-called euthanasia was merely a sideshow for a government that shrewdly awaited the cover of a world war before beginning to kill the handicapped.

We must cherish our safeguards, chiefly the ability of the judiciary to defend and protect the helpless and the dying. Despite differing reasons for their conclusions, courts on the whole have upheld the right of a patient to refuse treatment. Moreover, legislatures have it within their power to enact laws that enhance the rights of the dying, the best examples being the Humane and Dignified Death Act, the Right to Refuse Treatment Act, and the Uniform Rights of the Terminally Ill Act.

Such laws are critical in securing the rights of the hopelessly ill patient. An apparently uncomplicated ideal—dying naturally—has proved less simple in its application.

# *Appendices*

## I. FILMS DEALING WITH DYING

*Dark Victory* (1939)—Bette Davis, Geraldine Fitzgerald, George Brent, Humphrey Bogart, Ronald Reagan (dir. Edmund Goulding)

*On Borrowed Time* (1939)—Lionel Barrymore, Cedric Hardwicke, Beulah Bondi (dir. Harold S. Bucque)

*The Eddy Duchin Story* (1956)—Tyrone Power, Kim Novak, Victoria Shaw, James Whitmore, Rex Thompson (dir. George Sidney)

*On the Beach* (1959)—Gregory Peck, Ava Gardner, Fred Astaire, Anthony Perkins (dir. Stanley Kramer)

*Love Story* (1970)—Ali MacGraw, Ryan O'Neal (dir. Arthur Hiller)

*Brian's Song* (1971)—James Caan, Billy Dee Williams (dir. Buzz Kulik): Story of Brian Piccolo

*Harold and Maude* (1971)—Ruth Gordon, Bud Cort, Vivian Pickles, Ellen Geer (dir. Hal Ashby)

*Soylent Green* (1973)—Charlton Heston, Joseph Cotton, Edward G. Robinson, Leigh Taylor-Young, Chuck Connors (dir. Richard Fleischer)

*Sunshine* (1973)—Brenda Vaccaro, Christina Raines, Cliff DeYoung (dir. Joseph Sargent)

*Babe* (1975)—Susan Clark, Alex Karras (dir. Buzz Kulik): Story of Babe Didrikson Zaharias

*Death Be Not Proud* (1975)—Arthur Hill, Jane Alexander, Robby Benson (dir. Donald Wrye)

*Eric* (1975)—John Savage, Patricia Neal, Claude Akins, Mark Hamill (dir. James Goldstone)

*The Gathering* (1977)—Edward Asner, Maureen Stapleton, Lawrence Presman (dir. Randal Kleiser)

*A Love Affair: The Eleanor and Lou Gehrig Story* (1977)—Edward Herrmann, Blythe Danner (dir. Fielder Cook)

*First You Cry* (1978)—Mary Tyler Moore, Anthony Perkins, Florence Eldridge, Jennifer Warren (dir. George Schaefer)

*Little Mo* (1978)—Glynnis O'Connor, Michael Learned, Anne Baxter (dir. Daniel Haller): Story of Maureen Connelly

*Promises in the Dark* (1979)—Kathleen Beller, Marsha Mason, Ned Beatty (dir. Jerome Hellman)

*Act of Love* (1980)—Ron Howard, Robert Foxworth (dir. Jud Taylor)

*The Shadow Box* (1980)—Joanne Woodward, Christopher Plummer, James Broderick, Ben Masters, Melinda Dillon (dir. Paul Newman)

*A Matter of Life and Death* (1981)—Linda Lavin, Tyne Daly, Salome Jens, Gail Strickland (dir. Russ Mayberry): story of Joy Ufema

*On Golden Pond* (1981)—Henry Fonda, Katharine Hepburn, Jane Fonda, Doug McKeon (dir. Mark Rydell.

*Whose Life Is It Anyway?* (1981)—Richard Dreyfuss, John Cassavetes, Christine Lahti, Bob Balaban, Kenneth McMillan, Kaki Hunter (dir. John Badham)

*Six Weeks* (1982)—Dudley Moore, Mary Tyler Moore, Katharine Healy (dir. Tony Bill)

*Right of Way* (1983)—Bette Davis, James Stewart (dir. George Schaefer)

*Do You Remember Love* (1985)—Joanne Woodward, Richard Kiley, Geraldine Fitzgerald (dir. Jeff Bleckner)

*The Ultimate Solution of Grace Quigley* (1985)—Katharine Hepburn, Nick Nolte (dir. Anthony Harvey)

## II. ORGANIZATIONS DEALING WITH DEATH

Voluntary Euthanasia Society of England and Wales, 13 Prince of Wales Terrace, London W8 5PG

Voluntary Euthanasia Society of Scotland, 17 Hart Street, Edinburgh EH1 3RO

Concern for Dying, Room 831, 250 West 57th Street, New York, New York 10107

Hemlock Society, P.O. Box 66218, Los Angeles, California 90066

Society for the Right to Die, 250 West 57th Street, New York, New York 10107

Dying With Dignity, West, P.O. Box 46408, Station 6, Vancouver, British Columbia, Canada V6R 4G7

Dying With Dignity, East, 175 St Clair Avenue, West, Toronto, Ontario, Canada M4V 1P7

World Federation of Right to Die Societies, c/o Association pour le Droit de Mourir dans la Dignité (ADMD), 103 Rue la Fayette, Paris, France 75010

National Hospice Organization, Suite 902, 1901 North Fort Meyer Drive, Arlington, Virginia 22209

American Association of Suicidology, 2459 South Ash Street, Denver, Colorado 80222

Continental Association of Funeral and Memorial Societies (CAFMS), Suite 530, 2001 S Street, N.W., Washington, D.C. 20009

Memorial Society Association of Canada, Box 96, Station A, Weston, Ontario M9N 3M6

# Notes

## I: HISTORICAL PERSPECTIVE

1. John McManners, *Death and the Enlightenment* (New York: Oxford University Press, 1981), 4.
2. David W. Louisell, 'Euthanasia and Biathanasia: On Dying and Killing,' in *Death, Dying, and Euthanasia*, ed. Dennis J. Horran and David Mall (Washington, D.C.: University Publications of America, 1977), 385; Jonathan Gould and Lord Craigmyle, eds., *Your Death Warrant? The Implications of Euthanasia* (New Rochelle, N.Y.: Arlington House, 1971), 21.
3. *The Ethics of Aristotle*, trans. J. A. K. Thomson (New York: Penguin Books, 1980), III, vii: 130.
4. Ibid., V, xi: 200–1.
5. A. Alvarez, *The Savage God: A Study of Suicide* (New York: Bantam Books, 1976), 56.
6. Jerry B. Wilson, *Death by Decision: The Medical, Moral and Legal Dilemmas of Euthanasia* (Philadelphia: Westminster Press, 1975), 20.
7. Plato, *Republic*, trans. B. Jowett (New York: D. Van Nostrand, 1959), III: 297.
8. Ibid., V: 347
8. Libanius, quoted in Émile Durkheim, *Suicide: A Study in Sociology*, trans. John A. Spaulding and George Simpson (New York: Free Press, 1951), 330.
10. Plato, *Republic*, III: 295.
11. Ibid.
12. Ibid., 297.
13. 'The Arts,' in *Hippocrates*, trans. W. H. S. Jones (London: William Heinemann, 1923), 193.
14. Alvarez, *Savage God*, 58.
15. W. Mair, 'Suicide: Greek and Roman,' *Encyclopedia of Religion and Ethics*, ed. James Hastings (New York: Charles Scribner's Sons, 1925), XII: 30.
16. Wilson, *Death by Decision*, 21.
17. Quoted by Helen Silving, 'Suicide and the Law,' in *Clues to Suicide*, ed. Edwin S. Shneidman and Norman L. Farberow (New York: McGraw Hill, 1957), 80–1.
18. Alvarez, in *Savage God*, attributes Stoic dignity to 'the murderous squalor of Rome itself. When those calm heroes looked around them they saw a life so unspeakable, cruel, wanton, corrupt and apparently unvalued that they clung

to their ideals of reason much as the Christian poor used to cling to their belief in Paradise and the goodness of God despite, or because of, the misery of their lives on earth. Stoicism, in short, was a philosophy of despair' (64).

19. Seneca, *Epistulae Morales*, trans. Richard M. Gummere (London: William Heinemann, 1917) I, lvii, 32–6: 407–9.
20. A. Frenay, *The Suicide Problem in the United States* (Boston: Gorham, 1926), 66.
21. Alvarez, *Savage God*, 68.
22. Frenay, *Suicide Problem*, 66.
23. Robert M. Veatch, *A Theory of Medical Ethics* (New York: Basic Books, 1981), 128–30.
24. Helen Silving, in Shneidman and Farberow, *Clues to Suicide*, pp. 80–1 says: 'Up to this day, we do not know what crime suicide constituted, whether a crime *sui generis* or a particular instance of murder.... Another interesting feature of that crime is the manner in which it was formulated. In the case of all other offences, the common law defines the crime itself ('larceny is the felonious taking'; 'murder is the unlawful killing'). But in suicide, not the crime but the criminal is defined: *'felo de se* is he who kills.' Obviously, as was with Christian doctrine, so was the common law struggling with the dilemma of a crime in which the aggressor and the object of aggression are united in one person.'
25. Thomas Aquinas, *The 'Summa Theologica' of Saint Thomas Aquinas*, X, trans. Fathers of the Dominican Province (London: Burns, Oates, and Washbourne, 1929), II, ii, Q.64, a.5: 202–5.
26. Montaigne, 'A Custome of the Isle of Crea,' *Essays* (London: J. M. Dent and Sons, 1938), II: 27.
27. Thomas More, *Utopia*, trans. Paul Turner (New York: Penguin Books, 1981), 102.
28. McManners, *Death and the Enlightenment*, 411.
29. Montaigne, in Henry Romilly Fedden, *Suicide: A Social and Historical Study* (London: Peter Davies, 1938), 162.
30. In Gould and Craigmyle, *Your Death Warrant?* 23.
31. Francis Bacon, *The Advancement of Learning and Novum Organum* (New York: Colonial Press, 1900), 117.
32. John Donne, *Suicide*, ed. William A. Clebsch (Chico, Cal.: Scholars Press, 1983), 96.
33. Wilson, *Death by Decision*, 26.
34. Fedden, *Suicide: A Social and Historical Study*, 228–9.
35. Ibid., 230.
36. David Hume, *Essays, Moral, Political and Literary* (London: Oxford University Press, 1963), XXXI: 337.
37. Alvarez, *Savage God*, 165.
38. McManners, *Death and the Enlightenment*, 420.
39. Fedden, *Suicide: A Social and Historical Study*, 265.
40. Carl F. H. Marx, 'Medical Euthanasia,' trans. Walter Cane, *Journal of the History of Medicine* VII (1952): 405.
41. In Fedden, *Suicide: A Social and Historical Study*, 255.
42. McManners, *Death and the Enlightenment*, 414–15.
43. Ibid., 420.
44. In Milton D. Heifetz, *The Right to Die* (New York: G. P. Putnam's Sons, 1975), 99.
45. L. A. Tollemache, *Fortnightly Review*, 19 (1873).

46. Frank E. Hitchcock, 'Euthanasia,' *Transactions of the Maine Medical Association* X (1889): 42.
47. R. F. Rattray, 'The Right to Painless Death,' *Quarterly Review* CCLXXIV (January 1940): 40–1.
48. Emile Durkheim, *Suicide: A Study in Sociology*, trans. John A. Spalding and George Simpson (New York: The Free Press, 1951).
49. In O. Ruth Russell, *Freedom to Die* (New York: Human Sciences Press, 1977), 59.
50. 'Euthanasia Once More,' *Independent* 60 (February 1, 1906): 291.
51. *Outlook*, February 3, 1906.
52. *New York Times* (February 3, 1906).
53. In Fedden, *Suicide: A Study*, 268.
54. Abraham Jacobi, 'Euthanasia,' *Medical Opinion and Review*, XVIII (1912): 362–3.
55. In Wilson, *Death by Decision*, 28.
56. *British Medical Journal*, November 21, 1936.
57. *New York Times*, January 17, 1938.
58. *Collier's*, May 20, 1939, 13, 16.
59. *Time*, November 18, 1935, 54.
60. Anthony M. Turano, in 'Murder by Request,' *American Mercury* 423 (1935): 423–4, commented:

   The leading judicial decision on the subject [of mercy killings] is *The People vs. Frank C. Roberts*, which involved a devoted husband who released his wife from the prolonged death agonies of multiple sclerosis. Knowing that her condition was incurable, Mrs Roberts had repeatedly informed her relatives of her wish to die. She had also made an unsuccessful attempt to kill herself by drinking carbolic acid. Finally, her wasted body writhing in pain, she asked her husband to terminate her suffering as a *coup de grâce*. According to his confession, he dissolved a quantity of Paris green in a glass of water, and placed it at her bedside.
      Under ordinary rules of logic, the man should have received official commendation for his courage and humanity. But instead, he was convicted of wilful murder, and condemned to life imprisonment 'at hard labour and in solitary confinement.' The learned trial judge informed him: 'It doesn't make any difference whether she had that intention or not to commit suicide. You are a principal to committing the crime of murder. It was, indeed, an inhuman and dastardly act.' It is difficult to agree that a more kindly man would have forced his wife to squirm in agony until the last moment. The Supreme Court of Michigan solemnly approved the conviction on appeal.

61. Turano (ibid., 426–7) cites similar cases on the Continent:

   The same reluctance to punish benevolent homicide as wilful murder is increasingly evident in European countries, although the general policy of the law does not materially differ from the American codes. At Prague, as recently as 1934, Dr Paula Klaft-Salus, a woman physician, administered painless death to a fourteen-year-old boy whose body had been horribly mutilated in an explosion. Since the patient's mother had consented, both women were placed under arrest; but they were later released. In Denmark, Baroness von Duehen had been long afflicted with an incurable disease; her daughter administered a lethal dose of narcotics at her request. A jury decided that imprisonment for three months was a sufficient penalty. Jean Zysnowsky, a Polish writer living in France, was suffering intense pain from phthisis and internal cancer. His fiancee was constantly at his side, giving him every care, even submitting to a blood transfusion as a last resort. The patient had previously purchased a revolver, but, being too weak to pull the trigger, asked the girl for final proof of her love and charity. At length, she aimed the weapon, closed her eyes, and fired into his mouth, producing instantaneous death. A jury exonerated her after less than five minutes of deliberation.

The French *cause célèbre*, however, involved Richard Corbett, the son of an English banker. His aged mother was in the last stages of cancer, and her pain had become so acute that opiates had no effect. Having tried to persuade the doctors, day after day, to prescribe a deadly potion for the groaning patient, he finally induced permanent sleep by firing a single shot. In pleading his own case at the trial, Corbett refused to ask for clemency but argued that until physicians are permitted to follow the promptings of simple humanity, the next of kin have a legal right to administer euthanasia to hopelessly sick relatives. The jury brought in a verdict of acquittal.

62. *New York Times*, December 2, 1934.
63. In Abraham L. Wolbarst, 'The Doctor Looks at Euthanasia,' *Medical Record* 149. No. 10 (1939), 354.
64. In Art Carey, 'A Time to Die,' *Philadelphia Inquirer*, March 10, 1985.
65. *New York Times*, October 2, 1938.
66. Ibid., May 9, 1939.
67. Ibid., October 14, 1939.
68. Ibid., December 25, 1941.
69. 'Fortune Survey: Mercy Killings,' *Fortune* XVI (July 1937): 106.
70. 'The Quarters Poll,' ed. Mildred Strunk, *The Public Opinion Quarterly* XI (Fall 1947): 77.
71. *New York Times*, April 23, 1939.
72. For example, William G. Lennox wrote, in 'Should They Live?' *American Scholar* 454 (1938): 454ff:

The number of unproductive members which society can support is limited.... Those who are farsighted will study the growing problem of the unproductive and the socially useless.... First, select, preserve and improve the good; second, eliminate the bad.... Medical science tends to repeal the law which has been the mainstay of evolution—the survival of the fit.... If we are farsighted, we shall begin to do something about that portion of our population which is a heavy and permanent liability.... Congenital idiots or monsters.... incurably sick with heart, joint, or lung disease; the wrecks made by war, by machines, or by drink and drugs; and the aged.... There is a method (inhalation of nitrogen) which is speedy, symptomless, and ... without unpleasant after-effects.... In the betterment of race, medicine must play a part, education a part, religion a great part.... One of the guiding posts: 'The privilege of death for the congenitally mindless and for the incurably sick who wish to die. The boon of not being born for the potentially unfit.'

2: EUTHANASIA'S NAZI 'ALBATROSS'

1. Adolf Hitler, *Mein Kampf*, trans. Ralph Manheim (Boston: Houghton Mifflin, 1971), 296.
2. Ibid., 516.

3. Alexander Mitscherlich, *Doctors of Infamy* (New York: Henry Schuman, 1949), p. 92. See also Gerald Fleming's *Hitler and the Final Solution* (Berkeley: University of California Press, 1982), 20ff.
4. In William L. Shirer, '"Mercy Deaths" in Germany,' *Reader's Digest*, June 1941, 57.
5. Ibid., 56–7.
6. Fredric Wertham, 'The Geranium in the Window,' in *Death, Dying, and Euthanasia*, ed. Dennis J. Horan and David Mall (Washington, D.C.: University Publications of America, 1977), 618.
7. Mitscherlich, *Doctors of Infamy*, 106.
8. Fleming, *Hitler and the Final Solution*, 27.
9. Shirer, 'Mercy Deaths,' 57.
10. Fleming, *Hitler and the Final Solution*, 27.
11. Mitscherlich, *Doctors of Infamy*, 105–6.
12. Ibid., 112.
13. Ibid., 107.
14. Ibid., 109.
15. Ibid., 110.
16. Ibid., 140.
17. Ibid., 115.
18. Simon Wiesenthal, *The Murderers Among Us* (London: Heinemann, 1967), 274.
19. Gerald Reitlinger, *The Final Solution* (London: Vallentine, Mitchell, 1971), 133–4.
20. *New York Times*, July 7, 1985.
21. 'Biomedical Ethics and the Shadow of Nazism,' *Hastings Center Report Special Supplement*, August 1976, 12.
22. Mitscherlich, *Doctors of Infamy*, 113.
23. Wertham, 'The Geranium in the Window,' 606.
24. Leo Alexander, 'Medical Science Under Dictatorship,' *New England Journal of Medicine*, July 14, 1949, 44.
25. *Hastings Center Report*, 13.
26. Ibid., 3.
27. Joseph Fletcher, 'Ethics and Euthanasia,' in *To Live and To Die*, ed. Robert H. Williams (New York: Springer-Verlag, 1973), 114.
28. Marvin Kohl, 'Voluntary Beneficent Euthanasia,' in *Beneficent Euthanasia*, ed. Marvin Kohl (Buffalo: Prometheus Press, 1975), 137.
29. Winston S. Churchill, *The Second World War* (London: Cassell, 1959), 50.
30. Gitta Sereny, *Into That Darkness* (London: André Deutsch, 1974), 37.
31. Franklin H. Littell, 'Church Struggle and the Holocaust,' in *The German Church Struggle and the Holocaust*, ed. Franklin H. Littell and Hubert G. Locke (Detroit: Wayne State University Press, 1974), 24.
32. William Sheridan Allen, 'Objective and Subjective Inhibitants in the German Resistance to Hitler,' in *The German Church Struggle*, 123.
33. Sereny, *Into That Darkness*, 74–5.
34. Ibid.
35. Fleming, *Hitler and the Final Solution*, 30.
36. Ibid.
37. Sereny, *Into That Darkness*, 76.
38. Fleming, *Hitler and the Final Solution*, 23.
39. Alexander, 'Medical Science Under Dictatorship,' 40.

40. Howard Zinn, *People's History of the United States* (New York: Harper Colophon Books, 1980), 11.
41. *New York Times*, March 23, 1985.
42. *Hastings Center Report*, 15.

## 3: 1940 TO 1950

1. *New York Times*, May 23, 1941.
2. Ibid., December 15, 1947.
3. Joseph Fletcher, *Morals and Medicine* (Princeton: Princeton University Press, 1954), 187–8.
4. *Time*, November 18, 1946, 70.
5. *New York Times*, December 9, 1946.
6. Ibid.
7. Ibid., December 16, 1946.
8. Ibid., November 27, 1948.
9. W. G. Earengey, 'Voluntary Euthanasia,' *Medico-Legal and Criminal Review* (Cambridge) 8 (1940): 92.
10. Ibid.
11. Ibid., 101.
12. R. F. Rattray, 'The Right to Painless Death,' *Quarterly Review* (London) 274, 543 (January 1940): 39–49.
13. A. Hurst, 'Euthanasia,' *Quarterly Review* 274, 544 (April 1940): 319–24.
14. Frank Hinman, 'Euthanasia,' *Journal of Nervous and Mental Disease* 99 (1944): 641.
15. Ibid., 643.
16. Ibid., 646.
17. Sidney Katz, 'Are They Better Off Dead?' *Maclean's* (Toronto) 60, no. 21 (November 1, 1947): 72.
18. Ibid., 70.
19. Selwyn James, 'Euthanasia—Right or Wrong?' *Survey Graphic* 37 (May 1948): 242.
20. *New York Times*, January 1, 1949.
21. Ibid.
22. Ibid., January 1, 1949.
23. Russell, *Freedom to Die*, 287.
24. *New York Times*, December 18, 1950.
25. Ibid.
26. Ibid.
27. Ibid., June 27, 1942.
28. Ibid.
29. Ibid., August 8, 1946.
30. Ibid.
31. Ibid., January 8, 1949.
32. *Time*, December 2, 1946, 32.
33. *New York Times*, July 23, 1947.
34. Ibid., April 8, 1950.
35. Ibid., April 11, 1950.
36. *Time*, June 5, 1950, 20.
37. Ibid., February 6, 1950, 15.
38. Ibid., February 13, 1950, 21.

39. Ibid.
40. *New York Times*, February 24, 1950.
41. Ibid., March 7, 1950.
42. *Time*, January 1, 1950, 14.
43. *New York Times*, January 2, 1950.
44. Ibid., March 10, 1950.
45. Ibid., January 9, 1950.
46. Ibid., January 18, 1950.
47. Ibid., January 9, 1950.
48. Ibid.
49. Ibid.
50. *Time*, March 6, 1950, 20.
51. Alexander, 'Medical Science Under Dictatorship,' 44.

## 4: 1950 TO 1960

1. Gould and Craigmyle, *Your Death Warrant?* 44.
2. Ibid., 45ff.
3. *New York Times*, November 29, 1950.
4. Russell, *Freedom to Die*, 111.
5. *New York Times*, October 29, 1951.
6. Joseph Fletcher, 'Our Right to Die,' *Theology Today* 8 (May–July 1951): 202.
7. Ibid., 203.
8. Ibid., 204ff.
9. Ibid., 211.
10. Russell, *Freedom to Die*, 109.
11. *New York Times*, May 24, 1951.
12. John Sutherland Bonnell, 'The Sanctity of Life,' *Theology Today* 8 (May–June 1951): 197.
13. Ibid., 197–8.
14. Ibid., 199.
15. Ibid., 201.
16. *Christian Century* 67: 301.
17. *Catholic World*, 169 (April 1949): 3. *America*, February 23, 1951, 17.
18. Thomas Owen Martin, 'Euthanasia and Modern Morality,' *The Jurist* 437 (1951): 448.
19. *Hospital Progress* 31, no. 3 (March 1950): 91.
20. Ibid., 31, no. 4 (April 1950): 118.
21. *New York Times*, August 12, 1956.
22. Ibid., February 25, 1957.
23. Ibid., November 25, 1957.
24. Ibid.
25. Gerald Kelly, *Medico-Moral Problems* (St. Louis, Mo.: Catholic Hospital Association of the U.S. and Canada, 1958), 13–14.
26. Fletcher, *Morals and Medicine*, 187.
27. Ibid., 184.
28. Ibid., 181.
29. Ibid., 183.
30. K. R. Eissler, *The Psychiatrist and the Dying Patient* (New York: International Universities Press, 1955), 117.
31. Ibid., 120–1.

32. Ibid., 118.
33. A. Leslie Banks, 'Euthanasia,' *Bulletin of the New York Academy of Medicine* 26, 297 (1950): 302.
34. Walter C. Alvarez, 'Care of the Dying,' *Journal of the American Medical Association* 150 (September 13, 1952): 91.
35. 'Symposium on Euthanasia,' *Maryland State Medical Journal* 2, no. 3 (March 1953): 120–40.
36. George Boas, 'The Sanctity of Life,' ibid., 128–31.
37. Charles E. Orth, Jr., 'Legal Aspects Relating to Euthanasia,' ibid., 124.
38. Louis Krause, 'Medical Aspects Relating to Euthanasia,' ibid., 133.
39. Ibid., 135.
40. Ibid., 133.
41. John Farrell, 'The Right of a Patient to Die,' *Journal of the South Carolina Medical Association* 55, no. 7 (July 1958): 231.
42. Edward H. Rynearson, 'You are Standing at the Bedside of a Patient Dying of Untreatable Cancer,' *CA Bulletin of Cancer Progress*, 9 (May–June 1959): 85.
43. 'The Issues,' *New York University Law Review*, 31 (November 1956): 1157–1245.
44. Horace M. Kallen, 'An Ethic of Freedom,' ibid., 1169.
45. Joseph D. Hassett, S. J., 'Freedom and Order Before God: A Catholic View,' ibid., 1184.
46. Ibid., 1188.
47. Paul Ramsey, 'Freedom and Responsibility in Medical and Sex Ethics: A Protestant View,' ibid., 1201.
48. Ibid., 1204.
49. Emanuel Rackman, 'Morality in Medico-Legal Problems: A Jewish View,' ibid., 1213.
50. Phillips Frohman, 'Vexing Problems in Forensic Medicine: A Physician's View,' ibid., 1221–2.
51. Morris Ploscowe, 'The Place of Law in Medico-Moral Problems: A Legal View II,' ibid., 1245.
52. Harry Kalven, 'A Special Corner of Civil Liberties: A Legal View I,' ibid., 1236.
53. Ploscowe, ibid., 1238.
54. Kalven, ibid., 1237.
55. Gould and Craigmyle, *Your Death Warrant?* 27.
56. Glanville Williams, *The Sanctity of Life and the Criminal Law* (New York: Knopf, 1957), 317.
57. Ibid., 322.
58. Ibid.
59. Ibid., 324.
60. Ibid.
61. Ibid., 334.
62. Ibid., 340–1.
63. Russell, *Freedom to Die*, 288.
64. 'Who Signed for Euthanasia?' *America*, February 23, 1957, 573.
65. Russell, *Freedom to Die*, 133–4.
66. *New York Times*, February 17, 1950.
67. Ibid., March 23, 1950.
68. Ibid., March 30; March 31; April 2, 1953.
69. Ibid., August 7, 1953.

70. Ibid., March 13, 1952.
71. Ibid., May 10, 1959.
72. Ibid., May 6, 1959.
73. Ibid., May 5, 1952.
74. *Time*, July 27, 1953, 12.
75. *New York Times*, October 26, 1953.
76. *People v. Werner*, Criminal No. 58–3636, Cook County Court, Illinois, December 30, 1958; also partially reported in Glanville Williams 'Euthanasia and Abortion,' *University of Colorado Law Review*, 38 (Winter 1966): 186–7.

## 5: THE 1960S

1. *New York Times*, October 22, 1962.
2. *American Funeral Director*, April 1956, 43.
3. Paul Jacobs, 'The Most Cheerful Funeral in the World,' *The Reporter*, September 18, 1958, 72.
4. Richard Trubo, *An Act of Mercy: Euthanasia Today* (Los Angeles: Nash Publishing, 1973), 114.
5. Ibid., 108.
6. Perrin H. Long, 'On the Quantity and Quality of Life,' *Medical Times* 88, no. 5 (May, 1960): 614; Charles W. Blaker, 'Thanatopsis,' *Christian Century* 83 (December 7, 1966): 1506.
7. See especially: E. Paul Betowski, 'Prolongation of Life in Terminal Illness,' *CA* 10, no. 1 (January–February 1960): 25ff.; Long, 'On the Quantity and Quality of Life,' 615–16; A. A. Levisohn, 'Voluntary Mercy Deaths: Social-Legal Aspects of Euthanasia,' *Journal of Forensic Medicine* 8, no. 2 (April–June 1961): 74; F. J. Ayd, Jr., 'The Hopeless Case: Medical and Moral Considerations,' *Journal of the American Medical Association* 181, no. 13 (September 29, 1962): 1101; E. E. Filbey, 'Some Overtones of Euthanasia,' *Hospital Topics* 43 (September 1965): 57; *Medical Journal of Australia* II (October 8, 1966): 710; W. P. Williamson, 'Life or Death—Whose Decision?' *Journal of the American Medical Association* 197, no. 10 (September 5, 1966): 794; Adriaan Verwoerdt, 'Viewpoint,' *Geriatrics* 22, no. 8 (August 1967): 52 ff.; Duncan Vere, 'Why the Preservation of Life?' in Vincent Edmunds and C. Gordon Scorer, *Ethical Responsibility in Medicine: A Christian Approach* (London: E. & S. Livingstone Ltd., 1976), 59; Fred Rosner, 'Jewish Attitude Toward Euthanasia,' *New York State Journal of Medicine* 67, no. 18 (September 15, 1967): 2503; L. Kutner, 'Due Process of Euthanasia: The Living Will,' *Indiana Law Journal* 44, no. 4 (Summer 1969): 548.
8. Reported in Russell, *Freedom to Die*, 168. In 1906, Sir William Osler studied 500 dying patients. He found that slightly more than 20 per cent clearly expressed pain or bodily distress. The extent of the anxiety and mental distress was less clear.
9. 'Attitudes Toward Death in an Aged Population,' *Journal of Gerontology* 16, no. 1 (January 1961): 50.
10. Ibid.
11. Francis C. Jeffers and Claude R. Nichols, 'Attitudes of Older Persons Toward Death: A Preliminary Study,' ibid., 55.
12. 'Attitudes of and Towards the Dying,' *Canadian Medical Association Journal* 87 (September 29, 1962): 695.
13. Ibid., 698.

14. Russell, *Freedom to Die*, 170.
15. A. N. Exton-Smith, 'Terminal Illness in the Aged,' *The Lancet* 2 (August 5, 1961): 305–8.
16. J. M. Hinton, 'The Physical and Mental Distress of the Dying,' *Quarterly Journal of Medicine* (London) 32, no. 125 (January 1963): 1–21.
17. *British Medical Journal* 2 (August 17, 1963): 40–1.
18. J. M. Hinton, *Dying* (London: Penguin Books, 1967).
19. Ibid., 144.
20. Hinton, 'The Physical and Mental Distress of the Dying,' and 'Facing Death,' *Journal of Psychosomatic Research* 10 (July, 1966): 22–8.
21. C. Knight-Aldrich, 'The Dying Patient's Grief,' *Journal of the American Medical Association* 184, no. 5 (May 4, 1963): 331.
22. Ibid.
23. J. C. Quint, *The Nurse and the Dying Patient* (New York: Macmillan, 1967), 229.
24. B. G. Glaser and A. L. Strauss, *Awareness of Dying* (Chicago: Aldine, 1965).
25. Elisabeth Kübler-Ross, *On Death and Dying* (New York: Macmillan, 1969), 6.
26. Ibid., 39ff.
27. Elisabeth Kübler-Ross, *Questions and Answers on Death and Dying* (New York: Macmillan, 1974); *Death: The Final Stage of Growth* (Englewood Cliffs, N.J.: Prentice-Hall, 1975).
28. Kübler-Ross, *Death and Dying*, 276
29. 'Thanatopsis,' *CA Bulletin of Cancer Progress* 10, no. 1 (January–February 1960), 12.
30. Ibid., 32.
31. 'Voluntary Mercy Deaths,' *Journal of Forensic Medicine* 8, no. 2: 68.
32. Ibid., 69.
33. Ibid., 77.
34. Ibid., 58.
35. 'A Study of How Physicians Feel About Euthanasia,' *New Medica Materia* 4, no. 10 (October 1962): 31.
36. *American Journal of Psychiatry* 119, no. 11 (May 1963): 1104.
37. In Russell, *Freedom to Die*, 155.
38. 'Should Mercy Killing Be Permitted? Dr Leslie Wenger Says Yes,' *Good Housekeeping*, April 1967, 82.
39. 'Our Role in the Generation, Modification and Termination of Life,' *Archives of Internal Medicine* 124, no. 2 (August 1969): 229–30.
40. Ibid., 236.
41. Long, 'On the Quantity and Quality of Life,' 613–14.
42. Ibid., 616.
43. *Maclean's*, February 11, 1961, 30.
44. 'The Hopeless Case: Medical and Moral Considerations,' *Journal of the American Medical Association* 181, no. 13 (September 29, 1962): 1100.
45. Ibid., 1101.
46. 'A Time to Die,' *Medical Journal of Australia* II (October 8, 1966): 710
47. 'A Doctor's Moral Obligation to His Patient,' *New Zealand Journal of Medicine* 66: (October 1967): 686–8.
48. *Medical Journal of Australia* I, no. 3 (January 18, 1969): 127–8.
49. Williamson, 'Life or Death—Whose Decision?' 795.
50. David Karnofsky, 'Why Prolong the Life of a Dying Patient?' *CA Bulletin of Cancer Progress* 10, no. 1, (January–February 1960): 10.

51. *The Lancet*, II (August 12, 1961): 351–2.
52. Ibid., 351.
53. Ibid., II (December 8, 1962): 1205.
54. K. S. Jones, 'Death and Doctors,' *Medical Journal of Australia* II, no. 8 (September 1, 1962): 333.
55. David Daube, 'Sanctity of Life,' *Proceedings of the Royal Society of Medicine* 60 (November 1967): 1235–40.
56. 'Euthanasia—To Set You Straight,' *Minnesota Medicine*, 49, no. 8 (August, 1966): 1269.
57. Adriaan Verwoerdt, 'Euthanasia: A Growing Concern for Physicians,' *Geriatrics* 22, no. 8 (August 1967): 52.
58. Russell, *Freedom to Die*, 156–7.
59. Charles W. Blaker, 'Thanatopsis,' *Christian Century* 83 (December 7, 1966): 1506.
60. Joseph Fletcher, 'The Patient's Right to Die,' *Harper's* 221 (October 1960): 140.
61. Ibid., 143.
62. Joseph Fletcher, *Moral Responsibility: Situation Ethics at Work* (Philadelphia: Westminster Press, 1967), 27.
63. Ibid., 51.
64. In E. F. Torrey, *Ethical Issues in Medicine* (Boston: Little, Brown, 1968), 156.
65. Edgar Filbey, 'Some Overtones of Euthanasia,' *Hospital Topics* 43 (September 1965): 61.
66. In Vincent Edmunds and C. Gordon Scorer, *Ethical Responsibility in Medicine: A Christian Approach* (London: E. & S. Livingstone, 1967), 60.
67. Mary McDermott Shideler, 'Coup de Grace,' *Christian Century* 83 (December 7, 1966): 1500.
68. Ibid., 1502.
69. 'Thanatopsis'; ibid., 1504.
70. Ibid., 1505.
71. Russell, *Freedom to Die*, 209.
72. 'Details About Life and Death,' *Canadian Medical Association Journal* 93 (September 25, 1965): 719.
73. Russell, *Freedom to Die*, 207.
74. See Wilson's *Death by Decision*, 62–3.
75. See 'Murder for Mercy's Sake,' December 15, 1962, 1242–4: 'The Sacredness of Life,' March 9, 1963, 326–7; 'Freedom to Die,' January 11, 1964, 33.
76. Betowski, 'Prolongation of Life,' 25.
77. Ibid., 27.
78. 'Keeping the Dying Alive,' *America*, January 1, 1966, 6.
79. *New York Times*, June 17, 1963.
80. Fred Rosner, 'Jewish Attitude Toward Euthanasia,' *New York State Journal of Medicine* 67, no. 18 (September 15, 1967): 2504.
81. Ibid., 2505.
82. Ibid.
83. *Time*, July 11, 1960, 64.
84. *Newsweek*, November 19, 1962, 62.
85. *Look*, March 12, 1973, 76.
86. *New York Times*, November 2, 1964.
87. *La Presse Medicale* 72, no. 24 (May 16, 1964): 1458–60.

88. *New York Times*, October 7, 1965.
89. *Chicago Tribune*, August 9, 1967.
90. *New York Times*, January 25, 1969.
91. *Chicago Tribune*, August 10, 1967.
92. *Newsweek*, April 26, 1965, 58.
93. *Time*, April 23, 1965, 74.
94. *New York Times*, May 31, 1969.
95. Ibid., September 23, 1969.
96. Joseph Sanders, 'Euthanasia: None Dare Call It Murder,' *Journal of Criminal Law, Criminology and Police Science* 60, no. 3. (September 1969): 359.
97. Levisohn, 'Voluntary Mercy Deaths,' 76.
98. *Indiana Law Review*, Summer 1969, 543.
99. Ibid., 552.
100. Ibid., 549–50.
101. Ibid., 550.
102. Russell, *Freedom to Die*, 180.
103. Donald McKinney, unpublished letter, February 16, 1982.
104. Stephen J. Kuepper, *The Euthanasia Movement: A Brief History of the Organized Euthanasia Movement in the United States*, 1979, quoted in McKinney's letter.
105. Dale V. Hardt, *Death: The Final Frontier* (Englewood Cliffs, N.J.: Prentice-Hall, 1979), 73.
106. Russell, *Freedom to Die*, 192.
107. *New York Times*, September 24, 1967.
108. Ibid., September 23, 1967.
109. Ibid., March 8, 1969.
110. *Home News*, March 25, 1969.
111. London *Times*, March 8, 1969.
112. Ibid., March 26, 1969.
113. Ibid., March 27, 1969.
114. Russell, *Freedom to Die*, 185.
115. Sanders, 'Euthanasia,' 359.

## 6: THE EARLY 1970S

1. United Press International, August 31, 1975.
2. *Publishers Weekly*, February 24, 1974.
3. *National Observer*, March 4, 1972.
4. *New York Times*, July 21, 1974.
5. Ibid.
6. Robert Jay Lifton, *Living and Dying* (New York: Praeger Publishers, 1974), 97.
7. United Press International, August 31, 1975.
8. Norman K. Brown, 'The Preservation of Life,' *Journal of the American Medical Association* 211, no. 1 (January 5, 1970): 76–83.
9. Ibid., 97: 'the attitude expressed or implied is cultural rather than conditioned by frequent exposure to patients in terminal condition, and ... in this instance, the physicians spoke as members of society rather than as doctors.'
10. E. Harold Laws et al., 'Views on Euthanasia,' *Journal of Medical Education* 46 (June 1971): 540–42.

11. Anon., 'Euthanasia, ' *Journal of the American Medical Association* 218, no. 2 (October 11, 1971): 249.
12. Norman K. Brown et al., 'How Do Nurses Feel About Euthanasia and Abortion?' *American Journal of Nursing* 7 (July 1971): 1413–16.
13. *Life*, August 11, 1972, 38–9.
14. Ibid., 39.
15. *New York Times*, August 2, 1973 .
16. *Los Angeles Times*, December 25, 1973.
17. In Wilson, *Death by Decision*, 44.
18. In Hardt, *Death: The Final Frontier*, 75.
19. *Los Angeles Times*, April 3, 1975.
20. R. H. Williams, 'The End of Life in the Elderly,' *Postgraduate Medicine* 54, no. 6 (December 1973): 57.
21. Ibid. Other writers—several journalists and one congressman—bemoaned the plight of the chronically ill and the elderly, enduring, as one writer put it, 'a slow, dry death' in unsanitary, understaffed, unsafe nursing homes and institutions. See especially: David H. Pryor, 'Where We Put the Aged,' *New Republic*, April 25, 1970, 15–17; 'The Old in the Country of the Young,' *Time*, August 3, 1970, 49–54; 'Nursing Homes: The "End of the Line,"' *Washington Post*, April 4, 1971; 'Forest Haven: 200 Wait Mindlessly for Death,' *Washington Post*, May 26, 1971.
22. Arthur Schiff, 'Euthanasia? Yes, But What Kind?' *Medical Economics* 47 (May 25, 1970): 269.
23. Walter Sackett, 'Death with Dignity,' *Southern Medical Journal*, March 1971, 330–2.
24. Walter Sackett, 'I've Let Hundreds of Patients Die. Shouldn't You?' *Medical Economics* 50 (April 2, 1973): 92–114.
25. Joseph Fletcher, 'Ethics and Euthanasia,' *American Journal of Nursing* 73, no. 4 (April 1973): 674.
26. See Eric J. Cassell, 'Permission to Die,' *Bioscience* 23, no. 8 (August 1973): 475–8; 'Learning to Die,' *Bulletin of the New York Academy of Medicine* 49, no. 12 (December 1973): 1110–18.
27. For example, Franklin H. Epstein, 'No, It's Our Duty to Keep Patients Alive,' *Medical Economics* 50 (April 2, 1973): 97–114.
28. *New York Times*, April 24, 1972.
29. 'On Drinking the Hemlock,' *Hastings Center Report* 1, no. 3 (December 1971): 4.
30. Ibid., 5.
31. *New York Times*, September 25, 1971.
32. *Life*, January 14, 1972, 49.
33. *Chicago Tribune*, April 23, 1972.
34. *Good Housekeeping*, August 1974, 130.
35. *Chicago Tribune*, February 5, 1975.
36. *San Francisco Chronicle*, October 2, 1976.
37. *New York Times*, January 10, 1973.
38. *Newsweek*, January 22, 1973, 79.
39. *New York Times*, March 1, 1971.
40. *Washington Post*, August 19, 1973.
41. 'Plea for Beneficent Euthanasia,' *The Humanist* 3, no. 4 (July–August 1974): 4–5.
42. Russell, *Freedom to Die*, 158–9.

43. *New York Times*, January 13, 1973.
44. *Washington Post*, June 29, 1973.
45. Ibid., December 6, 1973.
46. Ibid., June 26, 1974.
47. *The Lancet*, January 30, 1971, 220.
48. 'Care of the Dying,' *British Medical Journal* 31, no. 2 (January 6, 1973): 29–41.
49. Personal communication from Frank Dungey, secretary, Voluntary Euthanasia Society, Wellington, New Zealand, May 19, 1985, and Tim Saclier, former president, Voluntary Euthanasia Society, September 14, 1985.
50. *New York Times*, December 26, 1971.
51. Ibid., January 16, 1972.
52. Ibid., April 18, 1976.
53. Ibid., November 6, 1973.
54. *Newsweek*, January 28, 1974, 45.
55. *New York Times*, February 6, 1974.
56. *Time*, July 16, 1973, 37.
57. United Press International, February 14, 1974.
58. Reuters, August 9, 1974.
59. Associated Press, October 26. 1974.
60. *New York Times*, October 24, 1975.
61. *Los Angeles Times*, March 22, 1975.
62. *Daily News*, February 28, 1982.
63. *New York Times*, February 26, 1975.
64. *Saturday Review*, June 14, 1975, 4.
65. *New York Times*, October 17, 1974.
66. *Los Angeles Times*, August 27, 1975.

## 7: SIGNIFICANT DEVELOPMENTS, LATE 1970S TO 1985

1. Joseph and Julia Quinlan with Phyllis Battelle, *Karen Ann* (New York: Bantam, 1977), 11.
2. *Los Angeles Times*, September 17, 1975.
3. Barbara A. Backer et al., *Death and Dying* (New York: John Wiley and Sons, 1982), 191.
4. In re Quinlan, 137 N.J. Supr. 277 (Ch. Div. 1975).
5. *New York Times*, April 1, 1977.
6. *Handbook of Living Will Laws, 1981–84* (New York: Society for the Right to Die, 1984), 1.
7. Ibid.
8. Ibid., 28.
9. Ibid.
10. Letter from Alice Mehling, executive director of Society for the Right to Die, August 1985, to Doris Portwood.
11. Statement, September 1980, from the president of Concern for Dying regarding the Third International Euthanasia Conference at Oxford. The statement was in defence of Concern's having been excluded from the programme because of their opposition to legislation.
12. Letter to T. Saclier, president of the Voluntary Euthanasia Society, Victoria, Australia, February 16, 1982.
13. Supreme Court of the State of New York, County of New York: Special Term,

Part I; Index No. 217/81, # 47, April 15, 1981. Society for the Right to Die, Plaintiff, against Concern for Dying.

14. Letter from T. Saclier to Ann Wickett, August 25, 1985.
15. The Hemlock Society.
16. Statement, September 1980.
17. Letter from Mrs Levinson, August 6, 1980, to Derek Humphry.
18. Statement issued by Concern for Dying, February 1985.
19. Letter from Donald McKinney, February 7, 1985, to Derek Humphry.
20. *Los Angeles Times*, December 14, 1977.
21. *Chicago Tribune*, March 24, 1977.
22. B. K. Singh, 'Correlates of Attitudes Toward Euthanasia,' *Social Biology* 26, no. 3: 247–54.
23. *San Francisco Chronicle*, April 10, 1978.
24. Ibid., March 15, 1983.
25. N. K. Brown and D. J. Thompson, 'Nontreatment of Fever in Extended-Care Facilities,' *New England Journal of Medicine* 300 (1979): 1246, in *Washington Post*, May 31, 1979.
26. *Washington Post*, April 26, 1984.
27. *New England Journal of Medicine* 308, no. 12 (March 24, 1983): 716–19.
28. Ibid., 719.
29. Bernadine Z. Paulshock, M.D., and Kristin Stitz, 'Allowing the Debilitated to Die,' *Journal of Family Practice* 18, no. 6 (1984): 46.
30. *Los Angeles Times*, September 18, 1978.
31. Alfred Jaretzki III, M.D., 'Death with Dignity—Passive Euthanasia,' *New York State Journal of Medicine* 4 (April 1976): 541–2.
32. Bruce E. Zawacki, M.D., 'The Doctor-Patient Covenant,' *The Journal of Trauma* 19, no. 11 (November 1979): 871–3.
33. E. Stanley Young, 'Care of the Dying—A Country Doctor Speaks Out,' *Journal of the Maine Medical Association* 69, no. 5 (May 1978): 144–5.
34. Joseph F. Zimring, M.D., 'Euthanasia and the Right to Die,' *New York State Journal of Medicine* 82, no. 8 (July 1982): 1263.
35. 'Terry Daniels' (pseudonym), *Chicago Tribune*, May 7, 1979.
36. Michele Anne Cawley, 'Euthanasia: Should It Be a Choice?' *American Journal of Nursing* 5 (May 1977): 861.
37. Anne J. Davis, 'To Make Live or Let Die,' *American Journal of Nursing* 3 (March 1981): 582.
38. 'Dilemmas in Practice,' *American Journal of Nursing* 11 (November 1982): 1768.
39. Ibid., 1770.
40. '"No Code": A Nurse's Viewpoint,' *Connecticut Medicine*, 47, no. 9 (September 1983): 568.
41. Ibid., 569.
42. 'Nurses Speak Out: Does a Terminal Patient Have the Right to Die,' *Good Housekeeping*, May 1984. Reprinted from the January/February 1984 and March/April 1984 issues of *Nursing Life*.
43. *New York Times*, March 10, 1985.
44. *Los Angeles Times*, January 6, 1985.
45. Bernard Towers, 'Report from America,' *Journal of Medical Ethics* 4 (1978): 96–8.
46. 'Guidelines for Discontinuance of Cardiopulmonary Life-Support Systems Under Specified Circumstances,' adopted March 1981.

47. *New York Times*, September 9, 1982.
48. *San Francisco Chronicle*, September 20, 1983; *Chicago Tribune*, September 21, 1983.
49. DNR Guidelines, issued by the Minnesota Medical Association, January 24, 1981; *St Paul Pioneer Press*, July 21, 1983.
50. *San Francisco Chronicle*, March 22, 1983.
51. 'Deciding to Forego Life-Sustaining Treatment,' President's Commission for the Study of Ethical Problems in Medicine and Biomedical and Behavioral Research,' March 21, 1983, 11ff.
52. Ibid.
53. Sidney H. Wanzer et al., 'The Physician's Responsibility Toward Hopelessly Ill Patients,' *New England Journal of Medicine* 310, no 15: 959.
54. Ibid., 955ff.
55. *Sacramento Bee*, April 12, 1983.
56. *Los Angeles Times*, January 1, 1985.
57. Ibid.
58. *New York Times*, June 18, 1984.
59. *New York Times*, June 16, 1984.
60. *Chicago Tribune*, January 16, 1985.
61. Robert M. Veatch, 'An Ethical Framework for Terminal Care Decisions,' *Journal of the American Geriatric Society* 32, no. 9 (September 1984): 665.
62. *New York Times*, June 16, 1984.
63. Veatch, 'An Ethical Framework,' 665.
64. In Britain, an attempt was made in December 1985 to modify the Suicide Act of 1961, which punishes assistance in suicide by a prison sentence of up to fourteen years. Lord Jenkins of Putney tabled an amendment in the House of Lords to the 1961 Act which read: 'It shall be a defence to any charge under this Act that the accused acted on behalf of the person who committed suicide and in so acting behaved reasonably and with compassion and in good faith.' Lord Kagan told the assembly that when he was a prisoner in a German concentration camp that it was not death, or even dying, which depressed and frightened him but the feeling of powerlessness. If the inmates could have managed to get hold of the means of committing suicide it would have given them the strength and courage to go on living. He argued that the same applied to the terminally ill. The amendment was defeated by forty-eight votes to fifteen.

## 8: COMPASSIONATE CRIMES

1. Annual report, Voluntary Euthanasia Society, 1985.
2. Letter from Glanville Williams to Nicholas Reed, June 22, 1979, quoted in Voluntary Euthanasia Society news release.
3. Evidence given at the Old Bailey, October, 1981. Author's notebook.
4. *Guardian*, October 31, 1981.
5. Evidence given at Hendon Magistrates' Court, April 1981. Author's notebook.
6. Reported in *Hemlock Quarterly*, July 1981.
7. Evidence given at the Old Bailey, October, 1981. Author's notebook.
8. *The Times*, October 28, 1981.
9. *Hemlock Quarterly*, July 1981.
10. Arthur Koestler, preface to 'A Guide to Self Deliverance,' Voluntary Euthanasia Society, 1981, 2.

11. *Guardian*, June 24, 1982.
12. *Statistical Abstracts of the U.S. 1985*. 105th ed.
13. 'Overdose—Will Psychiatrist Please See.' *The Lancet*, January 24, 1981.
14. *The Times Law Report*, April 29, 1983. Queen's Bench Division Attorney-General v. Able and others.
15. Chairman's annual report to Voluntary Euthanasia Society, 1984.
16. Ibid.
17. The *Daily Telegraph*, December 15, 1984.
18. *Guardian*, December 19, 1984.
19. *The Sunday Times*, December 6, 1984.
20. Hansard, December 11, 1985.
21. John Dawson, 'An Open and Gentle Death?' *BMA News Review*. Volume 12, No. 1, January 1986.
22. Conversations with the authors, March 8, 1986.

## 9: AN UPSURGE IN MERCY KILLING AND DOUBLE SUICIDE

1. *New York Times*, December 10, 1981.
2. United Press International, February 1, 1982.
3. *New York Times*, December 10, 1981.
4. *Dallas Morning News*, March 5, 1982.
5. *San Jose Morning News*, September 1, 1985.
6. *San Bernardino Sun*, July 16, 1985.
7. *Washington Post*, July 5, 1985.
8. Letter in *Hemlock Quarterly* 13 (October 1983).
9. 'In Memoriam,' by Diane Callahan, August 25, 1983 (unpublished).
10. 'Choices in Death for the Elderly,' speech to National Conference of the Hemlock Society, February 8, 1985.
11. *Associated Press Report*, June 19, 1984.
12. Ibid.
13. *Tampa Tribune*, June 22, 1979.
14. *Washington Post*, January 5, 1984.
15. *New York Times*, May 12, 1984.
16. *Washington Post*, May 24, 1979.
17. Ibid.
18. *Rochester Democrat & Chronicle*, August 27, 1985.
19. *Rochester Times Union*, August 27, 1985.
20. *Rochester Democrat & Chronicle*, September 8, 1985.
21. *New York Times*, April 25, 1983.
22. *Marin Independent Journal*, July 16, 1985.
23. Harold Harris, Preface, *Stranger on the Square*, by Arthur and Cynthia Koestler (New York: Random House, 1984).
24. *New York Times*, March 4, 1983.
25. George Mikes, *Arthur Koestler: The Story of a Friendship* (London: André Deutsch, 1983), 78–9.
26. Harris, *Stranger on the Square*.
27. Richard Seiden, 'Self-Deliverance or Self-Destruction?' adapted from presentation at the American Association of Suicidology plenary session, 'Suicide Manuals: Deliverance or Coercion?' Dallas, April 23, 1983.
28. *London Observer*, August 21, 1983.
29. Mikes, *Arthur Koestler*, 77.

30. *Los Angeles Times*, October 26, 1985.
31. Correspondence files of the Hemlock Society.


10: THE HANDICAPPED AND EUTHANASIA

1. *Oxford Mail*, June 13, 1981.
2. Haig in conversation with Derek Humphry, Oxford, September 1980.
3. *Oxford Mail*, June 13, 1981.
4. Unpublished letter from Larry Hill to Derek Humphry, August 9, 1984.
5. *Guardian*, June 13, 1981.
6. Ibid.
7. *Hartford Courant*, December 18, 1980.
8. Ibid., April 28, 1981.
9. *New London Day*, May 19, 1981.
10. *Los Angeles Times*, November 30, 1983.
11. *Associated Press Report*, October 16, 1983.
12. *Los Angeles Times*, November 3, 1983.
13. Ibid., November 30, 1983.
14. *San Francisco Chronicle*, December 5, 1983.
15. *Los Angeles Herald-Examiner*, December 6, 1983.
16. *Sacramento Bee*, December 6, 1983.
17. Ibid., December 2, 1983.
18. *New York Times*, December 6, 1983.
19. *Los Angeles Times*, December 6, 1983.
20. Ibid.
21. *Los Angeles Times*, December 7, 1983.
22, Ibid., December 10, 1983.
23. Ibid., December 17, 1983.
24. Ibid., December 3, 1984.
25. Ibid., January 20, 1984.
26. Ibid., February 7, 1984.
27. Ibid., April 9, 1984.
28. Ibid., May 2, 1984.
29. Ibid., November 12, 1984.
30. *Open Forum*, April 1984.
31. Ibid.
32. Ibid.
33. *Syracuse Post-State*, February 3, 1984.
34. Ibid.
35. *Los Angeles Times*, February 10, 1984.
36. *San Francisco Examiner*, December 20, 1983.
37. *Newsweek*, January 16, 1984, 72.
38. *Hemlock Quarterly* 14 (January 1984).
39. George Annas, 'When Suicide Prevention Becomes Brutality: The Case of Elizabeth Bouvia,' *Hastings Center Report*, 14 (April 1984): 20.
40. Bouvia v. County of Riverside. No. 159780 Supreme Court Riverside County, California, December 16, 1983.
41. Annas, 'When Suicide Prevention Becomes Brutality,' 46.
42. 'Correspondence,' *Hastings Center Report* 15 (April 1985): 49.
43. *The Times*, May 15, 1985.
44. *Daily Telegraph*, May 15, 1985.

45. *The Times*, May 15, 1985.
46. *Daily Telegraph*, May 15, 1985.
47. *Mail on Sunday*, May 26, 1985.

## 11: THE RIGHT-TO-LIFE VIEWPOINT

1. Roy White, 'Abortion Politics and the American Catholic Church,' *Conscience* (Catholics for a Free Choice), July 1981.
2. Connie Paige, *The Right to Lifers*, (New York: Summit Books, 1983), 57.
3. David Mall, 'Death and the Rhetoric of Unknowing,' in *Death, Dying and Euthanasia*, ed. Dennis Horan and David Mall (Washington, D.C.: University Publications of America, 1977), 651.
4. Steven Valentine, *National Right to Life News*, December 22, 1983.
5. Ibid.
6. C. Everett Koop, *The Right to Live, The Right to Die* (Ontario: Life Cycle Books, 1980), 122.
7. Ibid., 123.
8. Ibid., 139.
9. 'What About the Right to Die?' Life Cycle Books, 1982.
10. Malcolm Muggeridge and Alan Thornhill, *Sentenced to Life* (New York: Thomas Nelson Publishers, 1983), 15.
11. Malcolm Muggeridge, 'This Programme Courtesy of Lucifer Inc.,' in Roy Bonisteel, *Searching for Man Alive* (Ontario: Totem Books, 1980).
12. Malcolm Muggeridge, *Muggeridge: Ancient and Modern*, ed. Christopher Ralling and Jane Bywaters (London British Broadcasting Corp., 1981), 176.
13. Joseph J. Piccione, 'Last Rights: Treatment and Care Issues in Medical Ethics,' *Currents in Family Policy*, 1984, 20.
14. Merrill Simon, *Jerry Falwell and the Jews* (New York: Jonathan David Publishing, 1982), 154.
15. *Minneapolis Star Tribune*, April 21, 1985.
16. 'What About the Right to Die?' 4.
17. Thomas St Martin, 'Euthanasia: The Three in One Issue,' in *Death, Dying and Euthanasia*, 597.
18. *Executive Intelligence Review*, March 5, 1985.
19. In the Matter of Claire C. Conroy, Supreme Court of New Jersey, January 17, 1985.
20. *Barber and Nedjl v. Superior Court of the State of California for the County of Los Angeles*, 2 Civil No. 69350/1.
21. *Moral Majority Report on Human Life* 7 (May 1985).
22. *National Right to Life News*, January 1985.
23. Ibid.
24. *National Right to Life News*, February 1985.
25. Speech to the National Right to Life Convention banquet, 1985.

## 12: EUTHANASIA IN THE NETHERLANDS

1. Arthur Seyss-Inquart, 'Order of the Reich Commissar for the Occupied Territories Concerning the Netherlands Doctors' (gazette containing the order for the Occupied Netherlands Territories) December 1941, 1004–26.
2. Alexander, 'Medical Science Under a Dictatorship.'
3. William L. Shirer, *The Rise and Fall of the Third Reich* (London: Pan Books Ltd., 1960), 1356.

4. *Time*, March 5, 1973, 70.
5. Ibid.
6. Press release, Society for Voluntary Euthanasia, September 1978.
7. Jeanne Troup Meesters, *20/20 Vision* (television programme, Britain), July 6, 1985.
8. Press release, Society for Voluntary Euthanasia, September 1978.
9. Ibid.
10. Press release A104/81, January 16, 1981, Leeuwarden to Lawyer Spong, The Hague.
11. Letter to the authors, January 2, 1981.
12. Press release, Society for Voluntary Euthanasia, September 1978.
13. Eugene Sutorius, speech to Hemlock Society National Voluntary Euthanasia Conference, Santa Monica, Cal., February 8, 1985.
14. Judge Anka Sutorius, speech to the Hemlock Society National Voluntary Euthanasia Conference, February 8, 1985.
15. Ibid.
16. *20/20 Vision*, July 6, 1985.
17. *Hemlock Quarterly* 17 (October 1984).
18. Eugene Sutorius, Hemlock Society Conference, February 8, 1985.
19. *The Economist*, September 8, 1985.
20. Ibid.
21. Ibid.
22. Netherlands Bureau of Statistics, 1983.

## 13: EUTHANASIA AND HOSPICE

1. Robert G. Twycross, 'Hospice Care—Redressing the Balance in Medicine,' *Journal of the Royal Society of Medicine*, 73 (July 1980): 478.
2. Robert L. Kane et al., 'A Randomized Controlled Trial of Hospice Care,' *The Lancet* 8382 (April 21, 1984): 891–3.
3. National Center for Health Statistics, *Monthly Vital Statistics Report* 33 no. 9 (December 20, 1984): 21.
4. National Hospice Organization, 'NHO Testifies Before U.S. Health Data Committee, *Hospice News* 3 (January 1, 1985): 3.
5. C. Murray Parkes, 'Terminal Care: Hospital or Hospice,' *The Lancet* 8421 (January 19, 1985): 155–6; Claire B. Tehan, 'Hospice Home Care Programs,' in Charles Corr and Donna Corr, eds., *Hospice Care: Principles and Practices* (New York: Springer Publishing Co., 1983), 282–3.
6. National Hospice Organization, 'Standards of a Hospice Program of Care,' 1982, 1.
7. Twycross, 'Hospice Care,' 477.
8. 'Get a Second Opinion on Terminal Care,' *New York Times*, March 26, 1985.
9. Neil MacDonald, M.D., 'The Hospice Movement: An Oncologist's Viewpoint,' *CA* 34 (July–August 1984): 180.
10. Andrew B. Adams, M.D., 'Dilemmas of Hospice: A Critical Look at its Problems,' Ibid.
11. Pamela Gray-Toft and James G. Anderson, 'Hospice Care: A Better Way of Caring for the Living,' *Hospice U.S.A.*, 115.
12. Anne Munley, *The Hospice Alternative: A New Context for Death and Dying* (New York: Basic Books, 1983), 274–5.
13. Communication with the authors, 1982.

14. Milton D. Heifetz, M.D., with Charles Mangel, *The Right to Die: A Neurosurgeon Speaks of Death with Candor* (New York: G.P. Putman's Sons, 1975), 154–5.
15. West Australia Voluntary Euthanasia Society, 'The Case for Voluntary Euthanasia,' 1985, 62.
16. *60 Minutes*, CBS–TV, September 1980.
17. Polly Toynbee, 'In the Midst of Death We Are in Life', *Guardian*, February 20, 1984.
18. Communication with the authors, August 1985.
19. Gary A. Jacobsen, M.D., 'Hospice: What It Is Not', 203. *Career Journal for Clinicians* 34, no. 4 (July–August 1984): 203.

## 14: HIGH TECHNOLOGY: A MIXED BLESSING

1. Jerry Wilson, *Death by Decision: The Medical, Moral, Legal Dilemmas of Euthanasia* (Philadelphia: Westminster Press, 1975), 97.
2. Richard Taylor, *Medicine Out of Control: The Anatomy of a Malignant Technology* (Melbourne, Australia: Sun Books, 1979), 119.
3. H. David Banta et al., *Toward Rational Technology in Medicine* (New York: Springer Series on Health Care and Society, 1981), 28–9; Charles Sanders, 'Technology in Hospitals,' in *Medical Technology: The Culprit Behind Health Care Costs?*, ed. Stuart Altman and Robert Blendon (USDHEW PHS 79–3216, 1977), 62–6.
4. Banta, *Toward Rational Technology*, 5.
5. Lewis Thomas, 'The Technology of Medicine,' *New England Journal of Medicine*, December 9, 1971, 1367.
6. B. D. Cohen, 'Buying Time for the Terminally Ill,' *Newsday, Special Reprint*, April 15–April 19, 1984, 16.
7. *Life*, January 14, 1972, 49.
8. Gina Bari Kolata, 'Dialysis After Nearly a Decade,' in *Medical Ethics: A Clinical Textbook and Reference for Health Care Professionals*, ed. Natalie Abrams and Michael Brucker (Cambridge, Mass: MIT Press, 1983), 571.
9. *New York Times*, October 23, 1982.
10. David Thomasma, 'The Goals of Medicine and Society,' in *The Culture of Biomedicine*, ed. D. Heyward Brock (Newark, Del.: University of Delaware Press, 1984), 38.
11. Taylor, *Medicine Out of Control*, 120.
12. Thomasma, 'The Goals of Medicine,' 38.
13. Leon Kass, 'The New Biology: What Price Relieving Man's Estate,' *Science* 174 (November 19, 1971): 782.
14. D. S. Kornfeld, 'The Hospital Environment: Its Impact on the Patient.' *Advances in Psychosomatic Medicine* 8 (1972): 252–70.
15. David Ellison, *The Biomedical Fix: Human Dimensions of Bio-Medical Technologies* (Westport, Conn.: Greenwood Press, 1978), 17.
16. *San Francisco Chronicle*, August 15, 1982.
17. *Los Angeles Times*, May 15, 1985.
18. 'A Moratorium on Heart Transplants,' *Discover*, July 1985, 87.
19. Robert Derzon, 'Influences of Reimbursement Policies on Technology,' in *Critical Issues in Medical Technology*, ed. Barbara McNeil and Ernest Cravalho (Cambridge, Mass: Auburn House, 1982), 140.

20. Ivan Illich, *Medical Nemesis: The Expropriation of Health* (New York: Bantam Books, 1976), 100.
21. Sanders, 'Technology in Hospitals,' 59.
22. Ross Arnett and Carol Cowell et al., 'Health Spending Trends in the 1980's: Adjusting to Financial Incentives,' *Health Care Financing Review* 6 (Spring 1985): 23.
23. 'The Cost, Pain of Holding On,' *Sacramento Bee*, June 24, 1984.
24. E.g., Norman K. Brown, 'The Preservation of Life,' *Journal of the American Medical Association* 211 (January 5, 1970): 76–82; H. Feifel et al., 'Physicians Consider Death,' *American Psychological Association*, 75th Annual Convention (1967), 201–2.
25. Taylor, *Medicine Out of Control*, 2.
26. President's Commission for the Study of Ethical Problems in Medicine and Biomedical and Behavioral Research, *Deciding to Forego Life-Sustaining Treatment*, March 1982, 17–18.
27. See Joseph Fletcher, 'The Patient's Right to Die.'
28. Gerald Kelly, *Medico-Moral Problems* (St Louis: Catholic Hospital Association, 1958), 129.
29. David G. Lygre, *Life Manipulation: From Test Tube Babies to Aging* (New York: Walker and Company, 1979), 108.
30. 'Humana: Making the Most of Its Place in the Spotlight,' *Business Week*, May 6, 1985, 69.
31. Ibid., 68.
32. Stein, *Making Medical Choices*, 217–18.
23. Thomas Raffin, 'The Right to Live, The Right to Die,' *Stanford Magazine*, Spring 1983, 26.
34. Susanna Bedell et al., 'Survival After Cardiopulmonary Resuscitation in the Hospital,' *New England Journal of Medicine* 309 (September 8, 1983): 574.
35. President's Commission, 439–41.
36. *New York Times*, November 4, 1984.
37. Minnesota Coalition of Health Care Costs, *The Price of Life: Ethics and Economics*, December 1984, 12.
38. 'Optimum Care for Hopelessly Ill Patients,' in *Medical Ethics: A Clinical Textbook and Reference for Health Care Professionals*, ed. Natalie Abrams and Michael Brucker (Cambridge, Mass.: MIT Press, 1983), 314–15.
39. Richard Benton, *Death and Dying* (New York: Van Nostrand Reinhold, 1978), 241. Professional report by Mary Kathleen Chudleigh.
40. Illich, *Medical Nemesis*, 94.
41. Ibid., 97.
42. *Washington Post*, December 2, 1984.
43. Laurence Tancredi, 'Social and Ethical Implications in Technology Assessment,' *Critical Issues in Medical Technology*, 95–7.
44. John Robitscher, 'The Problems in Prolongation of Life,' in *Biomedical Ethics and the Law* ed. James Humber and Robert Almeder (New York: Plenum Press, 1979), 493.
45. Tancredi, 'Social and Ethical Implications,' 99.
46. *New York Times*, January 18, 1985.
47. Ibid.
48. Lygre, *Life Manipulation*, 111.

## 15: MERCY KILLING AND THE LAW

1. 184 1009, 37 S.E. 2d 43, 47 (1946).
2. 64 Cal. 2d 310, 322, 49 Cal. Rptr. 815, 822, 411 P.2d 911, 918 (1966).
3. John C. Hirschfield, 'Recent Decision,' *Notre Dame Lawyer* (May 1959): 461.
4. Helen Silving, 'Euthanasia: A Study in Comparative Criminal Law,' *University of Pennsylvania Law Review* 103 (1954): 354.
5. Ibid., 367–8.
6. Ibid., 387.
7. Anton Pestalozzi-Henggeler, 'Euthanasia Under the Swiss Penal Code,' *Southwestern Law Journal* 15, no. 3 (1961): 395
8. Ibid., 396.
9. Yale Kamisar, 'Some Non-religious Views Against Proposed "Mercy Killing" Legislation,' in Dennis J. Horan and David Mall, *Death, Dying, and Euthanasia*, 408.
10. Joseph Sanders, 'Euthanasia: None Dare Call It Murder,' *Journal of Criminal Law, Criminology, and Police Science* 44, no. 4 (September 1969): 359.
11. L. Kutner, 'Due Process of Euthanasia: The Living Will. A Proposal,' *Indiana Law Journal* 44, no. 4 (Summer 1969): 539–54.
12. Arval A. Morris, 'Voluntary Euthanasia,' *Washington Law Review* 45, no. 2 (1970): 239–71; Philip Small, 'Euthanasia—The Individual's Right to Freedom of Choice,' *Suffolk University Law Review* V (Fall 1970): 190–212.
13. Morris, 'Voluntary Euthanasia,' 266.
14. William P. Cannon, 'The Right to Die,' *Houston Law Review* 7 (May 1970): 661.
15. Howard W. Brill, 'Death with Dignity: A Recommendation for Statutory Change,' *University of Florida Law Report* XXII (1970): 373.
16. Edward M. Scher, 'Legal Aspects of Euthanasia,' *Albany Law Review* 36 (1972): 678.
17. Mustafa D. Sayid, 'Euthanasia: A Comparison of Criminal Laws of Germany, Switzerland, and the United States,' *Boston College International and Comparative Law Review* VI, no. 2 (1983): 551–3.
18. Ibid., 553.
19. Silving, 'Euthanasia: A Study,' 354.
20. H. Gulkin, personal communication to Derek Humphry, May 1985.
21. See Right Hon. Lord Justice Lawton, 'Mercy Killing. The Judicial Dilemma,' *Journal of the Royal Society of Medicine* 72 (June 1979): 460–1; Roger Leng, 'Mercy Killing and the CLRC,' *New Law Journal*, January 28, 1982, 76–8; Nicholas Reed, 'Mercy Killing,' *Polytechnic Law Review*, Winter–Spring 1982, 17–20.
22. Leng, 'Mercy Killing,' 76.
23. Ibid., 77.
24. Ibid.
25. Lawton, 'Mercy Killing,' 460.
26. Leng, 'Mercy Killing,' 78.

## 16. IS THERE A CONSTITUTIONAL RIGHT TO DIE?

1. Union Pacific Railroad v. Botsford, 141 U.S. 250, 251 (1891).
2. See Marc D. Hiller, *Medical Ethics and the Law* (Cambridge, Mass.: Ballinger Publishing Company, 1981), 200ff.
3. Slater v. Baker and Stapleton, 2 Wils. 359, 95 Eng. Rep. 860 (K.B. 1767).

4. Mohr v. Williams, 95 Minn. 261, 104 N.W. 12 (1905).
5. Schloendorff v. Society of New York Hospital, 211 N.Y. 125, 129–30, 105 N.E. 92, 90 (1914).
6. Griswold v. Connecticut, 381 U.S. 479 (1965).
7. Ibid., at 484.
8. Olmstead v. United States, 277 U.S. 471 (1928).
9. See Norman L. Cantor, 'A Patient's Decision to Decline Lifesaving Medical Treatment: Bodily Integrity Versus the Preservation of life,' *Rutgers Law Review* 26 (1971): 242ff. Also Edward M. Scher, 'Legal Aspects of Euthanasia,' *Albany Law Review* 36 (1972): 680–1.
10. Application of President and Directors of Georgetown College, 331 F.2d 1000 (D.C. Cir. 1964), cert. denied, 377 U.S. (1964).
11. Ibid.
12. Ibid., at 1016–18.
13. United States v. George, 239 F. Supp. 752 (D. Conn. 1965).
14. Ibid., at 754.
15. Raleigh Fitkin-Paul Morgan Memorial Hospital v. Anderson, 42 N.J. 421, 201 A.2d 537 (1964).
16. Ibid., at 538.
17. Powell v. Columbia Presbyterian Medical Center, 49 Misc. 2d 215, 267 N.Y.S. 2d 450 (Sup. Ct. 1965).
18. Ibid., at 451.
19. John F. Kennedy Memorial Hospital v. Heston, 58 N.J. 576, 279 A.2d 670 (1971).
20. Ibid., at 670.
21. *New York Times*, July 14, 1971.
22. Ibid., January 28, 1972.
23. Ibid.
24. Erickson v. Dilgard, 44 Misc. 2d 27, 252 N.Y.S. 2d 705, (Sup. Ct. 1962).
25. Ibid., at 706.
26. In re Brooks, 32Ill. 2d 361, N.E. 2d 345 (1965).
27. Ibid., at 435, 442.
28. *New York Times*, July 3, 1971.
29. Case No. 71–12678, Cir. Ct. of Dade County, Fla., July 2, 1971.
30. *New York Times*, July 14, 1971.
31. Winters v. Miller, 446 F.2d 65 (N.Y. 1971).
32. Ibid.
33. Guardianship of Gertrude Raasch, County Court for Milwaukee County, Probate Division, No. 455–996, decided January 25, 1972.
34. Guardianship of Delores Phelps, County Court for Milwaukee County, Probate Division, No. 459–207, decided July 11, 1972.
35. In re Yetter, No. 1973–533 at 4 (Pa. Northampton Co., June 6, 1973).
36. *New York Times*, June 8, 1973.
37. *Washington Post*, April 27, 1974.
38. Cert. denied, 371 U.S. 890 (1962).
39. 331 F.2d at 1008.
40. For an excellent discussion, see James F. Hoover, 'An Adult's Right to Resist Blood Transfusions: A View Through *John F. Kennedy Memorial Hospital v. Heston*,' *Notre Dame Lawyer* 47 (February 1972): 574ff.
41. Reynolds v. United States, 98 U.S. 145 (1878); Hill v. State, 38 Ala. App. 623, 88 So. 2d 179 (1956); Hardin v. State, 188 Tenn. 17, 216 S.W. 2d 708

(1948); Lawson v. Commonwealth, 291 Ky. 437, 164 S.W. 2d 972 (1942); State v. Massey, 229 N.C. 734, 51 S.E.2d 179 (1949); Brunn v. North Carolina, 336 U.S. 942 (1949).

42. See Hoover, 'An Adult's Right'; also William H. Baughman et al., 'Euthanasia: Criminal, Tort, Constitutional, and Legislative Considerations,' *Notre Dame Lawyer* 48, no. 5 (June 1973): 124ff.

43. One attorney, arguing that exercise of religious freedom should always be honoured if there is no danger of public commotion, concluded that the *Heston* court used the correct test—i.e., were religious beliefs subject to governmental restraint?—but came to the wrong result (Michael Sullivan, 'The Dying Person—His Right and Plight,' *New England Law Review* 8 (1973): 209). Another attorney, also arguing for the First Amendment right of religious freedom in such cases, offered the following aside: 'Assuming [such a right], it might be argued by atheists and individuals desiring to refuse medical treatment on other than religious grounds, that they are being unfairly discriminated against by a law that recognizes a right to die only if religiously motivated' (Scher, 'Legal Aspects,' 684).

44. Brooks, at 373–74.

45. ibid., at 442.

46. In re Quinlan, 137 N.J. Supr. 227 (Ch. Div. 1975).

47. See Thomas C. Oden, 'Beyond an Ethic of Sympathy,' *Hastings Center Report*, February 1967: 12.

48. In re Quinlan, 70 N.J. 10, 355 A.2d 647, Cert. denied 429 U.S. 922 (1976).

49. Ibid., at 661.

50. Ibid., at 651, 652, 666, 670.

51. Superintendent of Belchertown State School v. Saikewicz, Mass. Supreme Judicial Court, 370 N.E.2d 417, 1977.

52. Ibid., at 435.

53. Dockcry v. Dockcry, No. 51439, Chattanooga Tenn. Chancery Ct., Jan. 1977.

54. *Washington Post*, January 12, 1977.

55. *Chicago Tribune*, October 1, 1977; *Los Angeles Times*, October 1, 1977.

56. *Chicago Tribune*, December 28, 1977.

57. Ibid.

58. Perlmutter v. Florida Medical Center, 47 Fla. Supp. 190 (Broward County Cir. Ct. 1978).

59. Ibid., at 194.

60. 362 So. 2d at 161.

61. Ibid.

62. 379 So. 2d at 359.

63. In re Dinnerstein, 78 Mass. App. Ct. Adv. Sh. 736, 380 N.E.2d 134, 1978.

64. Ibid., at 139.

65. Grace R. Lane v. Rosaria Candura, 6 Mass. App. Ct. 377; 376 N.E. 2d, May 26, 1978.

66. *Chicago Tribune*, May 24, 1978.

67. *Chicago Tribune*, July 12, 1978.

68. Eichner v. Dillon, 73 A.D.2d 431, 426, N.Y.S.2d 517, 1980.

69. Ibid., at 517, 526.

70. In re Storar, 52 N.Y.2d 363, 420 N.E.2d 64, 438 N.Y.S. 266 (1981).

71. Ibid., at 426.

72. Ibid.

73. Ibid.
74. The intermediate appellate court outlined the following procedures for the withdrawal of extraordinary life-sustaining measures from the terminally ill and comatose patient: (1) the physicians attending the patient must certify that he is 'terminally ill and in an irreversible, permanent, or chronic vegetative coma, and that the prospects of him regaining cognitive brain function are extremely remote'; (2) a family member or someone having a close personal relationship with the patient may present the prognosis to an appropriate hospital committee, whereupon the committee shall approve or reject the prognosis. Upon confirmation of the prognosis, the attorney general and district attorney shall be given notice and have an opportunity to have examinations conducted by their own physicians. Finally a guardian *ad litem* shall be appointed to assure that the interests of the individual are protected. (Ibid., at 476–7.)
75. Ibid., at 276.
76. Leach v. Akron General Medical Center, 68 Ohio Misc. 1, 426 N.E.2d 809 (C.P. Summit Co. P. Div. 1980).
77. Ibid., at 812.
78. Ibid.
79. Ibid., at 816.
80. Ibid., at 815. Worth noting is the subsequent suit which the Leach family filed against Mrs Leach's doctor (Leach v. Shapiro, 13 Ohio App. 393, 395 469 N.E.2d 1047, 1051, Ct. App. 1984), the first time a family charged a doctor for keeping a patient alive against her wishes. Howard Sharpiro, an Akron neurologist, was accused of failing to get the family's consent before connecting Mrs Leach to a respirator in July 1980, and subsequently refusing to disconnect it when the family requested it. In September 1985, as the *New York Times* reported (September 18, 1985), Judge John Reece of Summit County Common Pleas Court decided in favour of Dr Shapiro.
81. In re Spring, 79 Mass. App. Ct. Adv. Sh. 2469, 2471, 399, N.E.2d 493, 496 (1979).
82. Ibid., at 498.
83. Ibid., at 499.
84. 79 Mass. App. Ct. Adv. Sh. 2469, 2484–85, 399 N.E.2d, 493, 503 (1979).
85. 80 Mass. Adv. Sh. at 1209, 405 N.E.2d at 120.
86. Ibid., at 121.
87. Ibid., at 120–21.
88. Severns v. Wilmington Medical Center, Inc., 421 A.2d 1334 (Del. Sup. Ct. 1980.
89. Ibid.
90. In re Storar, 52 N.Y.2d 363, 420 N.E.2d 64 438 N.Y.S.2d 266 (1981).
91. Ibid., at 64, 73, 438 N.Y.S.2d 266, 275 (1981).
92. Ibid., at 275–6.
93. Ibid.
94. Ibid.
95. Foster v. Tourtellotte, No. Cv 81-5046-RMT (MX) (C.D. Cal. Nov. 16, 1981).
96. Ibid.
97. Barber v. Superior Court, 147 Cal. App. 3d 1006, 195 Cal. Rptr. 484 (Ct. App. 1983).
98. Ibid., at 1016, Cal. Rptr. at 490.

99. Ibid., at 1021, 493.
100. Ibid., at 1013, 488.
101. Severns, at 1334, 1344, in Barber, at 1014, 489.
102. Welfare of Colyer, 99 Wash. 2d 114, 660 P.2d 738 (1983).
103. Ibid., at 144–45, 660 P.2d at 761.
104. Ibid., at 134, 749.
105. Ibid., at 127–8, 745–6.
106. In re Hamlin, 102 Wash. 2d 810, 689 P.2d 1372 (1984) (en banc).
107. Ibid.
108. John F. Kennedy Memorial Hospital v. Bludworth, 452 So.2d 921, 922 (Fla. 1984).
109. Ibid., at 925.
110. In re Torres, 357 N.W.2d 332, Sup. Ct. (en banc).
111. *New York Times*, November 4, 1984.
112. Bludworth, at 341, no.4.
113. In re Hier, 18 Mass. App. Ct. 200 (1984).
114. The appellate court made four key points: (1) They investigated the different medical possibilities for nourishing Mrs Hier, noting the technical difficulties associated with each. (2) The benefit/burden analysis set forth in *Barber* should be considered when weighing whether to discontinue medical nourishment. (3) The court discussed the substituted judgment doctrine, finding that Mrs Hier's obvious and persistent refusals were indicative of her wishes. (4) The court found no state interest outweighing the patient's wishes.
115. Bartling v. Glendale Adventist Medical Center, Case No. C500 735, June 22, 1984, Superior Court, Los Angeles CA (Dept. 86, Waddington, J.).
116. The case became: Bartling v. Superior Court, 2 Civil No. B007909, Supr. Ct. No. C500735.
117. Ibid.
118. *Los Angeles Times*, December 28, 1984. In a similar case in Maryland, reported in the *Washington Post* on March 5, 1984, Circuit Court Judge Robert S. Heise refused permission to seventy-five-year-old Edward Fitzgerald to be removed from his respirator, despite Fitzgerald's pleas that he would prefer death to the ventilator. Heise dismissed the hospital's petition that Fitzgerald's wish be granted, saying there was nothing in Maryland law that allowed 'death with dignity'.
119. In re Conroy, 188 N.J. Super. 523 (Ch. Div. 1983).
120. 190 N. J. Super. 453, 459–60 (1983).
121. *New York Times*, December 28, 1983.
122. In re Conroy, No. A-108, Slip op. at 62 (N.J. Jan. 17, 1985).
123. Ibid., at 77, 79, 80.
124. *New York Times*, October 23, 1985.
125. Courts have differed as to whether to justify refusing treatment on a constitutional or common-law basis, and will continue to do so until the United States Supreme Court deals with whether the constitutional right to privacy extends to the right to refuse life supports. It never may. However, the common-law right to bodily integrity is clearly developed, and no state interest can outweigh this right unless a legislature passes a statute specifically prohibiting such decisions from being made by or for terminally ill patients. This is unlikely, however, given the state of the Natural Death Act and Durable Power of Attorney statutes in many states, defending the rights of competent and incompetent patients to refuse treatment.

126. President's Commission, *Deciding to Forego Life-Sustaining Treatment*, 135.
127. Saikewicz, at 752–3. One theory, proposed by lawyer/ethicist George Annas, is that the court, faced with the task of justifying its previous decision to stop treatment, could not use the best interests test because most people would elect to have chemotherapy. Thus, substituted judgment was the only criterion to support the decision, despite the fiction of the imagined 'competent' Saikewicz. See Beth L. Rubin, 'Refusal of Life-Sustaining Treatment for Terminally Ill Incompetent Patients: Court Order or an Alternative,' *Columbia Journal of Law and Social Problems*, Spring 1985, 22ff.
128. Professor Annas, in 'Reconciling *Quinlan* and *Saikewicz*: Decision making for the Terminally Ill Incompetent,' *American Journal of Law and Medicine* 4 (Winter 1979): 367–96, has argued that the charges of a dichotomy between the two cases (or medical paternalism in *Quinlan* and legal imperialism in the latter) are basically unfounded and 'can be reconciled by the next supreme court that rules on the question.' Annas has maintained that much of the distortion is a result of a misinformed medical community, and that, in fact, the cases share a defence of the incompetent's right to refuse treatment based on the constitutional right to privacy, the rights of proxy decision-making, and physicians' ability to make medical judgments and courts' to reflect those of society. However, none of the recent court cases have adopted the reconciliation position outlined by Annas (although, notably, *Colyer* alluded to it), and many have gone on to apply one branch of the dichotomy or the other.
129. Joseph M. Vaccarino, 'If Your Patient Is Hopelessly Ill, Must You Go to Court?' *Legal Aspects of Medical Practice*, July 1978, 51.
130. Charles H. Baron, 'Assuring "Detached but Passionate Investigation and Decision": The Role of Guardians Ad Litem in *Saikewicz*-type Cases,' *American Journal of Law and Medicine* 4, no. 2: 129.
131. Severns, at 1338.
132. Spring, at 120.
133. Ibid., at 121–2.
134. Storar, at 381.
135. Eichner, at 276.
136. Quinlan, at 367.
137. Dinnerstein, at 139.
138. Storar, at 277.
139. Colyer, at 137, 660 P.2d at 751.
140. Hamlin, at 1378.
141. Bludworth, at 446–7.
142. Torres, at 341, no. 4.
143. Conroy, at 78.
144. Eichner, at 382–3.
145. Ibid.
146. Severns, at 1338.
147. Barber, at 1022.
148. Foster, No. Cv 81-5046-RMT.
149. 'Prisoner in the ICU: The Tragedy of William Bartling,' *Hastings Center Report*, December 1984, 29.
150. President's Commission, *Deciding to Forego Life-Sustaining Treatment*, 136.
151. Eichner v. Dillon, at 542.
152. Storar, at 266, 272.
153. John J. Paris, 'Sounding Board: The New York Court of Appeals Rules on

the Rights of Incompetent Dying Patients,' *New England Journal of Medicine*, 304, no. 23 (June 4, 1981): 1425.
154. Leach, at 811–12, 816.
155. Spring, N.E.2d at 502.
156. Spring, 405 N.E.2d at 122.
157. George J. Annas, 'Quality of Life in the Courts: Earle Spring in Fantasyland,' *Hastings Center Report*, August 1980, 9.
158. Spring, 405 N.E.2d at 122.
159. Annas, 'Quality of Life,' 10.
160. President's Commission, *Deciding to Forego Life-Sustaining Treatment*, 133.
161. Ibid., 135.
162. See Katherine A. Day, 'A Patient's Last Rights—Termination of Medical Care—An Analysis of New York's *In re Storar*,' *Albany Law Review* 46 (1982): 1380–1413; Kevin W. Bates, 'Live or Let Die; Who Decides an Incompetent's Fate? *In re Storar* and *In re Eichner*,' *Brigham Young University Law review*, 1982, 387–400.
163. Storar, 106 Misc. 2d 880, 433 N.Y.S.2d at 388.
164. Storar, 102 Misc. 2d 209, 423 N.Y.S.2d at 596.
165. Colyer, at 137, 660 P.2d at 751.
166. Hamlin, at 1377.
167. Hier, No. 84–592 (Mass. App. June 4, 1984).
168. George J. Annas, 'The Case of Mary Hier: When Substituted Judgment Becomes Sleight of Hand,' *Hastings Center Report*, August 1984, 25.
169. In re Conroy, at 47–50.
170. Ibid., at 50–1.
171. Ibid., at 51–2.
172. Ibid., at 52.
173. George J. Annas, 'When Procedures Limit Rights: From *Quinlan* to *Conroy*,' *Hastings Center Report*, April 1985, 24.
174. Spring, at 637, 405 N.E.2d at 121.
175. Bludworth, at 921, 926.
176. Rubin, 'Refusal of Life-Sustaining Treatment,' suggests one possible way to get around this: She observes (p. 57) that 'according to Professor Annas, clinicians had previously assumed that they needed to obtain a court-appointed guardian for an incompetenen in this type of situation. The physicians did not necessarily institute judicial guardianship proceedings in each case, but they tried to procure the consent of all family members who could be appointed as guardian, in the event of actual judicial guardianship proceedings. The physicians procured this consent in order to avoid going to court solely for [such] proceedings, and they hoped to prevent possible civil liability suits brought by family members who were unhappy with the decision or with the hospital care. This informal practice was quicker and more practical than going to court, and now, according to Professor Annas, "one question is whether that practice has become so customary that [it] actually is the law, and in California, it is the law."'
177. Annas, 'reconciling *Quinlan* and *Saikewicz*,' 390–2.
178. Rubin, 'Refusal of Life-Sustaining Treatment,' 53–4.
179. Lawyer/ethicist Alexander Capron, in a perceptive article, 'Ironies and Tensions in Feeding the Dying' (*Hastings Center Report*, October 1984, 32–5), holds that while the courts may have addressed the issue, what they have not addressed adequately is the symbolic nature of feeding. Capron pointed to the

dilemma in which, typically, there is the difficult task of weighing (p. 35) 'autonomy (which would often oppose feeding) with the impulse to paternalism (which would lead to feeding even resisting patients), all in the framework of community (which embodies our commitment to caring for each other).'

180. For an excellent article of cases involving these questions, see Rebecca Dresser, 'Discontinuing Nutrition Support: A Review of Case Law,' *Current Issues* 85, no. 10 (October 1985): 1289–92.
181. Legal Advisory Committee, Concern for Dying, Proposed Draft, 1982.
182. George J. Annas, 'Fashion and Freedom: When Artificial Feeding Should Be Withdrawn,' *American Journal of Public Health and the Law* 75, no. 6 (June 1985): 688.
183. *New York Times*, November 4, 1984.
184. Robert Veatch, 'Limits of Guardian Treatment Refusal: A Reasonableness Standard,' *American Journal of Law and Medicine* (1984) 9: 463.
185. President's Commission, *Deciding to Forego Life-Sustaining Treatment*, 165–9.
186. Rubin, 'Refusal of Life-Sustaining Treatment,' 66.

## 17. DEFINING DEATH

1. A. Keith Mant, 'The Medical Definition of Death,' in Toynbee et al., *Man's Concern With Death* (London: Hodder and Stoughton, 1968).
2. J. G. Smith, *Principles of Forensic Medicine* (London: Underwood, 1821), 16, as quoted in Mant, 'Medical Definition.'
3. Uniform Anatomical Gift Act, sect. 7(b).
4. Human Tissue Act, 1961, ch. 54.
5. Richard G. Benton, *Death and Dying: Principles and Practices in Patient Care* (New York: Van Nostrand Reinhold Co., 1978), 16.
6. Ibid., 17–18.
7. 'A Definition of Irreversible Coma,' *Journal of the American Medical Association* 205 (August 5, 1968): 337–40.
8. J. R. Hughes, 'Guidelines for the Determination of Death,' *Neurology* 32 (1982): 682.
9. Peter McL. Black, 'Brain Death,' *New England Journal of Medicine* 299 (August 17, 1978): 344.
10. William J. Curran, 'Legal and Medical Death—Kansas Takes the First Step,' *New England Journal of Medicine* 284 (February 4, 1971): 261.
11. Kansas Session Laws of 1970, ch. 378, in Ian McColl Kennedy, 'The Kansas Statute on Death—An Appraisal,' *New England Journal of Medicine* 285 (October 21, 1971): 946.
12. Alexander Morgan Capron and Leon R. Kass, 'A Statutory Definition of the Standards for Determining Human Death: An Appraisal and a Proposal,' *University of Pennsylvania Law Review* 121 (November 1972): 94.
13. Ibid., 111.
14. *ABA Annual Report*, February 1975, 231–2.
15. Dennis J. Horan, 'Euthanasia and Brain Death: Ethical and Legal Considerations,' *Annals of the New York Academy of Science* 315 (November 17, 1978): 366.
16. Royal Colleges and Faculties in the United Kingdom, *British Medical Journal* 2 (1976): 1069–70.

17. A. Mohandas and S. N. Chow, 'Brain Death: A Clinical Pathological Study,' *Journal of Neurosurgery* 35 (1971): 211.
18. AMA Interim Meeting, December 1979.
19. President's Commission for the Study of Ethical Problems in Medicine and Behavioral Biomedical Research, *Defining Death*, 1981, 2.
20. A. Earl Walker, *Cerebral Death*, 3rd ed. (Baltimore: Urban & Schwartzenberg, 1985), 154.
21. Ibid., 147.
22. Susan L. Brennan and Richard Delgado, 'Death: Mutliple Definitions or a Single Standard,' *Southern California Law Review* 54 (September 1981): 1325–8.
23. Walker, *Cerebral Death*, 154.
24. 'New York Hospitals Welcome Brain Death Ruling,' *New York Times*, October 31, 1984.
25. 124 Ariz. 182, 603 P. 2d 74 (1979).
26. 8 Or. App. 72, 491 P. 2d 1193 (1971); 47 Cal. App. 3d 954, 121 Cal. Rptr. 243 (1975).
27. Tucker v. Lower No. 2831 (Richmond, Va. L. & Eq. Ct. (May 23, 1972).
28. People v. Lyons, 15 Crim. L. Rptr. 2240 (Cal. Super. Alameda Co. 1974).
29. No. 578–23001 (Criminal Ct. of Baltimore, 1979).
30. Bacchiochi v. Johnson Memorial Hospital, 1981.
31. Peter S. Janzen, 'Law at the Edge of Life: Issues of Death and Dying,' *Hamline Law Review* 7 (June 1984): 435.
32. Walker, *Cerebral Death*, 187.
33. Ibid., 183.
34. Ibid., 182.
35. Ibid., 15.
36. Joseph Fletcher, 'New Definitions of Death,' *Prism* 13 (January 1974): 36.
37. S. S. Olinger, 'Medical Death,' *Baylor Law Review* 1 (1975): 25.
38. Horan, 'Euthanasia and Brain Death,' 367–8.
39. Walker, *Cerebral Death*, 143.
40. President's Commission, *Defining Death*, 2.

## 18: RELIGION AND EUTHANASIA

1. The Vatican's Declaration on Euthanasia, 1980.
2. Rabbi Immanuel Jakobovits, *Jewish Medical Ethics: A Comparative and Historical Study of the Jewish Religious Attitudes to Medicine and Its Practice* (New York: Philosophical Library, 1959), 345.
3. Ibid.
4. Ibid.
5. Ibid.
6. Gerald Larue, *Euthanasia and Religion* (Los Angeles: Hemlock Society, 1985), 67.
7. Doris Portwood, *Commonsense Suicide: The Final Right* (Los Angeles, Hemlock Society, 1983), 22.
8. John Donne, *Suicide*, William A. Clebsch (Chico, Cal.: Scholars Press, 1983).
9. William V. Rauscher, *The Case Against Suicide* (New York: St Martin's Press, 1981), 114.
10. P. R. Baelz, 'Suicide: Some Theological Reflections,' in *Suicide: The Philo-*

*sophical Issues*, ed. M. Pabst Battin and David J. Mayo (New York: St Martin's Press, 1980), 72.

11. Ibid., 79.
12. Ibid., 83.
13. Larue, *Euthanasia and Religion*.
14. Gerald Larue, Speech to the Fifth World Congress of the World Federation of Right to Die Societies, Nice, France, September 1984.
15. Ibid.
16. Daniel M. Wilner et al., *Who Believes in Voluntary Euthanasia?* (Los Angeles: Hemlock Society, 1983), 19.
17. Gerald Larue, *Euthanasia and Religion* (Los Angeles: Hemlock Society, 1985); Dale Hardt, *Death: The Final Frontier*.

## 19. HELPING ANOTHER TO DIE

1. Elisabeth Kübler-Ross, *Questions and Answers on Death and Dying* (New York: Macmillan, 1974), 58, 59.
2. *New York Daily News*, October 28, 1983.
3. Margaret Pabst Battin, *Ethical Issues in Suicide* (Englewood Cliffs, N.J.: Prentice-Hall, 1982), 190.
4. Joseph Fletcher, *Humanhood: Essays in Biomedical Ethics* (New York: Prometheus Books, 1979), 157.
5. Derek Humphry, *Let Me Die Before I Wake* (Los Angeles: Hemlock Society, 1982), 55.
6. Ibid., 41–42.
7. *Miami Herald*, May 19, 1985.
8. *Hemlock Quarterly* 10 (January 1985).
9. *Psychology Today*, January 1978. 16.
10. Lael Tucker Wertenbaker, *Death of a Man* (New York: Random House, 1957), 180.
11. Derek Humphry, *Jean's Way* (New York: Quartet 1978), 108.
12. Betty Rollin, *Last Wish* (New York: Linden Press, 1985), 234.
13. *Who Believes in Voluntary Euthanasia*, 22.
14. *Hemlock Quarterly* 4 (July 1981).
15. *Hemlock Quarterly* 5 (October 1981).
16. James Rachels, 'Active and Passive Euthanasia' *New England Journal of Medicine*, 1975, 292: 78–80.
17. Christiaan Barnard, *Good Life/Good Death: A Doctor's Case for Euthanasia and Suicide* (Englewood Cliffs, N.J.: Prentice-Hall, 1980), 69.
18. Speech to the 50th Anniversary Celebration of the Voluntary Euthanasia Society of England, April 14, 1985.
19. Arthur Boorman, 'To Live or Not to Live: The Moral and Practical Case Against Active Euthanasia,' *Canadian Medical Association Journal* 121 (August 18, 1979): 483.
20. Daniel Maguire, *Death by Choice* (New York: Doubleday, 1974), 119.
21. Fletcher, *Humanhood*, 156.
22. Boorman, 'To Live or Not to Live,' 485.
23. Matthew Conolly, 'Forming Up Against the Euthanasia Bandwagon,' *Los Angeles Times*, February 1, 1983.
24. *U.S. News & World Report*, November 3, 1975, 21.
25. *Face the Nation*, CBS Television, September 1, 1985.

26. Barnard, *Good Life/Good Death*, 73.
27. Peter V. Admiraal, *Hemlock Quarterly* 21 (October 1985).
28. *The Sunday Times*, March 1978.
29. Christiaan Barnard, Speech to the World Federation of Right to Die Societies, Nice, France, September 1984.
30. *Euthanasia: Murder of Mercy*, Churchill Films, 1985.
31. John H. Leversee, 'Hippocrates Revisited: A View from General Practice,' *Hippocrates Revisited: A Search for Meaning*, ed. Roger Burder (New York: Medcom, 1973).
32. Ludwig Edelstein, 'The Genuine Works of Hippocrates,' in Robert Veatch, *A Theory of Medical Ethics* (New York: Basic Books, 1981), 331.
33. Richard Kravitz, *The Pharos*, Winter 1984.
34. Humphry, *Let Me Die*, 25.
35. 'The Billfold Biopsy,' *60 Minutes*, CBS Television, July 27, 1985.

## 20. THE PATH AHEAD

1. Alexander Capron, 'Ironies and Tensions in Feeding and Dying,' *Hastings Center Report*, October 1984: 33.
2. *New York Times*, September 29, 1983.

# Bibliography

Aaron, Henry J., and William B. Schwartz, *The Painful Prescription: Rationing Hospital Care* (Washington, D.C.: Brookings Institute, 1984).

Abrams, Natalie, and Michael Brucker, eds., *Medical Ethics: A Clinical Textbook and Reference for Health Care Professionals* (Cambridge, Mass.: MIT Press, 1983).

Albertson, Sandra H., *Endings and Beginnings* (New York: Random House, 1980).

Alsop, Stephen, *Stay of Execution* (Philadelphia: J. B. Lippincott, 1973).

Altman, Stuart, and R. Blendon, eds., *Medical Technology: The Culprit Behind Health Care Costs?* DHEW Pub. No. (PHS) 79–3216, US DHEW 1977.

Alvarez, A., *The Savage God: A Study of Suicide* (New York: Bantam Books, 1976).

Backer, Barbara et al., *Death and Dying* (New York: John Wiley and Sons, 1982).

Bacon, Francis, *The Advancement of Learning and Novum Organum* (New York: Colonial Press, 1900).

Baer, Louis Shattuck, M.D., *Let the Patient Decide: A Doctor's Advice to Older Persons* (Philadelphia: Westminster Press, 1978).

Banta, H. David., et al., *Toward Rational Technology in Medicine* (New York: Springer Series on Health Care and Society, 1981).

Barnard, Christiaan, M.D., *Good Life/Good Death: A Doctor's Case for Euthanasia and Suicide* (Englewood Cliffs, N.J.: Prentice-Hall, 1980): *In the Night Season* Englewood Cliffs. N.J.: Prentice-Hall, 1978).

Battin, Margaret Pabst, *Ethical Issues in Suicide* (Englewood Cliffs, N.J.: Prentice-Hall, 1982).

and Roland W. Maris, *Suicide and Ethics* (New York: Human Sciences Press, 1983).

and David Mayo, eds., *Suicide: The Philosophical Issues* (New York: St Martin's Press, 1980).

Benton, Richard, *Death and Dying* (New York: Van Nostrand Reinhold, 1978).

Bonisteel, Roy, *Searching for Man Alive* (Toronto: Totem Books, 1980).

Bowers, Margaretta K., et al., *Counseling the Dying* (New York: Harper & Row, 1981).

Brock, Heyward, ed., *The Culture of Biomedicine* (Newark, Del.: University of Delaware Press, 1984).

Brown, Tom, *Jeanette: A Memoir* (Toronto: Lester and Orpen, 1978).

Burder, Roger, ed., *Hippocrates Revisited: A Search for Meaning* (New York: Mecom, 1973).

Caine, Lynn, *Widow* (New York: Bantam Books, 1975).

334

Churchill, Winston. *The Second World War* (London: Cassell, 1959).

Clark, Brian, *Whose Life Is It Anyway?* (New York: Avon, 1980).

Corr, Charles, and Donna Corr, eds., *Hospice Care: Principles and Practices* (New York: Springer, 1983).

Cousins, Norman, *Anatomy of an Illness as Perceived by the Patient* (New York: W. W. Norton, 1979).

Donne, John, *Suicide*, ed. William A. Clebsch (Chico, Cal.: Scholars Press, 1983).

Downing, A. B., ed., *Euthanasia and the Right to Die* (New York: Humanities Press, 1969).

Durkheim, Émile, *Suicide: A Study in Sociology*, trans. John A. Spaulding and George Simpson (New York: Free Press, 1951).

Edmunds, Vincent, and C. Gordon Scorer, *Ethical Responsibility in Medicine: A Christian Approach* (London: E. & S. Livingstone, 1967).

Eissler, K. R., *The Psychiatrist and Dying Patient* (New York: International Universities Press, 1955).

Ellison, David, *The Bio-Medical Fix: Human Dimensions of Bio-Medical Technologies* (Westport, Conn.: Greenwood Press, 1978).

Fedden, Henry Romilly, *Suicide: A Social and Historical Study* (London: Peter Davies, 1938).

Fleming, Gerald, *Hitler and the Final Solution* (Berkeley: University of California Press, 1982).

Fletcher, Joseph, *Humanhood: Essays in Biomedical Ethics* (New York: Prometheus Books, 1979).

   *Moral Responsibility: Situation Ethics at Work* (Philadelphia: Westminster Press, 1977).

   *Morals and Medicine* (Princeton, N.J.: Princeton University Press, 1954).

Frenay, A., *The Suicide Problem in the United States* (Boston: Gorham, 1926).

Gill, Derek, *Quest: The Life of Elisabeth Kübler-Ross* (New York: Harper & Row, 1980).

Glover, Jonathan, *Causing Death and Saving Lives* (New York: Penguin Books, 1978).

Gould, Jonathan, and Lord Craigmyle, eds., *Your Death Warrant? The Implications of Euthanasia* (New Rochelle, N.Y.: Arlington House, 1971).

Graham, Jory, *In the Company of Others* (New York: Harcourt Brace Jovanovich, 1982).

Grollman, Earl, *Concerning Death: A Practical Guide for the Living* (Boston: Beacon Press, 1974).

Gunther, John, *Death Be Not Proud: A Memoir* (New York: Modern Library, 1953).

Hardt, Dale, *Death: The Final Frontier* (Englewood Cliffs, N.J.: Prentice-Hall Inc., 1979).

Hastings, James, ed., *Encyclopedia of Religion and Ethics* (New York: Charles Scribner's Sons, 1975).

Heifetz, Milton D., M.D., with Charles Mangel, *The Right to Die: A Neurosurgeon Speaks of Death with Candor* (New York: G. P. Putnam's Sons, 1975).

Hinton, John, *Dying* (London: Penguin, 1967).

*Hippocrates*, trans. W. H. S. Jones (London: William Heinemann, 1923).

Hitler, Adolf, *Mein Kampf*, trans. Ralph Manheim (Boston: Houghton Mifflin, 1971).

Horan, Dennis J., and David Mall, eds., *Death, Dying and Euthanasia* (Washington, D.C.: University Publications of America, 1977).

Howe, Herbert M., *Do Not Go Gentle* (New York: W. W. Norton, 1980).

Humber, James, and Robert Almeder, eds., *Biomedical Ethics and the Law* (New York: Plenum Press, 1979).

Hume, David, *Essays, Moral, Political and Literary*, 2 vols. (London: 1961).

Humphry, Derek, *Let Me Die Before I Wake* (Los Angeles: Hemlock Society, 1984).

   with Ann Wicket, *Jean's Way* (New York: Fontana, 1978).

   ed., *Assisted Suicide: The Compassionate Crime* (Los Angeles: Hemlock Society).

Huttmann, Barbara, R. N., *Code Blue* (New York: William Morrow, 1982).

   *The Patient's Advocate: The Complete Handbook of Patient's Rights* (New York: Penguin Books, 1981).

Illich, Ivan, *Medical Nemesis: The Expropriation of Health* (New York: Bantam Books, 1976).

Jakobovitz, Rabbi Immanuel, *Jewish Medical Ethics: A Comparative and Historical Study of the Jewish Religious Attitudes to Medicine and Its Practice* (New York: Philosophical Library, 1959).

Kelly, Gerald, *Medico-Moral Problems* (St. Louis, Mo.: Catholic Hospital Association of the U.S. and Canada, 1958).

Kennedy, Betty, *Gerhard: A Love Story* (Toronto: Totem Books, 1976).

Koestler, Arthur, and Cynthia Koestler, *Stranger on the Square* (New York: Random House, 1984).

Kohl, Marvin, ed., *Beneficent Euthanasia* (Buffalo: Prometheus Books, 1975).

Koop, C. Everett, *The Right to Live, The Right to Die* (Toronto: Life Cycle Books, 1980).

Kübler-Ross, Elisabeth, *Death: The Final Stage of Growth* (Englewood Cliffs, N.J.: Prentice-Hall, 1975).

   *Questions and Answers on Death and Dying* (New York: Macmillan, 1974).

   *To Live Until We Say Goodbye* (Englewood Cliffs, N.J.: Prentice-Hall, 1978).

Kuepper, Stephen, J., *The Euthanasia Movement: A Brief History of the Organized Euthanasia Movement in the United States* (1979).

Larue, Gerald, *Euthanasia and Religion* (Los Angeles: Hemlock Society, 1985).

Lear, Martha W. *Heartsounds* (New York: Pocket Books, 1980).

Le Shan, Eda, *Learning to Say Goodbye: When a Parent Dies* (New York: Avon, 1978).

Lifton, Robert Jay, *Living and Dying* (New York: Praeger Publishers, 1974).

Littell, Franklin H., and Hubert G. Locke, *The German Church Struggle and the Holocaust* (Detroit: Wayne State University Press, 1974).

Lygre, David G., *Life Manipulation: From Test Tube Babies to Aging* (New York: Walker and Company, 1979).

McManners, John, *Death and the Enlightenment* (New York: Oxford University Press, 1981).

McNeil, Barbara, and Ernest Cravalho, eds., *Critical Issues in Medical Technology* (Mass.: Auburn Publishing Co., 1982).

Maguire, Daniel C., *Death by Choice* (New York: Schocken Books, 1975).

Marshall, George N., *Facing Death and Grief* (New York: Prometheus Books, 1981).

Marx, Reverend Paul, *Death Without Dignity: Killing for Mercy* (Collegeville, Minn.: Liturgical Press, 1978).

Mikes, George, *Arthur Koestler: The Story of a Friendship* (London: André Deutsch, 1983).

Mitchell, Page, *Act of Love* (New York: Bantam, 1977).

Mitscherlich, Alexander, *Doctors of Infamy* (New York: Henry Schuman, 1949).

Montaigne, *Essays* (London: J. M. Dent and Sons, 1939).

More, Thomas, *Utopia*, trans. Paul Turner (New York: Penguin Books, 1981).

Morgan, Ernest, *Dealing Creatively with Death: A Manual of Death Education and Simple Burial*, 10th ed. (Celo Press, 1984).

Morris, Sarah, *Grief and How to Live with It* (New York: Grosset and Dunlap, 1972).

Muggeridge, Malcolm, and Alan Thornhill, *Sentenced to Life* (New York: Thomas Nelson, 1983).

Munley, Anne, *The Hospice Alternative: A New Context for Death and Dying* (New York: Basic Books, 1983).

National Hospice Organization, *Standards of a Hospice Program of Care*.

Paige, Connie, *The Right to Lifers* (New York: Summit Books, 1983).

Piccione, Joseph, 'Last Rights: Treatment and Care Issues in Medical Ethics,' *Currents in Family Policy* (1984).

Plato, *Republic*, trans. Benjamin Jowett (New York: D. Van Nostrand, 1959).

Portwood, Doris, *Commonsense Suicide: The Final Right* (Los Angeles: Hemlock Society, 1983).

President's Commission for the Study of Ethical Problems in Medicine and Biomedical and Behavioral Research, *Deciding to Forego Life-Sustaining Treatment* (March 1982).

   *Defining Death* (1981).

   *Securing Access to Health* (March 1983).

Quinlan, Joseph, and Julia Quinlan, with Phyllis Battelle, *Karen Ann* (New York: Bantam, 1977).

Ralling, Christopher, and Jane Bywaters, eds., *Muggeridge: Ancient and Modern* (British Broadcasting Corp., 1981).

Rauscher, William V., *The Case Against Suicide* (New York: St. Martin's Press, 1981).

Reitlinger, Gerald, *The Final Solution* (London: Vallentine, Mitchell, 1971).

Rollin, Betty, *First You Cry*, (New York: Signet, 1977).

   *Last Wish* (New York: Linden Press/Simon & Schuster, 1985).

Roman, Jo, *Exit House: Choosing Suicide as an Alternative* (New York: Seaview Books, 1980).

Rossman, Parker, *Hospice: Creating New Models of Care for the Terminally Ill* (New York: Fawcett Columbine, 1980).

Russell, O. Ruth, *Freedom to Die: Moral and Legal Aspects of Euthanasia*, rev. ed. (New York and London: Human Sciences Press, 1977).

Ryan, Cornelius, and Kathryn Morgan Ryan, *A Private Battle* (New York: Fawcett Popular Library, 1980).

Segal, Erich, *Love Story* (New York: Harper & Row, 1970).

Sereny, Gitta, *Into That Darkness* (London: André Deutsch, 1974).

Sheely, Patrick F., *On Dying with Dignity*, (New York: Pinnacle, 1981).

Shirer, William L., *The Rise and Fall of the Third Reich* (London: Pan Books, 1964).

Shneidman, Edwin S., *Death: Current Perspectives* (California: Mayfield Publishing Co., 1984).

   *Voices of Death, Letter, Diaries and Other Personal Documents from People Facing Death that Prove Comforting Guidance for Each of Us* (New York: Harper & Row, 1980).

   and Norman Faberow, eds., *Clues to Suicide* (New York: 1957).

Simon, Merrill, *Jerry Falwell and the Jews* (New York: Jonathan David Publishing, 1982).

Society for the Right to Die, *Handbook of Living Will Laws, 1981–84* (New York: Society for the Right to Die, 1984).

Sommers, Herman M., and Anne Ramsay Sommers, *Doctors, Patients, and Health Insurance: The Organization and Financing of Medical Care* (Garden City, N.Y.: Doubleday, 1961).

Stein, Jane, *Making Medical Choices: Who Is Responsible?* (Boston: Houghton Mifflin, 1978).

Stoddard, Sandol, *Hospice Movement: A Better Way of Caring for the Dying* (New York: Stein and Day, 1978).

Taylor, Richard, *Medicine Out of Control: The Anatomy of a Malignant Technology* (Melbourne, Australia: Sun Books, 1979).

Torrey, E. F., *Ethical Issues in Medicine* (Boston: Little, Brown, 1968).

Toynbee, Arnold, and Daisaku Ikeda, *The Toynbee-Ikeda Dialogue* (New York: Kodansha International, 1984).

Trubo, Richard, *An Act of Mercy: Euthanasia Today* (Los Angeles: Nash Publishing, 1973).

Tuchman, Barbara, *A Distant Mirror* (New York: Ballantine Books, 1978).

Veatch, Robert M., *A Theory of Medical Ethics* (New York: Basic Books, 1981).

Walker, A. Earl, *Cerebral Death*, 3rd ed. (Baltimore: Urban and Schwarzenberg, 1985).

Wertenbaker, Lael, *Death of a Man* (New York: Random House, 1957).

West, Jessamyn, *The Woman Said Yes* (New York: Harcourt Brace Jovanovich, 1976).

Wiesenthal, Simon. *The Murderers Among Us* (London: Heinemann, 1967).

Williams, Glanville, *The Sanctity of Life and the Criminal Law* (New York: Alfred A. Knopf, 1957).

Williams, Robert, ed., *To Live and to Die* (New York: Springer-Verlag, 1973).

Wilner, Daniel, et al., *Who Believes in Voluntary Euthanasia?* (Los Angeles: Hemlock Society, 1983).

Wilson, Jerry B., *Death by Decision: The Medical, Moral, and Legal Dilemmas of Euthanasia* (Philadelphia: Westminster Press, 1975).

Zinn, Howard, *People's History of the United States* (New York: Harper Colophon, 1980).

Zorza, Victor, and Rosemary Zorza, *A Way to Die* (New York: Alfred A. Knopf, 1980).

# Index

Abimelech, 277
Abortion, 30, 49, 169–71, 172–74, 186
Abram, Morris, 122
Active euthanasia, 115, 117n, 152; and
    Hemlock Society, 113–14; hospice
    supporters and, 187, 191; vs. passive, 75,
    96, 288–91; physicians' surveys, 88–89,
    90, 291; Pope Pius XII on, 49–50;
    religious opposition to, 274–76, 280
Addison, Joseph, 9
Admiraal, Professor Pieter V., 289, 291
Advocates of the Developmentally Disabled,
    157–58
Africa, 29
Age, as factor in medical treatment, 257–58.
    See also Elderly
Agnostics, 171, 279
Ahithopel, 277
AIDS (Acquired Immune Deficiency
    Syndrome), 151, 198
Aldrich, C. Knight, 65, 66–67
Alexander, Leo, 25n, 26, 29, 43, 178
Alkmaar Court case, 182, 184–85
Allen, Samuel, 270
Allen, William Sheridan, 27–28
A.L.S. (amyotrophic lateral sclerosis), 190,
    233, 236, 240
Alsop, Stewart, 93–94
Altruistic suicide, 275, 277–78
Alvarez, Dr Walter C., 33, 52, 90
Alzheimer's disease, 139, 142, 147–48; and
    negotiated death concept, 297–98
America (magazine), 48, 77–78
America. See United States
American Academy of General Practice, 47
American Bar Association, 267–69
American Civil Liberties Union (ACLU),
    157–58, 160–61
American Council of Christian Churches, 47
American Hospital Association, 95, 115, 206

American Indians, 29
American Institute of Public Opinion, 18
American Journal of Psychiatry, 68
American Journal of Nursing, 117
American Medical Association (AMA), 53;
    definition of death, 268–69; and legalizing
    euthanasia, 12; on mercy killing, 97
American Nurses' Association, 119–20
American Physicians Association, 34
American Society of Law and Medicine, 202
Americans United for Life, 169, 175, 272
Anderson case, 22, 228
Anaesthesia, 49
Anaesthesiologists, 50, 205
Angiography, coronary, 194
Anglican Church, 275, 281
Annas, Professor George J., 163–64, 252,
    254, 256, 258–59, 261
Antibiotics, 74, 124, 189, 194–95, 261
Antidysthanasia, 75, 260
Application of President and Directors of
    Georgetown College, 220, 220n, 227, 227n
Aquinas, St Thomas, 6–7, 276–77
Arawak Indians, 29
Aristotle, 3, 5
Armenians, 29
Arras, John D., 148, 163
Ars Morendi, 88
Artificial breathing, 194. See also
    Respiration, artificial
Artificial feeding. See Force-feeding;
    Gastrotomy; Intravenous feeding;
    Nourishment and nutrition
Artificial hearts, 195, 197, 201–2
Aryan race, 19–20
Asclepius, 4
Assisted suicide, xi, 75, 88, 125, 140n, 224,
    282–94; accounts of, 284–87; opposition
    to, 274, 282–83; support for, 283–85
Association of American Physicians, 69

339

killing verdicts, 79–81, 98–99, 146–47,
166, 211–12, 215–16, 217
'Justifiable Euthanasia: A Manual for the
Medical Profession' (Admiraal), 180–81,
289

Kafri, Gizela, 80
Kallen, Horace M., 54
Kalven, Harry, 55
Kamisar, Yale, 212
Karnofsky, David, 72, 75, 92
Kass, Leon, 266–67, 269
Katz, Sidney, 36
Keedy, Judge Sanford, 237
Keene, Barry, 95
Kelly, Gerald, S. J., 48–49, 50, 200
Kennedy, Dr Foster, 14, 16
Kennedy Memorial Hospital court cases. See
Bludworth case; Heston, Jane and Delores
Kilbon, Ralph, 57
King, William, R., 155
Klein, Alfons, 24, 28
Knaus, Dr William, 199
Koestler, Arthur and Cynthia, 132, 149–51
Kohl, Marvin, 27
Koop, Dr C. Everett, 171, 176
Kopelman, Judge David H., 246–47
Kornfeld, D. S., 197
Kraai, Dr John, 147–48, 193n, 208–10, 217,
292
Kübler-Ross, Elisabeth, 65–67, 87, 91, 94n,
192, 282–83
Kuepper, Stephen, J., 83
Kutner, Louis, 82

Lack-of-causation defence, 41, 99, 211n, 215
Laforgues, 12
Lancet, The, 72–73, 133, 188
Landy, Francis, 242–43, 244
LaRouche, Lyndon, 174
Larue, Professor Gerald A., 278–79
Laski, Harold, 127
Laws and legislation (see also Euthanasia,
legalization attempts; Litigation; Mercy
killing; Right-to-refuse-treatment cases);
legal definition of death, 266–67, 268–69;
and life-support measures, 125–26; Living
Will and, 94–96, 111, 111n, 261; and
mercy killings, 44, 53, 61, 208–17;
proposals for change, 134, 136–38, 211–
12, 297; and right to die, 83, 110, 111, 127;
against suicide, 5–6, 9, 14–15, 275
Leach, Edna Marie, 236
Leach v. Akron General Medical Center, 236,
238, 253–54
Lebensunwerten Leben, 18, 20
Lecky, William, 10

Let Me Die Before I Wake (Humphry), 113–
14, 132–33, 138, 180
Leversee, Dr John H., 293
Levinson, Ann Jane, 112, 114, 114n
Levisohn, Dr Arthur A., 67–68, 82
Liability, 56, 251; civil vs. criminal, 218,
218n; of hospitals and physicians in
withholding treatment, 220–24, 227, 228,
238, 250, 259, 262; Quinlan case
immunity from, 231
Liège (Belgium) mercy killing trials, 79–80,
98
Life, quality of, 47, 196–97, 200, 201–2, 206;
and 'best interests' test, 247–48, 247n,
253, 255, 257–58, 260; rejected in
Saikewicz case, 231–32
Life magazine, 89–90, 92–93
Life-support systems, 61, 111, 114–15, 194,
199; analysis of, 247–63; and definition of
death, 264, 267–68; force-feeding as, 175;
guidelines for, 120–26, 203; murder
charge, 209; nurses' poll on, 119; in
Quinlan case, 102, 110, 229–31;
withdrawal of, and court decisions, 232–
47
Limburg, Bishop of, 23
Listowel, Lord, 127, 136
Litigation (see also Right-to-refuse-treatment
cases); Bouvia case, 155–61; Clinque case,
196; fear of, 123, 125, 273; new techniques
and, 201, 207; Warthen case, 119–20
Little, Sheila, 131
Living Wills, 82, 180, 204, 209, 243, 246,
253–55, 257n, 296–97; Bartling and, 245;
honouring of, 263; Human Life Alliance
opposition, 173; state legislation on, 94–
96, 111, 111n, 170, 214
Lobotomy, 48
'Locked-in-syndrome', 273
Long, Gordon, 39–40
Long, Dr Perrin H., 70, 74
Los Angeles County associations, 120
Los Angeles Times, 116, 124
Lutheran Church, 276, 281
Luxton, Dr R. W., 291
Lygre, David, 201
Lynn, Dr Joanne, 165
Lyons, Andrew, 270–71
Lyons, Mark, 127, 128–31, 135, 137, 153–54

McCall, Governor Tom, 94
McCormick, Monsignor Robert E., 33–34
McCullough, Laurence, 30
McKinney, Donald, 83, 95, 112n, 113–14,
114n
Macleod of Borve, Baroness, 137
McNath, Dr William, 84